Play
in Animals and Humans

Play

in Animals and Humans

Edited by
Peter K. Smith

Basil Blackwell

© Basil Blackwell Publisher Limited 1984

First published 1984
Basil Blackwell Publisher Limited
108 Cowley Road, Oxford OX4 1JF, England

Basil Blackwell Inc.
432 Park Avenue South, Suite 1505
New York, NY 10016, USA

British Library Cataloguing in Publication Data

Play in animals and humans.
 1. Play
 I. Smith, Peter K.
 155.4′18   BF717
 ISBN 0-631-13492-1

96602

Typesetting at The Spartan Press Ltd.
Printed in Great Britain by T.J. Press Ltd., Padstow

Contents

Part 4: The study of children's play

Part 5: Varied perspectives on play and games in humans

Editor's Preface

Play can be a source of enjoyment and fascination for both the participant and for the observer of others at play. Subjectively, play and games seem among the most valuable aspects of human experience. Objectively, play also presents some profound intellectual puzzles. What exactly do we even mean by play? Why do children and young animals play? If play has no obvious function, as most agree, are there in fact developmental benefits which research can uncover?

After some decades of relative neglect, the area of play research is burgeoning. What is more, a number of different disciplines converge on the topic of play. The most prominent are ethology and sociobiology, psychology, and anthropology. Other areas as diverse as sports sociology, exercise physiology, linguistics and communication science, and psychoanalysis, all have contributions to make.

In the general area of animal behaviour, ethological observation and sociobiological theory have come together in an exciting and fruitful combination. This has had a considerable impact on play research. Over the past ten years, there has been a great growth in the number of reports of play in different species; more intense observational and experimental studies of play in some laboratory species; and an upsurge of theorizing about, and modelling of, the circumstances in which animal play could occur, and its likely benefits. In a widely acclaimed book, Fagen (1981) brought together a vast amount of this observation and theory on animal play.

Somewhat separately, psychologists have been pursuing a variety of studies on play, with renewed vigour. These have included observational studies of play in infancy, with parents and later with peers; experimental investigations of object play; studies of the development of fantasy and sociodramatic play and their educational significance; and ecological influences on play. The majority of this work has been done on infants and preschool children. The extensive review by Rubin et al. (1983) documents work in these areas.

Apart from the investigations of Sutton-Smith and his colleagues, the study of the games of older children has not received a great deal of attention from psychologists. It is anthropologists and folklorists who have provided a wealth of information on toys and games in different societies. The book by Schwartzman (1978) gave a most thorough and incisive account of the anthropology of children's play, together with an overview of other approaches.

Many behavioural scientists are feeling the increasing irrelevance of disciplinary boundaries, such as those between ethology, psychology and anthropology. At certain times, some areas of research endeavour seem best delineated (in so far as any boundaries are necessary) by topic, rather than by the historical accident of professional discipline. My own feeling is that play, at present, is one such topic. Some attempts have been made to relate different perspectives on play (e.g. Lancy, 1980; Smith, 1982). Still, one's training in a particular discipline and one's professional affiliations are pervasive influences; it seems rare for published research or reviews on children's play to make any substantial link to the ethological work, or vice versa.

Yet the links between these areas are there, implicitly, in a number of ways. They can surely be developed and made more explicit. The links are at the levels of both description, and theory (though these are not fully separate, since current theory informs methods of description).

At a descriptive level, the painstaking methods of ethologists in studying animals in their natural habitats percolated through directly to the study of child development by the early 1970s (Blurton Jones, 1972). Less obviously, this probably also helped foster a climate of research opinion in which observation, rather than immediate experimentation, became acceptable again as a method in mainstream psychology. Child development research now is dramatically different in its balance of methods from what it was twenty years ago. Some methods developed by psychologists, such as sampling techniques, and the study of individual differences, are usefully directed back to ethology.

At a theoretical level, ideas such as the surplus energy theory of play linked animal and human play back in the nineteenth century. More recently, an influential theory has been that play enhances behavioural flexibility. Sources of evidence from both ethological and psychological work have (often separately) been adduced to support this.

The overall aim of the present book has been to bring together and review recent research on animal and human play, in the belief that the time is ripe to do so. The book has not turned out wholly as I originally envisaged. No doubt naively, I expected authors to provide chapters predominantly reporting observational or experimental data, which one might hope to see fitting into some provisional overall framework of theory. Instead, the different contributions seem to me positively to bristle with theoretical assumptions and speculations, some in agreement, some different but compatible, some in profound disagreement. In retrospect, I take this to be a very positive feature. It is much more exciting and healthy than a bland consensus of commonplace notions on play, such as were to be found in the literature not so very long ago.

I have arranged the book into five parts, within each of which I felt chapters related strongly to one another; for example, by illustrating different approaches to a similar problem. I have written a short introduction to each part, in which I have attempted not just to abstract the chapters, but to draw the reader's attention to certain issues where the authors might agree or disagree amongst themselves, or where some different viewpoint could usefully be alluded to. Obviously, I am solely responsible for the content of this introductory material.

In this preface, I should also like to draw out some issues which occur several times through the book, often in different parts. These are issues which surely characterize the study of play as it is presently conducted, and delineate the aims of the book in more specific terms.

1   The links between different disciplines. I have already alluded to some mutual influence between ethology and psychology. Both Humphreys and Smith, and Parker, make explicit use of ethological methods and of evolutionary theory in their chapters on rough-and-tumble play, and games, in humans. Wolf suggests ideas from children's play which may prove useful in animal study.

Similarly, the genesis and importance of play theories (such as the surplus energy and practice theories) receive attention, both at the beginnning of the book (Burghardt) and at the end (Sutton-Smith and Kelly-Byrne). The link between play and behavioural flexibility is important in several chapters (Hole and Einon; Fagen; Wolf; Smith and Simon).

2   The systematic study of why play occurs. Ethologists have traditionally asked four 'why' questions: those of development, causation, function and evolution. The first three of these receive very explicit treatment in reviews of kitten play (Martin), and monkey play (Chalmers) and inform many of the others.

3   The evolution of play. The most neglected of the four 'whys', this at last generates some informed and testable hypotheses in the chapters by Burghardt, and Byers. The chapter by Parker draws attention to the evolutionary origins of human games.

4   The study of play through the life-span. Many reviews of play are largely confined to infancy and early childhood. But in human play particularly, the study of play grades into the study of games in older children and adults. The chapters by Humphreys and Smith, Parker, Lancy, and Sutton-Smith and Kelly-Byrne, all consider human play in a context broader than that of early childhood. Parker, and Lancy, provide two quite different approaches to the study of human games.

5   The functions and developmental significance of play. This (and the related problem of defining what play is) provide perhaps the most pervasive issues in the book. In animals, notable techniques are the use of cross-species comparisons (Byers; Hole and Einon; Müller-Schwarze) and the use of deprivation experiments (Hole and Einon; Fagen). The attempts to measure the costs and the benefits of play also receive emphasis (Burghardt; Martin; Müller-Schwarze).

For both animal and human play, the strongest contender for a functional explanation has been that (in either general, or specific, ways) play is useful practice for adult activities. This view is well represented in the book (Byers; Partington and Grant; Humphreys and Smith; Parker) but it is also substantially challenged. Alternative theories, notably that of behavioural flexibility, are available. Play may serve different or additional functions (such as social cohesion) in certain species (Byers).

Even if play is useful for some purpose in a species, it may well be that it is not necessary: that there are other developmental ways of becoming an effective adult, apart from playing (e.g. Chalmers; Lancy). Furthermore, some benefits of play may be quite short term, for the use of the individual while young and not as an adult (Martin; Müller-Schwarze). And, as Hole and Einon point out, some 'play' may have no particular function, being a by-product of other selective processes.

The explanation of any biological functions of play (i.e. the benefits of play which natural selection has acted on) is of scientific interest; but, in human play certainly, it is not the end of the matter. Play can be put to new, culturally decided, uses. For example, we could foster sociodramatic play, or imaginary companions (Partington and Grant) for developmental ends (such as fostering cooperation, or creativity), whatever the selective origins of play in our evolutionary history. But here we come back full circle. Sutton-Smith and Kelly-Byrne argue that theories of play have been used culturally, and generally for the ends of adults rather than children. Adults may encourage aspects of play they find most socially acceptable, and use play theories to back this up.

The spirit of the time is clearly reflected in our popular views of play, and in our academic theories. Is there, nevertheless, real scientific progress in our understanding of play? I believe there is, but that must be left for the reader to judge.

I should like to thank Wladyslaw Sluckin for first suggesting the idea of this book to me; Helen, for her patience and encouragement; and James, Samuel and Benjamin, for being past, present and future playmates.

Peter K. Smith
Sheffield

REFERENCES

Blurton Jones, N. (ed.) (1972). *Ethological Studies of Child Behaviour*. Cambridge: Cambridge University Press.

Fagen, R. (1981). *Animal Play Behavior*. New York: Oxford University Press.

Lancy, D. F. (1980). Play in species adaptation. *Annual Review of Anthropology* 9, 471–95.

Rubin, K. H., Fein, G. G. and Vandenberg, B. (1983). Play. In P. H. Mussen and E. M. Hetherington (eds), *Handbook of Child Psychology (4th edn), Vol. 4*. New York and Chichester: Wiley.

Schwartzman, H. B. (1978). *Transformations: the Anthropology of Children's Play*. New York: Plenum Press.

Smith, P. K. (1982). Does play matter? Functional and evolutionary aspects of animal and human play. *Behavioral and Brain Sciences* 5, 139–84.

PART 1
Evolutionary Origins of Play

What are the evolutionary origins of play behaviour? When did play first evolve, and what selection pressures or evolutionary trends were responsible? Until now, these questions have received remarkably little scientific attention. Two previous collections, *Play – Its Role in Development and Evolution* (eds J. S. Bruner, A. Jolly and K. Sylva; Harmondsworth: Penguin Books, 1976), and *Evolution of Play Behavior* (ed. D. Müller- Schwarze; Stroudsberg: Dowden, Hutchinson and Ross, 1978) did not consider the evolution of play as such, although they did contain much information on play in different species. Indeed, evolutionary theorizing might have been premature until recently. The chapters in part one by Gordon Burghardt (chapter 1) and John Byers (chapter 2) break new ground in this area. That they can present plausible and testable scientific hypotheses indicates the progress that has been made, both in our general scientific knowledge of animals (e.g. reptile and mammal physiology and development) and in our data on play forms in different orders and families of mammals.

How can hypotheses about the origins of play proceed beyond speculative 'just so' stories? A starting point can be the observation that 'cold-blooded' animals, such as fishes, reptiles and amphibians, apparently do not play; whereas 'warm-blooded' animals, that is birds and mammals, may play (and, in mammals, often do play). Mammals evolved from reptiles some 150 million years ago. Reptiles, being exothermic, or poikilothermic, can only regulate their body temperature by extrinsic means, such as moving in and out of shade, or staying motionless. Birds and mammals, being endothermic, or homoiothermic, can regulate their body temperature within a narrow range by intrinsic means.

Thus, was the origin of play behaviour connected with the evolution of endothermy, and the benefits and costs of vigorous exercise? Burghardt carefully develops this possibility. While reptiles certainly explore, the energetic costs of vigorous play in reptiles, which would rely more on anaerobic metabolism than on increased breathing, may have been too great. Burghardt considers the use, from Spencer and Groos onwards, of the concepts of 'energy' and 'surplus', and he makes a strong case for their relevance in considering the apparently discontinuous origin of play between the reptiles and early mammals.

The evolution of endothermy in the therapsids (mammal-like ancestors) and early mammals, together with a gradual increase in brain size and intelligence, may in fact have provided the necessary preconditions for extended postnatal parental care (Hopson, 1973; Case, 1978a). Parental care of young birds and mammals involves provision of food and warmth. This facilitates much faster growth rates in the young of homoiothermic than of poikilothermic vertebrates (Case, 1978b). It seems in addition, from Burghardt's analyses, that young reptiles may channel extra food or energy into growth; whereas young birds or mammals may channel it into fat, and perhaps into 'behavioural fat', i.e. energy-consuming activities such as play.

If one argues that the proportion of time mammals spend in play is, relatively, rather small; and that play behaviour is readily displaced or reduced by other activities or by adverse conditions; then it could be concluded that any functions of play might be additional rather than essential, providing some extra practice perhaps, if conditions are good enough to allow it. Such practice could have become more useful in the evolution of mammals as brain size increased and as learning came to be more important in the development of behavioural repertoires.

Burghardt speculates that the play of early mammals would be based on behaviours essential to their reptilian ancestors. But if play does have some practice benefits, what might these have been for the evolving mammals, and hence what kinds of play would have evolved? We cannot examine extinct behaviour, but we can examine the types of play found across the mammals or, more readily, within all the families of a large order of mammals. Byers takes this approach with the hoofed mammals or ungulates. Tabulating a considerable amount of data, he finds that play mimicking flight behaviour is common throughout the ungulates, and may be the only form of play in some. He suggests that this was the ancestral form of play in ungulates, and perhaps in mammals generally. The forms of such play are consistent with it functioning as motor training, i.e. enhancing muscle growth, bodily efficiency, and neuromuscular coordination. Byers suggests that social play evolved with increased social living and polygyny (and hence male–male competition), as a means of motor training and specifically as practice for fighting skills, especially in males. Subsequently, he argues, these forms of play could be modified for other functions in different species, during the radiation of mammalian life forms. As an example, the form and occurrence of play in the collared peccary suggests to him that it could have been selected for to enhance cohesion of individuals in cooperative social groups.

Both Burghardt and Byers have produced interesting hypotheses about the evolutionary origins of play, hypotheses that can be supported or falsified by subsequent evidence. If the young of a small lizard species was found to engage in vigorous play, then Burghardt's thesis would be in trouble. Byers makes five predictions toward the end of his chapter, which are perfectly testable. Their hypotheses may or may not be correct, but they do put the study of phylogenesis of play on to a new scientific basis.

REFERENCES

Case, T. J. (1978a). Endothermy and parental care in the terrestrial vertebrates. *American Naturalist* 112, 861–74.

Case, T. J. (1978b). On the evolution and adaptive significance of postnatal growth rates in the terrestrial vertebrates. *Quarterly Review of Biology* 53, 243–82.

Hopson, J. A. (1973). Endothermy, small size and the origin of mammalian reproduction. *American Naturalist* 107, 446–51.

1 On the Origins of Play

Gordon M. Burghardt

TO DEFINE RAINBOWS AND HUNT FOR POTS OF GOLD

Play is a remarkably elusive concept of fluctuating scientific popularity, as is true of most enduring topics in psychology, such as mind, consciousness, intelligence, and instinct. And, as with these other phenomena, play has been extensively looked at in both humans and non-human animals (simply animals from here on) for evidence relating to the mental and behavioural continuity issues instigated by Darwin (Burghardt, 1978b), particularly in *The Descent of Man and Selection in Relation to Sex* (1871) and *The Expression of the Emotions in Man and Animals* (1872). The acknowledged doyen of play in the post-Darwinian era was Karl Groos, whose two volumes on play in animals (1898) and humans (1901) are virtually the only works of the period still cited.

Now while the recent revival of interest in play has led to many books and symposia (e.g. Bekoff, 1974; Bruner, et al., 1976; Fagen, 1981; Müller-Schwarze, 1978; Smith 1978; Sutton Smith, 1979; Symons, 1978) theoretical statements (e.g. Bekoff, 1976, 1978; Fagen 1976, 1977, 1978; Meyer-Holzapfel, 1956; Smith, 1982; Welker, 1971; Baldwin and Baldwin, 1977) and empirical research both descriptive (e.g. Biben, 1982) and experimental (e.g. Müller-Schwarze et al. 1982; Martin, 1984) it must be acknowledged at the outset that many questions of recognizing, describing, and classifying play are still unresolved. So too are issues concerning the function, ontogeny, motivation, and physiology of play.

It might thus seem premature to try to develop a coherent, even if speculative, view of the origin of play in the ancient world of vertebrate evolution, a world still far more mythical, and even mystical, to us than our concrete contact with frisky colts, wrestling puppies, and kittens chasing balls of yarn. All the outpouring of research on play of the last fifteen years, although providing more data and imaginative theory, has *not* answered the key questions. Instead we have a plethora of rather fragmented approaches: behaviouristic, ethological, sociobiological, biopsychological, psychoanalytic, and cognitive (see the anthology by Müller-Schwarze, 1978). But perhaps a return to a consideration of the evolutionary origins of the playful act, through a comparative perspective and biological attitude, may help to focus upon some core issues in the interminable debates on the function and mechanisms of readily acknowledged play. Thus my objective is to consider the transition from animals that don't play to animals that do. This transition, in spite of all the claims for a new era of evolutionary thinking about play, has been largely ignored. While I may seem occasionally unsympathetic to his views, Robert Fagen's writings, especially his book (1981), have been particularly useful and stimulating in preparing this chapter.

But what *is* play? Culled from many sources some of the claimed characteristics of play are: no obvious immediate function; pleasurable effect; sequentially variable; stimulation-seeking; quick and energetically expensive behaviour; exaggerated, incomplete, or awkward movement; most prevalent in juveniles; special 'play' signals; a breakdown in role relationships; mixing of behaviour patterns from several contexts; relative absence of threat or submission; and the relative absence of final consummatory acts (e.g. biting, intentional injury or killing, eating, copulation).

However, together with Martin (below, chapter 3), I find the definition of Bekoff and Byers (1981: 300) as good as any in reflecting how play is, in fact, usually recognized:

> *Play* is all motor activity performed postnatally that appears to be purposeless, in which motor patterns from other contexts may often be used in modified forms and altered temporal sequencing.

Most typical play can be reliably recognized and scored by independent observers, a fact sometimes used to argue for animal play being a *real* phenomenon. But play is definitely not a homogeneous category of behaviour. The three main and generally accepted (e.g. Bekoff and Byers, 1981; Smith, 1982) categories of play are:

Social play
Object play
Locomotor play

―――――――――

Curiosity
Exploration

Below them I have added curiosity and exploration. Together these form Berlyne's (1960) category of *ludic behaviour*. I have put them in decreasing order of apparent topographic complexity.

In all three play categories, the main focus of researchers has been on energetic physical movements. Conversely, in curiosity and exploration research the main focus has been on sensory experience, feedback, and information gathering (Hutt, 1966; Welker, 1971; Lorenz, 1981). Exploration typically refers to the movements of an animal through space where it attends to chemical, auditory, tactile, and visual stimuli in a rather cursory but often repetitive manner. Curiosity involves more active scrutiny of objects, including approach–withdrawal, manipulation, and careful, close, inspection with nose, paws, and mouth. Curiosity is structurally akin to object play, exploration with locomotor play.

All the dozens of postulated functions of play can be classified into three categories: those involving motor training, socialization, and enhanced cognitive abilities (Bekoff and Byers, 1981; Smith, 1982). But surprisingly, while such functions may, and probably do, exist, there is little hard, non-controversial evidence for any of them. Indeed the plethora of functions and scanty evidence makes it conceivable that single-minded searching for specific functions of play in extant animals may be misguided. Important to the views to be advocated here is the fact that locomotor play seems to be the most physiologically based, widespread, and ontogenetically earliest type of play. It is usually related to benefits, still unsubstantiated, derived from skill, practice, and exercise.

DISCONTINUITY

Many mammals engage in behaviours universally labelled as playful, but while play of some kind occurs in all *orders* of mammals (Fagen, 1981), its true extent among *species* is still unknown (Bekoff and Byers, 1981). Play occurs in birds but appears to be more limited than in mammals both in its diversity and the species engaging in it (Fagen, 1981). Typical play is also rare to non-existent in poikilothermic ('cold-blooded') vertebrates (fish, amphibians, reptiles, some neonate birds and mammals). Play is considered by virtually no one today a serious component of invertebrate behaviour, thus we can omit invertebrates; also plants and protista (unicellular organisms).

Few writers deal with this apparent dramatic and widespread occurrence of play in mammals and its absence, or unrecognizability, in poikilothermic vertebrates (cf. Hess, 1964). Fagen (1981) is one who holds that play is virtually ubiquitous in mammals and may be more common than we think in other groups. He points out that insufficient study of non-mammals and lack of objective criteria for recognizing play in non-mammals, as well as true biological differences, may all be involved in the lower incidence of play in birds and its virtual absence elsewhere. He argues that since vertebrates and invertebrates that do not play may have parental care, juvenile fighting, complex social cooperation, tool use, learning, environmentally-induced brain plasticity, and elevated aerobic metabolism in vigorous exercise, such conditions are not sufficient to explain the rarity of non-mammalian play. Yet those factors Fagen does assume are concomitants of play (endothermy, large brains, generalized learning, and long-term individual recognition), he also realizes fail to explain the absence of play in various birds and mammals.

In contrast to Fagen (1981), Bekoff and Byers (1981: 30; also Bekoff, 1983) flatly assert that 'fish, amphibians, reptiles, birds, and perhaps a large number of mammals' do not play. They note that primates and carnivores dominate play studies. Play has been described in only 20 out of 1687 species of rodents, they claim (but about 65 in Fagen, 1981; still less than 5%). Berger (1979) noted that play frequency differed between mountain and desert populations of Bighorn sheep by a factor of 9:1, thus showing the difficulties of making comparisons even within a species, let alone quantitative comparisons across genera, families, and orders (see also Baldwin and Baldwin, 1974, on differences among squirrel monkey populations). Ghiselin's (1974) dogmatic but unsupported view that play is found only in social animals having families, but not all of them (e.g. ants) seems to beg too many questions to be helpful in any comparative perspective. In any event, *the apparent occurrence of play in all orders of mammals indicates its probable existence in the earliest mammals. Thus reptiles, being ancestral to both birds and mammals, are the key group to consider in developing hypotheses about play evolution.* This statement does not prejudge whether play has a monophyletic or polyphyletic origin.

Ewer (1968) asks why, if play is advantageous, do not all mammals play? She points out three constraints. First, the need for quick oriented movements in normal behaviour. This applies most to predators, fast moving arboreal species, and prey species in open terrain. Second, there needs to be a period of protected childhood during which the use of behaviour patterns in their appropriate 'earnest situation does not yet arise' (Ewer 1968: 301). and third, the capacity for relatively rapid learning is needed. Fagen's extensive discussion of life-history strategy and mathematical models has helped us realize that for many reasons play might not occur.

We also need to realize that the lack of play in any mammal species may have causes separate from the lack of play in non-homoiothermic vertebrates. Different kinds of play may have varying prominence in the lives of animals, have dissimilar evolutionary histories, and have diverse ontogenies. Too much of the play literature pays no more than lip-service to the diversity of play and the need for truly comparative analyses (Bekoff and Byers, 1981; Burghardt, 1982).

We should approach play in extant animals in a manner similar to other behavioural phenomena. Current phenotypes are a varying mix of phylogenetic inertia and species, population, or individual adaptation to current conditions of life. Homologies, convergencies, and different mixes of genetic and environmental variables may all be involved. Of course, with play the appropriate structural characteristics are not agreed upon and the functions little understood. This underlines a danger in attempts to treat all play as a unitary or natural category (e.g. Fagen 1981: 480), which may obscure real differences in the processes involved and their origin.

Play in the typical mammalian way is, at best, rare or very subtle in reptiles, a subtlety that is incompatible with most characterizations of locomotor, object, or social play. Fagen (1976) predicts that crocodilians, because of their parental care, should play; also varanid lizards because of their high metabolic rate relative to other reptiles. Meagre support is available for these predictions. I suggest here that we need to consider the entire constellation of life-history characteristics, not just isolated features, in approaching the discontinuity issue.

Many reptiles are large, long-lived, and have slow development (Burghardt, 1978a), three characteristics often associated with mammalian play. Also mammals as a group (or even just the playful ones) do not appear to possess any learning ability alien to all reptiles (Burghardt, 1977a). Crocodilians do have a rather long period of parental care (even the minimum estimates are longer than the life expectancies of many 'playful' mammals). They have never, however, been reported to engage in social play. Iguanas, also large and long- lived, engage as juveniles in many social behaviours, some quite sophisticated, but play has never been observed (e.g. Burghardt, 1977b). There is one report of object play in one alligator (Lazell and Spitzer, 1977) and many reptiles do explore. I also briefly reported possible slow-motion manœuvres in neonate chameleons that could be viewed as social play (Burghardt, 1982). But the discontinuity in terms of 'vigorous' play behaviour appears real. A large part of this chapter will be devoted to explaining why; but it is also true that our perceptual limitations and anthropomorphism may be blinding us (Hess, 1964), important factors that I am not able to discuss here.

PLAY AND CURIOSITY

Most recent play specialists in ethology and sociobiology do not seriously consider the relationship of play to exploration and curiosity (cf.

Burghardt, 1982 and Smith, 1982). But many earlier writers did so explicitly (e.g. Groos, 1898; Meyer-Holzapfel, 1956) as do those interested in psychological issues (e.g. Baldwin and Baldwin, 1977; Berlyne, 1960; Lorenz, 1981; Weisler and McCall, 1976; Welker, 1971). Meyer-Holzapfel, for instance, states that 'exploratory behaviour may be a *precursor of play* as appetitive behavior' (1956, English translation in Müller-Schwarze, 1978: 259). She appends a comprehensive scheme incorporating behaviour, level of motivation, drive specificity, and adequacy of play object. Baldwin and Baldwin (1977: 343) assert: 'Clearly a multifactor theory of play is needed to account for the complex intertwining of variables that affect exploration and play.'

There seems to be two reasons for the current reluctance of play researchers (rather than theorists) to associate play and exploration. First, exploration is linked clearly to information-gathering whereas play, by definition, has no such immediate function. Second, in animals that are very playful such as kittens (West, 1977) and children (Hutt, 1966), exploration has been shown to precede play and to be more representative of novel rather than familiar situations.

But if this distinction is so clear, why have so many theorists linked exploration and play? One reason is that without careful experimental work the distinction is difficult to make and is often arbitrary; in any event it appears impossible to make early in ontogeny. Another reason is that everyone assumes that animals *must* learn and improve at least some abilities through play. For Hutt (1966) and West (1977), exploration involves learning about stimuli; play involves learning about responses and movement coordination. Thus play *is*, in spite of its definition, functionally akin to exploration. What about the *delayed* character of play's benefits? Well, the phenomenon of 'latent learning' (Tolman, 1948) is an example of the delayed benefits of exploration.

In contrast to play, curiosity and exploration certainly do occur in vertebrates other than mammals and birds. For example, tongue-flicking in snakes is a well-studied chemosensory investigatory behaviour (e.g. Chiszar et al., 1976). Newly hatched green iguanas (*Iguana iguana*) orient and explore (Burghardt et al., 1976; Drummond and Burghardt, 1982), and they even seem curious. A group of hatchlings no more than three days old once walked up to and all over my open camera case, tongue-touching it repeatedly, while I quietly filmed them. A large anolis lizard endemic to small and remote Malpelo Island has been characterized (Rand et al., 1975: 30) as 'particularly bold and curious'.

In short, while reptiles may not engage in play as typically recognized in mammals, they certainly do engage in exploration, investigation, and even curiosity. Any play that we do see in reptiles will most likely combine such investigatory behaviour with serious precocial activities such as food recognition, and thus be very difficult to identify (figure 1.1, top).

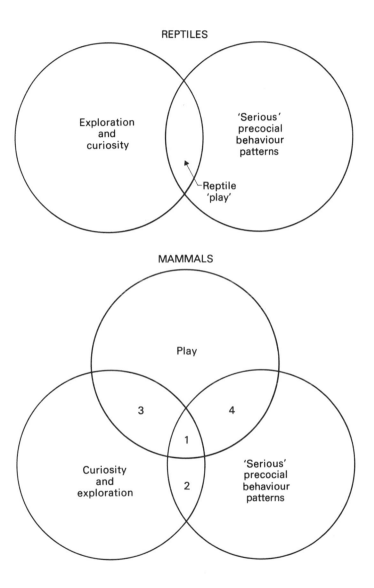

FIGURE 1.1 Simplified diagram depicting the transition between reptiles and mammals in the evolution of play

ORIGINS AND PRECURSORS

By origins of play I refer to the evolutionary factors that led to or made possible play behaviour. Unlike Welker, I put a different gloss on his true enough assertion that 'play and exploration have their origins early in ontogeny' (1971: 172). What we need in addition to careful descriptive, ontogenetic, neurobiological, and experimental studies of play in neonates and young of 'playful' species, is a more comparative perspective involving animals that do *not* play at all, or play in debatable ways. That is, those cases where we are not sure play is even occurring might be particularly fruitful.

As I have previously emphasized in a discussion of the ontogeny of communication (Burghardt, 1977c), questions about origin, modification, and maintenance involve separate but integrated processes in the resulting behavioural phenotype. Is exploration a necessary ontogenetic precursor of play? Are prenatal movements precursors of postnatal activity? The seemingly straightforward continuity position advocated by many developmentalists is not at all so easily supported (see the papers and discussion in Immelmann et al., 1981; especially Bateson, 1981 and Sackett et al., 1981).

As a specific example concerning play, Bekoff and Byers (1981: 300) postulate that 'the phylogenetic oldest function of postnatal outwardly purposeless motor behavior (play) was probably the facilitation of neuromuscular development'. These authors try to draw a continuity between prenatal motility and postnatal play. By claiming that natural selection shaped the various play behaviours in mammalian orders from neuromuscular responses, they can avoid the criticism that most neonatal behaviours have little topographic similarity to prenatal movements.

To date, even postnatal developmental studies of playful species seem to offer little help in understanding evolutionary origins. Cats, one of the favourite subjects for play research, seem to have a highly complex play repertoire involving conspecifics, prey, and locomotion. Bateson (1981) has shown that the types of social play engaged in by kittens each have their own developmental waxing and waning. Thus, play in animals that show it so clearly (cats, dogs, primates) may evidence such an elaboration of play of different kinds that the search for evolutionary precursors is doomed to drive us to bewilderment. The study of mammals and birds showing one or a few types of play behaviour in well-defined contexts may be much more appropriate for uncovering evolutionary origins.

In fact, little has been written on the evolution of play. This may seem a bold and rash assertion given two recent collections of papers (Bruner, et al., 1976; Müller-Schwarze, 1978) and a major monograph, Fagen, 1981 (the first since Groos, 1898), wherein the author claims to have made play studies evolutionary by combining modern views on evolution and social behaviour with recent position statements on behavioural development and the sophisticated use of cost–benefit analysis. At the risk of seeming to disparage current enthusiasms, I feel that we will never be successful in either explaining minor variants of play or understanding the forest, as contrasted with the desert, until serious headway is made on the discontinuity issue.

EVOLUTIONARY EXPLANATIONS AND ARMCHAIR (COMPUTER) THEORY

The only apparent attempt to detail specific reasons as to why only homoiotherms play has been briefly presented by Fagen (1976: 208–9). Starting from the safe assumption (empirically supported, see below) that poikilotherms have lower metabolic requirements than homoiotherms, he asserts that homoiotherms (1) eat a greater variety of foodstuffs than poikilotherms, (2) eat more volume, and (3) spend more time foraging for it. Homoiotherms thus will spend more time and energy on less desirable food items and hence there will be 'greater selective pressure for increased physical capacity in homoiotherms than in like sized poikilotherms and, consequently they will evidence stronger tendencies to play'.

This view predicts that metabolic rate should be correlated with prey diversity, not prey type. While Fagen claims some suggestive trends, McNab (1980) in fact found basal metabolic rate to be correlated with diet (folivore, frugivore, insectivore, etc.). If poikilotherms are more 'r'-selected, hence opportunistic, should not exploration and foraging be enhanced? Fagen's argument also ignores the continuum in reptile foraging from sit and wait to active searching. Thus there are alternative explanations and I deem Fagen's food hypothesis unlikely.

But interesting questions do arise. Are there correlations in mammals among the types and frequency of play, degrees of dietary diversity, foraging requirements, predatory risks, habitat type, and social organiz- ation? Multivariate studies similar to those by Clutton-Brock and Harvey (1977) on sexual dimorphism in primates are what we really need. But for now there are too few data, although carnivores and primates (omnivores) are usually considered most socially playful, and ungulates (herbivores) seem to engage in much locomotor play.

Fagen (1978: 398) presents another brief resume of an apparently unpublished 'formal mathematical model' of the evolution of animal play behaviour. The model turns out to be based on a 'nonzerosum game model of animal playfighting' where cheating, reciprocity, escalation strategy, encounters (random or non-random) were viewed in a game-theory approach looking for evolutionary stable strategies. The model predicts that 'play fighting is most likely to have evolved and should be observed most frequently in family-living animals, where positively assortative, non-random encounters between playful young are inevitable'. As stated, of course, the animals must be 'playful' to begin with and non-mammals are not discussed. Fagen compounds our disappointment by allowing that 'factors other than those already considered can help explain evolution of social play behavior'. We also learn, in the last paragraph, that we are only discussing 'truly reciprocal play' and not the 'solitary or companion-oriented play . . . found in almost all mammals'. The results are similar to what he found with an alternative model (Fagen, 1977) 'resting on quite different premises'.

Fagen's (1977) model 'predicts that not all animal species will exhibit play behavior, that play should be more frequent in K-selected species than in r-selected species, that young animals should tend to devote more time and energy to play than older animals, that adults of some species should play, and that in the ontogeny of animals exhibiting play, behavior patterns required in adulthood should appear in play as soon as or soon after they appear in the animal's general behavioral repertoire' (1977: 411–12). Fagen claims support for the first three predictions and a failure for the fourth. The results of McNab (1980, 1983) make us also question the K- and r-selected dichotomy (the second prediction) as animals maximizing r (the exponential population growth constant) have higher basal metabolic rates.

Fagen (1978) defends the large amount of such theorizing in play research. He points out that 'mathematical formalism' is needed to make 'vague theory operational'. True as this may be, to date almost all the resulting 'predictions' themselves seem premature, *post hoc*, or vague, and are rarely applied to specific species and contexts. Hypothetical graphs abound. Computer simulations are run on crude estimates and the results found acceptable only if they accord with what we already think we know. Cleverness in modelling is in itself no substitute for answering specific questions with comparative data. And a plethora of models with similar conclusions lends no support to the importance of any of the postulated evolutionary scenarios, even *if* comparative data on play diversity in mammals followed the predictions. Bekoff (1978) has listed a page of empirically testable non-trivial questions on social play alone. We need theory that directly aids in the intelligent gathering of empirical data.

I have been critical of such theorizing here, not because it cannot offer important insights, but because of the great temptation to rely on it too heavily and the willingness of empirical workers to be intimidated by its authority. 'Analysis of play using hypothetico-deductive evolutionary theory may offend ethologists and comparative psychologists who prefer data to mathematical models and physiological metaphors to evolutionary logic' (Fagen 1981: 480). It is not the models but the priorities that some find offensive.

Fagen's attitude seems misguided in at least four respects. First, it sets up opposition between data and theory, proximate mechanisms and functional evolutionary issues, that need not exist (and does not for many scientists). Second, it holds that mathematical models are superior to non-mathematical ones, whereas this is true only to the extent that the ideas behind the models approximate reality, are adequately formalized, and allow testable predictions. Third, ethologists and psychologists are well aware, as most sociobiologists advocating this line (e.g. Fagen, 1981; Wilson, 1975) appear not to be, of the history of animal learning theory based upon an explicit hypothetico-deductive approach, which prematurely developed elegant formalisms (e.g. Hull, 1943). The recent trend in learning theory has been to study specific phenomena, constructing modest mini-theories in close reciprocity with experimental findings. And fourth, 'truths' derived from evolutionary 'logic' usually end up being qualified, as the 'logic' resides in our mental, or computer, manipulation of what we think we know about evolution, not the evolutionary process itself.

It might seem, after the above, very risky to present some theoretical ideas. And so it is. My approach, presaged in a brief commentary (Burghardt, 1982), will be to take one of the earliest and still ubiquitous notions in play theory, energy, and show how, properly rehabilitated, it may be an important factor in the evolutionary origins of play. I will focus on reptiles and mammals, although supporting data from amphibians and birds could be marshalled. Some simplifications are necessary, not only for reasons of space, but in order to keep a straightforward question from becoming profound, and thus dooming all hopes of at least side-stepping toward a general theory (Borgatta, 1954).

SPENCER AND SURPLUS ENERGY

The earliest serious theory of play was the 'surplus energy' theory most effectively championed by Herbert Spencer, although Groos (1898) credits Schiller, the playwright, with priority (see also Elias, 1973). We

Gordon M. Burghardt

know it best today through the elegant debunking by Groos (1898) from which it never recovered. Before seeing if resuscitation is possible, or even useful, it is instructive to examine the debate. I will rely on Spencer's statement in the third (last) edition of his *Principles of Psychology* (1898, original 1880) where it occurs in the final chapter (of 75) titled 'Aesthetic Sentiments'.

According to Spencer, animal play is the forerunner to aesthetics and art, which like them, does not 'subserve, in any direct way, the processes conducive to life' (1898: 627). However, immediate gratification (i.e. play is pleasurable) and 'maintained or increased ability due to exercise' (ibid: 628) are involved. Note that he lists both a proximate explanation (pleasure) and a function (exercise).

The core of Spencer's view of animal play is revealed in the following (1898: 628–9):

> Inferior kinds of animals have in common the trait, that all their forces are expended in fulfilling functions essential to the maintenance of life. They are unceasingly occupied in searching for food, in escaping from enemies, in forming places of shelter, and in making preparations for progeny. But as we ascend to animals of high types having faculties more efficient and more numerous, we begin to find that time and strength are not wholly absorbed in providing for immediate needs. Better nutrition, gained by superiority, occasionally yields a surplus of vigour. The appetites being satisfied, there is no craving which directs the overflowing energies to the pursuit of more prey, or to the satisfaction of some pressing want. . . . Thus it happens that in the more evolved creatures, there often recurs an energy somewhat in excess of immediate needs, and there comes also such rest, now of this faculty and now of that, as permits the bringing of it up to a state of high efficiency by the repairs which follow waste.

Spencer elaborates this final point by discussing his theory of nerve centres in which those undischarged through behaviour for long periods of time becomes 'unusually ready to undergo change, to yield up molecular motion' (1898: 629), in other words, become more ready to be performed via threshold lowering. This view, though more mentalistic, is astonishingly prescient of Lorenz's *action specific energy* model (Lorenz, 1981).

> Every one of the mental powers, then, being subject to this law, that its organ when dormant for an interval longer than ordinary becomes unusually ready to act . . . it happens that a simulation of those activities is easily fallen into, when circumstances offer it in place of the real activities. Hence play of all kinds – hence this tendency to superfluous and useless exercise of faculties that have been quiescent. Hence, too, the fact that these uncalled for

exertions are most displayed by those faculties which take the most prominent parts in the creature's life. Observe how this holds from the simplest faculties upwards (Spencer, 1898: 629–30).

Spencer gives examples of gnawing rats, stretching cats, licking giraffes, chasing and wrestling dogs, kittens with cotton balls, sports and 'make-believe' games in children, and games of skill and conversational bantering (repartee) in human adults. Again, all these are performed because of both immediate pleasure from the activity itself and 'partly for the accompanying satisfaction of certain egoistic feelings which find for the moment no other sphere' (1898: 631).

Now there are problems with Spencer's views involving circular logic, levels of explanation, and the varied use of the energy concept itself. But more of modern hindsight later. First let us look at Spencer's key contemporary critic.

GROOS AND THE PLAY INSTINCT

Groos (1898) claimed that the surplus energy theory was faulty in many respects. Mark Baldwin, in his preface to the English edition, claimed that Groos' criticism of Spencer 'put this theory permanently out of court' (iii). Groos was more circumspect, claiming in *his* preface that the surplus energy view 'is certainly of great value, but is not fully adequate' (1898: xix). None the less, the first chapter of his book is devoted to reducing the theory to sufficient rubble that it could easily be cleared away to make room for his new ideas.

Here is Groos' (1898: 6) summary of the surplus energy theory, which differs from Spencer's version in its emphases.

1　The higher animals being able to provide themselves with better nourishment than the lower, their time and strength are no longer exclusively occupied in their own maintenance, hence they acquire a superabundance of vigour.

2　The overflow of energy will be favored in those cases where the higher animals have need for more diversified activities, for while they are occupied with one, the other special powers can find rest and reintegration.

3　When in this manner, the overflow of energy has reached a certain pitch, it tends to discharge.

4　If there is no occasion at the moment for the correlative activity to be seriously exercised, simply imitative activity is substituted, and this is play.

Groos attacks on several fronts. First he points out that the imitative aspect (4) will not hold for the first manifestations of play in young animals and children. Play is thus more a *premonition* of serious activities to come than an *imitation* of past performed serious behaviour.

Groos second major criticism derives from the oft-claimed exuberance of young animals in comfortable conditions. He quotes many authors delightfully to this effect. For example, Hudson (1895, after Groos 1898: 10):

> We see that the inferior animals, when the conditions of life are favourable, are subject to periodical fits of gladness, affecting them powerfully, and standing out in vivid contrast to their ordinary temper, and we know what this feeling is – this periodic intense elation which even civilized man occasionally experiences when in perfect health, especially when young. There are moments when he cannot keep still, when his impulse is to sing and shout aloud and laugh at nothing, to run and leap and exert himself in some extravagant way.

While Groos acknowledges that this 'physical and mental overflow of energy' is 'one of the most important characteristics of play' (1898: 11) he claims that it cannot be the sole answer because 'it does not explain how it happens that all the individuals of a species manifest exactly the specific kind of play expression which prevails with their species, but differs from every other' (ibid: 12). What does explain this, *contra* Spencer and imitation, is instinct.

Groos's next move is to counter the view that 'a condition of surplus energy still appears as the conditio sine qua non, that permits the force of the instinct to be so augmented' (ibid: 15). This he disproves by pointing out that play occurs in 'tired' animals when a potent stimulus appears, as when a kitten chases a piece of paper that blows past 'even if it has been exercising for hours and its superfluous energies are entirely disposed of' (ibid: 19). Thus, by the end of his treatment Groos has reduced energy to being, at best, 'a particularly favorable condition for play' (ibid: 22).

But for Groos the major failing of surplus energy was that it didn't account for the 'biological significance of play', which, he goes on to argue throughout the book, is practice of adult behaviour. As seen in the spirited commentaries on Smith's (1982) attempt to answer this question 84 years later, the jury is still out, and perhaps Spencer should not be faulted for avoiding the issue.

The differences between Groos and Spencer were actually more apparent than real. Spencer was primarily concerned with the proximate reasons for play while Groos was far less interested (and sophisticated) concerning them, but was an enthusiastic evolutionist interested in ultimate factors. This proximate/ultimate dichotomy exists in most areas of behaviour study today, including play research as shown by Fagen's (1981) book that continues the Groos line with a relative lack of interest in causation, while Baldwin and Baldwin (1977), for example, represents the non-evolutionary proximate factor attitude. As classical ethology teaches (Tinbergen, 1963), both approaches are necessary. (See Martin, below, chapter 3, for an analysis of the four ethological queries in relation to play.)

Not all writers were convinced by Groos's anti-energy views. McDougall (1924) claimed that play is not an instinct. His fairly cogent reasons, echoed frequently today, are as follows: (1) since play involves behaviour from several 'motor mechanisms', it is 'the expression not of one instinct but of many, or of all' (1924: 170); (2) practice is ruled out as mature animals play long after the serious patterns are present; (3) behaviourally and emotionally, play differs from the real thing (e.g. presence of biting inhibitions and lack of anger); and (4) the situations (setting factors) differ. As an alternative to instinct, not citing Spencer, McDougall (1924: 171) states that:

> Play is activity for its own sake, or more properly, it is a purposeless activity, striving toward no goal. Whence, then comes the energy that sustains it? The answer, I think, is that the well fed and well rested animal especially the young animal, has a surplus of nervous energy which works through the channels of the various motor mechanisms.

He derives play from the stereotyped movements of caged animals, fidgety schoolboys, and the frisky antics of horses released from stables. 'It is the primal *libido* or vital energy flowing not in the channels of instinct, but overflowing, generating a vague appetite for movement and finding outlet in any or all of the motor mechanisms in turn' (1924: 172).

A major problem is that all these early theories, and many recent ones, suffer from confusing the causal and functional dynamics of elaborate play in today's creatures with the precursors and preadaptations that allowed natural selection to shape complex play from non-play. Let me use an analogy to reiterate this important point. One can study for years the ear and hearing in mammals and never have much to say about the evolutionary origin of the ear and hearing, whereas comparative studies of poorly hearing vertebrates uncovered the connection between a tiny bone in our middle ear and the jaw-bone of salamanders, a rather unexpected evolutionary origin, to say the least.

ENERGY AND PLAY: THE CURRENT SCENE

Discussions of energy have fallen upon hard times in writings on play. While many modern writers refer to energy in their treatments of play (e.g. Ewer, 1968; Hediger, 1964) it is done uncritically and usually with the goal of telling us that play is energetically costly and thus *must* be important (see Martin, 1982, 1984). Bekoff and Byers (1981: 324) noted that play may be very energetic *and* deplete a limited energy store, and admirably provide some suggestions for research. But Bekoff (1976) explictly dismissed the surplus energy theory as untestable. Müller-Schwarze (1978) briefly discussed energy and refers to play as 'behavioral fat'. In Fagen's lengthy monograph on animal play (1981) neither 'energy' nor 'surplus energy' made it into the 16-page double-columned index, although energy in the colloquial sense was utilized repeatedly. There were also no entries dealing with metabolic rate and only one under 'physiological'. The Müller-Schwarze anthology (1978) refers to the Spencerian position, of necessity in a historical collection, but otherwise energy is almost totally neglected in all the included classical papers except for Leyhausen (1973, original 1965; discussed below).

In spite of the dearth of technical concern with energy of most play researchers, I think that recent physiological studies and a more critical use of energy concepts can help to identify the physiological and behavioural requisites for play in the mammalian way, and facilitate the formulation of a plausible evolutionary scenario.

Differing connotations of energy and surplus

It is first necessary to clarify years of confusion in the use of the terms 'energy' and 'surplus' (table 1.1). Vigorous or sustained rapid behaviour is often referred to as energetic, with behaviour that is more vigorous being considered more energetic. This energetic behaviour has costs for the animal. What kind of costs? – costs in time and energy. But now the term 'energy' is being used in a second way, as denoting a metabolic resource, energy stored in muscle and fat, that can be converted into behaviour, behaviour that may or may not be energetic. 'Energetic' behaviour in the first sense necessitates an efficient respiratory and circulatory system as well as the neuromuscular capacity for rapid movement. Such behaviour also, of course, eventually draws on metabolic reserves. First, adequate nutritional state, second physiological performance. Even a fat tortoise can only move slowly.

'Energy' is also used in a motivational sense to characterize hypothesized general or specific moods, drives, or instincts responsible for the proximate occurrence of play, as in concepts such as 'arousal' or 'action specific energy'. These uses, although controversial (e.g. Hinde, 1970), have been common in traditional ethological and psychological theory. Thus, if play involves a motivation for a *specific* set of activities, then just as with drives (or response tendencies) to perform feeding, sexual, nest building and other behaviours, we can study changes in threshold, deprivation effects, and so on. Alternatively we can postulate *general* arousal or drive states. Thus, Groos (1898) discredited an exuberance (arousal) view of play but advocated specific instincts. Leyhausen (1973) uses the concept of 'drive surplus' in a similar manner. Spencer (1898) himself, we have seen used both as he developed his threshold lowering model. Table 1.1 illustrates these four uses of 'energy'.

TABLE 1.1   Various connotations of the terms 'energy' and 'surplus' in reference to play

Energy	Surplus
1 As vigorous (energetic) behaviour	1 Elevated activity level (hyper-activity, fidgety)
2 As metabolic potential (i.e. from food)	2 Excess available metabolic reserves
3 As specific motivation, drive, or instinct	3 Excess accumulated motiva-tion or action-specific energy
4 As general motivation or drive	4 High level of arousal

Similarly, 'surplus' is variously referred to as hyperactivity, unneeded stored metabolic reserves, as a dammed up, near excessive, general arousal level, or as excessive drive, mood, or motivational 'energy' for the performance of specific acts (e.g. vacuum activities). Table 1.1 lists the different uses of 'surplus' associated with the different uses of 'energy'.

Note that the metabolic potential usage is primary to *both* motivational usages of energy and surplus. We know that food deprived animals do play less (Baldwin and Baldwin, 1976; Müller-Schwarze et al., 1982). The *vigorous behaviour* connotation is more descriptive, but tied to our anthropocentric time scale. It is my contention that these usages have been confused by Spencer, Groos, McDougall, and others down to the present, leading to the remarkable misunderstanding of energy consider-ations today. We will begin by considering energy as metabolic potential in reptiles and mammals.

METABOLIC ENERGY

It is our impression that reptiles spend much of their time, even when 'active' in the field, remaining quiescent for long periods or making only slow and deliberate movements. . . This relative inactivity is punctuated by rapid and explosive bursts, fuelled by anaerobic metabolism. The contrast between sedentary, sometimes immobile behavior and intense and rapid activity, which makes reptiles such fascinating animals to watch, finds its basis in differential metabolic support for these behavioral modes. (Bennett, 1982: 193)

Physiologists would have us restrict the use of energy to the joules or calories of metabolism (cf. Martin, 1982). To do this we need to begin by distinguishing a number of concepts. Throughout I will rely on the writings of Bennett (1982), Bennett and Dawson (1976), Pough (1980), and McNab, (1980, 1983). Lizards are the primary focus here both because more work has been done with them and because, as a group, they are structurally and ecologically diverse and occupy niches most similar to terrestrial mammals. The following terms, modified from Bennett (1982), will aid in our discussion:

1   *Basal metabolic rate* (BMR). Minimal metabolic rate when fasting under optimal environmental conditions. All metabolic rates may be measured indirectly (by oxygen consumption) or directly (by heat production).
2   *Resting metabolic rate* (RMR). The level of oxygen consumption or heat production when an animal is not engaged in any overt activity.
3   *Aerobic metabolism.* Release of metabolic energy by use of external (gaseous) oxygen, generally obtained through breathing, lungs, and associated systems.
4   *Aerobic scope.* The range of oxygen consumption rate between minimum and maximum aerobic oxygen utilization.
5   *Anaerobic metabolism.* Release of metabolic energy by the breakdown of stored glycogen to lactic acid. This occurs when insufficient molecular oxygen is available through ordinary respiration.
6   *Anaerobic scope.* Rate of lactic acid formation during the onset of vigorous activity (usually the first 30 sec).
7   *Anaerobic capacity.* The amount of lactic acid formed during longer activity bouts, usually those preceding exhaustion.
8   *Maximum sustainable activity.* The level of exertion (often measured in locomotion rate) an animal can carry out continuously without building up an oxygen deficit.

9 *Energy costs of activity.* Amount of energy (joules or calories) needed to perform a given behaviour. Should be measured as a *rate* of energy output, as in metabolic rate (i.e. watts = joules/sec) (Martin, 1984). The net cost of activity is the difference between the total energy expenditure rate during activity less the RMR.

10 *Total metabolic scope.* The difference between BMR and maximum combined contributions of aerobic and anaerobic metabolism.

Aerobic metabolism

Resting metabolism is about ten times lower in reptiles than in homoiotherms (Bennett and Dawson, 1976). Oxygen consumption in all animals is related to size, activity level, and body temperature. For example, RMR in all reptiles studied is 5.6 times higher at 40°C than at 20°C (Bennett, 1982). Aerobic scope is strongly size-dependent in lizards. For instance, a 10 g lizard can increase its oxygen consumption up to 7.2 times its resting level, but a 1 kg lizard can only increase it 3.6 times. Even monitor lizards, whose metabolic rates are the highest recorded in reptiles and which, under some conditions, overlap mammalian BMRs, are limited. Animals averaging 714 g, at prime activity temperatures of 30°C and 40°C could only increase oxygen consumption about 4.2 and 2.3 times respectively (calculated from Bartholomew and Tucker, 1964). Thus, if larger body and absolute brain size are positively correlated with play, as has been argued for mammals (Fagen, 1981) then the larger reptiles are at a physiological disadvantage, *vis-à-vis* smaller reptiles.

While accepting the views of Fagen (1976) and Symons (1978) on the exercise function of play, Bekoff and Byers claim that the essential question is 'whether the training responses produced by this type of exercise conferred a selective advantage that led to the evolution of play in animals' (1981: 317). It is thus interesting to note that in the one lizard (*Sceloporus occidentalis*) studied, and not as in mammals, aerobic scope was unaffected by 6–8 weeks of daily physical activity (Gleeson, 1979). These lizards are thus characterized as metabolically inflexible. Admittedly, one should not generalize to an entire class from one species, but if measures of stamina are not substantially increased by activity in reptiles, one of the several postulated exercise benefits for play in mammals is inapplicable to reptiles. It also is inconsistent with Fagen's (1981: 266) hypothesis that somatic (bone and muscle) plasticity evolved *because* young reptiles are 'highly motile upon hatching'. Note that activity is not the same as play. While exercise in terms of activity does seem to provide benefits for mammals, play activity has not yet been shown to provide this.

Cost of activity

While reptiles, as compared to mammals, have reduced metabolic scope, the calculated cost of walking 1 km is much less in lizards than in mammals (Bennett, 1982). For instance, at 0.1 km/hr a 10 g lizard will expend 0.98 kilojoules and a 10 g mammal will expend 7.46 kilojoules, a better than seven-fold difference. However, the cost of activity to the mammal includes thermoregulation, a major factor in the much higher BMR and RMR of mammals. The relative metabolic costs of endothermy go down rapidly with increasing body size. This relates to why the cost of locomotion increases with increasing body weight in both lizards and mammals, but more slowly in mammals. Thus, a hundredfold increase in body weight (to 1000 g) leads to a 39.6 times energy expenditure increase in a lizard but only a 30.2 times increase in a mammal (calculated from Bennett, 1982). In addition, the cost of locomotion per unit distance travelled decreases sharply as locomotory speed increases. Thus a tenfold increase in speed (from 0.1 km/hr to 1.0 km/hr) leads to a reduction in energy cost per distance covered of 51% for the 10 g lizard and of 59% for a 1000 g lizard. For the mammal, however, the reduction in cost for the 10 g animal is 82% and for the 1000 g animal 86%. Hence, at 1 km/hr and 1000 g, the relative cost for a mammal to move 1 km, compared to the lizard, has declined from a 7.6 times lizard advantage to only a 2.0 times one. Note that this is superimposed on an animal with only about 10% of the RMR of the mammal to begin with.

Although I have not seen it pointed out, these calculations showing relatively greater efficiency of rapid locomotion and large size may help us to understand the growing indication that small homoiotherms in a lineage (genus, family) appear to play less frequently or less complexly than larger species, e.g. rats and mice (Poole and Fish, 1975). Lizards are generally much smaller than mammals. Few lizards (mainly varanids and iguanas) have adult sizes larger than 3 kg, and only one (komodo dragon) more than 100 kg. Most mammals other than bats and rodents are considerably larger than lizards and many mammals top 100 kg. Indeed, 79% of all lizard adults weight less than 20 g, with 36% weighing 5 g or less. Adult mammals, because of endothermic constraints, rarely weigh as little as 5 g (Pough, 1980). Thus mammals, by virtue of their larger size alone, may have greater physiological preadaptations for play.

Many snakes and turtles, and all crocodilians, do grow larger than the typical lizard, so the point may not hold for them. However, snakes have a particularly energy-efficient locomotor style; crocodilians are largely aquatic and this also greatly cuts locomotor costs, something true of aquatic turtles too. Land turtles, with their armoured shells and omnivorous diet, need not run fast to avoid predators, find food, or compete with conspecifics. It might be thought that reptiles, not having the enormous costs of endothermy to bear, should have more energy available for activity. But the metabolic reserves they do have are not readily available for rapid sustained behaviour due to their reduced aerobic abilities. Rand and Rand (1976) discuss the energy problems faced by nesting iguana females in digging their extensive burrows.

Physiological limitations may also be related to locomotor efficiency and play in homoiotherms. Flying in birds is a much more efficient mode of locomotion than is walking in birds. While light weight is an asset for flying, the smallest birds often have extremely high metabolic costs due to thermoregulation; hummingbirds, the smallest species, have apparently never been observed playing (Fagen, 1981). Conversely aquatic mammals, large and in an energy-efficient medium, seem to be among the most playful of all mammals.

Anaerobic metabolism

'Intense activity [in reptiles] can be supported only anaerobically and is required in precisely those instances which are of the greatest significance to survival and reproduction (e.g. escape, pursuit, courtship, territorial defense)'. (Bennett, 1982: 189) Anaerobic metabolism refers to the production of energy by means not involving inspired O_2. Lactic acid is produced and occurs in reptiles not only in the initial burst of activity but even after only 5 sec of intense activity (Bennett, 1982). While relying on anaerobic metabolism has many advantages for the energy-conserving life-style of reptiles, in terms of behavioural performance it is largely associated with lowered capacity for sustained vigorous behaviour, rapid exhaustion, and long recovery times (Bennett, 1982).

Anaerobic scope, and to a lesser degree, anaerobic capacity, are generally greater in reptiles than in amphibians. Interestingly, reptiles have greater anaerobic capacities than the mammals studied to date. But the only ontogenetic studies indicate that anaerobic capacity and associated maximal duration of activity are reduced in neonate as compared to adult natricine snakes (Pough, 1977, 1978). Maturation leads to a fourfold to sevenfold increment in time to complete exhaustion. What this means, of course, if these findings can be generalized, is that at the time in life play is most common and, presumably, adaptive, a reptile's physiology may just not be capable of performing.

A typical characteristic of play is that it occurs in sustained bouts of active, repetitive movements. In small lizards, anaerobic metabolism provides at least 80–90% of the total ATP (energy) production in the first

30 sec of vigorous activity. In the mammals studied, anaerobic metabolism accounted for only 8–25% of total ATP production (Bennett, 1982). Thus 'the development of high aerobic capacities in mammals has not resulted in increased capacities for burst activity, but rather in the expansion of capacities for routine and sustainable activity' (Bennett, 1982: 189). Strict locomotor–respiratory synchronization is another factor recently postulated as 'a vital factor in the sustained aerobic exercise of endothermic mammals' (Bramble and Carrier, 1983: 251). Reptiles have, apparently, not yet been examined, but my prediction is that synchrony will be shown, if at all, only in slow, steady locomotion, as evidenced by foraging lizards.

In any event, even rather routine activities in reptiles may involve anaerobic metabolism. For example, Feder and Arnold (1982) found that it was substantially relied on during attack and ingestion of typical salamander prey by garter snakes. Pough has argued that the reliance on anaerobic metabolism in reptiles is a specialized strategy to avoid the high resting metabolic rates needed in 'maintaining an aerobic system capable of delivering large amounts of energy during exercise' (1980: 96).

Total metabolic scope

Energy budgets in the field are largely unknown for reptiles other than lizards (Congdon, et al., 1982). Nagy (1982) in his review of studies on iguanid lizards, calculated that during its activity season a typical 100 g lizard expends about 6–9% the energy of a 100 g rodent and only 3% that of a 100 g bird. The high cost of homoiothermy for mammals and birds helps to explain these differences. When annual energy requirements are considered, the energy requirements of the lizard, as compared to the mammal, are approximately halved (to 2–4%). Again, this seems due to the ability of reptiles to hibernate or aestivate at near-zero BMRs.

Nagy claims that the general similarity of lizard and mammal tissues and morphology should lead to equal potential food consumption. Even allowing for the faster food processing time of mammals, given their higher metabolic rate '. . . the lizard should be capable of obtaining far more surplus energy . . . than the mammal' (1982: 57). Nagy's view is that the lizards shunt this surplus to growth and reproduction. We will come back to this important point.

Metabolic rate in mammals

A different approach is McNab's (1980, 1983) attempt to explain the wide diversity in metabolic rate in mammals. He found that while body size is the most important variable in BMR, diet and reproductive output are major factors when body size is held constant. Edentates (ant-eaters) have very low BMRs, followed closely by arboreal folivores (e.g. sloths) and browsers. Play is not prominent in such lower BMR mammals (Fagen, 1981). I think this is due to limitations on both aerobic activity and the costs of obtaining and processing a low nutritive diet, often toxic. Average daily metabolic rate (ADMR) or field metabolic rate (FMR) are better measures for such comparisons (e.g. Nagy, 1982) but too few data are available.

Nectar specialists and frugivores (some bats) and carnivores (but not insectivores) have the highest metabolic rates (McNab, 1980). While the aerobic scope ratio of most mammals is about six, in the low BMR mammals the scope is reduced to as little as two. McNab also found that at constant body size, species with a higher metabolic rate had higher population growth constants (r_m). Thus McNab believes that, within mammals at least, those with lower metabolic rates do not shunt energy towards reproduction (either number or size of offspring). Furthermore, under relatively constant conditions, when ecologically equivalent mammals with differing metabolic rates are paired in the laboratory or in 'natural' introductions in the field (snowshoe and arctic hares, carnivorous marsupials and placentals) the higher BMR animals always displace the lower BMR ones. Why then do some low metabolic animals (e.g. opossums) survive and thrive? Because, McNab asserts, they can deal with uncertain environments better than higher metabolic rate species. This argument is similar to those touting the superiority of reptiles in variable or harsh environments (such as deserts) (e.g. Regal, 1978; Pough, 1980; Burghardt and Rand, 1982).

Fagen (1981) sees a precise parallel between the evolution of play and brain size. Such a parallel can, omitting some extremes, also be found with play and metabolic rate. That brain size and metabolic rate may be hard to disentangle is underscored by a recent report showing a positive relation between brain size and metabolism in mammals (Armstrong, 1983).

ENERGY AND MOTIVATION

Early writers such as Spencer and McDougall viewed play as an overflow of energy. This overflow is sometimes characterized as a general arousal and then the problem is to explain the specific types of play engaged in. Groos avoided this by postulating 'instincts' separate from general energy overflow. Other writers claimed that play could be derived from incomplete, awkward, or premature aspects of 'normally motivated' behaviour because specific play behaviours seemed to have a 'drive' of their own (e.g. Meyer-Holzapfel, 1956). The question then becomes one of establishing whether or not there are specific play drives.

One way to go about this is to deprive animals of play experience. In one of the first studies Müller-Schwarze (1968) found that locomotor play in black-tailed deer was not pent up after deprivation, and he argued for a general readiness to be active, not a specific motivation. Chepko (1971) found that confining domestic goats, thus eliminating alternative physical activity, resulted in a substantial increase in play. Thus play in both species may be mediated largely by general activity drive.

Another approach is to see if the opportunity to play is reinforcing to an animal. Will an animal learn a new task based upon the reward of play? Harlow (1953) established this in terms of investigatory–manipulatory 'motives' in monkeys. Humphreys and Einon (1981) showed that social play was reinforcing in laboratory rats, and as effective as food in learning a T-maze discrimination.

Armed with this information we can now delve into the murky waters of motivational play theory. A current autochthonous (independent) motivation for play in some animals does not rule out its evolutionary origin from motivation supplied from different sources (allochthonous). The significance of early ethological discussions of ritualization, displays, and displacement activities (Tinbergen 1952) is based on this recognition. Lorenz (1981), while accepting a specific motivation for play in some cases, derives others from 'dammed up' motor patterns, as in locomotion and vacuum activities. 'In these most primitive forms of play, it is not necessary to assume a special motivation. However, there are all kinds of possible transitions from such primitive forms of play to the more sophisticated and complicated ones in which motor patterns belonging to entirely different functional systems are produced in a haphazard succession' (1981: 330).

Ewer (1968) states that play is not 'in earnest' and 'since the genuine motivation is absent, there is no defined endpoint and the actions may be repeated over and over again; in practice it is this repetition that constitutes one of the most obvious characteristics of play' (1968: 288). She concludes 'that play has no biological objective other than its own performance' (ibid: 288). Note the confusion here between function (not in earnest) and causation (motivation absent), further confounded by the reinforcement value of play itself, which makes us unclear as to what 'genuine motivation' really means. Presumably she is arguing that the topographic movements seen are not in their usual 'serious' context. Following (but probably unaware of) Spencer, Ewer (1968: 288) came to believe that 'different types of play may have different thresholds, with some not appearing until the activity level is high'.

Meyer-Holzapfel (1956: 462) concludes 'that play behavior arises from a general non-specific activity drive, a readiness to be active in any manner whatsoever'. In contrast, Leyhausen (1973) claims that play derives from independent motivations for different predatory behaviours, with those later in the sequence (e.g. killing and eating) having higher thresholds, hence being less likely to be performed. Thus play involves the earlier stages (e.g. pouncing, stalking) that are less likely to be 'seriously' expressed in captivity, but are most likely to be performed repeatedly in the field. In this way 'drive surplus' accumulates that is expressed in play. Bekoff (1974) argues, based on observations of canids, that there is a drive for play that may be variously exhibited in social, self-directed, object contexts.

Ewer (1968: 293) combines these views and postulates both a 'general play drive' and 'accumulation of motivations for individual actions' (see also Eibl-Eibesfeldt, 1982, for a systems diagram of a similar model). The acceptance of the former for Ewer is largely based on the 'enthusiasm with which learned games may be performed'. Interestingly, the appetitive early stages in an 'instinct' are precisely where Craig (1918) long ago postulated that learning should occur. Biben's (1979) experiments on predation and play in cats show the difficulty in evaluating such causal motivation models and underscore the need for careful experimentation.

The view of play as due to low levels of motivation and thus as providing incomplete or developmental precursors of adult behaviour, as held by Kruijt (1964) in his analysis of 'play' fighting in jungle fowl, has sometimes been dismissed by pointing to the rapidity and diversity of play (Lorenz, 1981) and its persistence in adults long after the 'relevant earnest patterns are fully matured and in use' (Ewer, 1968: 294). Yet the i dea has persisted. Craig (1918) mentioned doves 'toying' with nest material early in the reproductive cycle. In Kruijt's analysis such behaviour in neonates may help develop behaviour systems through increasing interaction and integration of causal factors initially autonomous. This, of course, is a variant of the motor training hypothesis and is a process I will later recast phylogenetically.

MAMMALS AND REPTILES COMPARED: A SURPLUS RESOURCE APPROACH

How prominent is play in a mammal's time budget? Fagen (1981) estimates 1–10% under natural conditions. He also lists various costs. Martin (1982, 1984) points out that the net energy costs of play, in terms of an increase over RMR, may actually be rather small. His careful studies of kittens showed that play occupied about 9% of the time, and accounted for about 4% of the daily energy expenditure, excluding growth. He concludes that this relatively minor cost may thus mean that play may at best provide minor benefits. If this is true of such intense and complex play as found in kittens, then the incipient play we are considering here in reptiles or archaic mammals need provide even fewer benefits.

Further support for the less than critical role of play in mammals is shown by how easily play is suppressed under adverse conditions (food shortage, heavy predator pressure, bad weather) with no documented loss of fitness (Baldwin and Baldwin, 1974; Berger, 1979; Fagen, 1981). This means, not that play has no long-term benefits, but that any that do exist pale in relation to immediate demands.

A short-term decrease of 33% in energy intake (milk) in white-tailed deer fawns led to a decrease in play (35%) and general activity (9%) but an increase in grazing (62%) such that estimated total energy consumption remained about the same (Müller-Schwarze et al., 1982). Since the animals could compensate for a one-third reduction in milk, an implication of the experimental results is that healthy mammals in a resource-rich environment have considerable reserves: an energy bank. Reliance on a less rich food (grass) resulted in a reduction in the frequency of play. Similarly Baldwin and Baldwin (1976) experimentally demonstrated that making food difficult to obtain reduced play in squirrel monkeys to 1% of the free-access baseline level. Such results seem to model the findings of Baldwin and Baldwin (1974) and Berger (1979) on natural populations. Reptiles, we have seen, do not have the physiological capacity to perform sustained vigorous movement without drawing on anaerobic sources. The costs (e.g. predator risks, diversion from possibility of other activities) of doing this for 'play' are much higher for animals relying on anaerobic rather than aerobic metabolism.

Fagen (1976) explicitly brings out energy and life-history considerations in mammalian play and notes that neonate ectothermic altricial mammals appear not to play because of the time and energy demands of feeding, competition, and of maintaining body temperature. As mammals mature, however, these factors recede in importance and 'exercise play will begin at that stage in ontogeny when the long-term benefits of exercise outweigh the short-term costs of such diversion of time and energy' (1976: 201). We have seen that exercise *may* not result in improved locomotor endurance in reptiles.

Young reptiles have much greater indeterminate growth than do young mammals. By this I mean that while the maximum size of a reptile might be set, its neonatal and juvenile growth rate is much less so (Andrews, 1982). For example sibling young reptiles (e.g. snapping turtles) can remain in good health even if one remains near birth weight while a sibling increases in size tenfold. The advantages to reptiles of putting all excess energy into growth processes and outpacing possible predators, particularly when defended, if at all, by parents themselves physiologically limited, would seem to outweigh rather slight and delayed assumed benefits of play. Neonate mammals and birds, on the other hand, with rather determinate growth, protection, increased resting and active metabolic rates, and high energy (e.g. milk, insects) consumption accompanied by few costs in obtaining it, may, in 'good times' accumulate more energy than can be effectively utilized for growth. This leads to a source of energy for less than critical activities. Supporting this idea is the observation that well-fed young birds and mammals often become fat, well-fed reptiles just grow faster.

Very young mammals and birds often have to regulate their body temperature through external sources of heat and at this stage do not clearly appear to play. This indicates that altricial mammals and birds have metabolic limitations that may make excess activity, as in play, maladaptive. Reptiles' reliance on external heat sources throughout their lives, along with anaerobic metabolism, is their primary physiological difference from mammals (Pough, 1980). Together these combine to make play in reptiles a possible bankruptcy strategy, not a judicious use of accrued interest. While reptiles may have fat deposits, their ability to withdraw and spend them rapidly is severely constrained.

None the less, reptiles do have the requisite behavioural and motivational processes (arousal, curiosity, classical instinctive and learning mechanisms) for us to see how play could easily evolve when bank transactions could be more rapidly and efficiently processed and competing demands (e.g. basking, defence) reduced. Regal (1978) sees the most mammal-like behaviour in those lizards that have moved into an active foraging mode. Indeed he postulates endogenous activity cycles as an evolutionary mechanism to get the animal up and going. Exploratory behaviour he finds more prominent precisely in these species.

The frequent observation that play occurs only when animals are in a 'relaxed field', sated, warm, content, and so forth supports the view that play of various kinds originated in animals with (1) sufficient metabolic resources; (2) an efficient aerobic system; (3) a relatively familiar and often risk-free juvenile environment; (4) the ability to accumulate more energy than can be shunted to growth; (5) escape from the need to behaviourally thermoregulate to bring the body to the optimum for vigorous behaviour; (6) innate precocial exploratory and arousal mechanisms; (7) specific motivational and behavioural systems; and (8) relatively high survival rate of offspring (as compared to reptiles with comparable life-spans). Thus metabolic and behavioural physiology set the stage for the retention and elaboration of once-critical reptilian abilities in a less demanding context, where slight but advantageous improvements in a myriad of situations could be favoured. Play today is thus a heterogeneous phenomenon; available surplus resources have made the evolution of vigorous play possible. Many of the primary physiological and life-history contrasts between mammals and reptiles discussed here can be summarized as follows:

	Mammals	Reptiles
1	Play research focuses on pure 'delayed' benefits, vigorous motor activity.	Highly likely that any 'play' will also have a current benefit. Play may occur on a different time scale.
2	High basal and resting metabolic rates.	Low basal and resting metabolic rates.
3	Capable of sustained vigorous activity (aerobic metabolism). Costs of activity go down rapidly with increased body size.	Vigorous behaviour sporadic and short-lived. Reliance on anaerobic metabolism for sustained activity. Costs of activity go down more slowly with increased size.
4	Rapid recuperation after sustained activity and thus short period of vulnerability.	Recuperation from sustained activity (to normal lactic acid levels) measured in hours. Extended period of vulnerability.
5	Exercise increases cardiovascular and endurance functions.	No evidence for physiological benefits of exercise.
6	Endothermy provides high resting metabolism allowing rapid onset of play.	Ectothermy allows a low energy (conservation) life-style. The behaviours needed to raise body temperature to aerobic optimum often incompatible with play.
7	Neonates have food, heat, shelter and protection provided by parent.	Neonates must provide for all their own resources.

8	Neonatal period available to develop or perfect functional social, feeding, locomotor, or antipredator skills.	Most behaviours necessary for survival need to be highly functional at birth. Skill improvement can, however, occur.
9	'Relaxed field' common in juveniles.	'Relaxed field' rare in juveniles.
10	Play occurs most frequently when well fed, often after feeding.	Postingestion behaviour in reptiles characterized by lethargy and distended stomachs, basking or hiding out of harm's way.
11	Relatively determinate juvenile growth allows for excess metabolic energy in 'good times'.	Relatively indeterminate juvenile growth allows most energy intake to be channelled into growth.
12	Relatively few offspring, especially in the most 'playful' families.	Relatively more offspring produced, with higher mortality, over equivalent adult lifespans.

BOREDOM AND DEGENERATION: SIDESTEPS TOWARD A THEORY

Now if my characterization of reptile and mammal life history strategy and play behaviour is even roughly accurate, how did the situation in the top diagram of figure 1.1 evolve to that in the bottom diagram, in which play is now specified as separable from both exploration and serious precocial activity? I will now briefly suggest a scheme.

Could not the earliest play be related to what we colloquially refer to as escaping boredom? Play in homoiotherms does appear to be partly a function of a biological need for exercise not adequately satisfied when food is plentiful and predators scarce. Exploration and play have been noted to be more prevalent in animals in perceptually impoverished environments (reviewed in Bekoff, 1972). Comparative evidence suggests that locomotor-rotational play is the most widespread and common form of play in mammals and birds. Play may be but one method to obtain a functional end. For example, the role of play in exercise might

only be important in animals not obtaining sufficient exercise through other means, such as foraging. Play must thus be, in Müller-Schwarze's (1978) term, behavioural fat, serving as a homeostatic exercise reserve, with mechanisms that *appear* to produce behaviour 'for its own sake' evolving subsequently, including social, socially facilitated, and sexually dimorphic play.

But what, then, leads to the similarity within species in the kinds of play behaviour observed? Is it not conceivable that the types of play seen in mammals and birds are derived from degenerated systems of instinctive behaviour? Altricial mammals do not have the need to engage in the same serious behaviour as juvenile reptiles. However, incipient mammals must certainly have had the neural, sensory, motivational, and motor processes for performing many specific precocial activities. With the advent of parental care, natural selection for the maintenance of these was relaxed as the performance of such behaviour patterns became less necessary and even maladaptive. Conceivably therefore, in the absence of strong selection, the degree of hard-wired proficiency in these behaviours decreased while other, more experientially based, supports increased. This can, simplistically, be viewed as a shift from closed to open genetic programmes (Burghardt, 1977c).

Thus, we have young mammals, parasites on their parents, (Galef, 1981), nutritionally well off and often with a surplus of metabolic reserves, that, unlike in reptiles, could be activated quickly with aerobic metabolism. The remnants of behaviour patterns, physiological mechanisms, and motivations, coupled with exploratory tendencies, were readily triggered as the enforced inactivity associated with parental care led to 'boredom' and lowered thresholds. Remember that these behaviour systems once essential to their new-born reptile ancestors, while not very useful to neonate mammals themselves, were, however, still highly useful to adult mammals. Relaxed selection on neonates would lead to less precise releasing situations and altered thresholds. Well-integrated sequences of behaviour could become altered in temporal patterning and behaviour patterns from different motivational sources jumbled. Any 'superfluous' activity, not detrimental to survival, was now available to take over secondarily as *one* means to maintain, practice or refine behaviour. Such activity, facilitated by both metabolic and motivational 'energies', if you will, allowed greater learning to enter these behavioural contexts and larger brains made the degree of motor control available to the mammal much higher than that available to the reptile. This fits our impression that while reptiles are capable of very remarkable and precise behaviour, as in prey capture, the repertoire of such behaviour is very limited in any *individual* reptile, and is largely locked into stereotyped 'instinctive' systems.

Note that by this view play did not arise *directly* as a somewhat mysterious means of incorporating flexibility, modifiability, plasticity, or innovation within a behavioural repertoire, but was a serendipitous bonus for having to find other ways to do what reptiles did 'naturally'. Reptiles were on this earth and highly successful for millions of years. Snakes didn't even begin their major radiation until after all those bright, furry little mammals were scurrying about. Reptiles are thus at one peak of adaptive fitness; in order to reach an even hgher (in some sense) peak, early endotherms had to descend into a valley and find a new way up.

Consider figure 1.1 more closely. The numbers of the intersecting circles represent varying mixtures of play, exploration, and serious precocial activities, not of course in any measure of their importance. As one unobvious prediction from the theory outlined here, virtually all mammalian play should involve behaviour patterns reflective of past neonatal ancestry, that is, represent functions that reptiles had to perform as neonates in the absence of parental care. And so we find play involving locomotion, predation, social interaction, manipulating objects, etc. and, in fact, a linking of varying degrees between exploration, curiosity, and motoric play. On the other hand, play is virtually never, if ever, discussed in terms of those neonatal behaviour patterns that are critical to survival in the young mammal or bird, but rare or absent in adults. We don't read about gaping play in altricial birds. Their competition for food with siblings is dead serious. Suckling behaviour and teat competition in young mammals is also in earnest, as is thermoregulatory huddling behaviour of baby chicks or rat pups. These are all behaviour patterns that evolved in neonate homoiotherms in conjunction with parental care. Fagen (1981: 295) mentions similar behaviours that do not occur in play, without explanation.

Play is a surprisingly inefficient process with a lot of slack. Is it not reasonable to consider play a collection of jerry-built mechanisms for maintaining, in varying ways, continuity for homoiothermic and behavioural systems bridging the periods of juvenile dependence and adult independence? The deterioration of neonatal instinctive behavioural patterns through parental care and the increased aerobic metabolic ability made possible by homoiothermy, led to a reorganization of developmental processes such that play, as well as other experiential alternatives, was not only available to homoiotherms but *had* to be exploited by them. The perplexing individual variability we see in mammalian play may reflect the fact that the 'serious' activity that much play has become (and hence is not recognized as play) may be more important than the motley category we yet call animal play.

CONCLUSIONS

Energy and surplus resources are critical concepts in play theory that merit attention. Play originated from boredom and deteriorated behaviour, an outrageous speculation that may, after all, also be true of the writer and his thesis.

ACKNOWLEDGEMENTS

This chapter is dedicated to Eckhard H. Hess. Preparation was supported, in part, by NSF Grants BNS 78-14196 and BNS 82-17569. Many thanks are due to Denise Breeding, Karen Fawver, and Marty Trewhitt for cheerfully typing several drafts. The following thoughtfully commented on an earlier version: Marc Bekoff, Carl Gans, Neil Greenberg, Stan Rand, Peter Smith, Sandra Twardosz, and especially Paul Martin.

REFERENCES

Andrews, R. M. (1982). Patterns of growth in reptiles. In C. Gans and F. H. Pough (eds), *Biology of the Reptilia, Vol. 13, Physiology D*, pp. 273–320. London: Academic Press.

Armstrong, E. (1983). Relative brain size and metabolism in mammals. *Science* 220, 1302–4.

Baldwin, J. D. and Baldwin, J. I. (1974). Exploration and social play in squirrel monkeys (*Saimiri*). *American Zoologist* 14, 303–15.

Baldwin, J. D. and Baldwin, J. I. (1976). Effects of food ecology on social play: a laboratory simulation. *Zeitschrift für Tierpsychologie* 40, 1–14.

Baldwin, J. D. and Baldwin, J. I. (1977). The role of learning phenomena in the ontogeny of exploration and play. In S. Chevalier-Skolnikoff and F. E. Poirier (eds), *Primate Biosocial Development: Biological, Social and Ecological Determinants*, pp. 343–406. New York: Garland.

Bartholomew, G. A. and Tucker, V. A. (1964). Size, body temperature, thermal conductance, oxygen consumption, and heart rate in Australian varanid lizards. *Physiological Zoology* 37, 341–54.

Bateson, P. (1981). Discontinuities in development and changes in the organization of play in cats. In K. Immelmann, G. W. Barlow, L. Petrinovich and M.Main (eds), *Behavioral Development: The Beilefeld Interdisciplinary Project*, pp. 281–95. Cambridge: Cambridge University Press.

Bekoff, M. (1972). The development of social interaction, play, and metacommunication in mammals: an ethological perspective. *Quarterly Review of Biology* 47, 412–34.

Bekoff, M. (ed.) (1974). Social play in mammals. *American Zoologist* 14, 265–436.

Bekoff, M. (1976). Animal play: problems and perspectives. In P. P. G. Bateson and P. H. Klopfer (eds), *Perspectives in Ethology, Vol. 2*, pp. 165–88. New York: Plenum.

Bekoff, M. (1978). Social play: structure, function, and the evolution of a cooperative social behavior. In G. M. Burghardt and M. Bekoff (eds), *The Development of Behavior: Comparative and Evolutionary Aspects*, pp. 367–83. New York: Garland STPM.

Bekoff, M. (1982). The development of behavior from evolutionary and ecological perspectives: towards a generic social biology. In E. S. Gollin (ed), *The Comparative Development of Adoptive Skills: Evolutionary Implications*. New York: Academic Press.

Bekoff, M. and Byers, J. A. (1981). A critical reanalysis of the ontogeny and phylogeny of mammalian social and locomotor play: an ethological hornet's nest. In K. Immelmann, G. W. Barlow, L. Petrinovich and M. Main (eds), *Behavioral Development. The Beielefeld Interdisciplinary Project*, pp. 296–337. Cambridge: Cambridge University Press.

Bennett, A. F. (1982). The energetics of reptilian activity. In C. Gans and F. H. Pough (eds), *Biology of the Reptilia. Vol. 13, Physiology D*, pp. 155–99. London: Academic Press.

Bennett, A. F. and Dawson, W. R. (1976). Metabolism. In C. Gans and W. R. Dawson (eds), *Biology of the Reptilia. Vol. 5, Physiology A*, pp. 127–223. London: Academic Press.

Berger, J. (1979). Social ontogeny and behavioural diversity: consequences for Bighorn sheep *Ovis canadensis* inhabiting desert and mountain environments. *Journal of Zoology (London)* 188, 251–66.

Berlyne, D. E. (1960). *Conflict, Arousal, and Curiosity*. New York: McGraw-Hill.

Biben, M. (1979). Predation and predatory play behaviour of domestic cats. *Animal Behaviour* 27, 81–94.

Biben, M. (1982). Object play and social treatment of prey in bush dogs and crab-eating foxes. *Behaviour* 79, 201–11.

Borgatta, E. F. (1955). Sidesteps towards a nonspecial theory. *Psychological Review* 61, 343–52.

Bramble, D. M. and Carrier, D. R. (1983). Running and breathing in mammals. *Science* 219, 251–9.

Bruner, J. S., Jolly, A. and Sylva, K. (eds) (1976). *Play: Its Role in Development and Evolution*. New York: Basic Books.

Burghardt, G. M. (1977a). Learning processes in reptiles. In C. Gans and D. Tinkle (eds), *Biology of the Reptilia. Vol. 7, Ecology and Behavior A*, pp. 555–681. London: Academic Press.

Burghardt, G. M. (1977b). Of iguanas and dinosaurs: social behavior and communication in neonate reptiles. *American Zoologist* 17, 177–90.

Burghardt, G. M. (1977c). Ontogeny of communication. In T. E. Sebeok (ed), *How Animals Communicate*, pp. 67–93. Bloomington, Ind.: Indiana University Press.

Burghardt, G. M. (1978a). Behavioral ontogeny in reptiles: whence, whither, and why? In G. M. Burghardt and M. Bekoff (eds), *The Development of Behavior: Comparative and Evolutionary Aspects*, pp. 149–74. New York: Garland

STPM.

Burghardt, G. M. (1978b). Closing the circle: the ethnology of mind. *Behavioral and Brain Sciences* 1, 562–3.

Burghardt, G. M. (1982). Comparison matters: curiosity, bears, surplus energy, and why reptiles do not play. *Behavioral and Brain Sciences* 5, 159–60.

Burghardt, G. M., Greene, H. W., and Rand, A. S. (1977). Social behavior in hatchling green iguanas: life at a reptile rookery. *Science* 195, 689–91.

Burghardt, G. M. and Rand, A. S. (1982). Introduction. In G. M. Burghardt, and A. S. Rand (eds), *Iguanas of the World: Their Behavior, Ecology and Conservation*, pp. 1–4. Park Ridge, NJ: Noyes Publ.

Chepko, B. D. (1971). A preliminary study on the effects of play deprivation on young goats. *Zeitschrift für Tierpsychologie* 28, 517–26.

Chiszar, D., Carter, T., Knight, L., Simonsen, L. and Taylor, S. (1976). Investigatory behavior in the plains garter snake (*Thamnophis sirtalis*) and several additional species. *Animal Learning and Behavior* 4, 273–8.

Clutton-Brock, T. H. and Harvey, P. H. (1977). Primate ecology and social organization. *Journal of Zoology (London)* 183, 1–39.

Congdon, J. D., Dunham, A. E. and Tinkle, D. (1982). Energy budgets and life histories of reptiles. In C. Gans and F. H. Pough (eds), *Biology of the Reptilia Vol. 13, Physiology D*, pp. 233–71. London: Academic Press.

Craig, W. (1918). Appetites and aversions as constituents of instinct. *Biological Bulletin* 34, 91–107.

Darwin, C. (1871). *The Descent of Man and Selection in Relation to Sex*. London: Murray.

Darwin, C. (1872). *The Expression of the Emotions in Man and Animals*. London: Murray.

Drummond, H. and Burghardt, G. M. (1982). Orientation in dispersing hatchling green iguanas, *Iguana Iguana*. In G. M. Burghardt and A. S. Rand (eds), *Iguanas of the World: Their Behavior, Ecology and Conservation*, pp. 271–91. Park Ridge, NJ: Noyes.

Eibl-Eibesfeldt, I. (1982). The flexibility and affective autonomy of play. *Behavioral and Brain Sciences* 5, 160–2.

Elias, J. A. (1973). Art and play. In P. P. Wiener (ed), *Dictionary of the History of Ideas*, pp. 99–107. New York: Charles Scribner's Sons.

Ewer, R. F. (1968). *Ethology of Mammals*. New York: Plenum.

Fagen, R. (1976). Exercise, play, and physical training in animals. In P. P. G. Bateson and P. H. Klopfer (eds), *Perspectives in Ethology Vol. 2*, pp. 189–219. New York: Plenum.

Fagen, R. (1977). Selection for optimal age-dependent schedules of play behaviour. *American Naturalist* 111, 395–414.

Fagen, R. (1978). Evolutionary biological models of animal play behavior. In G. M. Burghardt and M. Bekoff (eds), *The Development of Behavior: Comparative and Evolutionary Aspects*, pp. 385–404. New York: Garland STPM.

Fagen, R. (1981). *Animal Play Behavior*. New York: Oxford University Press.

Feder, M. E. and Arnold, S. J. (1982). Anaerobic metabolism and behavior during predatory encounters between snakes (*Thamnophis elegans*) and salamanders (*Plethodon jordani*). *Oecologia* 53, 93–7.

Galef, B. G. (1981). The ecology of weaning: parasitism and the achievement of independence by altricial mammals. In D. J. Gubernick and P. H. Klopfer (eds), *Parental Care in Mammals*, pp. 211–41. New York: Plenum Press.

Ghiselin, M. R. (1974). *The Economy of Nature and the Evolution of Sex*. Berkeley: University of California Press.

Gleeson, T. T. (1979). The effects of training and captivity on the metabolic capacity of the lizard *Sceloporus occidentalis*. *Journal of Comparative Physiology* 129, 123–8.

Groos, K. (1898). *The Play of Animals*. New York: D. Appleton.

Groos, K. (1901). *The Play of Man*. New York: D. Appleton.

Harlow, H. F. (1953). Mice, monkeys, men, and motives. *Psychological Review* 60, 23–32.

Hediger, H. (1964). *Wild Animals in Captivity*. New York: Dover.

Hess, E. H. (1964). On anthropomorphism. In A. Abrams, H. H. Garner, and J. E. P. Tolman (eds), *Unfinished Tasks in the Behavioral Sciences*, pp. 174–80. Baltimore: Williams and Wilkins.

Hinde, R. A. (1970). *Animal Behaviour* (2nd edn). New York: McGraw-Hill.

Hull, C. (1943). *Principles of Behavior*. New York: Appleton-Century.

Humphreys, A. P. and Einon, D. F. (1981). Play as a reinforcer for maze-learning in juvenile rats. *Animal Behaviour* 29, 259–70.

Hutt, C. (1966). Exploration and play in children. In P. A. Jewell and C. Loizos (eds), *Play, Exploration and Territory in Mammals*, pp. 61–81. London: Symposium Zoological Society.

Immelmann, K., Barlow, G. W., Petrinovich, L. and Main, M. (eds) (1981). *Behavioral Development. The Bielefeld Interdisciplinary Project*. Cambridge: Cambridge University Press.

Kruijt, J. P. (1964). Ontogeny of social behaviour in Burmese red jungle fowl. *Behaviour Supplement 12*.

Lazell, J. D., Jr. and Spitzer, N. C. (1977). Apparent play in an American alligator. *Copiea* 1977, 188.

Leyhausen, P. (1973). On the function of the relative hierarchy of moods (as exemplified by the phylogenetic and ontogenetic development of prey catching in carnivores) (1965). In K. Lorenz and P. Leyhausen (eds), *Motivation of Human and Animal Behavior. An Ethological View*, pp. 144–247. New York: Van Nostrand.

Lorenz, K. Z. (1981). *The Foundations of Ethology*. New York: Springer-Verlag.

McDougall, W. (1924). *An Outline of Psychology* (2nd edn). London: Methuen.

McNab, B. K. (1980). Food habits, energetics, and the population biology of mammals. *American Naturalist* 116, 106–24.

McNab, B. K. (1983). Ecological and behavioral consequences of adaptation to various food resources. In J. F. Eisenberg and D. G. Kleiman (eds), *Advances in the Study of Mammalian Behavior*, pp. 664–97. Pittsburgh: American Society of Mammalogists.

Martin P. (1982). The energy cost of play: definition and estimation. *Animal*

Behaviour 30, 294–5.

Martin, P. (1984). The time and energy costs of play behaviour in the cat. *Zeitschrift für Tierpsychologie* 64, in press.

Meyer-Holzapfel, M. (1956). Über die Bereitschaft zu Spiel-und Instinkt-handlungen. *Zietschrift für Tierpsychologie* 13, 442–62 (partial translation in Müller-Schwarze, 1978).

Müller-Schwarze, D. (1968). Play deprivation in deer. *Behaviour* 31, 144–68.

Müller-Schwarze, D. (ed) (1978). *Evolution of Play Behavior*. Stroudsburg Pa: Dowden, Hutchinson and Ross.

Müller-Schwarze, D., Stagge, B. and Müller-Schwarze, C. (1982). Play behavior: persistence, decrease and energetic compensation during food shortage in deer fawns. *Science* 215, 85–7.

Nagy, K. A. (1982). Energy requirements of free-living iguanid lizards. In G. M. Burghardt and A. S. Rand (eds), *Iguanas of the World: Their Behavior, Ecology, and Conservation*, pp. 49–59. Park Ridge, NJ: Noyes.

Poole, T. B. and Fish, J. (1975). An investigation of playful behaviour in *Rattus norvegicus* and *Mus musculus* (Mammalia). *Journal of Zoology (London)* 175, 61–71.

Pough, F. H. (1977). Ontogenetic change in blood oxygen capacity and maximum activity in garter snakes (*Thamnophis sirtalis*). *Journal of Comparative Physiology B*. 166, 337–45.

Pough, F. H. (1978). Ontogenetic changes in endurance in water snakes (*Natrix spiedon*): physiological correlates and ecological consequences. *Copeia* 1978, 69–75.

Pough, F. H. (1980). The advantages of ectothermy for tetrapods. *American Naturalist* 115, 92–112.

Rand, A. S., Gorman, G. C. and Rand, W. M. (1975). Natural history, behavior, and ecology of *Anolis agassizi*. In J. B. Graham (ed), *The Biological Investigation of Malpelo Island, Columbia. Smithsonian Contributions to Zoology* 176, 27–38.

Rand, W. M. and Rand, A. S. (1976). Agonistic behaviour in nesting iguanas: a stochastic analysis of dispute settlement dominated by the minimization of energy cost. *Zeitschrift für Tierpsychologie* 40, 279–99.

Regal, P. (1978). Behavioral differences between reptiles and mammals: an analysis of activity and mental capabilities. In N. Greenberg and P. D. MacLean (eds). *Behavior and Neurology of Lizards*, pp. 183–202. DHEW Publ. No. (ADM) 77-491, Rockville, Md.

Sackett, G. P., Sameroff, A. J., Cairns, R. B. and Suomi, S. J. (1981). Continuity in behavioral development: theoretical and empirical issues. In K. Immelmann, G. W. Barlow, L. Petrovich and M. Main (eds), *Behavioral Development. The Bielefeld Interdisciplinary Project*, pp. 23–57. Cambridge: Cambridge University Press.

Smith, E. O. (ed) (1978). *Social Play in Primates*. New York: Academic Press.

Smith, P. K. (1982). Does play matter? Functional and evolutionary aspects of animal and human play. *Behavioral and Brain Sciences* 5, 139–55.

Spencer, H. (1898). *The Principles of Psychology*, vol. II, pt. 2. New York: D.

Appleton.

Sutton-Smith, B. (ed) (1979). *Play and Learning*. New York: Gardner Press.

Symons, D. (1978). *Play and Aggression. A Study of Rhesus Monkeys*. New York: Columbia University Press.

Tinbergen, N. (1952). 'Derived' activities. Their causation, biological significance, origin, and emancipation during evolution. *Quarterly Review of Biology* 27, 1–32.

Tinbergen, N. (1963). On the aims and methods of ethology. *Zeitschrift für Tierpsychologie* 20, 410–33.

Tolman, E. C. (1948). Cognitive maps in rats and men. *Psychological Review* 55, 189–208.

Weisler, A. and McCall, R. B. (1976). Exploration and play. Résumé and redirection. *American Psychologist* 31, 492–508.

Welker, W. I. (1971). Ontogeny of play and exploratory behaviors: a definition of problems and a search for new conceptual solutions. In H. Moltz (ed), *Ontogeny of Vertebrate Behavior*, pp. 171–213. New York: Academic Press.

West, M. J. (1977). Exploration and play with objects in domestic kittens. *Developmental Psychobiology* 10, 53–7.

Wilson, E. O. (1975). *Sociobiology. The New Synthesis*. Cambridge, Mass.: Belknap Press, Harvard University.

2 Play in Ungulates

John A. Byers

Coming cautiously one day over a rimrock at Spanish Lake, I saw a group of seven antelope kids with their mothers on the hard shore-edge of the receding lake. The mothers were contentedly resting in the warm June sun, apparently at ease and unaware of my approach. The kids were having a great time in a quite highly organized game. Rushing away across the flat rim of the lake shore, as though started by a lifting of a barrier on a race track, they ran neck and neck, swung in a wide arc and then thundered back, their tiny hooves beating in unison as they soared rather than ran, their bodies parallel to the earth. Upon nearing the starting point they drew up to a stiff-legged stop at their mothers' sides, gazed with dreamy eyes around the immediate vicinity, then wheeled away on another flight, with apparently enough power and enthusiasm to drive them to the summit of the Rocky Mountains 1,000 miles away. (Einarsen, 1948: 122)

Einarsen's description of play in pronghorn (*Antilocapra americana*) emphasized what all ungulate young do when they play. They run. Often, as Einarsen suggested, they seem to run as fast as they can. Anticipating the hypothesis I shall advance here, I would like to be able to say that the more an ungulate species shows cursorial adaptations in morphology, the more its young run in play. The anecdotal play literature hints at such a correlation, but real data are lacking. Nevertheless, the simple observation that all ungulate young run in play is in itself revealing. The observation means that a strong selective advantage goes to individuals that run during development; this meaning, in turn, waves the red flag lettered 'motor training' in front of our eyes.

The term 'ungulate' is taken commonly to include exclusively the orders Artiodactyla and Perissodactyla (see glossary under table 2.1). This is a phylogenetically artificial category, which cannot rightfully exclude, if these two orders are lumped together, other extant members of the grand order Ungulata (Eisenberg, 1981): the aardvarks, whales, hyraxes, elephants, and sea cows. However, the Artiodactyla and

Perissodactyla are united in a functional sense; both groups comprise ungulate lineages in which there has been specialization for herbivory, involving high-crowned cheek-teeth and digestion assisted by microbial symbionts, and in which the evolutionary trajectory away from predation has involved an increase in body size, extreme cursorial specializations, and often, the formation of large conspecific aggregations. Because the Artiodactyla and Perissodactyla are convergent in these respects, the extent to which there has been convergence in the form of play is of interest, and this is my rationale for considering these two orders while excluding the other Ungulata.

Debate about the function or functions of play is as heated now as it has ever been (see Smith, 1982 and Commentary). I think much of the controversy results from attempts to identify a single function for all mammalian play, without specification of in what sense 'single function' is implied. For instance, one might flatly state that the function of play in mammals is motor training (this term refers to several developmental effects of exercise, including bone remodelling and enhanced muscle growth, cardiovascular and respiratory efficiency, and neuromuscular coordination: see Byers, 1980; Bekoff and Byers, 1981). A critic would rightfully point to the gentle interactive play (Fagen 1981) that occurs in many primates and ask how it is explained by the motor training hypothesis. One might engage in a furious bout of data jamming to get such a square peg of observation to fit into the round hole of theory (Bekoff, 1983), but it would probably be a waste of time.

I will sidestep into morphology for a moment to more clearly illustrate this point. Having studied pronghorn skeletons, and in particular the bones of the hand, I might flatly state, 'the function of the mammalian manus is to provide an elongated distal limb segment which increases stride length and thus running speed'. Of course, equally slow-witted students of other species would claim I was wrong and would propose alternative unitary functions of the mammalian manus, each consistent with the species studied: anteaters – a powerful digging instrument; bats – wings; dolphins – fins; humans – manipulation of controls in video arcades. Clearly, I and the others would be correct with respect to the species we studied but ridiculously narrow in our generalizations. In fact, there is no single function of the mammalian manus, and one cannot arrive at a very satisfying understanding of this character by advocating one function over another, or even by compiling a list of the various functions it performs. However, all becomes elegantly clear when we consider the structure of the therapsid manus, and then trace its modification in each mammalian order.

Now the problem concerning proposals for a single function of play should be clear. If we mean, when we say that play has *a* function in mammals, that it has the same set of effects in all species, then we are clearly in the company of those who would send a pronghorn to rip up an anthill, fly from Boise to Pocatello, swim to Hawaii, or score high on Missile Command. If however, we mean that play probably had an ancestral form and function that has been retained, with varying degrees of modification, in the present-day mammals, we make what I consider a reasonable supposition. Of course, there are no fossils of play behaviour, so the suggestion that all mammalian play is derived from a common ancestral form never can be accepted with the same confidence that we accept homology in the mammalian hand. Nevertheless, the suggestion is heuristic. It implies that study of the function of play in any species should begin by identifying in what respects play structure conforms to the presumed ancestral function in mammals, then it should analyse the elements of play that are not satisfactorily explained in this way to ascertain the ways in which play has become specialized and the likely selective pressures that have led to the specialization.

All that is required to make such a programme of research to work is common agreement on the ancestral function of play in mammals. Is this likely? I argue that it is, and that the function everyone sooner or later will come to accept as ancestral is motor training. My main reason for this dogmatic assertion, in addition to the evidence that motor training is a primary function of play in several modern mammals (see Bekoff and Byers, 1981; Fagen, 1981; Smith, 1982), is that I can imagine the evolution of play due to motor training benefits without requiring the small-bodied, insectivorous, late Cretaceous mammals (see Kielan-Jaworowska et al., 1979) to have any particular sort of social organization or Encephalization Quotient (Jerison, 1973). I suggest that the other plausible functions of play are not good candidates for the ancestral condition because they require either specializations, or uniform selection pressures, that most likely were not present in mammals at this time. For instance, the hypothesis that play functions to promote cohesion among individuals, to qualify as the ancestral function, requires that at the time play appeared, all mammalian lineages were experiencing selection for increased sociality. This is not likely. In fact, if we take the near-ubiquity of play in all mammalian orders as evidence that play or its precursor became common in the Cretaceous, before the separation of modern orders, the cohesion hypothesis seems impossible, because the diets of these animals, as inferred from tooth structure (Lillegraven et al., 1979) would have required a dispersed social organization (Eisenberg, 1981).

Of course, the near-ubiquity of play does not logically require common ancestry. Play in all orders might have arisen by convergence. If so, there are two possible evolutionary routes. The more likely is that convergence, as seems to be the situation in other examples of the phenomenon, resulted from responses in different lineages to a common set of selection pressures. This again implies a single, ancestral function for play. The difference between this and the previous scenario is that we must now find a set of selection pressures that could have worked similarly on all the diverging orders in the Cenozoic. Once again, I argue that the motor training hypothesis provides the only selective regime that could have done so.

Finally, we must consider the logically possible, but dubious, proposition that play appeared after lines leading to the modern orders were established, that it arose in response to different selection pressures in different taxa, and that subsequently, the great similarities in the form of play among all orders were produced by modifications in response to a new, common set of selection pressures. Such an evolutionary history of play is exactly the reverse of what I originally proposed and what I believe to be the likely sequence of events in the evolution of play – that is, common ancestry, with increasing divergence in form that reflected the changing selection pressures that accompanied radiation and specialization.

Currently, evidence is not sufficient to implicate decisively one of the three evolutionary origins of play just outlined. However, I suggest that research concerning the functions of play will make the best progress when it attempts to trace descent with modification, in an effort to support the following hypothesis: play originally appeared in the mammals as a form of motor training, and in many modern species still retains this function. In some taxa, play too has become specialized, in response to new selection pressures associated with morphological or behavioural specializations, and now genuinely has multiple functions. This hypothesis is testable by comparison. If we examine play in a family, order, or larger taxon we should see clear evidence for motor training in all, or most, species, and also should see types of play poorly explained by motor training in the species that are morphologically or behaviourally most specialized. The ungulates clearly show such a pattern, and, in the remainder of the chapter, I shall demonstrate this.

THE STRUCTURE OF UNGULATE PLAY

In this section, I provide a description of the most frequently observed ungulate play motor patterns, along with tabular summaries of the number of species, in each family, that perform them. I must acknowledge a great head start given to me in this task by Robert Fagen's (1981) extensive literature review, which led me to several important references.

Ungulate play, although often spectacular and dramatic, is relatively simple in form. For the most part, it closely mimics, out of context, two classes of behaviour: flight and intraspecific agonistic competition. Correct (in fact, perfect) performance of the motor patterns involved in both classes has clear adaptive significance, and much ungulate play is nothing more than the repetitive performance, during development, of these patterns. I shall refer to the behaviour that mimics flight as locomotor-rotational (see Wilson and Kleiman, 1974) play, and the behaviour that mimics agonistic competition as social play. Locomotor-rotational (LR) and social (S) play often occur close to each other in time; LR and S patterns may even alternate with each other (Berger, 1980; Byers, 1977). However, play bouts, in the few species for which data are available, appear to have species-specific, predictable structures (Berger, 1980; Byers, 1977; Müller-Schwarze, 1968) in which LR patterns are clumped in time, and are preceded or followed by clumped S patterns. The organization of play into discrete bouts is common in ungulates; an emerging generalization is that bouts tend to occur at predictable times of day, especially at dawn or dusk (Brownlee, 1954; Byers, 1977; Dubost, 1971; Estes and Estes, 1979; Geist, 1963; Jarman and Jarman, 1973; Koford, 1957; Lumia, 1972; Mackler and Buechner, 1978; Mungall, 1976; Underwood, 1979).

Locomotor-rotational play

Table 2.1 shows eight principal motor patterns performed by ungulates in LR play, and the number of species in each family for which I judged there to be a reliable report that each motor pattern occurs. The blanks, or small numbers, in table 2.1 do not necessarily mean that a pattern does not occur or is infrequent in a family; many of the references cited offer only brief and probably fragmentary descriptions of play. My impression, while working on the tables, was that the more lengthy the discussion of play in an article, the greater the number of motor patterns that were mentioned. For instance, Owen-Smith (1974, 1975) and Schenkel and Schenkel-Hulliger (1969) offered short accounts of play in general articles on ecology and social behaviour of, respectively, the white rhinoceros (*Ceratotherium simum*) and black rhinoceros (*Diceros bicornis*). For these two species, the only LR play pattern reported was running. The paper by Mackler and Buechner (1978), in contrast, specifically concerned play in the Indian rhinoceros (*Rhinoceros uni-*

TABLE 2.1 Distribution of locomotor-rotational play motor patterns in the ungulate families. Entries are the number of species in which the motor pattern has been reported.

	Run	Leap or jump	Rear, rear and pirouette	Head shake, head jerk, neck twist	Heel kick, torso twist	Fast turns, fast stops	Whirl	Wallow	References
Perissodactyla									
Tapiridæ	X			X			X		Frädrich and Thenius, 1972
Rhinocerotidæ	3	1		1		?	1	1	Mackler and Buechner, 1978; Owen-Smith, 1974, 1975; Schenkel and Schenkel-Hulliger, 1969
Equidæ	4	1		1	1	1			Fagen, 1981; Fagen & George, 1977; Feist and McCullough, 1976; Joubert, 1972; Klingel, 1967, 1968, 1974a, b; Schoen et al., 1976; Tyler, 1972
Artiodactyla									
Suidæ	4	1		2		2	1		Frädrich, 1965, 1974; Fraser, 1978; Kingdon, 1979; Oliver, 1980
Tayassuidæ	1	1		1		1	1		Byers and Bekoff, 1981; Dobroruka and Horbowyjova, 1972
Hippopotamidæ	2	1	2	1		1	1		Fagen, 1981; Kingdon, 1979; Wilson and Kleiman, 1974
Tragulidæ	1	1		1		1			Dubost, 1975
Camelidæ	3	1	1		1	2			Gauthier-Pilters and Dagg, 1981; Koford, 1957; Pilters, 1954
Giraffidæ	2	1	?	1	1				Leuthold, 1979; Pratt and Anderson, 1979; Walther, 1962

								References
Cervidae	9	9		5	5	5	1	Altmann, 1963; Barrette, 1977; Darling, 1937; Dubost, 1971; Espmark, 1969, 1971; Geist, 1963; Lent, 1966; Michael, 1968; Miller, 1975; Miller and Gunn, 1981; Müller-Schwarze, 1968; Müller-Schwarze et al., 1982; Schaller, 1967; Struhsaker, 1967
Antilocap-ridae	1	1	1	1	1			Autenreith and Fichter, 1975; Einarsen, 1948
Bovidae	26	14	7	9	12	4	2	Allsopp, 1978; Berger, 1980; Brandborg, 1955; Brownlee, 1954; Byers, 1977, 1980; Chepko, 1971; Dane, 1977; David, 1975; Dubost and Feer, 1981; Estes, 1969; Estes and Estes, 1979; Geist, 1971; Hanks et al., 1969; Jarman and Jarman, 1973; Kingdon, 1982; Kramer, 1969; Lent, 1969; Lentfer, 1955; Leuthold, 1970; Leuthold and Leuthold, 1973; Lumia, 1972; Mungall, 1976; Owen, 1973; Rudge, 1970; Sachs and Harris, 1978; Schaller, 1977; Scheurmann, 1975; Sinclair, 1977; Spinage, 1969; Tener, 1965; Underwood, 1979; Verheyen, 1955
Total	57	31	13	24	21	17	6	4

Key X – present but number of species unclear   ? – presence suggested, but not definitive

Glossary of terms

Ungulate: hoofed mammal; Perissodactyla: odd number of toes; Artiodactyla: even number of toes; Tapiradae: tapirs; Rhinocerotidæ: rhinoceroses; Equidae: horses, zebras, wild asses; Suidæ: pigs, warthogs; Tayassuidæ: peccaries; Hippopotamidæ: hippopotamuses; Tragulidæ: mouse deer, chevrotains; Camelidæ: camels; Giraffidæ: giraffe, okapi; Cervidæ: deer; Antilocapridæ: pronghorns; Bovidæ: antelope, sheep, goats, cattle.
The Artiodactyls contain two suborders: the Suina (families Suidæ, Tayassuidæ and Hippopotamidæ); and the Ruminantia (ruminants) (families Tragulidæ, Camelidæ, Giraffidæ, Cervidæ, Antilocapridæ, and Bovidæ).

cornis) and reported five (possibly six) LR patterns. It would be unwise to conclude that play in the Indian rhinoceros is more diverse than play in either the white or black rhinoceros. Table 2.1 should be regarded as a provisional picture of the distribution of LR play patterns in the ungulate families. With this caution in mind, I offer the following remarks on the motor patterns.

Run

As table 2.1 shows, running is documented in 57 species, or about one-third of the ungulates. All references to ungulate play mention running, and it seems reasonable to conclude that, when play in all ungulate species has been described, this activity will be found to be ubiquitous, or nearly so. Although running may involve close pursuit of another animal (listed as 'chase' in table 2.2 for social play), in the form as reported in table 2.1 it is an individual activity, clearly not directed toward conspecifics. Stotting, four-footed bounding, is an alarm gait confined to the Cervidae, Antilocapridae, and Bovidae. It also appears in the play of these three families (Cervidae, 3 species; Bovidae, 8 species). Alarm signals (piloerection or vocalization) also are occasionally given in running play in these three families and in the Tayassuidae.

Leap or jump

Leaping (leaving the ground and travelling no horizontal distance) or jumping (travelling some horizontal distance while off the ground) is reported in all families except the Tapiridae and Rhinocerotidae. Information on tapirs is scanty, and I would not conclude that the pattern is absent in this family. However, Mackler and Buechner's (1978) detailed description of play in an Indian rhinoceros calf did not mention leaping or jumping, so the absence here may be real.

Rear, rear and pirouette

In this movement, the animal rocks backward into a bipedal position. It may then fall forward, jump forward, or pirouette (turn while bipedal to face a new direction before returning to all fours). Pronghorn fawns typically perform several rear-pirouettes in quick succession (personal observation). The pattern appears to be genuinely absent in the Suidae, Tayassuidae, Tragulidae, and Cervidae.

Head shake, head jerk, neck twist

In this movement, the animal shakes its head from side to side, or rapidly elevates its snout, or rapidly rotates its head to one side, so that the snout points perpendicularly left or right. With increasing intensity, rotation of the head involves the neck, and finally most of the vertebral column. Vigorous neck twists performed in the midst of a jump may turn most of the body parallel to the ground. Movements of this sort appear in all families, with the possible exception of the Camelidae.

Heel kick, torso twist

In this movement, the hind legs are rapidly kicked back, and also usually up and to one side. As in neck twists, as intensity increases, the vertebral column is torqued. Heel kicks performed in mid-air result in some of the most striking movements performed in animal play. Heel kicks, like rear-pirouettes, change the animal's direction of travel. These movements appear not to occur in the morphologically conservative ungulates; they are confined to the ruminants (excepting the Tragulidae) and the Equidae. This suggests that heel kicks may be linked to cursorial specialization.

Fast turns, fast stops

In these movements the animal, while running, rapidly changes direction by 90° or more, or comes to an abrupt halt. Fast turns and stops are less distinct motor patterns than they are ways of running and, for this reason, probably are reported in fewer species than the actual number in which they occur. Table 2.1 indicates that these manœuvres are not reported in Tapiridae, Hippopotamidae, or Giraffidae, but I prefer to regard this as a tentative conclusion.

Whirl

A whirling animal turns rapidly in a circle while remaining in place. The movement is scattered idiosyncratically across families; its occurrence is not obviously linked to morphology.

Wallow

A wallowing animal thrashes on the ground, performing movements associated with deposition or uptake of scent. These movements seem to

TABLE 2.2 Distribution of social play motor patterns in the ungulate families. Entries are the number of species in which the motor pattern has been reported.

	Butt, clash, spar	bite, slash	Push, neck-fight	Paw, foreleg kick	Mount	Charge, lunge	Mouth-mouth Naso-naso contact	Chase	References
Perissodactyla									
Tapiridæ	3								Frädrich and Thenius, 1972
Rhinocero-tidæ		1	X		1		2		Mackler and Buechner, 1978; Owen-Smith, 1974, 1975; Schenkel and Schenkel- Hulliger, 1969
Equidæ		4	1	1	1	4			Fagen, 1981; Fagen & George, 1977; Feist and McCullough, 1976; Joubert, 1972; Klingel, 1967, 1968, 1974a, b; Schoen et al., 1976; Tyler, 1972
Artiodactyla									
Suidæ		4					4	3	Frädrich, 1965, 1974; Fraser, 1978; Kingdon, 1979; Oliver, 1980
Tayassuidæ		1		1		1	1	1	Byers and Bekoff, 1981; Dobroruka and Horbowyjova, 1972
Hippopota-midæ		1				1	1		Fagen, 1981; Kingdon, 1979; Wilson and Kleiman, 1974
Tragulidæ									Dubost, 1975
Camelidæ	3	3	3	2	3	3			Gauthier-Pilters and Dagg, 1981; 1981; Koford, 1957; Pilters, 1954

Family									References
Giraffidæ	5		2		1				Leuthold, 1979; Pratt and Anderson, 1979; Walther, 1962
Cervidæ	5		5	3	3	1	4		Altmann, 1963; Barrette, 1977; Darling, 1937; Dubost, 1971; Espmark, 1969, 1971; Geist, 1963; Lent, 1966; Michael, 1968; Miller, 1975; Miller and Gunn, 1968; Müller-Schwarze, 1968; Müller-Schwarze et al., 1982; Schaller, 1967; Struhsaker, 1967
Antilocap-ridæ	1		1		1	1		1	Autenreith and Fichter, 1975; Einarsen, 1948
Bovidæ	19	7		3	10			8	Alsopp, 1978; Berger, 1980; Brandborg, 1955; Brownlee, 1954; Byers, 1977, 1980; Chepko, 1971; Dane, 1977; David, 1975; Dubost and Feer, 1981; Estes, 1969; Estes and Estes, 1979; Geist, 1971; Hanks et al., 1969; Jarman and Jarman, 1973; Kingdon, 1982; Kramer, 1969; Lent, 1969; Lentfer, 1955; Leuthold, 1970; Leuthold and Leuthold, 1973; Lumia, 1972; Mungall, 1976; Owen, 1973; Rudge, 1970; Sachs and Harris, 1978; Schaller, 1977; Scheurmann, 1975; Sinclair, 1977; Spinage, 1969; Tener, 1965; Underwood, 1979; Verheyen, 1955
Total	28	14	15	13	20	10	8	8	

Key X – present but number of species unclear

occur only in the play of the Rhinocerotidae and Suina. They illustrate the close association between olfaction and play, pointed out by Wilson (1973) and Wilson and Kleiman (1974).

Social play

Table 2.2 shows the distribution of the eight most commonly performed social play motor patterns. Note that no social play has been observed in the Tragulidae and that, in general, fewer cells are filled in table 2.2 than in table 2.1 (proportions filled: table 2.1, 0.73; table 2.2, 0.43, arcsin test for the equality of two percentages t = 4.28, p < .001). There are fewer motor patterns per family in social vs locomotor-rotational play (Mann–Whitney T = 29.5, p < 0.01) and each motor pattern tends to be represented in fewer families (Mann – Whitney T = 15.5, p < 0.05). There are no motor pattens, such as running in LR play, that are found in the social play of all families. The apparent explanation for these differences is that social play, with the exception of mounting, mimics adult agonistic competition; because the ungulate families differ more in the kinds of weapons they possess (and therefore the kind of fighting individuals employ) than in their rather universal method of avoiding predators (flight), social play is more family-specific than LR play. In the few ungulates for which data are available, males engage in significantly more social play than females (Berger, 1980; Byers, 1980; Reinhardt and Reinhardt, 1982; Sachs and Harris, 1978; Sinclair, 1977). Byers (1980), presenting evidence that social play in ibex (*Capra ibex sibirica*) is most consistent with the motor training hypothesis, predicted that most polygynous ungulates, in which the development of fighting strength and skill is more closely linked to male, than to female, reproductive success, should show such sexual dimorphism in play.

Butt, clash, spar

Head to head butting, head to body butting, butting preceded by rearing on the hind legs, and wrestling with horns or antlers in contact are included in this category. These play motor patterns appear only in the horned or antlered ungulates, and closely resemble fighting between adult males.

Bite, slash

Play motor patterns in this category include inhibited or mock biting or, in the Suina, in which the adult canine teeth are large, sharp and often procumbent, upward thrusting head movements. Such movements in play appear to be confined, with the exception of the Rhinocerotidae, to the families in which biting or slashing is a major form of adult combat.

Push, neck-fight

Individuals engaged in these patterns stand side by side and push back and forth, with shoulders and/or necks in contact. The distribution across families is not easily explained.

Paw, foreleg kick

These patterns involve one animal striking another with one or both front hooves. When the movement is gentle, it is usually referred to as pawing; when forceful, as kicking or striking. For the most part, the patterns are confined to families in which this is a form of combat between adults. An exception is in the collared peccary (*Tayassu tajacu*) in which pawing by one animal elicits play in a reclined partner (Byers and Bekoff, 1981).

Mount

Mounting is the only pattern I have listed as social play that does not obviously mimic adult agonistic behaviour. Play mounting strongly resembles mounting that occurs in mating. It seems to be performed much more frequently by juvenile males than juvenile females (Berger, 1979; Byers, 1977, 1980; Kitchen, 1974). It seems to be absent in the Suina and Tragulidae. Descriptions of play in the Giraffidae are insufficient to form a conclusion on the presence or absence of the pattern in this family. If play mounting is a form of motor training, one would predict it to occur more in juvenile males than females; also one would expect a positive correlation between the frequency of play mounting in a species and the extent to which rapid copulations-on-the-run occur during the rut (J. Hogg, personal communication).

Charge, lunge

An animal performing play patterns in this category runs directly at a conspecific, or, from a standing start, leaps at it. Such patterns are mentioned infrequently, except in descriptions of play in families Equidae and Camelidae.

Mouth–mouth, naso–naso contact

Individuals performing these patterns bring their snouts or open mouths in gentle contact, often while rotating their heads from side to side. Such patterns appear to be confined to the Rhinocerotidae and the Suina.

Chase

In preparing table 2.2, I listed a species as showing chasing in its play only if the word 'chase' was used in the original description, or if the description clearly distinguished this activity from play running. Because running play in ungulates may be 'contagious' (individuals tend to run when another conspecific runs), running play and chasing play may not be completely distinct. However, I draw the line between these two forms of play based on a facilitation–interaction distinction: play running may involve facilitation, in which running in one individual sets off running in another, but it does not involve interaction, in which each movement in a series performed by one individual is closely followed by a corresponding response in another individual. Play chasing, in contrast, is interactive; the chased animal frequently changes direction as if to avoid the chaser, and the chaser closely follows these direction changes. This kind of play interaction currently is only known in the Suidae, Tayassuidae, and Cervidae.

EVOLUTIONARY INTERPRETATION OF UNGULATE PLAY

I suggested earlier that modern ungulate play reveals an evolutionary history in which motor training was the ancestral function and in which morphological or behavioural specializations in some groups were followed by modification of play, in some instances to the extent that play acquired new functions. Having reviewed the structure of ungulate play I can now evaluate this hypothesis. Patterns of similarity in ungulate play suggest that the ancestral form comprised the locomotor-rotational patterns Run, Leap or Jump, Head Shake, Fast Turns. These patterns are common in all ungulates for which descriptions exist, and they are the only play patterns shown by the tragulid *Hyemoschus aquaticus* or water chevrotain (Dubost, 1975). Descriptions of play in other species of Tragulidae are unavailable, but would be valuable, because of the plesiomorphic morphology (and therefore, presumably, behaviour) in this family. None of the LR play patterns, with the exception of Wallow, require a functional explanation other than motor training. That is, by the programme of research outlined earlier, the motor training hypothesis is sufficient to explain the nature of all the LR patterns, except Wallow. For all these patterns, with the possible exception of Head Shake, I believe the motor training hypothesis is necessary as well.

The next hypothetical stage in the evolution of ungulate play involved performance, in play, of motor patterns involved in adult agonistic competition. I propose that social play appeared after LR play because: (1) social play apparently does not exist in *Hyemoschus aquaticus* (Dubost, 1975); (2) social play is more family-specific than LR play; and (3) selection pressures for early rehearsal of adult competitive patterns probably did not appear (whether the benefit of the rehearsal involved motor training or anything else) until social groups and the potential for polygyny had appeared. Ancestors of both Artiodactyla and Perissodactyla were small-bodied folivores and frugivores (Romer, 1967), and therefore probably had dispersed social organizations, similar to those of their modern-day equivalents, the tragulids, duikers (Cephalophinae), and muntjacs (*Muntiacus* sp.). These species collectively are called 'small-solitary-forest-ruminants' by Barrette (1977) (see also Dubost, 1968, and Jarman, 1974 for explanations of the relationship between ecology and social organization in these animals). As the equids and ruminants moved into savannah-steppe habitats, and began to feed on grasses, predation presumably created strong selection for clumped spacing of individuals (Brown and Orians, 1970; Hamilton, 1971). Such selection was not opposed by pressures related to food competition because grasses are not economically defendable (Jarman, 1974). Herds thus became common, and with them, the potential for males to gain multiple matings per reproductive season. This situation presumably led to the evolution of sexual dimorphism in body size, horns and antlers, and competitiveness (Emlen and Oring, 1977; Darwin, 1871; Jarman, 1974), because success in winning fights appears to be closely correlated with mating success (Clutton-Brock et al., 1982). I suggest that the selection for fighting skill also led to performance of adult fighting movements early in life, a phenomenon we recognize as social play. Thus, it is plausible that social play appeared after LR play, and I propose that social play also originally emerged because of motor training selective pressures. This hypothesis predicts that: (1) social play should be rare or absent in the small-solitary-forest-ruminants; (2) in polygynous species, social play should occur frequently, and there should be a positive correlation between variance in male reproductive success and the amount of social play performed; (3) social play should be much more prevalent in males than in females; (4) details of social play, such as play partner preferences (Byers, 1980) should reflect design for motor training benefits; (5) social play should be modified or reduced in social species in which polygyny is reduced.

Evidence currently is not sufficient to confirm or reject prediction (1). Social play has not been observed in tragulids (Dubost, 1975), but it does occur in muntjacs, *Muntiacus muntjak* (Dubost, 1971). Studies of play in the duikers would be of great interest. Predictions (2), (3), and (4) are supported by some evidence. In bighorn sheep, *Ovis canadensis*, (Berger, 1980), Siberian ibex (Byers, 1980), and Boran cattle, *Bos indicus* (Reinhardt and Reinhardt, 1982), all highly polygynous species, males play more than females and play most frequently with equal-sized male partners. Also, in Siberian ibex (Byers, personal observation), bighorn sheep (Geist, 1971), blackbuck, *Antilope cervicapra* (Dubost and Feer, 1981; Mungall, 1976), wildebeest, *Connochaetes taurinus* (Estes, 1969), pronghorn, *Antilocapra americana* (Kitchen, 1974), and impala, *Aepyceros melampus* (Leuthold, 1970), all highly polygynous species, social play in males persists well past sexual maturity in a slightly modified form, most commonly called sparring. This kind of behaviour typically makes up a huge proportion of the social interactions of these males. Finally, is there evidence for prediction (5)? There is, and I present it in the next subsection.

Play in the collared peccary

With the evolutionary stage set by the establishment of both social and LR play, the possibility emerges that either can be modified to serve new functions, different from motor training. I believe that when more careful studies of the structure of ungulate play are done, many examples will be found. Social or LR patterns will be found to be performed in contexts and in such a manner that motor training will be neither a necessary nor a sufficient functional explanation. This is apparently the situation in the collared peccary *Tayassu tajacu*. Peccaries are the best example known to me of a species in which all play no longer is satisfactorily explained by motor training.

Social organization and behaviour in this species are described in Byers and Bekoff (1981), Byers (1983) and Sowls (1974). Peccaries live in permanent, mixed-sex herds in which the sex ratio is 1:1. There is little immigration or emigration. Herd ranges are exclusive and non-overlapping. Within herds several forms of apparent altruism exist; these include food sharing, cooperative defence against predators, and cooperative nursing. Also, males show little observable competition over œstrous females. Small inter-individual distances are maintained, and all individuals in a herd move, feed, and rest in close synchrony. Because of the close-knit nature of herds, kin selection may have been an important force in the evolution of peccary social behaviour.

What do peccaries do in play? The basic categories of motor patterns are shown in tables 2.1 and 2.2, under the family Tayassuidae. In LR play, peccaries run, jump, head jerk, show fast stops and turns, and wallow. In social play they engage in mock biting and fighting, paw each other in soliciting play, charge and lunge, engage in extensive mouth-to-mouth contact, and conduct frequently reversed chases. None of the play patterns alone, except wallowing, seems to require a functional explanation other than motor training. Howeve, when one considers the structure of peccary play bouts, other functional explanations are required. In my observations (Byers and Bekoff, 1981; Byers, 1983) play most frequently occurred as a coordinated herd activity which centred on sites I called playgrounds. Seventy-two per cent of all play motor patterns observed took place in this context. Playgrounds were circular patches of earth approximately 2 m in diameter, in or near herd bedgrounds. They were trampled and rooted bare and heavily scent-marked. Adults as well as juveniles participated in herd play bouts and an average 42% of all herd members were involved in any one bout. Sixty-four per cent of such bouts were initiated by adults, and adults performed 55% of all play motor patterns observed. There were far fewer juveniles than adults in each herd, however, and juveniles actually played at higher rates than adults (Byers, 1983). Herd play bouts also showed a significant temporal correlation with scent-marking. Twenty-four scent marking acts (29% of all observed) took place immediately before, or during, herd play bouts. If scent-marking were evenly distributed in time, the number of acts expected during the 1.85 hours of play observed would be less than one. Play also occurred away from playgrounds (28% of all play motor patterns observed) but in these instances it was of considerably shorter duration than bouts at playgrounds (100 sec vs 392 sec) and was performed mostly by juveniles.

Play in peccaries is thus quite different from play in the majority of ungulates, in which this behaviour is rather strictly the province of juveniles and sub-adult males. The coordinated nature of herd play bouts, the strong participation by adults, and the apparent control of play by olfactory cues which herds deposit on traditional playgrounds, are features poorly explained by the motor training hypothesis and which demand another functional explanation. I suggest that herd play in peccaries is a genuine example in which the much maligned and debated functional hypothesis – social cohesion – (see Byers and Bekoff, 1981: Fagen, 1981) is upheld. Most peccary social behaviour clearly reveals an evolutionary history of strong selection for sociality and group cohesion and it is therefore likely that play has been modified to promote and maintain social bonds between individuals. It is especially significant that juvenile peccaries engaged in no forms of amicable contact among themselves except play, until 2–3 months of age (Byers, 1983). In contrast, agonistic behaviour appeared shortly after birth in disputes over suckling access. Play appears to be the only form of active social interaction between juvenile peccaries and could promote the social bonds that result in cooperative, cohesive adults.

SUMMARY

In this paper, I suggest that needless controversy over the function of mammalian play has arisen from failure to distinguish between biological effects and ancestry. It is unlikely that all play has the same set of biological effects, but likely that play had a common ancestry, or, at least, a common ancestral function. I argue that motor training is the most plausible ancestral function of play and that, with the morphological and behavioural specializations that accompanied the mammalian radiations, play probably became modified to the extent that it now has new and different functions in some groups. The ungulates show such a progression. Distribution of play motor patterns across families suggests that locomotor- rotational play, which mimics flight, appeared first and was followed by social play, which mimics adult agonistic competition. In most instances the motor training hypothesis is both necessary and sufficient to explain both locomotor-rotational and social play. However, in the collared peccary, social play occurs as a coordinated herd activity that strongly involves adults; the motor training hypothesis does not satisfactorily explain this kind of play and the highly social nature of peccaries suggests that play may have been modified to promote group cohesion. Similar specializations in other species probably will be found as study of ungulate play proceeds.

REFERENCES

Allsopp, R. (1978). Social biology of the bushbuck (*Tragelaphus scriptus* Pallas 1776) in the Nairobi National Park, Kenya. *East African Wildlife Journal* 16, 153–66.

Altmann, M. (1963). Naturalistic studies of maternal care in moose and elk. In H. L. Rheingold (ed.), *Maternal Behavior in Mammals*. New York: John Wiley.

Autenreith, R. E. and Fichter, E. (1975). On the behavior and socialization of pronghorn fawns. *Wildlife Monographs* 42, 1–111.

Barrette, C. (1977). Some aspects of the behaviour of muntjacs in Wilpattu National Park. *Mammalia* 4, 1–29.

Bekoff, M. (1983). The development of behavior from evolutionary and ecological perspectives: towards a generic social biology. In E. S. Gollin (ed),

The Comparative Development of Adaptive Skills: Evolutionary Implications. New York: Academic Press.

Bekoff, M. and Byers, J. A. (1981). A critical reanalysis of the ontogeny and phylogeny of mammalian social and locomotor play: an ethological hornet's nest. In K. Immelmann, G. Barlow, M. Main and L. Petrinovich (eds), *Behavioral Development. The Bielefeld Interdisciplinary Project.* Cambridge: Cambridge University Press.

Berger, J. (1979). Social ontogeny and behavioural diversity: consequences for bighorn sheep *Ovis canadensis* inhabiting desert and mountain environments. *Journal of Zoology (London)* 188, 251–66.

Berger, J. (1980). The ecology, structure and function of social play in bighorn sheep (*Ovis canadensis*). *Journal of Zoology (London)* 192, 531–42.

Brandborg, S. M. (1955). *Life History and Management of the Mountain Goat in Idaho.* Boise: Idaho Department of Fish and Game.

Brown, J. L. and Orians, G. H. (1970). Spacing patterns in mobile animals. *Annual Review of Ecology and Systematics* 1, 239–62.

Brownlee, A. (1954). Play in domestic cattle in Britain: an analysis of its nature. *British Veterinary Journal* 110, 48–68.

Byers, J. A. (1977). Terrain preferences in the play of siberian ibex kids (*Capra ibex sibirica*). *Zeitschrift für Tierpsychologie* 45, 199–209.

Byers, J. A. (1980). Play partner preferences in siberian ibex, *Capra ibex sibirica*. *Zeitschrift für Tierpsychologie* 53, 23–40.

Byers, J. A. (1983). Social interaction of juvenile collared peccaries, *Tayassu tajacu (Mammalia: Artiodactyla). Journal of Zoology (London)* 201, 83–96.

Byers, J. A. and Bekoff, M. (1981). Social, spacing, and cooperative behaviour of the collared peccary, *Tayassu tajacu. Journal of Mammalogy* 62, 767–85.

Chepko, B. D. (1971). A preliminary study of the effects of play deprivation on young goats. *Zeitschrift für Tierpsychologie* 28, 517–28.

Clutton-Brock, T. H., Guinness, F. E. and Albon, S. D. (1982). *Red Deer. Behavior and Ecology of Two Sexes.* Chicago: University of Chicago Press.

Dane, B. (1977). Mountain goat social behavior: social structure and 'play' behavior as affected by dominance. In W. Samuel and W. G. Macgregor (eds), *Proceedings of the First International Mountain Goat Symposium.* British Columbia: Ministry of Recreation and Conservation.

Darling, F. F. (1937). *A Herd of Red Deer.* London: Oxford University Press.

Darwin, C. (1871). *The Descent of Man and Selection in Relation to Sex.* London: Murray.

David, J. H. M. (1975). Observations on mating behaviour, parturition, suckling and the mother–young bond in the bontebok (*Damaliscus dorcas dorcas*). *Journal of Zoology (London)* 177, 203–23.

Dobroruka, L. J. and Horbowyjova, R. (1972). Notes on the ethology of collared peccary, *Dicotyles tajacu* (Linnaeus, 1766) in the Prague Zoological Garden. *Lynx* 13, 85–94.

Dubost, G. (1968). Les Niches écologiques des forêts tropicales sud-americaines et africaines, sources de convergences remarquables entre Rongeurs et Artiodactyles. *La Terre et la Vie* 1, 3–28.

Dubost, G. (1971). Observations éthologiques sur le Muntjak *(Muntiacus muntjak* Zimmerman 1780 et *M. reevesi* Ogilby 1839) en captivité et semi-liberté. *Zeitschrift für Tierpsychologie* 28, 387–427.

Dubost, G. (1975). Le comportement du Chevrotain africain, *Hyemoschus aquaticus* Ogilby (Artiodactyla, Ruminantia). *Zeitschrift für Tierpsychologie* 37, 449–501.

Dubost, G. and Feer, F. (1981). The behavior of the male *Antilope cervicapra* L., its development according to age and social rank. *Behaviour* 76, 62–127.

Einarsen, A. S. (1948). *The Pronghorn Antelope and its Management.* Washington, DC: The Wildlife Management Institute.

Eisenberg, J. F. (1981). *The Mammalian Radiations. An Analysis of Trends in Evolution, Adaptation, and Behavior.* Chicago: University of Chicago Press.

Emlen, S. T. and Oring, L. W. (1977). Ecology, sexual selection, and the evolution of mating systems. *Science* 197, 214–23.

Espmark, Y. (1969). Mother–young relations and development of behaviour in roe deer (*Capreolus capreolus* L.). *Viltrevy* 6, 461–529.

Espmark, Y. (1971). Mother–young relationship and ontogeny of behaviour in Reindeer (*Rangifer tarandus* L.). *Zeitschrift für Tierpsychologie* 29, 42–81.

Estes, R. D. (1969). Territorial behaviour of the wildebeest (*Connochaetes taurinus* Burchell, 1823). *Zeitschrift für Tierpsychologie* 26, 284–370.

Estes, R. D. and Estes, R. K. (1979). Birth and survival of wildebeest calves. *Zeistschrift für Tierpsychologie* 50, 45–95.

Fagen, R. (1981). *Animal Play Behavior.* New York: Oxford University Press.

Fagen, R. and George, T. K. (1977). Play behavior and exercise in young ponies (*Equus caballus* L.). *Behavioral Ecology and Sociobiology* 2, 267–9.

Feist, J. D. and McCullough, D. R. (1976). Behaviour patterns and communication in feral horses. *Zeitschrift für Tierpsychologie* 41, 337–71.

Frädrich, H. (1965). Zur Biologie und Ethologie des Warzenschweines (*Phacochoerus aethropicus* Pallas) unter Berucksichtigung des Verhaltens anderer Suiden. *Zeitschrift für Tierpsychologie* 22, 375–93.

Frädrich, H. (1974). A comparison of behaviour in the Suidae. In V. Geist and F. Walther (eds), *The Behaviour of Ungulates and its Relation to Management.* Morges: International Union for Conservation of Nature and Natural Resources.

Frädrich, H. and Thenius, E. (1972). Tapirs. In *B. Grizmek's Animal Life Encyclopedia* 13, 17–33.

Fraser, D. (1978). Observations on the behavioural development of suckling and early-weaned piglets during the first six weeks after birth. *Animal Behaviour* 26, 22–30.

Gauthier-Pilters, H. and Dagg, A. I. (1981). *The Camel: Its Evolution, Ecology, Behavior, and Relationship to Man.* Chicago: University of Chicago Press.

Geist, V. (1963). The North American moose (*Alces alces andersoni*). *Behaviour* 20, 377–416.

Geist, V. (1971). *Mountain Sheep. A Study in Behavior and Evolution.* Chicago: University of Chicago Press.

Hamilton, W. D. (1971). Geometry for the selfish herd. *Journal of Theoretical*

Biology 31, 295–311.

Hanks, J., Price, M. S. and Wrangham, R. W. (1969). Some aspects of the ecology and behaviour of the Defassa waterbuck (*Kobus defassa*) in Zambia. *Mammalia* 33, 471–94.

Jarman, P. J. (1974). The social organization of antelope in relation to their ecology. *Behaviour* 48, 215–67.

Jarman, M. V. and Jarman, P. J. (1973). Daily activity of impala. *East African Wildlife Journal* 11, 75–92.

Jerison, H. J. (1973). *Evolution of the Brain and Intelligence*. New York: Academic Press.

Joubert, E. (1972). Activity patterns shown by mountain zebra *Equus zebra harmannae* in southwest Africa with reference to climatic factors. *Zoologica Africana* 7, 309–31.

Kielan-Jaworowska, Z., Bown, T. M. and Lillegraven, J. A. (1979). Eutheria. In J. A. Lillegraven, Z. Kielan-Jaworowska and W. A. Clemens (eds), *Mesozoic Mammals. The First Two-Thirds of Mammalian History*. Berkeley: University of California Press.

Kingdon, J. (1979). *East African Mammals: an Atlas of Evolution in Africa. Vol. 3. Part B: Large Mammals*. London: Academic Press.

Kitchen, D. W. (1974). Social behavior and ecology of the pronghorn. *Wildlife Monographs* 38, 1–96.

Klingel, H. (1967). Soziale Organisation und Verhalten freilebender Steppenzebras. *Zeitschrift für Tierpsychologie* 24, 580–624.

Klingel, H. (1968). Soziale Organisation und Verhaltensweisen von Hartmann – und Bergzebras (*Equus zebra hartmannae* und *E. z. zebra*). *Zeitschrift für Tierpsychologie* 25, 76–88.

Klingel, H. (1974a). Soziale Organisation und Verhalten des Grevy-Zebras (*Equus grevyi*). *Zeitschrift für Tierpsychologie* 36, 47–70.

Klingel, H. (1974b). A comparison of the social behaviour of the Equidae. In V. Geist and F. Walther (eds). *The Behaviour of Ungulates and its Relation to Management*. Morges: International Union for Conservation of Nature and Natural Resources.

Koford, C. B. (1957). The Vicuna and the puna. *Ecological Monographs* 27, 153–219.

Kramer, A. (1969). Soziale Organisation und Sozialverhalten einer Gemspopulation (*Rupicapra rupicapra* L.) der Alpen. *Zeitschrift für Tierpsychologie* 26, 889–964.

Lent, P. C. (1966). Calving and related social behaviour in the barren-ground caribou. *Zeitschrift für Tierpsychologie* 23, 701–56.

Lent, P. C. (1969). A preliminary study of the okavango Lechwe (*Kobus leche leche* Gray). *East African Wildlife Journal* 7, 147–57.

Lentfer, J. W. (1955). A two-year study of the rocky mountain goat in the Crazy Mountains, Montana. *Journal of Wildlife Management* 19, 417–29.

Leuthold, B. M. (1979). Social organization and behaviour of giraffe in Tsavo East National Park. *African Journal of Ecology* 17, 19–34.

Leuthold, W. (1970). Observations on the social organization of Impala

(*Aepyceros melampus*). *Zeitschrift für Tierpsychologie* 27, 693–721.

Leuthold, W. (1977). *African Ungulates. A Comparative Review of Their Ethology and Behavioural Ecology*. Berlin: Springer-Verlag.

Leuthold, W. and Leuthold B. M. (1973). Notes on the behaviour of two young antelopes reared in captivity. *Zeitschrift für Tierpsychologie* 32, 418–24.

Lillegraven, J. A., Kielan-Jaworowska, Z. and Clemens, W. A. (1979). *Mesozoic Mammals. The First Two-Thirds of Mammalian History*. Berkeley: University of California Press.

Lumia, A. R. (1972). The relationship between dominance and play behaviour in the american buffalo *Bison bison*. *Zietschrift für Tierpsychologie* 30, 416–19.

Mackler, S. F. and Buechner, H. K. (1978). Play behaviour and mother–young relationships in captive indian rhinoceroses (*Rhinoceros unicornis*). *Der Zoologische Garten* 48, 177–86.

Michael, E. D. (1968). Playing by white-tailed deer in south Texas, USA, *Odocolleus virginianus* behavioral activities. *American Midland Naturalist* 80, 535–7.

Miller, F. L. (1975). Play activities of black-tailed deer in north-western Oregon. *Canadian Field-Naturalist* 89, 149–56.

Miller, F. L. and Gunn, A. (1981). Play by peary caribou *Rangifer tarandus pearyi* calves before during and after helicopter harassment. *Canadian Journal of Zoology* 59, 823–7.

Müller-Schwarze, D. (1968). Play deprivation in deer. *Behaviour* 31, 144–62.

Müller-Schwarze, D., Stagge, B. and Müller-Schwarze, C. (1982). Play behavior: persistence, decrease, and energetic compensation during food shortage in deer fawns. *Science* 215, 85–7.

Mungall, E. C. (1976). *The Indian Blackbuck Antelope: a Texas View*. College Station: Texas Agricultural Experiment Station.

Oliver, W. L. R. (1980). *The Pigmy Hog. The Biology and Conservation of the Pigmy Hog Sus (porcula) salvanius and the hispid hare Caprolagus hispidus*. Jersey, UK: Jersey Wildlife Preservation Trust.

Owen, S. (1973). Behaviour and diet of a captive royal antelope, *Neotragus pygmaeous* L. *Mammalia* 37, 56–65.

Owen-Smith, N. (1974). The social system of the white rhinoceros. In V. Geist and F. Walther (eds), *The Behaviour of Ungulates and its Relation to Management*. Morges: International Union for Conservation of Nature and Natural Resources.

Owen-Smith, N. (1975). The social ethology of the white rhinoceros (*Ceratotherium simum*) (Burchell 1817). *Zeitschrift für Tierpsychologie* 38, 337–84.

Pilters, H. (1954). Untersuchungen über angeborene Verhaltensweisen bie tylopoden, unter besonderer Berücksichtigung der neuweltlichen formen. *Zeitschrift für Tierpsychologie* 11, 213–303.

Pratt, D. M. and Anderson, V. (1979). Giraffe cow–calf relationships and social development of the calf in the Serengeti. *Zeitschrift für Tierpsychologie* 51, 233–51.

Reinhardt, V. and Reinhardt, A. (1982). Mock fighting in cattle. *Behaviour* 80, 1–13.

Romer, A. S. (1967) *Vertebrate Paleontology* (3rd edn). Chicago: University of Chicago Press.

Rudge, M. R. (1970). Mother and kid behaviour in feral goats (*Capra hircus* L.). *Zeitschrift für Tierpsychologie* 27, 687–92.

Sachs, B. D. and Harris, V. S. (1978). Sex differences and developmental changes in selected juvenile activities (play) of domestic lambs. *Animal Behaviour* 26, 678–84.

Schaller, G. B. (1967). *The Deer and the Tiger*. Chicago: University of Chicago Press.

Schaller, G. B. (1977). *Mountain Monarchs. Wild Sheep and Goats of the Himalaya*. Chicago: University of Chicago Press.

Schenkel, R. and Schenkel-Hulliger, L. (1969). *Ecology and behaviour of the black rhinoceros (Diceros bicornis* L.). Hamburg: Paul Parey.

Scheurmann, E. (1975). Beobachtung zur Fortpflanzung des *Gayal Bibos frontalis* Lambert, 1837. *Zeitschrift für Säugetierkunde* 40, 113–27.

Schoen, A. M. S., Banks, E. M., and Curtis, S. E. (1976). Behaviour of young Shetland and Welsh ponies (*Equus caballus*). *Biology of Behavior* 1, 192–216.

Sinclair, A. R. E. (1977). *The African Buffalo. A Study of Resource Limitation of Populations*. Chicago: University of Chicago Press.

Smith, P. K. (1982). Does play matter? Functional and evolutionary aspects of animal and human play. *Behavioral and Brain Sciences* 5, 139–55.

Sowls, L. K. (1974). Social behaviour of the collared peccary *Dicotyles tajacu* (L.). In V. Geist and F. Walther (eds), *The Behaviour of Ungulates and its Relation to Management*. Morges: International Union for Conservation of Nature and Natural Resources.

Spinage, C. A. (1969). Naturalistic observations on the reproductive and maternal behaviour of the uganda defassa waterbuck *Kobus defassa ugandae* Neumann. *Zeitschrift für Tierpsychologie* 26, 39–47.

Struhsaker, T. T. (1967). Behaviour of elk (*Cervus canadensis*) during the rut. *Zeitschift für Tierpsychologie* 24, 80–114.

Tener, J. S. (1965). *Musk oxen in Canada. A Biological and Taxonomic Review*. Canadian Wildlife Service.

Tyler, S. J. (1972). The behaviour and social organization of the New Forest ponies. *Animal Behaviour Monographs* 5, 85–196.

Underwood, R. (1979). Mother–infant relationships and behavioural ontogeny in the common eland (*Taurotragus oryx oryx*). *South African Journal of Wildlife Research* 9, 27–45.

Verheyen, R. (1955). Contribution à l'éthologie du waterbuck *Kobus defassa ugandae* Neumann et de l'antilope harnachée *Tragelaphus scriptus* (Pallas). *Mammalia* 19, 309–19.

Walther, F. (1962). Uber ein spiel bei *Okapia johnstoni*. *Zeitschrift für Säugetierkunde* 27, 245–51.

Wilson, S. C. (1973). The development of social behaviour in the vole (*Microtus agrestis*). *Zoological Journal of the Linnaean Society* 52, 45–62.

Wilson, S. C. and Kleiman, D. G. (1974). Eliciting play: a comparative study. *American Zoologist* 14, 341–70.

PART 2
The Study of Play in Mammals

Some form of play has been observed in most, if not all, mammals which have been studied in detail (though it may be the case that some mammals, such as small rodents, do not play; perhaps because of energetic costs, Burghardt, chapter 1). However, our knowledge of play across mammalian families and orders is very unbalanced. For example, in the many species of bats, play is barely described, in part no doubt because of observational difficulties. Some species, for example the larger ungulates, are readily observed in the wild, and a reasonable amount of data now exist on the form and occurrence of ungulate play (Byers, chapter 2; also Müller-Schwarze, below, chapter 6). Other species have been studied very intensively in laboratory conditions. Prime examples of the laboratory study of play are of the cat, a predatory felid; and of the rat, an omnivorous rodent.

In this part, play in kittens is reviewed by Paul Martin (chapter 3), and play in the rat, and in rodents generally, by Graham Hole and Dorothy Einon (chapter 4). In both kittens and rats, several investigators have documented the development of play by careful laboratory observations; and some very sophisticated rearing manipulations have been carried out to examine the effects of environment on play behaviour. Play has also been studied extensively in the primates (monkeys and apes). It is probably amongst primates that we find at present the best balance between laboratory and field studies. While laboratory studies allow detailed recording of behaviour and control of the environment, field studies allow a fuller range of natural behaviour and more understanding of its adaptive significance. Neil Chalmers (chapter 5) reviews play in monkeys, especially baboons and rhesus monkeys, and marmosets.

Any reader considering these three chapters on mammalian play will be struck by the concern over the description and definition of play, and of the various approaches taken by the different authors. It is often claimed that observers can agree on what is or is not play when watching a particular species; but even if this is so, what does it prove? Only that the observers share certain preconceptions, which they may not be able to make explicit. The definition of play is important, not just for helping observers agree, but for clarifying our theories and thinking about the causation, development and function of play behaviour. This does not mean that a single or all-embracing definition is easy, or attainable, or even desirable.

Martin follows a well-established distinction between 'structural' and 'functional' descriptions. Such descriptions concentrate on the form of behaviour, or its (lack of) obvious purpose, respectively. Chalmers is less certain about the usefulness of this distinction; he prefers to measure certain aspects or parameters of behaviour when certain questions are being investigated. Hole and Einon end up with three criteria for play: its lack of immediate function, its context, and the incorporation of unique behaviour patterns. Their chapter provides a detailed description of behavioural patterns in some rodent species, and a very careful consideration as to whether certain behaviours are or are not usefully considered as play. Their distinction between two types of play-fighting ('rough-and- tumble', and 'not very serious fighting' or NVSF) illustrates the theoretical importance of careful description.

In a very influential article, Tinbergen (1963) argued that the ethological study of behaviour can be organized around four types of question: the causation of behaviour, its development, its function, and its evolution. Both Martin and Chalmers organize their chapters along these lines (although neither specifically addresses the evolution of play; cf. part 1). The methods of study of the proximate (immediate) causation of behaviour, and the ways of describing development, are well exemplified in their chapters.

All three chapters address the possible functions of play behaviour. As Martin soon points out, 'function' can be used in a weak sense (any beneficial consequence of the behaviour) or a strong sense (the reasons for which the behaviour was originally selected).

It is usually argued that experimental manipulations which enhance or deprive an animal of play experience only tell us about function in the weak sense, whereas consideration of design features tells us about function in the strong sense. Design features can include the actual forms of play, and cross-species comparisons, e.g. of fighting play in rodents (Hole and Einon). Chalmers, however, thinks that the distinction between these two sources of evidence is mistaken. He argues that the strongest evidence for function would come from studying the differences in viability or fecundity of playful and non-playful individuals, about which we have little information. This would be a very direct source of evidence, but even so, viability or fecundity might be little affected by variations in play experience if (as Martin suggests) the benefits of play are small, or short-term, and/or obtainable by alternative means. This last possibility (of alternative pathways to the same final state: equifinality or homeorhesis) poses particular problems for correlational studies of play effects. A few studies have compared variations in early play experience with specific aspects of later behaviour (such as predatory ability, amount of fighting, or social skills). The results of some of these studies are not very encouraging for functional theories of play. However, besides the difficulties mentioned, it is also possible in these studies that some relevant later behaviours were not being assessed (cf. Chalmers, figure 5.6; and Fagen, chapter 7). It is also possible that some behaviours do indeed have no direct function. Hole and Einon make a case for this possibility with the sexual 'play' of rodents; it is less plausible, as they point out, for play in which distinctive signals have evolved, as in rough- and-tumble and play-chasing.

The questions commonly addressed by ethologists (definition, causation, development and function) are useful conceptual tools; but they inter-relate with each other in complex ways, and there is a lively debate on definitional and functional issues, as the chapters in this part clearly demonstrate.

REFERENCES

Tinbergen, N. (1963). On aims and methods of ethology. *Zeitschrift für Tierpsychologie* 20, 410–33.

3 The (Four) Whys and Wherefores of Play in Cats: a Review of Functional, Evolutionary, Developmental and Causal Issues

Paul Martin

> But some instincts one can hardly avoid looking at as mere tricks, or sometimes as play.
>
> (Charles Darwin, quoted by Fagen, 1981)

In 1945 one rueful commentator on play research remarked that 'the richness of the observational evidence is in sharp contrast to the poverty of scientific knowledge' (Beach, 1945). In 1981, one of the foremost students of animal play described his subject as 'the ugly duckling of behavioral science' (Fagen, 1981), with the unhappy implication that the intervening 36 years had done little to remedy the matter. In sallying forth into the convoluted and vexed debate that surrounds play, it is prudent to go armed with as many mental aids and simplifying rules as possible. Two are particularly valuable.

The first, which has become the touchstone of ethology, is the logical distinction between four different sorts of question that can be asked about a behaviour pattern: 'What is it for?' (*function*); 'How did it evolve?' (*evolution*); 'How did it arise during the ontogeny of the individual?' (*ontogeny* or *development*); and 'What are the proximate factors eliciting and controlling it?' (*proximate causation* or *control*) (Tinbergen, 1963; Hinde, 1982). This review will comment separately on the play of cats in relation to these four questions.

A second useful distinction is the one Fagen (1974) has drawn between two complementary styles in the study of animal play: the *structuralist* approach, which emphasizes the form and temporal patterning of the motor acts used in play; and the *functionalist* approach, which stresses the biological consequences of play. Differentiating between these is particularly useful when discussing definitions of play.

Defining the problem

The protracted debate about the definition of play has yet to produce agreement as to what actually constitutes play. Most researchers seem to take the pragmatic line that it is still possible to study play without a satisfactory definition and it has become unfashionable in recent years to quibble over precise definitions. In general, the statement that an animal is playing seems to be arrived at by a subjective interpretation on the part of a human observer – usually as a result of the apparent lack of any immediate benefits from the animal's behaviour (a functional distinction). Play, once recognized, is then frequently characterized solely in terms of the particular motor patterns involved (a structural description; see Chalmers, 1980). Seldom is any explanation given as to why the particular set of motor patterns described was classified as play, however. A further problem about the use of the term 'play' is the tendency to generalize its meaning: it would appear that, as far as some writers are concerned, 'play' covers most activities performed by juvenile animals. Clearly, to have any practical use as a discrete behavioural category, the meaning of 'play' must be restricted to something more specific than all unaccountable juvenile behaviour.

An expedient approach to defining play seems to have been taken by most students of play in cats. For example, Barrett and Bateson (1978) describe seven distinct categories of playful motor activity solely in terms of their appearance, but note in passing that the observer had to rely on 'a strong subjective sense of certainty about when an animal is playing', together with contextual cues. West (1974), together with most others in this field (e.g. Collard, 1967; Smith and Jansen, 1977; Guyot et al., 1980; Bateson et al., 1981), simply lists structural definitions of the motor activities recorded as play, leaving the play/non-play distinction as entirely implicit. Caro (1979) describes in structural terms a number of motor patterns occurring in predatory behaviour and defines social play as the same items directed at siblings, making no other explicit distinction between the two types of behaviour. Biben's (1979) account is unusual, in that it includes a definition of play with prey in terms of its consequences rather than its appearance: play is defined as active behaviour where prey is manipulated or approached but not injured. Finally, some prefer to avoid the issue entirely – perhaps assuming the meaning of play to be self-evident – and give no definition at all (Koepke and Pribram, 1971; Villablanca and Olmstead, 1979).

Clearly, there are major problems with defining play. No single characteristic is universal to all behaviour termed play. Thus play behaviour forms a polythetic classification: one in which a large proportion of properties is shared, but no single property defines the group (Sokal, 1974). Structural definitions are weak, because of the enormous diversity of motor patterns potentially constituting play in different species. Functional definitions remain elusive because the functions of play are unknown (Bekoff and Byers, 1981). In keeping with common practice, I will give one published definition of play (one which seems more honest than most and probably most representative of much of the play literature): 'Play is all motor activity performed postnatally that *appears* (my italics) to be purposeless, in which motor patterns from other contexts may often be used in modified forms and altered temporal sequencing' (Bekoff and Byers, 1981). Object play and social play are taken simply to refer to play directed at objects and conspecifics, respectively.

To end this section on a note of optimism, it should be said that observers do, in practice, find play easy to recognize (although see Millar, 1981, for a contrary viewpoint) and a high level of inter-observer concordance has usually been found in studies of play in cats (Koepke and Pribram, 1971; Caro et al., 1979; Bateson and Young, 1979, 1981; Guyot et al., 1980). Some prominent motor patterns exhibited in kittens' play are illustrated in figure 3.1.

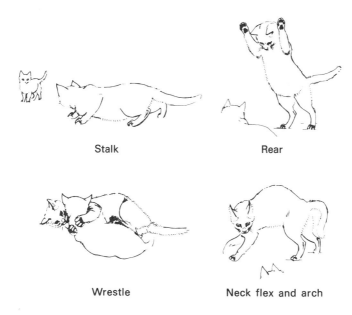

Stalk   Rear

Wrestle   Neck flex and arch

FIGURE 3.1 Some of the motor patterns exhibited in the play behaviour of young domestic cats

(Taken from Barrett and Bateson, 1978, by kind permission of the authors and E. J. Brill, Leiden)

FUNCTION AND EVOLUTION

The possible function of play was a troublesome enigma long before the 'adaptationist programme' (Gould and Lewontin, 1979) of modern biology came into ascendancy. The mystery of play's function is made all the more insoluble because play is usually distinguished by a human observer precisely because of a *lack* of any obvious biological function. Before joining this affray, however, it is worth restating the different meanings which may be attached to the term 'function' (Hinde, 1975, 1982; Clutton-Brock, 1981).

In its weakest sense, the function of a behaviour pattern is simply a consequence which appears beneficial – of which there may be many. Function in the strong sense refers to the particular beneficial consequences which critically influence the chances of survival and reproduction and upon which natural selection acts to maintain the pattern, in a population of individuals which differ with respect to that behaviour pattern. Since selection can act on more than one consequence, a behaviour pattern can have multiple functions. Furthermore, selection may currently be acting on different consequences from those for which the behaviour was originally selected. It is important not to confuse the issue of function (the current effects on survival and reproduction) with the issue of evolution (the changes in gene frequencies during the course of species history). As Gould and Vrba (1982) have pointed out, the historical origins of a phenotypic character cannot simply be inferred from its current usage. Unfortunately, biologists discussing adaptation have sometimes failed to recognize this distinction between the historical genesis of a character and the way in which the character may currently enhance the animal's fitness (see also Lewin, 1982). Thus, play may have numerous beneficial consequences, but these cannot necessarily be equated with functions (in the strong sense) and the current functions of play may be different from those for which play was originally selected. If playing is a character that now enhances fitness, but did not originally evolve for its current role, then it would – in Gould and Vrba's (1982) proposed terminology – be an exaptation rather than an adaptation.

Speculation as to the functions of play in animals has, of course, been prodigious: one review lists thirty functions that have been attributed to play, ranging from the provision of physical exercise to the establishing of dominance relationships (Baldwin and Baldwin, 1977). With effort, however, this impressive list may be reduced in length and Bekoff and Byers (1981) have condensed the various hypotheses into three main categories: motor training, socialization and cognitive training. It would not be appropriate to discuss the plethora of relevant information from other species here, for which the reader is referred to one of many comprehensive reviews (e.g. Loizos, 1967; Bekoff, 1976a; Baldwin and Baldwin, 1977; Bekoff and Byers, 1981; Fagen, 1981). Suffice it to say that solid evidence for any of the functional hypotheses is scarce (Bekoff and

Byers, 1981), although it must also be admitted that there have been few rigorous tests of any hypotheses.

Of most relevance to play in cats are functional hypotheses in the 'play as motor training' category, which state that play enhances the animal's subsequent ability to perform particular motor acts. Since there is a profusion of evidence suggesting that play is neither necessary nor sufficient for the development of many abilities (e.g. Bekoff, 1976a; Baerends-van Roon and Baerends, 1979; Caro, 1980b), such theories usually propose that play helps to perfect existing or future motor patterns. Cats are, of course, formidable hunters and many of the motor patterns that appear in play resemble in form those used in catching and killing prey (Rosenblatt and Schneirla, 1962; Egan, 1976; Leyhausen, 1979). Not surprisingly, therefore, many hypotheses about play in cats have invoked links between play and later predatory behaviour, with play seen as direct practice for adult predation (e.g. Egan, 1976; Moelk, 1979).

Object play in kittens

Kittens are renowned for playing with objects. From the third week of life, when kittens first tentatively paw at movable objects, object play develops into a pronounced interest in mouthing, patting, poking, batting and leaping over any suitable toy (Gruber et al., 1971; West, 1977; Moelk, 1979). Favourite toys tend to be prey-like in their physical properties and there are undoubtedly some similarities between many of the motor patterns employed in object play and those used in dealing with prey. This has led some writers (e.g. Egan, 1976) to regard object play as a category of behaviour that is not distinct from true predation and to suggest that object play functions as direct training for hunting.

To date, there has been only one attempt to subject the practice hypothesis of object play in kittens to a direct experimental test. Caro (1980b) repeatedly allowed kittens to play with small movable objects during the period from 4 to 12 weeks after birth and subsequently tested the same kittens on their ability to catch live prey at the age of six months. Predatory ability, as assessed by 13 different behavioural measures, was compared with that of a control group which had not played with objects as kittens. Both groups of kittens were raised in the presence of their mothers and littermates and therefore had opportunities for social play. There were very few noteworthy differences between the control and object-playing kittens when they were tested at six months of age and Caro concluded that object play seemed to have little significant effect on adult predatory abilities.

The failure of this experiment to demonstrate any effect of object play on subsequent predatory skills could, of course, have many different explanations – some of which Caro (1980b) has discussed. For example, the object-playing kittens may have been given insufficient experience of play or unsuitable toys to play with; the measures of predatory behaviour may not have been appropriate; kittens may only need a minimal amount of object play experience to become competent predators and the control kittens may have received this in some other way; social play may have compensated for the lack of object play in the controls. Until these other explanations are substantiated, however, Caro's (1980b) results are consistent with the assertion that early object play experience in kittens has no important effects on adult predatory skills. A lack of any significant correlations between play and later predatory success has also been demonstrated by Vincent and Bekoff (1978) in a study of coyotes (*Canis latrans*).

Social play in kittens

Social play is a prominent feature of kittens' behaviour and consists of stalking, chasing, displaying, pouncing and a variety of body-contact motor patterns, involving the mother or siblings as play partners (Rosenblatt and Schneirla, 1962; West, 1974, 1979; Barrett and Bateson, 1978; Moelk, 1979). Several of the motor patterns that appear in social play – such as West's (1974) 'belly-up', 'stand-up' and 'chase' categories – can also be seen in adult intraspecific fighting. However, these patterns occur in different combinations in the two contexts and, furthermore, fighting and social play include motor patterns that are not common to both (West, 1974). The most striking similarity, however, is between social play and predatory behaviour, which have many elements in common – stalking, chasing, pouncing, rolling and biting, for example (Rosenblatt and Schneirla, 1962; West, 1974; Leyhausen, 1979). It is frequently suggested, therefore, that social play – like object play – serves to practise adult predatory skills. Unfortunately, no direct evidence is yet available from studies of play in cats that can be used to test this hypothesis.

Indirect evidence comes from Caro's (1979, 1981b) work on the relations between social play in kittens, from 4 to 12 weeks of age, and predatory ability assessed at 6 months. Remarkably few significant correlations were found between measures of kittens' social play and their subsequent predatory behaviour (Caro, 1979). There was, however, a hint that some aspects of social play became increasingly associated with certain features of predatory behaviour in older kittens, while other measures of social play became less closely associated (Caro, 1981b).

The most obvious test of any hypothesis which proposes that a particular form of early experience has important benefits is to deny all opportunity for such experience and record the consequences. Deprivation experiments of this sort suffer from considerable methodological problems, however, the most notable of which is that of confounding variables (Bekoff, 1976b; Bateson, 1981a). Social deprivation introduces many interrelated effects, such as changes in all types of social interaction, exercise, sensory stimulation, arousal and, possibly, nutrition (Bekoff, 1976b). A kitten cannot *selectively* be deprived of social play. Many of the inevitable side-effects of social play deprivation may be far more damaging to the young animal than the loss of play experience itself. Kittens raised in social isolation or weaned extremely early are known to behave abnormally and a strong fear response to any novel object (such as live prey) would tend to obscure any underlying deficit in predatory skills which may also be present (Kuo, 1930; Seitz, 1959; Baerends-van Roon and Baerends, 1979). One hopeful way of circumventing some of the problems of social deprivation is the use of psychoactive drugs to modify the behaviour of play partners: a method used by Einon and colleagues in studies of play in rats (Einon et al., 1978). Even in this type of experiment, though, confounding variables are still present, since the drugged play partners are undoubtedly different from normal conspecifics in many ways. It remains uncertain in such experiments, therefore, whether it is social play *per se* – as opposed to some other form of experience – which is important for normal development.

Most functional discussions of play emphasize its supposed long-term effects: the juvenile is generally assumed to pay the immediate costs of play (in terms of time, energy and risk of injury) while the benefits accrue to the adult. It is, of course, convenient to ignore the possible short-term effects of play if – as is often the case – play is recognized precisely because of an apparent *lack* of immediate benefits.

One possible short-term benefit of social play in kittens has been mooted by West (1979). Females of semi-altricial species such as the cat generally give birth to more than one young per litter and a nest site serves, among other things, to keep the young together while the mother is away hunting. Very young kittens tend to huddle together and can orientate towards the home nest site (Rosenblatt, 1976). As the kittens grow older and become highly mobile, social play – by maintaining contact between littermates in the vicinity of the nest site – may have the beneficial consequence of keeping the litter together in one place. One way of testing this notion further would be to investigate whether there was any relation, in populations of feral cats, between the amount of social play shown by different litters and kitten mortality. West's idea implies that feral kittens which engaged in less social play would – other things being equal – be more likely to get separated from the litter or lost:

a family that plays together stays together. Note that no long-term effect of play on adult behaviour is necessarily predicated by this idea.

Play with prey and play by adult cats

In addition to the current absence of solid supporting evidence, another headache for those who favour practice-type functional hypotheses of play is that adults of many species also play – although usually much less than juveniles. The object play of adult cats is well known (West, 1974; Leyhausen, 1979), but probably the most puzzling form of play exhibited by adult cats is play with living or dead prey. This apparently pointless 'crazy capering', which can completely interrupt prey-catching, may include walking or leaping around the prey, vocalizing, grooming, head-rubbing, rolling and batting or carrying the prey (Baerends-van Roon and Baerends, 1979; Biben, 1979). Kittens may also play with prey. Leyhausen (1979) distinguishes between three different forms of play with prey: 'restrained play', said to be low intensity play due to fear of the prey; 'overflow play' with small prey (chasing, catching and throwing), supposedly due to an accumulation of prey-catching propensities; and 'relief play' (leaping around or over dead prey), which is said to occur after a particularly large or difficult prey has been killed. As structural descriptions Leyhausen's categories are almost certainly valid, but the accompanying causal explanations are based on highly questionable energy models of motivation and lack supporting evidence (Biben, 1979).

One dubious solution to the problem of why cats, both young and old, play with prey is to regard play and true predation simply as graded aspects of the same behaviour. Egan (1976) contends that play occurs in response to prey-like stimuli, uses motor patterns similar in form to prey-catching and is influenced by some of the same causal factors, concluding from this that play is not fundamentally distinct from predatory behaviour, but differs from true predation only by a matter of degree (and, of course, result). According to this notion, playing with objects results from a response to prey-like stimuli when the 'consum-matory stimuli' are lacking, while play with prey manifests an inexperi-enced animal's tendency to respond to prey stimuli when the training or motivation to kill are absent. To argue that there is a continuum between play and predation does not, however, explain why experi-enced adult cats play with live prey which are, manifestly, prey-like. More importantly, a common function cannot be inferred from similar-ities in appearance between two activities.

Evidence relevant to the debate about the function of playing with prey comes from a purely causal analysis which suggests that playing with prey may result from motivational conflict. Play often occurs when cats have difficulty with prey and appear to be in conflict between opposing tendencies to attack and abandon the prey (Baerends-van Roon and Baerends, 1979) and cats may sometimes exhibit a playful response to unfamiliar prey (Caro, 1980a). Direct evidence for the 'conflict' causal hypothesis has been furnished by Biben (1979), who investigated the effects of experimentally manipulating both hunger and prey size on the likelihood that adult cats would kill prey with which they were presented. Biben found that cats played least with prey when they were both hungry and dealing with small prey, in which case an immediate kill tended to result. Play was most likely to occur when cats were either (1) satiated and given small (easy) prey, or (2) very hungry but confronted with large or difficult prey. Cats were more likely to kill prey when hungry, but less likely if the prey was large and difficult. Prey size and hunger therefore worked in opposition to one another and together accounted for nearly all of the variability in the killing response. The interaction between hunger and prey size demonstrated by Biben may, incidentally, account for earlier failures to find any simple relation between hunger and killing in cats (Kuo, 1930; Leyhausen, 1979). Possibly at odds with the 'conflict' idea, however, are the results of a limited and inconclusive experiment in which the benzodiazepine tranquillizer diazepam (Valium) was found to induce play with prey in cats which normally killed prey immediately (Langfeldt, 1974).

Biben's (1979) results imply that a cat deprived of prey (and therefore of play with prey) is less likely to play, since hunger would encourage an immediate kill. Thus Egan's (1976) assertions that object play, play with prey and prey-killing are not causally distinct and that object play is unaffected by hunger are at odds both with Biben's results and with a mass of evidence, from many species, that play is depressed by food shortage (e.g. Baldwin and Baldwin, 1974, 1976; reviewed by Fagen, 1981: 370).

What might the benefits be to a kitten of playing with prey? Some kittens can kill prey at their first encounter (Yerkes and Bloomfield, 1910; Kuo, 1930; Leyhausen, 1979), but there is substantial individual variation in the time needed to become a competent predator and in the developmental route leading up to this. Such variation depends in part on early experience with prey, the presence of littermates and the mother's behaviour (Kuo, 1930; Baerends-van Roon and Baerends, 1979; Caro, 1980a,b,c). Individual variation seems to lie not so much in the actual prey-killing acts themselves, but in the complex appetitive sequence which leads up to killing: identifying and assessing the prey, orienting towards it and timing the first moves (Baerends-van Roon and Baerends,

1979). Playing with prey, when there is an underlying conflict between attack and escape, would tend to maintain contact with the prey and increase familiarity with prey-killing. In an inexperienced kitten, this mechanism might hasten the first attainment of successful prey-killing and would – if this were the case – constitute a facilitatory developmental determinant of predatory behaviour (see Bateson, 1981a, 1983). At the time of weaning, a feral kitten might find itself having to kill for its immediate survival and any process which facilitated these intitial kills could be an important asset. This hypothetical benefit of playing with prey need have no obvious long-term consequences for adult prey-catching abilities. It is interesting to note, in relation to this suggestion, that experimental evidence now suggests that certain aspects of the development of play in kittens are linked to the time of weaning. In particular, simulating early weaning is found – somewhat surprisingly – to increase the frequency of play (Bateson and Young, 1981; Bateson et al., 1981; Martin, 1982b; see Bateson, 1981b).

The costs and benefits of play

Play behaviour clearly has many consequences: kittens execute numerous motor patterns, interact with conspecifics, obtain physical exercise, are aroused and stimulated and become familiar with properties of the physical and social environment. It does not follow, however, that play is *necessary* for any of these effects to occur and there may be alternative mechanisms for acquiring important information or experience, such as observational learning (Berry, 1908; Marvin and Harsh, 1944; John et al., 1968; Chesler, 1969). Furthermore, there is currently no unequivocal evidence that play has any major long-term benefits for animals of any species (Bekoff and Byers, 1981; Fagen, 1981). The possibility therefore arises that the crucial importance of play for normal development – the *sine qua non* of some writers – may be an overstatement.

Uncritical assumptions about the major adaptive importance of play are frequently based on the unsupported assumption that play is very costly in terms of time, energy and risk of injury (Martin 1982a, 1984). Since animals are generally assumed not to perform a particular type of behaviour unless, on average, its benefits outweigh its costs, it follows that if play has major costs then it must have major benefits. Unfortunately, although the notion that play has major costs has achieved widespread and largely unquestioning acceptance, the limited empirical evidence which is available suggests that this is not necessarily justified.

In a recent experimental study, the amount of time spent playing by 10–12-week-old kittens and the accompanying net expenditure of metabolic energy on play have been measured using a variety of techniques, including indirect (oxygen consumption) calorimetry (Martin, 1984). Under conditions normally conducive to play – ample food, lack of disturbance and with mother and littermate present – kittens were found to spend roughly 9% of their total time playing. The associated net energy expenditure accounted for about 4% – and at most 9%– of total expenditure. Thus, even in well-nourished, undisturbed, disease- and predator-free juveniles of a reputedly playful domesticated species, play was found to account for relatively little time and to involve only a small additional energy expenditure. This conclusion probably applies to most species which play – indeed, it is likely that kittens expend more time and energy on play than the young of most mammals (see Fagen, 1981: 273; Martin, 1982a, 1984). Of course, even a 1% additional energy expenditure might constitute a major cost as far as a starving animal was concerned, but starving animals generally do not play. The possible magnitude of the costs associated with risk of injury during play (which is often mentioned anecdotally) has yet to be estimated. Thus, the doctrine that play has major costs (and must, therefore, have major benefits) is perhaps worthy of more critical scrutiny. Indeed, given the limited evidence which is currently available, it could be argued with equal plausibility that play is an activity which has only marginal costs and marginal benefits.

DEVELOPMENT

An important principle in the study of ontogeny is that organisms must be adapted to their environment at *all* stages in the life cycle and not just as adults. Thus the behaviour of juveniles must be suited to their current needs, as well as possibly preparing them for adulthood (Williams, 1966; Oppenheim, 1980; Galef, 1981). The developing animal is not merely a half-built version of the adult, but may have specific characteristics suited to its particular niche: suckling, for example, is not an incomplete version of adult feeding, but has many unique features both in terms of its form and underlying control (Blass and Teicher, 1980; see Galef, 1981).

Some early behaviour may be concerned specifically with acquiring information or skills needed in later life: 'behaviour used in development' (Bateson, 1976). Play has frequently been suggested as an example of 'behaviour used in development', or 'scaffolding' used to build adult behaviour (Bateson, 1981b). It could be argued, however, that this emphasis on the long-term effects of play reflects an implicit view of ontogeny in which all juvenile behaviour is seen as a preparation for adult life and the immediate problems facing the juvenile are ignored. This view of ontogeny is certainly consistent with practice hypotheses about the funcion of play. However, another implication of the 'scaffolding' analogy is that if the scaffolding (play) is dismantled when its job is done, no obvious counterpart need be found in adult behaviour, nor need there be any straightforward connection between the scaffolding and adult behaviour. In other words, particular motor patterns might be concerned with achieving different ends at different stages in development. Thus initial correlations between similar aspects of behaviour (say, different measures of social play) might break down as the same patterns became concerned with different roles later in life (say, predatory and aggressive behaviour).

Several measures of play in kittens are positively correlated with one another up until about two months of age, but after this time many of these associations break down (Barrett and Bateson, 1978; Caro, 1981b). Furthermore, with the exception of cat contact patterns, measures of play before two months of age are poorly correlated with the same measures after this age (Barrett and Bateson, 1978). These results led Barrett and Bateson (1978) to propose that different aspects of play might be coming under separate types of control later in development: a suggestion lent credence by Caro's (1981b) finding that some measures of social play become more closely associated with certain measures of predatory behaviour after two months of age. However, few statistically significant correlations have been found between social play and predatory behaviour at any age (Caro, 1981b). Furthermore, there are a variety of explanations for changes in correlations between measures of behaviour with age which are concerned simply with the methods of classification and measurement (see Bateson, 1981b).

Another useful concept in the study of ontogeny is that of equifinality (Bateson, 1976). This is simply the idea that a particular developmental steady state (say, normal adult behaviour) may potentially be reached by a number of different developmental routes. Thus differences between individuals when young may not predict corresponding differences between the same individuals when adult. For example, a kitten which did not play might still become a competent predator if there were alternative routes converging on that same state: early differences between kittens in their play experience might therefore have been ironed out by the time they have become adults. In practice, kittens who are poor predators often do catch up to some extent by the time they are adults (Caro, 1979). Similarly, Baerends-van Roon and Baerends (1979) comment that, despite large variations between individuals in the timing and nature of early predatory behaviour, there are remarkably few differences in the eventual behaviour of the adult cats.

Thus play may not be a unique developmental tactic. In other words, play may be one way in which a developing animal may acquire certain benefits, but not the only way. Support for this idea comes from Fagen's (1977, 1981) cost–benefit models of play as a component of life-history strategies. A major conclusion was that alternative developmental routes were common and some of these did not include play at all. Furthermore, different patterns of development, some involving play and others involving no play, often 'evolved' in different populations living in the same environment.

The idea of equifinality has proved fruitful in the study of child development, where some doubt has been cast on the supposition that early trauma necessarily has immutable effects or that there is only one way in which, say, to acquire language (Clarke and Clarke, 1976; Dunn, 1976). It is important to distinguish equifinality (the idea that different developmental routes may converge on the same steady state) from the idea that there may also be more than one possible steady state in any given environment (see Schaffer and Rosenzweig, 1977; Hinde, 1982: 121).

The timing of play in development

The age at which kittens first play is both arbitrary (depending on the particular definition, if any, of play that is used) and probably variable (depending on environmental conditions). Villablanca and Olmstead (1979) note that some playful social interactions may start as early as 10–15 days after birth, while Rosenblatt (1972) and Moelk (1979) describe simple play as appearing in the third week. Most writers, however, agree that recognizable social play appears at about four weeks of age and develops in parallel with improvements in sensory and locomotor abilities as well as with changes in feeding and social behaviour (West, 1974; Kolb and Nonneman, 1975; Baerends-van Roon and Baerends, 1979; Villablanca and Olmstead, 1979; Martin, 1982b). Object play first appears soon after social play, but does not become a prominent feature of play until kittens are 6–8 weeks old (Barrett and Bateson, 1978; Moelk, 1979).

West (1974), who recorded eight distinct motor patterns constituting social play, found that individual patterns first appeared in a solitary context at about three weeks, while sequences involving more than one pattern and more than one kitten first appeared at about five weeks. All patterns were present by six weeks. Barrett and Bateson (1978) recorded the frequencies of seven discrete facets of social and object play in kittens from 4–12 weeks of age. Some measures (such as wrestling and stalking) increased over this period, while others (such as cat contact and arching) decreased. The most striking change, however, was a considerable increase in the frequency with which objects were patted or bitten playfully, which took place 7–8 weeks after birth. The various changes in the frequencies of play measures with age could not readily be accounted for in terms of general aspects of behaviour, since no correlations were found between measures of play and measures of overall activity, timidity (emergence latency), distress (vocalizations), or proximity to the mother (Barrett and Bateson, 1978).

Social play in kittens declines from 12–16 weeks of age onwards, following a peak at about 12 weeks (West, 1974; Guyot et al., 1980; Caro, 1981a). From four months of age onwards, kittens spend less time with their littermates and at about this time some feral cat mothers are reported to leave their kittens (West, 1974). The eventual waning of social play could be related to the departure of the mother under natural conditions and the dispersal of the kittens (West, 1974, 1979). However, in some populations of feral cats male kittens may stay with their natal group until they are 18 months to three years old (Liberg, 1980). Moreover, a progressive drop in social play after a certain age is also found under laboratory conditions where the opportunities for social play do not change (Koepke and Pribram, 1971). Object play shows no obvious decline after three months of age (West, 1974; Caro, 1981a).

Although the study of ontogeny and the study of function are logically distinct, there may none the less be valuable interbreeding between the two. One promising area is the survival value of the patterns and processes of development: the functional approach to studying ontogeny (Tinbergen, 1963; Fagen, 1981; Bateson, 1982). Bateson (1981b) has argued that different types of play are concerned with acquiring different types of skill or experience and should therefore occur at different times during ontogeny. Functional reasoning therefore suggested that changes in the time at which kittens are weaned should alter the way in which their play behaviour develops (Bateson and Young, 1981). To investigate whether there was any causal connection between the way in which play develops and the timing of weaning, various aspects of weaning were experimentally manipulated and the consequences for the development of play in kittens were recorded. Weaning was manipulated either by gradual and progressive separation of kittens from their mothers (Bateson and Young, 1981), or by using the lactation-blocking drug bromocriptine to interrupt mother cats' milk production (Bateson et al., 1981; see Martin and Bateson, 1982). Both types of manipulation affected the development of play in the kittens, most notably by producing an increase in the frequency of some play measures. Similarly, Koepke and Pribram (1971) found that the development of play was accelerated in kittens fed with a stomach tube and allowed to suck only from an anaesthetized, non-lactating female. The functional implications of the relations between weaning and the development of play in cats are as yet unclear (for a discussion of this issue see Bateson, 1981b; Bateson and Young, 1981).

PROXIMATE CAUSATION

There are several indications that play in kittens is not a homogeneous category in terms of the underlying proximate causal factors (Barrett and Bateson, 1978). Different measures of play show different developmental trends and few associations between one another in older kittens (Barrett and Bateson, 1978; Caro, 1981b). Furthermore, object play and social play are not affected in the same way by early manipulation of the rearing environment (Guyot et al., 1980), nor by simulating aspects of early weaning at different ages (Martin and Bateson, in press). Comparable conclusions have been drawn about play in other species as well: for example, in olive baboons components of behaviour that appear subjectively to be playful form at least two distinct groups in terms of the underlying causal factors (Chalmers, 1980).

There is some indication, especially in older kittens, that play fighting may grade continuously into fighting in earnest. Friendly bouts of social play may occasionally turn into apparently aggressive encounters (see Ewer and Wemmer, 1974; Voith, 1980; Bateson, 1981b). Contrary to what might be expected, kittens are not necessarily 'relaxed' when playing and may, if unexpectedly grabbed by a human observer during play, exhibit a violent startle reaction.

Before about three months of age, kittens' play is greatly depressed if their mother is temporarily removed from the observation room (Barrett and Bateson, 1978), but the presence or absence of the mother has little effect on the play of older kittens (Caro, 1981a). The factors which most successfully elicit object play are familiar to all owners of a pet cat: small, movable, prey-like objects. When presented with an unfamiliar object, kittens tend first to investigate without manipulating the object. As familiarity with the object follows on from exploration, the tendency to play becomes more established (West, 1977). This, together with the finding that there is no correlation between which objects are explored most and which are played with most, suggests that play and exploration may safely be distinguished from one another (West, 1977). Manipulatory and exploratory activities are rewarding in their own right for kittens (Miles, 1958).

Sex differences

Remarkably few sex differences have been recorded for *any* measure of kittens' behaviour and even the difference in growth rate between the sexes is not fully established until about two months of age (Latimer and Ibsen, 1932; Kolb and Nonneman, 1975; West, 1977; Barrett and Bateson, 1978; Caro, 1979; Guyot et al., 1980; Levine et al., 1980). A sex difference does, however, emerge for some play measures if the sex ratio of the litter is taken into account. Males, together with females from mixed-sex litters, show significantly higher frequencies of object play than females from all-female litters after two months of age (Barrett and Bateson, 1978). Female kittens who have a brother make significantly more object contacts than brotherless females and are statistically indistinguishable from males on this measure. Although a female's behaviour is influenced by the sex of her littermates, the same is not true for males: the object play of male kittens is not significantly affected by the number of female littermates. Caro (1981a) has found a comparable disparity between females from all-female litters and other kittens for some measures of social play after three months of age and has also shown that the number of brothers has a graded effect on the 'maleness' of a female kitten's play.

One reason why females with brothers play more might simply be that males have a short-term stimulating effect on the play behaviour of the whole litter by, for example, being more active. To test this possibility Bateson and Young (1979) compared the object play of kittens in the presence and absence of their littermates. They found that females with brothers made as many object contacts as males regardless of whether or not their brothers were present at the time. It appears, therefore, as though any influence that male kittens may have on their sisters is relatively long-lasting.

Two plausible suggestions have been raised by Bateson and Young (1979) in relation to this effect. One possibility is that mothers of all-female litters may somehow be different from other mothers and their kittens reflect this difference. Interestingly, Caro (1981a) comments that all-female litters of three or more kittens are rare, whereas all-male litters are relatively common. Some systematic information on this point would be valuable. Evolutionary theory predicts that mothers in good condition should produce relatively more sons than daughters, so the low incidence of play in all-female litters might be associated with poor maternal condition (Trivers and Willard, 1973; Clutton-Brock and Albon, 1982). A second possibility, supported by a growing body of experimental evidence from work with rodents, is that female foetuses can be partially masculinized by prenatal exposure to testosterone in the uterus. This results from proximity to male foetuses and can have long-term effects on the behaviour of females (Gandelman et al., 1977; vom Saal and Bronson, 1980; Meisel and Ward, 1981). It is possible, however, that differences in placental and uterine structure might preclude this effect from operating in other species of mammal.

Play signals

Most mammals have identifiable visual, auditory, tactile or olfactory signals that serve to initiate or maintain social play or to denote that 'what follows is play' (Fagen, 1981). These play signals are sometimes the only motor patterns which are specific to play. A kitten often holds its mouth open while engaged in social play and Fagen (1981: 164) regards this open-mouth display as a typical example of a mammalian play-face. Certain motor patterns, such as the half-crouch and pounce, are frequently used to initiate social play bouts, while other patterns, such as chases or horizontal leaps, are often used to terminate social play (West, 1974).

COMMENTS ON PRESENT AND FUTURE WORK, AND CONCLUSIONS

Those studying play face the same fundamental problem as those studying the neural bases of behaviour: no single technique or experiment will ever resolve the major issues on its own. Rather, a combination of different approaches, each excluding different possibilities, offers the most hopeful research strategy. Social isolation or deprivation techniques have numerous methodological problems and seem to offer poor prospects. Less drastic experimental methods include manipulation of food accessibility (e.g. Baldwin and Baldwin, 1976), selective manipulation of early experience (e.g. Baerends-van Roon and Baerends, 1979; Caro, 1980b) or the use of drugs to alter the behaviour of play partners (e.g. Einon et al., 1978). The development of play in cats could also profitably be studied more closely in relation to neurological, sensory and locomotor development (Villablanca and Olmstead, 1979; Martin, 1982b).

In much of the literature on play in cats it is not always clear whether measurements were based on individual kittens, or whether litter-mean values were used for statistical analysis. The use of individuals as single data points ignores the possible correlations between members of the same litter and tends therefore to overestimate the statistical significance of any differences found between groups of animals (Abbey and Howard, 1973). For several measures of play in kittens, within-litter variance is known to be significantly less than between-litter variance, making any assumption of statistical independence between members of the same litter highly dubious (Barrett and Bateson, 1978). The simplest precaution against spurious statistical significance is to use litter-mean values as data points.

Quantitative descriptions of domestic cats' behaviour stem mainly from laboratory studies and are open to the criticism that artificial conditions may produce misleading results (although see Berman, 1980). More information is sorely needed about the behaviour of wild, feral or semi-independent cats so that laboratory results can be related to behaviour under more natural conditions (see Wilson and Weston, 1947; Laundré, 1977; MacDonald and Apps, 1978; Panaman, 1981; G. Kerby, in preparation). One powerful technique in field studies is to compare the behaviour of different populations of the same species which live in different environments and attempt to relate intraspecific behavioural variation to ecological factors (e.g. Baldwin and Baldwin, 1974; Berger, 1980). Another approach is to compare the behaviour of related species (for descriptions of play in other felids see Cooper, 1942; Schenkel, 1966; Schaller, 1972; Ewer and Wemmer, 1974; Wasser, 1978; Leyhausen, 1979; and Fagen, 1981).

More direct tests of the various functional hypotheses about play are obviously needed, as well as more information about the costs of play and not just its hypothesized benefits (see Bekoff, 1976a; Fagen, 1981; Martin, 1982a, 1984). Tests of functional hypotheses would benefit from an open-minded approach: in particular, the notion that play has major costs and must, therefore, have major benefits should not be accepted unquestioningly. A final point is that undue emphasis has, arguably, been placed on the long-term effects of play, while possible short-term effects have usually been ignored. In the cat, for example, the popular practice hypothesis maintains that kittens pay the immediate costs of playing but benefit by becoming more skilful when they grow up. There is currently no solid evidence to support this hypothesis, however. An alternative hypothesis – equally unsupported by empirical evidence as yet, but none the less equally plausible – is that play may be selected for because of its immediate benefits to the young animal (whatever they may be) and need make no straightforward contribution to the development of adult behaviour. As Fagen (1981) has so cogently argued, the study of animal play behaviour will advance more rapidly when explicit, testable hypotheses are placed in direct competition with one another.

ACKNOWLEDGEMENTS

This chapter was written while I was supported by a Medical Research Council research studentship at Cambridge University and revised while I held a Harkness Fellowship at Stanford University. I am very grateful to Pat Bateson, Tim Caro, Gillian Kerby, Trevor Poole and Harriet Sants for reading and commenting on an earlier version.

REFERENCES

Abbey, H. and Howard, E. (1973). Statistical procedure in developmental studies on species with multiple offspring. *Developmental Psychobiology* 6, 329–35.

Baerends-van Roon, J. M. and Baerends, G. P. (1979). *The Morphogenesis of the Behaviour of the Domestic Cat*. Amsterdam: North-Holland.

Baldwin, J. D. and Baldwin, J. I. (1974). Exploration and social play in squirrel monkeys (*Saimiri*). *American Zoologist* 14, 303–15.

Baldwin, J. D. and Baldwin, J. I. (1976). Effects of food ecology on social play: a laboratory simulation. *Zeitschrift für Tierpsychologie* 40, 1–14.

Baldwin, J. D. and Baldwin, J. I. (1977). The role of learning phenomena in the ontogeny of exploration and play. In S. Chevalier-Skolnikoff and F. E. Poirier (eds), *Primate Biosocial Development*. New York: Garland.

Barrett, P. and Bateson, P. (1978). The development of play in cats. *Behaviour* 66, 106–20.

Bateson, P. P. G. (1976). Rules and reciprocity in behavioural development. In P. P. G. Bateson and R. A. Hinde (eds), *Growing Points in Ethology*. Cambridge: Cambridge University Press.

Bateson, P. (1981a). Ontogeny. In D. McFarland (ed.), *The Oxford Companion to Animal Behaviour*. Oxford: Oxford University Press.

Bateson, P. (1981b). Discontinuities in development and changes in the organization of play in cats. In K. Immelmann, G. W. Barlow, L. Petrinovich and M. Main (eds), *Behavioral Development. The Bielefeld Interdisciplinary Project*. Cambridge: Cambridge University Press.

Bateson, P. (1982). Behavioural development and evolutionary processes. In, King's College Sociobiology Group (eds), *Current Problems in Sociobiology*. Cambridge: Cambridge University Press.

Bateson, P. (1983). Genes, environment and the development of behaviour. In T. R. Halliday and P. J. B. Slater (eds), *Animal Behaviour, Volume 3: Genes, Development and Learning*. Oxford: Blackwell.

Bateson, P., Martin, P. and Young, M. (1981). Effects of interrupting cat mothers' lactation with bromocriptine on the subsequent play of their kittens. *Physiology and Behavior* 27, 841–5.

Bateson, P. and Young, M. (1979). The influence of male kittens on the object play of their female siblings. *Behavioral and Neural Biology* 27, 374–8.

Bateson, P. and Young, M. (1981). Separation from the mother and the development of play in cats. *Animal Behaviour* 29, 173–80.

Beach, F. A. (1945). Current concepts of play in animals. *American Naturalist* 79, 523–41.

Bekoff, M. (1976a). Animal play: problems and perspectives. In P. P. G. Bateson and P. H. Klopfer (eds), *Perspectives in Ethology, Vol. 2*. New York: Plenum.

Bekoff, M. (1976b). The social deprivation paradigm: who's being deprived of what? *Developmental Psychobiology* 9, 499–500.

Bekoff, M. and Byers, J. A. (1981). A critical reanalysis of the ontogeny and phylogeny of mammalian social and locomotor play: an ethological hornet's nest. In K. Immelmann, G. W. Barlow, L. Petrinovich and M. Main (eds), *Behavioral Development. The Bielefeld Interdisciplinary Project*. Cambridge: Cambridge University Press.

Berger, J. (1980). The ecology, structure and functions of social play in Bighorn sheep (*Ovis canadensis*). *Journal of Zoology (London)* 192, 531–42.

Berman, C. M. (1980). Mother–infant relationships among free-ranging rhesus monkeys on Cayo Santiago: a comparison with captive pairs. *Animal Behaviour* 28, 860–73.

Berry, C. S. (1908). An experimental study of imitation in cats. *Journal of Comparative Neurology* 18, 1–25.

Biben, M. (1979). Predation and predatory play behaviour of domestic cats. *Animal Behaviour* 27, 81–94.

Blass, E. M. and Teicher, M. H. (1980). Suckling. *Science* 210, 15–22.

Caro, T. M. (1979). Relations between kitten behaviour and adult predation. *Zeitschrift für Tierpsychologie* 51, 158–68.

Caro, T. M. (1980a). The effects of experience on the predatory patterns of cats. *Behavioral and Neural Biology* 29, 1–28.

Caro, T. M. (1980b). Effects of the mother, object play, and adult experience on predation in cats. *Behavioral and Neural Biology* 29, 29–51.

Caro, T. M. (1980c). Predatory behaviour in domestic cat mothers. *Behaviour* 74, 128–48.

Caro, T. M. (1981a). Sex differences in the termination of social play in cats. *Animal Behaviour* 29, 271–9.

Caro, T. M. (1981b). Predatory behaviour and social play in kittens. *Behaviour* 76, 1–24.

Caro, T. M., Roper, R., Young, M. and Dank, G. R. (1979). Inter-observer reliability. *Behaviour* 69, 303–15.

Chalmers, N. R. (1980). The ontogeny of play in feral olive baboons (*Papio anubis*). *Animal Behaviour* 28, 570–85.

Chesler, P. (1969). Maternal influence in learning by observation in kittens. *Science* 166, 901–3.

Clarke, A. M. and Clarke, A. D. B. (1976). *Early Experience: Myth and Evidence*. London: Open Books.

Clutton-Brock, T. H. (1981). Function. In D. McFarland (ed), *The Oxford Companion to Animal Behaviour*. Oxford: Oxford University Press.

Clutton-Brock, T. H. and Albon, S. D. (1982). Parental investment in male and female offspring in mammals. In King's College Sociobiology Group (eds), *Current Problems in Sociobiology*. Cambridge: Cambridge University Press.

Collard, R. R. (1967). Fear of strangers and play behavior in kittens with varied social experience. *Child Development* 38, 877–91.

Cooper, J. B. (1942). An exploratory study on African lions. *Comparative Psychology Monographs* 17, 1–48.

Dunn, J. (1976). How far do early differences in mother–child relations affect later development? In P. P. G. Bateson and R. A. Hinde (eds), *Growing Points in Ethology*. Cambridge: Cambridge University Press.

Egan, J. (1976). Object-play in cats. In J. S. Bruner, A. Jolly and K. Sylva (eds), *Play: Its Role in Development and Evolution*. Harmondsworth: Penguin.

Einon, D. F., Morgan, M. J. and Kibbler, C. C. (1978). Brief periods of socialization and later behavior in the rat. *Developmental Psychobiology* 11, 213–25.

Ewer, R. F. and Wemmer, C. (1974). The behaviour in captivity of the African civet, *Civettictis civetta* (Schreber). *Zeitschrift für Tierpsychologie* 34, 359–94.

Fagen, R. (1974). Selective and evolutionary aspects of animal play. *American Naturalist* 108, 850–8.

Fagen, R. (1977). Selection for optimal age-dependent schedules of play behavior. *American Naturalist* 111, 395–414.

Fagen, R. (1981). *Animal Play Behavior*. New York: Oxford University Press.

Galef, B. G. (1981). The ecology of weaning: parasitism and the achievement of independence by altricial mammals. In D. J. Gubernick and P. H. Klopfer (eds), *Parental Care in Mammals*. New York: Plenum.

Gandelman, R., vom Saal, F. S. and Reinisch, J. M. (1977). Contiguity to male foetuses affects morphology and behaviour of female mice. *Nature* 266, 722–4.

Gould, S. J. and Lewontin, R. C. (1979). The spandrels of San Marco and the Panglossian paradigm: a critique of the adaptationist programme. *Proceedings of the Royal Society of London, Series B* 205, 581–98.

Gould, S. J. and Vrba, E. S. (1982). Exaptation – a missing term in the science of form. *Paleobiology* 8, 4–15.

Gruber, H. E., Girgus, J. S. and Banuazizi, A. (1971). The development of object permanence in the cat. *Developmental Psychology* 4, 9–15.

Guyot, G. W., Bennett, T. L. and Cross, H. A. (1980). The effects of social isolation on the behavior of juvenile domestic cats. *Developmental Psychobiology* 13, 317–29.

Hinde, R. A. (1975). The concept of function. In G. Baerends, C. Beer and A. Manning (eds), *Function and Evolution in Behaviour*. Oxford: Clarendon Press.

Hinde, R. A. (1982). *Ethology*. New York: Oxford University Press.

John, E. R., Chesler, P., Bartlett, F. and Victor, I. (1968). Observation learning in cats. *Science* 159, 1489–91.

Koepke, J. E. and Pribram, K. H. (1971). Effect of milk on the maintenance of sucking behavior in kittens from birth to six months. *Journal of Comparative and Physiological Psychology* 75, 363–77.

Kolb, B. and Nonneman, A. J. (1975). The development of social responsiveness in kittens. *Animal Behaviour* 23, 368–74.

Kuo, Z. Y. (1930). The genesis of the cat's responses to the rat. *Journal of*

Comparative Psychology 11, 1–35.

Langfeldt, T. (1974). Diazepam-induced play behavior in cats during prey killing. *Psychopharmacologia* 36, 181–4.

Latimer, H. B. and Ibsen, H. L. (1932). The postnatal growth in body weight of the cat. *Anatomical Record* 52, 1–5.

Laundré, J. (1977). The daytime behaviour of domestic cats in a free-roaming population. *Animal Behaviour* 25, 990–8.

Levine, M. S., Hull, C. D. and Buchwald, N. A. (1980). Development of motor activity in kittens. *Developmental Psychobiology* 13, 357–71.

Lewin, R. (1982). Adaptation can be a problem for evolutionists. *Science* 216, 1212–13.

Leyhausen, P. (1979). *Cat Behavior: The Predatory and Social Behavior of Domestic and Wild Cats*. Translated by B. A. Tonkin. New York: Garland.

Liberg, O. (1980). Spacing patterns in a population of rural free roaming domestic cats. *Oikos* 35, 336–49.

Loizos, C. (1967). Play behaviour in higher primates: a review. In D. Morris (ed.), *Primate Ethology*. London: Weidenfeld & Nicolson.

MacDonald, D. W. and Apps, P. J. (1978). The social behaviour of a group of semi-dependent farm cats, *Felis catus*: a progress report. *Carnivore Genetics Newsletter* 3, 256–68.

Martin, P. (1982a). The energy cost of play: definition and estimation. *Animal Behaviour* 30, 294–5.

Martin, P. H. (1982b). Weaning and behavioural development in the cat. Unpublished Ph.D. thesis, University of Cambridge.

Martin, P. (1984). The time and energy costs of play behaviour in the cat. *Zeitschrift für Tierpsychologie* 64, in press.

Martin, P. and Bateson, P. (1982). The lactation-blocking drug bromocriptine and its application to studies of weaning and behavioral development. *Developmental Psychobiology* 15, 139–57.

Martin, P. and Bateson, P. (in press). The influence of experimentally manipulating a component of weaning on the development of play in domestic cats. *Animal Behaviour*.

Marvin, J. H. and Harsh, C. M. (1944). Observational learning by cats. *Journal of Comparative Psychology* 37, 71–9.

Meisel, R. L. and Ward, I. L. (1981). Fetal female rats are masculinized by male littermates located caudally in the uterus. *Science* 213, 239–42.

Miles, R. C. (1958). Learning in kittens with manipulatory, exploratory and food incentives. *Journal of Comparative and Physiological Psychology* 51, 39–42.

Millar, S. (1981). Play. In D. McFarland (ed.), *The Oxford Companion to Animal Behaviour*. Oxford: Oxford University Press.

Moelk, M. (1979). The development of friendly approach behavior in the cat: a study of kitten–mother relations and the cognitive development of the kitten from birth to eight weeks. In J. S. Rosenblatt, R. A. Hinde, C. Beer and M. C. Busnel (eds), *Advances in the Study of Behavior* 10, 163–224.

Oppenheim, R. W. (1980). Metamorphosis and adaptation in the behavior of developing organisms. *Developmental Psychobiology* 13, 353–6.

Panaman, R. (1981). Behaviour and ecology of free-ranging female farm cats (*Felis catus* L.). *Zeitschrift für Tierpsychologie* 56, 59–73.

Rosenblatt, J. S. (1972). Learning in newborn kittens. *Scientific American* 227, 18–25.

Rosenblatt, J. S. (1976). Stages in the early behavioural development of altricial young of selected species of non-primate mammals. In P. P. G. Bateson and R. A. Hinde (eds), *Growing Points in Ethology*. Cambridge: Cambridge University Press.

Rosenblatt, J. S. and Schneirla, T. C. (1962). The behaviour of cats. In E. S. E. Hafez (ed.), *The Behaviour of Domestic Animals*. London: Bailliere, Tindall & Cox.

Schaffer, W. M. and Rosenzweig, M. L. (1977). Selection for optimal life histories II: multiple equilibria and the evolution of alternative reproductive strategies. *Ecology* 58, 60–72.

Schaller, G. B. (1972). *The Serengeti Lion: a Study of Predator–Prey Relations*. Chicago: University of Chicago Press.

Schenkel, R. (1966). Play, exploration and territoriality in the wild lion. *Symposia of the Zoological Society of London* 18, 11–22.

Seitz, P. F. D. (1959). Infantile experience and adult behavior in animal subjects. II: Age of separation from the mother and adult behavior in the cat. *Psychosomatic Medicine* 21, 353–78.

Smith, B. A. and Jansen, G. R. (1977). Maternal undernutrition in the feline: behavioral sequelae. *Nutrition Reports International* 16, 513–26.

Sokal, R. R. (1974). Classification: purposes, principles, progress, prospects. *Science* 185, 1115–23.

Tinbergen, N. (1963). On aims and methods of ethology. *Zeitschrift für Tierpsychologie* 20, 410–33.

Trivers, R. L. and Willard, D. E. (1973). Natural selection of parental ability to vary the sex ratio of offspring. *Science* 179, 90–2.

Villablanca, J. R. and Olmstead, C. E. (1979). Neurological development in kittens. *Developmental Psychobiology* 12, 101–27.

Vincent, L. E. and Bekoff, M. (1978). Quantitative analyses of the ontogeny of predatory behaviour in coyotes, *Canis latrans*. *Animal Behaviour* 26, 225–31.

Voith, V. L. (1980). Play behavior interpreted as aggression or hyperactivity: case histories. *Modern Veterinary Practice* 61, 707–9.

vom Saal, F. S. and Bronson, F. H. (1980). Sexual characteristics of adult female mice are correlated with their blood testosterone levels during prenatal development. *Science* 208, 597–9.

Wasser, S. K. (1978). Structure and function of play in the tiger. *Carnivore* 1, 27–40.

West, M. (1974). Social play in the domestic cat. *American Zoologist* 14, 427–36.

West, M. J. (1977). Exploration and play with objects in domestic kittens. *Developmental Psychobiology* 10, 53–7.

West, M. J. (1979). Play in domestic kittens. In R. B. Cairns (ed.), *The Analysis of Social Interactions*. Hillsdale, NJ: Lawrence Erlbaum.

Williams, G. C. (1966). *Adaptation and Natural Selection*. Princeton: Princeton

University Press.

Wilson, C. and Weston, E. (1947). *The Cats of Wildcat Hill*. New York: Duell, Sloan & Pearce.

Yerkes, R. M. and Bloomfield, D. (1910). Do kittens instinctively kill mice? *Psychological Bulletin 7*, 253–63.

4 Play in Rodents

Graham J. Hole and Dorothy F. Einon

INTRODUCTION

Although they comprise the largest order of mammals (with roughly 3,000 known species), we know little about the social behaviour of rodents, including their play. The laboratory rat remains the only readily-obtainable rodent whose play has been studied in any depth. The play of less than a dozen species has been examined in some detail, and that of maybe twenty others has been noted in passing. A more appropriate title for this paper would thus not be 'Play in rodents' but rather 'Play in the rat, with some observations on a few other rodent species'.

Problems in assessing play's distribution

Researchers into play have often sought correlations between the nature and frequency of play shown by a species, and that species' taxonomic position and ecology (e.g. Fagen, 1981; Smith, 1982). Efforts are made to determine whether play occurs in particular taxonomic groupings but not others, and to see if animals with similar social systems, occupying comparable ecological niches, also show similar play. Although this technique has generally been used on the level of comparisons between orders of mammals, it could be used very profitably *within* the order of rodents, as the latter constitutes a grouping of sufficient size and ecological diversity to make such comparisons worthwhile, and yet the animals concerned still share some affinities on the basis of their common phyletic origins. However, at present, this approach suffers from such severe methodological limitations that it must be used with great caution.

Firstly, there are the usual problems of cross-species comparison. For example, it is difficult to estimate the relative frequencies of play, or even to decide whether or not a given species shows *any* play. Fagen (1981) has pointed out that different species (or even different populations, age-groups or sexes *within* a species) may differ in their degree of shyness and hence show apparent differences in their levels of play which are in fact nothing more than an artefact due to their varying reactions to the presence of a human observer. Furthermore, many species may play when the animals are out of sight, in their burrows, up trees or in foliage cover. The problems of observing wild rodents are analogous to those discussed by Aldrich-Blake (1970) for forest-living primates.

A second major problem in making comparisons stems from our knowing so little about social behaviour generally (let alone play) of the vast majority of rodents. It is futile to attempt to draw any firm conclusions about rodent play on the basis of our minute sample of 20 species.

Finally there is the problem of determining exactly what is being compared across species. It has been commonplace in play research to evade the problem of definition, researchers assuming that what they personally consider 'playful' would be universally accepted as such. Studies which are directly concerned with 'play' at least give detailed descriptions of the behaviours concerned, and some rationale for describing them as 'playful'. The problem is far worse when trying to interpret studies in which play was not the primary concern. If play is not mentioned, is this because it was not seen to occur? Because the observer's definition was different from ours? Or simply because, although play occurred, it was not reported because the observer was not interested in such behaviour? Failure to define play adequately has led to unnecessary confusion in this area, and has effectively made valid cross-species comparisons impossible.

Currently, there are two schools of thought. The first is that all homoiotherms (or at least, all mammals) play, a stance leading to a readiness to label as 'play' all juvenile behaviours lacking an obvious immediate function. The second is that all mammals do *not* play, and that there is no general category of 'play' behaviour. We incline towards the second view. While not denying that there *may* be a general category of 'play' behaviour, we feel the case for adopting such a position is at present unproved – that indiscriminate use of the word 'play' is unhelpful, leading to global theorizing without any sound empirical basis. At present, it seems safest to maintain a distinction between the various behaviours which have been subsumed under the general heading of 'play'.

Reports of animal 'play' fall into at least three general categories: firstly, play with objects (either of a manipulative-cum-investigative kind or by a young predator with prey surrogates); secondly, locomotor play (e.g. running, frisking, and gambolling); and, lastly, social play (play-fighting and play-chasing). Of these three, only the latter two are unequivocally known to occur in rodents. Accounts of object play in rodents (e.g. Ferchmin, Eterovic and Levin, 1980; and Ferron, 1975) concern behaviours which most researchers would call 'exploration'.

We shall now consider a number of rodent behaviours which have at some time been claimed to be 'playful', and assess the evidence for these claims. Is it, or is it not, the case that certain behaviours are usefully described as 'playful'?

LOCOMOTOR-ROTATIONAL MOVEMENTS

The simplest type of 'play' consists of the 'locomotor-rotational' movements (LRMs) originally described by Wilson and Kleiman (1974): body-twisting, running, jumping, and head-shaking, sometimes accompanied by limited social behaviour, for example nosing the partner. LRMs have been reported in three species of South American caviomorph rodent (*Octodon degus*, *Octodontomys gliroides*, and *Pediolagus salinicola*), and in bank voles (*Clethrionomys glareolus*) (Wilson, 1973). According to Wilson (1973), they also occur in house mice (*Mus musculus*), wood mice (*Apodemus sylvaticus*), and gerbils (*Meriones unguiculatus*), but not in the brown rat, (*Rattus norvegicus*). The 'frisky hops' of Argentinian cavies (Rood, 1972) may be similar behaviours.

LRMs may be closely related to olfactory investigation, enhancing odour dissemination and/or occurring in response to it. In the caviomorphs, LRMs are complemented by sandbathing and urination, and sniffing a conspecific's odour is likely to result in head-shaking and body-twisting. Companion-oriented LRMs, in *Octodon* and *Octodontomys*, involve sniffing specific areas of the companion's body, which may enhance perception of individual odours: and the solo play of *P. salinicola*, which involves sniffing sand at communal urinating and sandbathing sites, may enhance perception of group odours. Similarly, in voles, companion-oriented LRMs seem both to facilitate olfactory investigation and themselves to be stimulated by it. They occur only in spring-born voles; autumn-born young lack a secretion on the back of the head which stimulates 'play', but will play if this is administered to them (Wilson, 1973) – which further suggests that LRMs have some olfactory significance.

LRMs may have some communicative function (or, at least, represent a response to olfactory communications), but they apparently lack any true social interaction. What Wilson and Kleiman call 'companion-oriented play' in *Octodon* and *Octodontomys* merely involves sniffing at a conspecific's body. Also, the LRMs are rarely followed directly by the same behaviour in a nearby animal. Similarly, the most interactive behaviour shown by the bank vole is when 'occasionally a 'play interaction' developed, when two voles made play movements while nosing each other several times' (Wilson, 1973).

Non-playful analogues of LRMs

Should LRMs be considered a form of 'play'? Consider the following behaviours which resemble LRMs.

'Popcorn' behaviour (sporadic hopping, jerking and jumping) is shown by many young rodents, for example mice (Fox, 1965), rats (Bolles and Woods, 1964), Chinese hamsters (*Cricetulus griseus*), and gerbils (Einon, unpublished); and the fat sand rat (*Psummomys obesus*) (Daly and Daly, 1975). Popcorn behaviour occurs for a short period of about a week or ten days, at a time when the young rodent first becomes mobile. It is induced by disturbance, and the end of the period in which it is observed seems to coincide with the development of the adult response to disturbance, that of 'freezing'. There is a considerable literature which suggests that in the rat this period of popcorn corresponds to a stage in development at which there is maturation of the arousal mechanisms of the CNS, but not of the inhibitory mechanism (Campbell et al., 1969). Kicking in human infants may be a comparable phenomenon. As with popcorn behaviour, kicking is not particularly related to the stimuli which trigger it: in the first months of life, it may be elicited by fussiness, feeding, interactions with a caregiver or an object, or even changes in position. As the child matures, it may respond to some of these stimuli more appropriately, but when highly aroused, it may revert to kicking in 'a display highly evocative of what is later called a temper tantrum' (Thelen, 1981). Again, as with popcorn behaviour, no one suggests that this behaviour should be called 'play'.

A second group of behaviours which superficially resemble LRMs are found in the responses of isolation-reared guinea-pigs and rats to an oestrous female (Gerall, 1963; Coulon, 1971). Head-shaking, leaping, body-twitching and other 'hyperexcitable' behaviours may be shown. These may be an extension of the immature animals' responses to stimulation: Rood (1972) and Coulon (1971) note that they occur in young animals and sexually-aroused males – both groups which are highly stimulated. Moreover, Einon et al. (1978) have shown that similar behaviours can be induced in adult rats by intense auditory and visual stimulation.

Another class of 'LRM-like' behaviours are those shown by rats and mice in response to psychomotor stimulants. Chance's (1948) description of the behaviour of amphetamine-dosed mice is strikingly similar to Wilson and Kleiman's (1974) descriptions of LRM 'play', even using terms such as 'head-shaking' and 'rotational movements'.

Most observers would not describe any of these behaviours as 'play'; but it is difficult to distinguish them from the 'playful' LRMs described earlier. Now, we do not wish to imply that LRMs, popcorn behaviour, and the aberrant behaviour of adult isolates or drugged mice share any underlying mechanism, but merely to suggest the possibility that they are all responses to high stimulation levels. If this is so, why consider LRMs as 'play', but not the others? If not on the basis of eliciting stimuli, could it be on functional grounds? Unfortunately, here too, there seems to be no valid means of differentiating between them.

Popcorn behaviour may serve anti-predator functions, as anyone who has opened a cage of 16-day-old mice will know. The behaviour of the collared lemming (*Dicrostonyx groenlandicus*) when cornered by a predator is reminiscent of popcorn behaviour: 'an explosive initial leap . . . [following which] . . . *the animal would bound about in an erratic unpredictable manner.*' (Brooks and Banks, 1973; our italics). Apparently-similar behaviour was observed by Elliott (1978) when one chipmunk was chased from another's territory: 'If cornered he may suddenly catapult wildly in the air, performing an aerial somersault.' Such behaviour may be highly effective in evading an adversary.

There thus seem to be no valid criteria, either on functional or structural grounds, by which LRMs can be clearly differentiated from other behaviours of similar appearance which have traditionally not been regarded as instances of play.

SOLITARY RUNNING: 'ESCAPE PLAY'

A second class of 'playful' locomotor movements may be characterized by the 'jinking' play of the African ground squirrel *Xerus erythropus* (Ewer, 1966), which involves zig-zag running with rapid, unpredictable changes of direction interspersed with vertical, twisting jumps. Similar behaviour has been reported for the house mouse (Wolff, 1981), and the green acouchi, *Myoprocta pratti* (Morris, 1962). If we consider popcorn behaviour as 'not-play' because it may have immediate functions, we would also have to exclude 'escape play'. Many instances may prove to be 'serious' escape behaviour performed by immature animals, for which the human observer has failed to notice the cause. As Ewer (1966) points out, animals such as ground squirrels are very timid: 'At any noise the animal will retreat, *indeed it may do so without obvious cause . . .*' (our italics). Given that the only factor distinguishing escape play from 'real' escape behaviour seems to be that the observer has failed to identify an eliciting stimulus for the flight, it would seem premature to consider this type of behaviour as 'play'.

PLAY-FIGHTING

Probably the behaviour which most people would agree is 'playful', is play-fighting – behaviour apparently similar to adult aggression but lacking aggressive intent. Actually the term 'play-fighting' has been used to describe two broad classes of non-serious fighting.

The first of these is 'rough-and-tumble' playful wrestling, in which two animals engage in prolonged ventral–ventral contact, one attempting to hold down the other on his back, while the one held down struggles to get free and to attain the on-top position. There is some degree of reciprocity, either within or across bouts, so that a given animal 'dominates' roughly as much as he is 'dominated'. 'Self-handicapping' may occur, so that a larger animal 'submits' to a smaller or weaker playmate. Bouts frequently include more than two animals, with a rapid interchange of partners. They may break from wrestling to chase each other (particularly around objects) and chases are frequently returned, so that the chaser of one moment suddenly becomes the one who is chased. Wrestling is performed with exaggerated movements, and there is inhibited biting and a lack of pain, aggressive or threat signals. These features, together with the initial high pounce which initiates the bout, seem to inform the interactants of the encounter's 'playful' nature. At present, the best example we have of rodent rough-and-tumble play is that of young rats (Small, 1899); this strongly resembles accounts of play-fighting in other mammalian orders. Other rodents known to show rough-and-tumble play include the black rat, *Rattus rattus* (Ewer, 1971); the black-tailed prairie dog, *Cynomys ludovicianus* (King, 1955); the Columbian ground squirrel *Spermophilus columbianus* (Steiner, 1971); and the social marmot species – the alpine marmot, *Marmota marmota*, the olympic marmot, *M. olympus*, the hoary marmot, *M. caligata*, and the yellow-bellied marmot, *M. flaviventris* (Barash 1973, 1974a, 1976; Armitage 1974; Nowicki and Armitage 1979).

A second category of 'playful' fighting is represented by what we call 'not very serious fighting' (NVSF). This differs from rough-and-tumble play in a number of ways. Firstly, the fighting patterns themselves lack the 'exuberance' of rough-and-tumble; the animals are less 'bouncy', and NVSF looks less 'enjoyable' – very subjective terms reflecting a subtle difference between the two behaviours. Chases are less likely to be returned, and there is less hiding behind objects or pouncing of the initiator from objects on to his partner. NVSF involves much less physical contact; postures involving rearing and 'boxing' are more common, the two animals facing each other standing bipedally and pushing or slapping at each other with their forepaws until one backs down.

Rough-and-tumble and NVSF can also be distinguished on contextual grounds. Einon (unpublished data) compared NVSF in hamsters and gerbils to rough-and-tumble in rats, ferrets, weasels and kittens. Rough-and-tumble occurs in no specific place, although in many animals small holes or boxes are frequently used if they are available. The initiator is the animal which approaches its partner, or on occasions the two animals may approach each other. Bouts are not initiated (at least in our experience) by the animal which is *approached*. In contrast, the NVSF of young hamsters occurs in particular locations: at the nest, food hopper or water bottle (see also Rowell, 1961). NVSF is almost always intiated by the animal which is *approached*. Rowell (1961) reports that play in hamsters may develop from mutual grooming (which in gerbils (Daly and Daly, 1975) is related to serious fighting) and from food snatching, and that older pups may initiate play by an attack upon younger pups. NVSF thus seems to bear closer affinities to adult aggression than does rough-and-tumble play, and to be much more like an adult's defence of a resource.

Although there are real – though subtle – distinctions between these two categories of play-fighting, in practice it may often be difficult to distinguish between them. Some animals apparently show only NVSF, and no rough-and-tumble play. This seems to be the case for mice, gerbils and in both golden and chinese hamsters (Einon et al., 1981): and, as far as we can tell from published reports, for the caviomorph rodents *Octodon, Octodontomys*, and *Pediolagus* (Wilson and Kleiman, 1974); bank voles (Wilson, 1973); the Australian conilurine rodents (Happold, 1976): Argentinian cavies (Rood, 1972); chipmunks (Elliott, 1978) and other non-social squirrels (Horwich, 1972; Balph and Stokes, 1963); and non-social marmots such as the woodchuck (Barash, 1974b). However, the converse does not seem to hold true: most rodents which rough-and-tumble also show NVSF, and the distinction between the two may become clouded.

At present, the most detailed account we have of the way in which rough-and-tumble and NVSF relate to each other in development, has been provided by Meaney and Stewart (1981) for the laboratory rat. In the rat, NVSF follows rough-and-tumble play in ontogeny, so that play increasingly comes to resemble adult aggression. Play which is clearly rough-and-tumble begins at about 21 days of age. After 30 days, wrestling rapidly declines, and it is virtually absent from the interactions of adult rats. However, by about 40 days, NVSF becomes more frequent. Behaviours related to directed confrontation, such as lateral attacks and mutual upright 'boxing' (rare in animals less than 30 days old) become increasingly common, so that by 46 days of age, boxing is six times more frequent than wrestling. Older rats always play in pairs rather than in the earlier, larger groups; and by 40 days, the encounters become more one-sided, with the animal that is pounced upon becoming almost immediately dominated for the whole of the encounter. Rat play thus becomes increasingly hard to differentiate from 'real' fighting, as the animals mature.

Steiner (1971) reports that with increasing age, the play-fights of Columbian ground squirrels involve 'less and less exchange of roles' and that 'the outcomes become more predictable'. He also notes a trend towards increased violence, and that if play is violent it frequently ends in an unreturned chase. As with the rat, the lateral display and rearing with boxing, and the occurrence in 'play' of pain and threat vocalizations, seem to link NVSF with serious adult fighting. However, from Steiner's descriptions it is not clear exactly how much of the Columbian ground squirrel's 'play' is rough-and-tumble, how much is NVSF, and what the relation is between them.

The reports on marmot play illustrate the ambiguities which occur when terms such as 'play-fighting' are used without being explicitly defined. Both Armitage and his associates (Armitage, 1974; Nowicki and Armitage, 1979) and Barash (1973, 1974a) use the term 'play-fighting' in their descriptions of the juvenile social behaviour of marmots. However, as far as we can tell from the published data, they are using the same term to describe different behaviours. Armitage's 'play-fighting' in the yellow-bellied marmot is apparently the same as our 'rough-and-tumble'.

We suspect that what Barash calls 'playfighting' corresponds to our category of NVSF, and that, though there is a preceding period of rough-and-tumble play, he pays it scant attention. There are a number of indirect indications that this may be so. With increasing age, hoary, alpine and Olympic marmots all show an increase in the frequency with which the upright posture of 'playfighting' is performed, the behaviour reaching its peak in yearlings and intergrading into serious fighting in adults (Barash 1973, 1974a, 1976). Whereas the upright posture often occurs in adults, rough-and-tumble does not, being confined to a short period immediately after the young first emerge from their burrows. It may well be that the Columbian ground squirrel and the social marmots show the same ontogenetic patterning of play-fighting as we described earlier for the rat, early rough-and-tumble being followed by NVSF which in turn intergrades into 'serious' fighting. However, without more information on the context of play-fighting, detailed descriptions of the behaviours concerned, and a rationale for why the original authors considered these patterns 'playful', this can only be a tentative suggestion.

The functions of play-fighting

What are the functions of rough-and-tumble and NVSF? The most obvious answer is that both are practice for adult fighting. Advocates of this hypothesis (Smith, 1982; Symons, 1978) emphasize the importance to the animal of winning fights as an adult, and the advantages in learning fighting skills in play where physical damage, loss of rank or loss of resources do not follow. Others (e.g. Bekoff, 1977; Eibi-Eibesfeldt, 1975) claim that the context of rough-and-tumble play is too different from that of real fighting for the former to be effective practice for the latter.

Part of the problem here is that NVSF and rough-and-tumble are being treated as a single category of behaviour: characteristics of rough-and-tumble are being used to support one argument, and features of NVSF are being used to support another. If they are considered separately, the situation becomes clearer. Rough-and-tumble is obviously *not* good practice for adult fighting; but NVSF may be, since it involves all of the behaviours found in adult aggressive encounters. Taylor (1980) has shown that those animals which play-fight most also fight most. This may be simply because these animals are more active, and engage in all other behaviours more often, too; but this may not be the only explanation, since both Meaney and Stewart (1981) and Panksepp (1981) report that dominance relationships can be seen in rat play from about 40 days of age. So, NVSF may be practice for adult fighting (and/or involved in dispersal – see sexual play, below).

It is hard to see rough-and-tumble play in this light: there is no competition for resources, no dominance over a partner, and an absence of many of the more common fighting postures such as lateral display and boxing. Rough-and-tumble is intiated by one animal pouncing upon another and it involves role reversals, neither of which occur in 'real' fighting. The distribution of rough-and-tumble within rodents also suggests that something other than fighting practice is involved. To some extent, the presence of rough-and-tumble is correlated with sociality. Rough-and-tumble has not been reported to occur in the more solitary squirrels (e.g. the chipmunk (Elliott, 1978); grey squirrel, *Sciurus carolinensis* (Horwich, 1972); or the Uinta ground squirrel, *Spermophilus* armatus (Balph and Stokes, 1963)). Nor, apparently, is it found in solitary marmots (the woodchuck, Barash 1974b) or hamsters (Einon et al., 1981, and unpublished data). Rough-and-tumble is seen in more social species such as the brown rat (Poole and Fish, 1975; Meaney and Stewart, 1981) and the black rat (Ewer, 1971); the social squirrels (Columbian ground squirrel, McDonald, 1977; Californian ground squirrel, Steiner, 1971); black-tailed prairie dog (King, 1955); and the social marmots (Olympic marmot, Barash 1973; yellow-bellied marmot, Armitage 1974). These species show a complexity and interactiveness in their social behaviour which is not apparent in those social species which do not rough-and- tumble.

So, from the distribution of rough-and-tumble within the order of rodents, one might speculate that it may facilitate the development of complex social behaviour. However, this cannot be its only function, since it is also found in solitary predators such as the polecat (Poole, 1966), weasels and mink, *Mustela vison* (Einon, personal observations). Interestingly, the only *solitary* and *omnivorous* mustelid (the skunk, *Mephitis mephitis*) may not engage in rough-and-tumble play (Fagen, 1981).

Whatever the primary function of rough-and-tumble, it does have some incidental benefits. In a series of experiments, Einon and her colleagues have shown that many of the effects of isolating rats prior to sexual maturity may be due to depriving them of rough-and-tumble play (Einon and Morgan, 1977, 1978; Einon et al., 1978, 1981). Rats isolated between 20 and 45 days of age are more active and slower to habituate (Einon and Morgan, 1977), to extinguish (Dalrymple-Alford and Benton, in press) or to reverse a previously-learned discrimination (Rosenzweig, 1971; Morgan, 1973).

That rough-and-tumble play is implicated in these effects is suggested by the fact that the period in which isolation is effective coincides with that in which rats show almost all of their rough-and-tumble play. But the most conclusive evidence is that merely one hour a day of rough-and-tumble play seems to protect an isolate from the effects of social deprivation, unlike daily contact with a drugged, non-playing, peer (Einon et al., 1978). Such isolation-induced effects are found in species which show rough-and-tumble play, such as rats (Einon et al., 1978, 1981) and ferrets (Chivers and Einon, 1981), but not in species which do not rough-and-tumble, such as mice, guinea-pigs, gerbils (Einon et al., 1981), or golden and Chinese hamsters (Einon, unpublished data). These experimental findings probably reflect wider underlying differences between playing and non-playing animals: social and behavioural flexibility, or less reactivity to novel stimuli and situations are obvious (if vague) suggestions.

'PLAY-CHASING'

How does 'play-chasing' differ from 'serious' chasing – i.e. pursuit with a purely aggressive intent? Firstly, play-chasing involves role-reversal: there is rapid alternation of who chases and who is chased. Secondly, the usual contextual features associated with agonistic encounters are absent: not only is there no contest for resources, but it is the *initiator* of the chase who flees. Typically, play-chasing is elicited by the initiator of the encounter 'teasing' the partner, by pushing and nudging him in an attempt to incite him to chase.

Such behaviour has been reported to occur in older *Galea* and *Cavia* (cavy) juveniles, by Rood (1972). However, in many studies, play-chasing is either mentioned merely in passing or else is described with little attempt to differentiate it from other locomotor 'play'. In the house mouse Wolff (1981) calls play-chasing 'social play' when it is directed towards another animal, and 'solitary play' when it occurs in a solitary animal. However, from his description, and the fact that he also calls it 'play-fleeing', 'solitary play' seems similar to Ewer's (1966) 'jinking' play – i.e. it may be an anti-predator escape behaviour. Similarly, the 'locomotor play' of the black rat (Ewer, 1971), and the similar 'hop-skip' behaviour of the African giant rat *Cricetomys gambianus* (Ewer, 1967) occur as social activities, with one youngster chasing another, but may also occur as solitary behaviours. A further complication is that in many species which show social play-fighting, play-chasing may occur within and between bouts. This is the case for the brown rat (personal observations) and the yellow-bellied marmot (Armitage, 1974; Nowicki and Armitage, 1979).

We consider play-chasing as 'play' because it has all the features which we regard as characteristic of play – it is directed towards another animal, involves reciprocity, has a playful context and involves unique behaviour-patterns (i.e. the 'teasing' behaviours). One function of play-chasing may be to act as an appetitive behaviour for play-fighting, one animal inciting another to chase it, and then turning to engage the chaser in rough-and-tumble. However, in view of the way in which play-chasing has been considered along with other kinds of locomotor play, it is difficult at present to say much about its distribution or functions.

OTHER 'PLAYFUL' JUVENILE SOCIAL BEHAVIOURS

Crawling under and over siblings

Crawling under and over siblings, either in the nest or elsewhere, is a behaviour which at first sight might be interpreted as 'playful'. However, it has a number of possible immediate functions. One may be temperature regulation (Alberts, 1978), even after the animal has developed other means of controlling its temperature. Even in adults, thermoregulation may be achieved by behavioural means. Alternatively, crawling over and under siblings may be involved in kin recognition. It is known that young can recognize littermates (Porter and Doane, 1979; Porter and Wyrick, 1979; Hepper, 1983). In many species, chemical marking occurs by rubbing the flank or ventral surface over an object or by pushing the head under an object or individual. Such marking could occur in the course of walking or climbing over peers, or by nosing or crawling under them. It is therefore possible that crawling over and under siblings may have immediate, olfactory functions, as with LRMs. We feel it is premature to call such behaviours 'play'.

Mouth-wrestling and 'greeting' behaviours

A similar criticism can be levelled at mouth-wrestling, greeting and kissing. Social squirrels greet each other (Armitage, 1962; King, 1955; Müller-Using, 1956) and kissing and tasting have been observed in the young of solitary squirrels (Elliott, 1978). Chipmunks press their mouths together, tilting their heads from side to side (Elliott, 1978). On one occasion, Elliott reports that, when two juveniles from different litters encountered each other on the midline between burrows, they touched noses and locked their mouths together for an instant, but then leapt backwards and hastily retreated. He suggests that they were frightened because they did not recognize each other's taste. Barash (1973) observed similar behaviour in the Olympic marmot. Members of this species move from burrow to burrow each morning, greeting individuals within the extended family group. When Barash removed a juvenile so that it missed this greeting ceremony, it was not readily accepted back by its group; Barash therefore suggests that the greeting ceremony may serve as a daily reminder of the smell of other group members. Other rodents also greet each other in this way, for example cavies (Rood, 1972; Wilson and Kleiman, 1974). In a number of cases, prolonged greeting has been observed to escalate into fighting (Daly and Daly, 1975; Barash, 1973), in much the same way as prolonged anogenital sniffing may precede fighting in dogs. So, again one should be wary of calling this 'play', simply because it occurs in young animals; it may well have functions related to olfactory activity, in a similar manner to the LRMs discussed previously.

Mouth-wrestling consists of the animals locking their jaws together and often swaying from side to side. This is seen in chipmunks, in greeting (Elliott, 1978); and also, in gerbils, and the South American caviomorph

Octodontomys (Wilson and Kleiman, 1974). This behaviour may be exaggerated greeting, tasting or kissing; alternatively, it may be NVSF (see above).

SEXUAL PLAY

Sexual play involves the movements of copulation but without intromission, mounting and thrusting being the most common elements. Female sexual play involves the male components of mounting and thrusting, rather than adult female sexual behaviours such as lordosis and ear wiggling (Meaney and Stewart, 1981; Happold, 1976). Although lordosis is sometimes shown by female rats at the age of 40+ days (Meaney and Stewart, 1981), female rats are sexually mature at this time, so that it is unlikely that this is play. Mounting may be directed towards both young males and females. In the rat, its onset is sudden (Meaney and Stewart, 1981), and it is not preceded in ontogeny by any 'premounting' play.

It is not clear whether sexual play is influenced by the animal's current hormonal state. However, in the few cases for which we have data, mounting by males and females is accompanied by increased anogenital investigation, e.g. the conilurine rodents *Notomys alexis* and *Pseudomys albocineus* (Happold, 1976). In rats, the onset of mounting is preceded by attraction towards the female; anogenital sniffing and social grooming increase, and play-preferences shift from male–male to male–female (Meaney and Stewart, 1981).

A correlation between testosterone levels and the amount of aggression shown by male rodents has been demonstrated on a number of occasions (e.g. Bronson, 1964; Beer and Meyer, 1951), and a relationship between dominance, aggression, territorial behaviour and sexual behaviour has also been frequently noted (e.g. Barash, 1973). In seasonal breeders such behaviours are influenced by the presence of circulating testosterone (see Beer and Meyer, 1951). However, there has been little consideration of the possibility that changes in play may reflect the presence of circulating testosterone. Although this relationship may not hold for all species, e.g. the cavy *Galea* (Rood, 1972), in a number of species male sexual play occurs at the same time that play-fighting begins to get more 'serious', e.g. the rat (Meaney and Stewart, 1981), the fat sand rat (Daly and Daly, 1975), the Olympic marmot (Barash, 1973a) and the cavy *Microcavia* (Rood, 1972). The seriousness of the later play-fighting, which gradually merges into adult fighting (Barash, 1973a; Elliott, 1978; Daly and Daly, 1975; Meaney and Stewart, 1981) may well be directly related to plasma testosterone levels, as also appears to be the case in cattle (Reinhart and Reinhart, 1982). Clearly this area needs further study.

Sexual play is almost certainly in some way related to the development of adult, or sub-adult, levels of circulating testosterone, and with the development of the oestrous cycle in females, but what is its function? Is it practice for adult activity? Isolating young male rats and guinea pigs between weaning and puberty does retard (but not eliminate) their sexual behaviour (see Larsson, 1978; and Gerall, 1963); they are slower to mate, or may not mate at all on their first attempt. Once they have successfully mated, subsequent matings are not slower. However, lack of sexual play is not apparently the cause of these effects. For one thing, isolation of members of social species such as the rat and the guinea-pig obviously deprives them of more than just sexual play. It is known that isolation can disrupt social behaviours in a number of species of rodent, for example increasing aggression in mice (DeFeudis, 1975) and altering social interactions in marmots (Barash, 1973) and rats (Lore and Flannelly, 1978). Isolated rats are more timid (Einon and Tye, 1975) and thus it is

TABLE 4.1   The effects of social isolation at different ages on rat sexual behaviour

Age at which isolated	Behaviour pattern			
	Mount	Mount+ thrust*	Intromission**	Ejaculation**
Socially housed from 21 to 65 days	33.3 (6)	38.6 (7)	61.1 (11)	38.9 (7)
Isolation from 21 to 35 days	38.9 (7)	27.8 (5)	27.8 (5)	5.6 (1)
Isolation from 36 to 50 days	44.4 (8)	61.1 (11)	77.8 (14)	66.7 (12)
Isolation from 51 to 65 days	44.4 (8)	22.2 (4)	38.9 (7)	33.3 (6)
Isolation from 21 to 65 days	16.7 (3)	5.6 (1)	5.6 (1)	0.0 (0)

Figures before the brackets are percentages of the total no. of subjects within that condition who showed the relevant sexual behaviour-pattern within a 30–minute trial period: figures in brackets are the raw data from which the percentages were obtained. * = $p > 0.05$; ** = $p > 0.01$ (x^2, with 4 d.f.), N = 18 for each condition.

perhaps not surprising that they take longer to approach an oestrous female. Depriving rats of social companions at the age when they are most likely to engage in sexual play does not seem to have any lasting effects on sexual behaviour. In a recent series of experiments we have isolated rats for 15 days, starting from 21, 35 or 50 days of age, and then observed their sexual behaviour with a receptive female at 65 days of age. The results are presented in table 4.1.

We have found some deficits in the sexual behaviour of rats which were isolated prior to 35 days of age (i.e. *before* sexual play appears, and before the surge in testosterone), but no impairment in animals isolated between the ages of 35 and 50 days – when most sexual play occurs. Meaney and Stewart (1981) report that by 50 days of age, mounts are correctly oriented; thus the deficits shown by animals isolated from 50 days of age on (but housed socially before that time), must be due to isolation affecting factors other than the development of their sexual behaviour. All other groups were housed in social conditions at the time of testing. DeCatanzaro and Gorzalka (1979) have also shown deficits in the sexual behaviour of rats isolated at maturity – i.e. *after* sexual play had occurred. Thus there is no evidence from these deprivation studies that sexual play is a necessary form of practice for adult sexual behaviour, at least in the rat.

In any case, sexual practice would not be necessary in the rat. Rats are social and breed throughout the year. If a young inexperienced male needed to 'practice' before approaching experienced females, he could do so with younger females, who are sexually mature at 35–40 days. Copulatory practice of this sort is known to occur in young horses (Tyler, 1972). Such practice, with receptive females, would be more informative than that obtained by mounting immature partners in play. One might ask, as Symons (1977) has for play-fighting, what advantage young male and female rats can gain from mounting partners which do not take up the lordoesis posture, without which the orientation of the mount would be incorrect and penetration would be unlikely to occur. And how, without penetration, could the young rat 'learn' the correct orientation for mounting? Since both mounting and thrusting appear in their mature forms from the first time they are observed (Sachs and Meisel, 1979; Meaney and Stewart, 1981), is there any need to practice mounting when it is incorrectly oriented and cannot lead to intromission?

Perhaps the rat is not a good example on which to consider the advantages of social play. Seasonal breeders, such as the marmots and squirrels, may well need to practice with conspecifics – particularly if they are solitary as adults. Consider the Eastern chipmunk, *Tamias striatus* (Elliott, 1978). The chipmunk is born in the spring or summer. From the time the litter disperses (at about 45 days) until they breed in the following spring, there is little interaction between individuals and very little physical contact with either sex. Hence the short period of sexual play in their first year may serve as very necessary practice – particularly since if they do not mate in their first spring, they may not mate at all that year. But is sexual play the only possible form of practice? If mating were confined to dominant males, the young and inexperienced males would have little chance of practice with mature females. Elliott, however, could find little evidence for this: in fact, in the case of two females that he watched throughout oestrus, it was the subordinate males who were most successful in achieving copulation. In chipmunks, as in other squirrels (e.g. the grey squirrel (Horwich, 1972); the tassle-eared squirrel, *Sciurus aberti ferreus* (Farentinos, 1972); the red squirrel, *Tamiasciurus hudsonicus* and the Douglas squirrel, *T. douglasi* (Smith, 1968)) an oestrous female attracts up to about 10 or 12 males, all of whom may mate with her. Interestingly, in the first two hours of oestrus, although there were 13 copulations, these were not apparently accompanied by ejaculation. If this female is typical, there would therefore seem to be a period early in oestrus in which there are potential opportunities for 'sexual practice' to occur. The important factor in effective mating did not appear to be competition with the other males (this always curtailed copulation), but rather finding the female alone. So, although the brief period of mounting and thrusting in the previous year may serve as practice for adult copulatory activity, it seems more likely that practice occurs when the animals first mate.

Why then does sexual play occur? The first possibility is that sexual play may simply reflect the onset of sexual maturity. As adult levels of circulating hormones are reached, and as sexual reflexes mature, so sexual behaviour gradually develops. This seems to be the case in the rat. In seasonally breeding rodents, the testes enlarge gradually during the spring, and there is an associated rise in testosterone levels (Bronson, 1964). However, this does not explain why seasonal breeders such as squirrels play sexually, since they do not become sexually mature until the spring following sexual play. Nor does it explain why there are two surges in testosterone in the rat, one at 35 days and the other at 50 days. A second hypothesis, which can account for both of these facts, is that the early surge in testosterone (and presumably a similar increase in testosterone levels in some marmots during their first summer) is a means of encouraging dispersal. Barash (1973) reports that the main factor in producing dispersal in marmots is a gradual increase in aggression between the young. In chipmunks (Elliott, 1978) and the round-tailed ground squirrel, *Spermophilus tereticaudus* (Dunford, 1977), sexual play and NVSF both occur prior to dispersal at about 3 months of age. The situation is similar for grey squirrels (Thompson, 1978; Horwich, 1972), which disperse in their first autumn. Meaney and Stewart (1981) claim that there is evidence of dominance relationships emerging in the play of rats after about 45 days of age, but that the more agonistic behaviours (such as lateral display) occur from as little as 35 days. This early dominance in fighting may persist in adulthood. If it is the case that the function of this early surge in testosterone is to increase inter-litter aggression, in order to encourage dispersal (in the chipmunk this may only be to neighbouring burrows, while in the rat it may be even less) then perhaps sexual play actually has no direct function. It may simply be an epiphenomenon reflecting the onset of circulating testosterone, whose function is to increase aggression rather than practice sexual behaviour.

Once again, the laboratory rat is the only rodent for which we have any detailed data to assess this hypothesis. Where both testosterone levels and mounting were measured in the same study (Sachs and Meisel, 1979), the onset of mounting at 40 days occurrred about 5 days after the surge in testosterone. In Meaney and Stewart's (1981) study, the development of dominance showed close parallels with the development of mounting. Finally, both Beach (1945) and Soderston et al. (1977) report that administration of testosterone to prepubertal male rats advances the onset of mounting.

Although this area clearly needs much more extensive study, the possibility that sexual play correlates with the onset of circulating testosterone in the male rat raises the question of whether one should call such behaviours 'play'.

CONCLUSION

We thus have a number of different juvenile behaviours which have been labelled 'play'; and the previous sections should make it abundantly clear that this ambiguity in the use of the term has created a great deal of confusion. We contend, therefore, that the use of the term 'play' should be more restricted than it has been up to date, in order to avoid further misunderstanding. We define play according to three basic criteria.

Firstly, the behaviour should have no *immediate* function; its benefits should be deferred until later in ontogeny. This is quite a weak basis for considering a behaviour as 'play'. As Beach (1945) pointed out, it is impossible to prove conclusively that a behaviour has *no* immediate function. But, in practice this is quite a widely-used criterion for identifying play; the behaviours which we have discussed have in common only that none of them has an immediately obvious function. As we have pointed out, some 'play' behaviours do have immediate functions – for example, LRMs and escape play, and possibly NVSF. Labelling these 'play' adds nothing further to our understanding of them, and obscures their relationship to other adult and juvenile activities. The immediate functions of play-chasing and rough-and-tumble are rather more obscure.

The context of a behaviour can be important in deciding whether or not it should be considered playful. Rough-and-tumble play and playful chasing occur within a context of amicable behaviours. When one looks at the context of the other so-called 'playful' behaviours, the justification for identifying them as playful is less clear. LRMs follow olfactory activity. Escape play *may* occur in situations in which a conspecific adult would flee. The context of NVSF resembles that of adult aggression. Furthermore, LRMs and escape play lack the 'directedness' of the other kinds of play behaviour. Rough-and-tumble, play-chasing, NVSF and sexual play all involve activities which are clearly directed towards a particular aspect of the animal's environment. It may be significant that this 'directedness' is a quality which these behaviours share with that other large category of juvenile behaviours which we feel confident to describe as play – the predatory object play shown by carnivores such as ferrets, kittens and puppies.

The most powerful criterion for considering a behaviour as 'play' is the extent to which it employs unique behaviour patterns. By this criterion, rough-and-tumble and play-chasing are the strongest candidates for being called play. Behaviours serving a metacommunicative function, informing the partner that the interaction is 'playful' rather than 'hostile', are unique to play. In contrast, sexual play is distinguishable from adult sexual behaviour only in being imperfectly performed and incompletely executed by juveniles. LRMs share many of their features with the behaviour patterns shown by highly-aroused animals in other situations. And escape play has nothing to distinguish it, structurally, from its 'serious' counterparts.

By all of these criteria, rough-and-tumble play and play-chasing stand out as the phenomena to which we feel the term 'play' should be restricted. However, this is not a hard and fast distinction: from the descriptions we have at present, it seems likely that these different types of 'play' may often overlap to varying extents. For example, the rat shows popcorn behaviour at about 15 days; play-chasing and rough-and-tumble from about 21 to 40 days; and then gradually comes to show NVSF and sexual play from then until the cessation of any clearly-playful behaviour at about 60 days. Nevertheless, regardless of any fuzziness around the edges of our classification, it seems clear that different types of 'playful' behaviour are validly differentiated from one another; to lump them together can only cause problems.

We believe that the clue to 'the function of play' rests within the pattern of its taxonomic distribution; we will understand function when we understand the distribution. However, while the present situation persists – in which any juvenile behaviours of indeterminate function are called 'play' – we feel that most of the significant information about play's distribution will be missed. Our understanding of play will not be furthered by anecdotal reports, nor by using the word 'play' in a loose sense, but only by careful description. If we cannot define play, and it is obvious from this review that we cannot to everyone's satisfaction, then at least we must accurately describe behaviours with clear justification of our claim that they are playful.

In short, the prevailing tendency to call all juvenile behaviour which serves no obvious function 'play' is legitimate, given the usual broad definitions of play: legitimate, but not informative. Caution is in the end more productive.

REFERENCES

Alberts, J. R. (1978). Huddling in rat pups: multi-sensory control of contact behaviour. *Journal of Comparative and Physiological Psychology* 92, 220–30.

Aldrich-Blake, F. P. G. (1970). Problems of social structure in forest monkeys. In J. H. Crook (ed.), *Social Behaviour in Birds and Mammals*. London: Academic Press.

Armitage, K. B. (1962). Social behaviour of a colony of the yellow-bellied marmots (*Marmota flaviventris*). *Animal Behaviour* 10, 319–31.

Armitage, K. B. (1974). Male behaviour and territoriality in the yellow-bellied marmot. *Journal of Zoology (London)* 172, 233–65.

Balph, D. F. and Stokes, A. W. (1963). On the ethology of a population of Uinta ground squirrels. *American Midland Naturalist* 69, 106–26.

Barash, D. P. (1973). The social biology of the Olympic marmot. *Animal Behaviour Monographs* 6, 171–245.

Barash, D. P. (1976). Social behaviour and individual differences in free-living alpine marmots (*Marmota marmota*). *Animal Behaviour* 24, 27–35.

Barash, D. P. (1974a). The social behaviour of the hoary marmot (*Marmota caligata*). *Animal Behaviour* 22, 256–61.

Barash, D. P. (1974b). Mother–infant relations in captive woodchucks (*Marmota monax*). *Animal Behaviour* 22, 446–8.

Beach, F. A. (1945). Current concepts of play. *American Naturalist* 79, 217–38.

Beer, J. R. and Meyer, R. K. (1951). Seasonal changes in endocrine organs and behaviour patterns of the muskrat. *Journal of Mammalogy* 32, 173–91.

Bekoff, M. (1977). Mammalian dispersal and ontogeny of individual behavioral phenotypes. *American Naturalist* 111, 715–32.

Bolles, R. G. and Woods, R. J. (1964). The ontogeny of behaviour in the albino rat. *Animal Behaviour* 12, 427–41.

Brooks, R. J. and Banks, E. M. (1973). Behavioural biology of the collared lemming *Dicrostonyx groenlandicus* (Traill): an analysis of acoustic communication. *Animal Behaviour Monographs* 6, 1–83.

Bronson, F. H. (1964). Agonistic behaviour in woodchucks. *Animal Behaviour* 12, 470–8.

Campbell, B. A., Lytle, D. D., and Fibiger, H. C. (1969). Ontogeny of adrenergic and cholinergic inhibitory mechanisms in the rat. *Science* 166, 637–8.

Chance, M. R. A. (1948). A peculiar form of social behaviour induced in mice by amphetamine. *Behaviour* 1, 64–71.

Chivers, S. M. and Einon, D. F. (1981). Effects of early social experience on activity and object investigation in the ferret. *Developmental Psychobiology* 15, 75–80.

Coulon, J. (1971). Influence de l'isolement social sur le comportement du cobaye. *Behaviour* 38, 93–120.

Dalrymple-Alford, D. and Benton, D. (in press). Behavioural inhibition and time of isolation in rats. *Quarterly Journal of Experimental Psychology*.

Daly, M. and Daly, S. (1975). Behaviour of *Psummomys obesus* (Rodentia: Gerbillinae) in the Algerian Sahara. *Zeitschrift für Tierpsychologie* 37, 298–321.

DeCatanzaro, D. and Gorzalka, B. B. (1979). Postpubertal social isolation and male sexual behavior in rodents: facilitation or inhibition is species dependent. *Animal Learning and Behavior* 7, 555–61.

DeFeudis, F. V. (1975). Cerebral biochemical and pharmacological changes in differentially housed mice. In W. B. Essman and L. Valzelli (eds), *Current Developments in Psychopharmacology*, vol. 1. New York: Spectrum Publications.

Dunford, C. (1977). Social system of round-tailed ground squirrels. *Animal Behaviour* 25, 885–906.

Eibl-Eibesfeldt, I. (1975). *Ethology: the Biology of Behaviour* (2nd edn). New York: Holt, Rinehart and Winston.

Einon, D. F., Humphreys, A. P., Chivers, S. M., Field, S. and Naylor, V. (1981). Isolation has permanent effects upon the behavior of the rat, but not the mouse, gerbil or guinea-pig. *Developmental Psychobiology* 14, 343–55.

Einon, D. F. and Morgan, M. J. (1977). A critical period for social isolation in the rat. *Developmental Psychobiology* 10, 123–32.

Einon, D. F. and Morgan, M. J. (1978). Habituation under different levels of stimulation in socially reared and isolated rats: a test of the arousal hypothesis. *Behavioral Biology* 22, 553–8.

Einon, D. F., Morgan, M. J. and Kibbler, C. C. (1978). Brief periods of socialization and later behavior in the rat. *Developmental Psychobiology* 11, 213–25.

Einon, D. F. and Tye, N. C. (1975). Chlordiazepoxide and isolation-induced timidity in rats. *Psychopharmacologia* 44, 83–5.

Elliott, L. (1978). Social behavior and foraging ecology of the eastern chipmunk (*Tamias striatus*) in the Adirondack mountains. *Smithsonian Contributions to Zoology* 265.

Ewer, R. F. (1966). Juvenile behaviour in the African Ground Squirrel (*Xerus erythropus* E. Geoff.). *Zeitschrift für Tierpsychologie* 23, 190–216.

Ewer, R. F. (1967). The behaviour of the African giant rat (*Cricetomys gamianus* Waterhouse). *Zeitschrift für Tierpsychologie* 24, 6–79.

Ewer, R. F. (1971). The biology and behaviour of a population of free-living rats (*Rattus rattus*). *Animal Behaviour Monographs* 4, 125–174.

Fagen, R. M. (1981). *Animal Play Behavior*. New York: Oxford University Press.

Farentinos, R. C. (1972). Social dominance and mating in the tassel-eared squirrel (*Sciurus aberti ferreus*). *Animal Behaviour* 20, 316–26.

Ferchmin, P. A., Eterovic, V. A. and Levin, L. E. (1980). Genetic learning deficiency does not hinder environment-dependent brain growth. *Physiology and Behavior* 24, 45–50.

Ferron, J. (1975). Solitary play of the red squirrel (*Tamiasciurus hudsonicus*). *Canadian Journal of Zoology* 53, 1495–9.

Fox, M. W. (1965). Reflex-ontogeny and behavioural development of the mouse. *Animal Behaviour* 13, 234–41.

Gerall, A. A. (1963). An exploratory study of the effect of social isolation variables on the sexual behaviour of male guinea-pigs. *Animal Behaviour* 11, 274–82.

Happold, M. (1976). The ontogeny of social behaviour in four Conilurine rodents (Muridae) of Australia. *Zeitschrift für Tierpsychologie* 46, 265–78.

Hepper, P. G. (1983). Sibling recognition in the rat. *Animal Behaviour*, 31, 1177–91.

Horwich, R. M. (1972). The ontogeny of social behaviour in the grey squirrel (*Sciurus carolinensis*). *Zeitschrift für Tierpsychologie, Supplement 8*.

King, J. A. (1955). Social behavior, social organization and population dynamics in a black-tailed prairie dog town in the Black Hills of South Dakota. *University of Michigan Contributions of the Laboratory of Vertebrate Biology*, No. 67.

Larsson, K. (1978). Experiential factors in the development of sexual behavior in male rats. In J. Hutchinson (ed.), *Biological Determinants of Sexual Behaviour*. New York: Wiley.

Lore, R. and Flannelly, W. (1978). Rat societies. *Scientific American* 236, 106–18.

McDonald, D. L. (1977). Play and exercise in the Californian ground squirrel (*Spermophilus beecheyi*). *Animal Behaviour* 25, 782–4.

Meaney, M. J. and Stewart, J. (1981). A descriptive study of social development in the rat. *Animal Behaviour* 29, 34–45.

Morgan, M. J. (1973). Effects of postweaning environment on learning in the rat. *Animal Behaviour* 21, 429–42.

Morris, D. (1962). The behaviour of the green acouchi (*Myoprocta pratti*) with special reference to food hoarding. *Proceedings of the Zoological Society of London* 139, 701–32.

Müller-Using, D. (1956). Zum Verhalten des murmeltieses (*Marmota marmota* (L.)). *Zeitschrift für Tierpsychologie* 13, 135–42.

Nowicki, S. and Armitage, K. B. (1979). Behaviour of juvenile yellow-bellied marmots: play and social integration. *Zeitschrift für Tierpsychologie* 51, 85–105.

Panksepp, J. (1981). The ontogeny of play in rats. *Developmental Psychobiology* 14, 327–32.

Poole, T. B. (1966). Aggressive play in polecats. *Symposium of the Zoological Society of London* 18, 23–44.

Poole, T. B. and Fish, J. (1975). An investigation of playful behaviour in *Rattus norvegicus* and *Mus musculus* (Mammalia). *Journal of Zoology (London)* 175, 61–71.

Porter, R. H. and Doane, H. M. (1979). Responses of spiny mice weanlings to conspecific chemical cues. *Physiology and Behavior* 23, 75–8.

Porter, R. H. and Wyrick, M. (1979). Sibling recognition in spiny mice *Acomys cahirinus*, influence of age and isolation. *Animal Behaviour* 27, 761–6.

Reinhart, V. and Reinhart, A. (1982). Mock fighting in cattle. *Behaviour* 81, 1–13.

Rood, J. P. (1972). Ecological and behavioural comparisons of three genera of Argentine cavies. *Animal Behaviour Monographs* 5, 1–83.

Rowell, T. E. (1961). The family group of golden hamsters: its formation and breakup. *Behaviour* 17, 81–94.

Rozensweig, M. R. (1971). Effects of environment on the development of brain and behavior. In E. Tobach, L. R. Aronson and E. Shaw (eds), *Biopsychology of Development*. New York: Academic Press.

Sachs, B. D. and Meisel, R. L. (1979). Pubertal development of penile reflexes and copulation in male rats. *Psychoneuroendocrinology* 4, 287–296.

Small, W. (1899). Notes on the psychic development of the young white rat. *American Journal of Psychology* 11, 80–100.

Smith, C. C. (1968). The adaptive nature of social organization in the genus of tree squirrels (*Tamiasciurus*). *Ecological Monographs* 35, 31–63.

Smith, P. K. (1982). Does play matter? Functional and evolutionary aspects of animal and human play. *Behavioral and Brain Sciences* 5, 139–84.

Soderston, P., Damassa, D. A. and Smith, E. R. (1977). Sexual behavior in developing male rats. *Hormones and Behavior* 8, 320–41.

Steiner, A. L. (1971). Play activity in Columbian ground squirrels. *Zeitschrift für Tierpsychologie* 28, 247–61.

Symons, D. (1977). The question of function: dominance and play. In E. O. Smith (ed.), *Social Play in Primates*. New York: Academic Press.

Symons, D. (1978). *Play and Aggression*. New York: Columbia Univeristy Press.

Taylor, G. J. (1980). Fighting in juvenile rats and the ontogeny of agonistic behavior. *Journal of Comparative and Physiological Psychology* 94, 953–61.

Thelan, E. (1981). Kicking, rocking and waving: contextual analysis of rhythmical stereotypes in normal human infants. *Animal Behaviour* 29, 3–11.

Thompson, D. C. (1978). Regulation of a Northern grey squirrel population. *Ecology* 59, 708–15.

Tyler, S. J. (1972). The behaviour and social organization of New Forest ponies. *Animal Behaviour Monographs* 5, 85–196.

Wilson, S. (1973). The development of social behaviour in the vole (*Microtus agrestis*). *Zoological Journal of the Linnean Society* 52, 45–62.

Wilson, S. C. and Kleiman, D. G. (1974). Eliciting play: a comparative study. *American Zoologist* 14, 341–70.

Wolff, R. J. (1981). Solitary and social play in wild *Mus musculus* (Mammalia). *Journal of Zoology (London)* 195, 405–12.

5 Social Play in Monkeys: Theories and Data

Neil Chalmers

INTRODUCTION

In this chapter, I shall not set out to review play in monkeys, since Fagen's (1981) and Smith's (1982) recent reviews and theoretical discussions of play make such an exercise untimely. Instead, I shall discuss what I see to be the most important question currently facing those who study play, namely the relationship between theory and data. I shall take my examples from the literature on monkey social play, since it illustrates many of the problems that currently exist in the field of play research.

Fagen (1981) in his exhaustive review of play argues that data have currently outstripped theory, and in response to the imbalance that he perceives he has erected a massive theoretical framework which, he proposes, should order future collection of data on play. I shall here argue that the major problem in the field of play at present is neither a lack of theory nor a lack of data, but a mismatch between the two; that data have been collected in the past without reference to an adequate theoretical framework, and that theories have been erected with little concern for promoting the collection of data that would test them.

The chapter is divided into four main sections, dealing respectively with (1) definitions and descriptions of monkey social play; (2) the proximate causes of social play; (3) the ontogeny of social play; (4) the functions of social play. In each section I give examples of data and theories, and consider the relationship between the two. For brevity, I refer to social play throughout simply as 'play'.

DEFINITIONS AND DESCRIPTIONS OF PLAY

Many discussions of play begin with the complaint that it is a very difficult behaviour to define. Definitional problems of play are discussed in other chapters (e.g. Martin; Hole and Einon), but I here take the view that many such problems arise from the mistaken belief that to define a behaviour is an end in itself rather than a means to an end. If one believes this with respect to play and tries to erect a single, universally applicable definition under which all that is play is distinguished from all that is not, one is bound to be disappointed. It is more fruitful, I would argue, to tailor one's definition of play to the investigation in hand, and not to attempt to construct an absolute dichotomy between behaviours that are playful and those that are not. For example, investigators who are interested in the ontogenetic relationships among play and other social behaviours in monkeys may choose to define play in terms of motor patterns such as wrestling, carrying, or mouthing, whose appearance during play to some extent resembles components of behaviour in these other social contexts (Lancaster, 1972; Chevalier-Skolnikoff, 1974; Owens, 1975; Chalmers, 1980b). By contrast, investigators who are interested in the role of play in the development of relationships or social skills may choose to define play in terms of strategies with respect to play partners. Symon's (1978) analysis of social play in rhesus monkeys (*Macaca mulatta*) in terms of advantage-seeking provides an example.

Whatever definition one adopts, the task of analysing play is made easier if, following Rosch (1978), one concentrates on 'clear cases' rather than on 'boundaries'; that is, if one selects behaviours that are clearly rather than debatably playful. For example, Chalmers (1980a) used this approach in his description of play ontogeny in the savannah baboon *Papio anubis*, where he identifies five behaviours, collectively termed 'play markers', which, few people would dispute, are components of social play. In this chapter, I am therefore going to assume that a fruitful way in which to conduct research into play is to select aspects of behaviour that appear to observers to be indisputedly playful, and that are appropriate to the research questions under investigation.

It is not useful to describe play, any more than it is to define it, in a theoretical vacuum. There are many different ways of describing play, and the kind of description chosen will depend upon the nature of the research question under investigation. Thus a person interested in reconstructing the evolution of play within a taxonomic group such as the primates will wish to describe the motor patterns, including gestures and vocalizations, used in social play across many species (see Byers, above, chapter 2, for such a reconstruction of the evolution of ungulate play). By contrast an investigator interested in the function of play will probably wish to describe the outcome of playful interactions, both in the short and long term, and the distribution of an individual's play among its potential play-partners. Somebody analysing the immediate causation of play will probably wish to measure the frequency with which specific components of play are performed under different experimental conditions, and also the short-term temporal patterning of components within play interactions. Finally, a person interested in the ontogeny of play will wish to measure changes in the frequency and form of specific components of play with age, and the relationship between these changes and those of components of other systems of behaviour.

Description of play should therefore be for a purpose, and not an end in itself. If one accepts this position, then it follows that the distinction that is sometimes made between the 'structuralist' and 'functionalist' approaches to play (Fagen, 1974; M. Bekoff, 1976), is not a useful one. 'Structuralists' are supposed to concentrate their energies upon describing play, and 'functionalists' upon discovering its functions, 'including underlying behavioural mechanisms and/or possible adaptive significance' (Fagen, 1974). It should be clear from the examples given above, that for any investigation of play to be fruitful, there must be an appropriate selection of descriptive parameters within the context of the particular set of questions that are being investigated. Moreover, this set of questions need not be limited purely to issues of function. Specific instances of the relationship between description and theory are described in more detail in the next three sections of this chapter.

PROXIMATE CAUSES OF PLAY

Many different questions can be asked about the proximate causes of play. What conditions are required if an animal is to play? What factors initiate and terminate play? What dictates which of several components of play will be performed at any one instant during a playful interaction? For feeding, drinking, sexual behaviour, and other well-researched behaviours, the study of causation has progressed beyond the stage of *ad hoc* investigations of individual causal agents to the elaboration of formal causal models (see Toates, 1980, for a review). In such models, the effects of the various causal factors on the behaviour of interest are considered collectively rather than one by one, and the aim of the approach is to postulate a set of interactive relationships among these factors that will adequately explain the observed characteristics of the animal's behaviour.

Research into the proximate causation of play has not proceeded beyond an examination of individual causal factors on an *ad hoc* basis. Such research as has been carried out on monkeys has shown that an individual's propensity for play varies with its age and sex. Moreover, the play of an individual of a given age and sex can be affected by factors both external and internal to it.

The age changes in play are described more fully in the next section. Sex differences in the quality and quantity of play have been reported for several monkey species (see reviews by Mitchell, 1977; Fagen, 1981; Smith, 1982). Although there are exceptions among some species, males of a given age tend to play more frequently and more vigorously than females of the same age. For example, Owens (1975) found that young male olive baboons (*Papio anubis*) performed more social play than females, and that males performed more wrestling than females (wrestling being an activity that involves active rough-and-tumble from both play partners) whereas females performed more mauling than males (mauling being an activity in which one partner wrestles while the other is passive).

Social play can be affected by both physiological, notably hormonal, factors and by features of the external environment. One of the most striking hormonal effects observed is that produced by testosterone propionate on the rhesus monkey foetus. If the mother of a genetically female foetus is injected with the androgen between the 46th and 90th day of pregnancy, the neonate is a pseudohermaphrodite: its external genitalia are masculine in appearance, whereas its internal reproductive organs are female. These pseudohermaphrodites are intermediate between unandrogenized genetic females and normal genetic males, in the frequency with which they perform rough-and-tumble play and with which they initiate play (Goy and Phoenix, 1971; Phoenix, 1974).

Numerous external factors influence social play. For example, Levy (1979) found that rhesus monkeys living under semi-natural conditions on Cayo Santiago island, Puerto Rico, played less during hot weather than at other times. She also found that play was less frequent during the mating season, a time of considerable turbulence within the rhesus groups, than at other times. Lee (1981) found that play in vervet monkeys (*Cercopithecus aethiops*) was extremely rare during the dry season, but that it rose substantially as the vegetation became more lush after the start of the rainy season. Play tended not to occur during rain showers, and Lee puts forward evidence that the rain exerts its effect through increasing the protein content of the animals' diet.

An additional important stimulus to play is the presence of other playful animals. In wild vervets, *Cercopithecus aethiops* (Lee, 1981), captive rhesus monkeys, *M. mulatta* (White, 1977), and wild baboons, *Papio cynocephalus* (Cheney, 1978), the amount of play that individuals perform varies from month to month according to a similar pattern despite the differing ages of the individual concerned. Indeed, Cheney (1978) found this similarity to be greater than that obtained when the percentage of time spent playing by the same individuals was plotted against their age (figure 5.1).

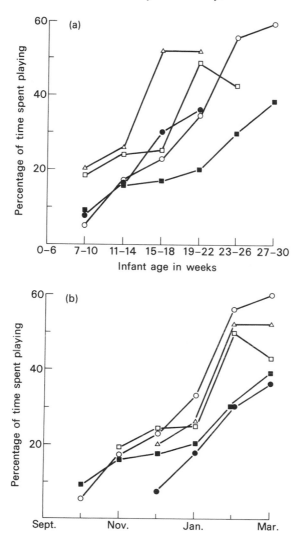

FIGURE 5.1 The proportion of observation time that five wild infant baboons (*Papio cynocephalus*) spent playing (a) at various ages and (b) during each of five months. Two infants were born in August, one in September and one in October of the same year.
(From Cheney, 1978)

Play can be suppressed by other behaviours. Squirrel monkeys (*Saimiri sciureus*) living in Panamanian forests may play little if food is in short supply, and hence if the animals have to spend a lot of their time searching for food (Baldwin and Baldwin, 1973). Baldwin and Baldwin (1976) were able to mimic this situation in the laboratory by presenting a captive *Saimiri sciureus* group with food in a form that was extremely inaccessible to the animals in comparison with their normal circumstances. The amount of time that the animals in the group spent feeding increased greatly under this latter condition, and the amount of time that young animals played was significantly reduced.

There is also evidence showing that the nature of the play component that an individual performs at any moment in an interaction depends in part on the nature of the component it has just performed. Thus Chalmers and Locke-Haydon (1981) showed that when captive common marmosets (*Callithrix jacchus*) play, certain components (wrestle, chase and grasp) follow each other in direct succession more often than would be expected if they were to be ordered at random with respect to one another, and following, patrolling and stationary episodes less often (figure 5.2). Stevenson and Poole (1982) using a different form of sequence analysis for the same species also conclude that components of behaviour during play are arranged in non-random sequences.

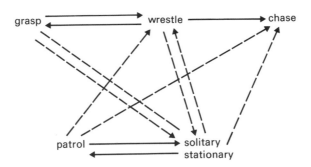

FIGURE 5.2 Components of play bouts in captive marmosets (*Callithrix jacchus*) that followed each other in direct succession significantly more often (solid arrows) and significantly less often (dashed arrows) than expected under a hypothesis of random sequencing.
(From Chalmers and Locke-Haydon, 1981)

Other factors influencing the temporal properties of social play are also becoming clear. Thus Chalmers (1980a) compared the durations of playful and non-playful interactions of wild baboons (*Papio anubis*) and found playful interactions to be significantly longer. Moreover, the rate at which individuals changed their behvaiour from one component to another was faster during the course of playful than non-playful interactions. Also, individuals continued to change their behaviour after a change in the partner's behaviour, rather than breaking off the interaction, more often during playful than non-playful interactions. These results suggest that the performance of a play component by one individual stimulates its partner to change its behaviour in turn from an existing to a new play component. Hence the interaction tends to be self-prolonging.

Chalmers and Locke-Haydon (1981) carried out a more detailed analysis of the temporal patterns of play components in captive groups of the common marmoset (*Callithrix jacchus*). They chose five unambiguously playful behaviour patterns (which can for convenience be called 'play markers') and found that for each marmoset infant examined, the intervals between the termination of each play marker and the onset of each subsequent play marker were not distributed randomly. Instead, there was a predominance of short intervals, with a long tail of larger ones. From this it was possible to produce non-arbitrary definitions of a play bout for each individual, and then to investigate the temporal patterning of play bouts. It was found, again, that play bouts tended to be clustered together in time, with long gaps between them (figure 5.3). The clusters of bouts can be called 'play sessions'. Typically, play bouts last about 15 to 35 seconds, whereas play sessions can contain many bouts and last for several minutes.

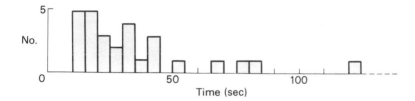

FIGURE 5.3 Histogram of intervals between play bouts in a captive juvenile marmoset (*C. Jacchus*).
(From Chalmers and Locke-Haydon, 1981)

To explain the causal factors behind this temporal patterning, Chalmers and Locke-Haydon suggest that it is necessary to postulate internal, time-dependent causal processes operating at at least two levels. One process would operate within play sessions, and would be responsible for switching an animal between the respective states of 'within play bout' and 'between play bouts'. The other process would operate by switching an animal between the respective states of 'within play session' and 'between play sessions'.

Given the information currently available on the causal factors affecting play performance, the next state of analysis must be to adopt a modelling approach. That is, having defined a set of unambiguous components of social play, it will be necessary to investigate how variables such as 'nature of last component performed by self', 'duration from onset of play bout', 'duration from onset of play session', etc. interact to produce interactions with the properties that are observed in a selected species. The earliest attempts at modelling in ethology and comparative psychology invoked unitary drives, variation in whose intensity affected the quality of the behaviour under examination. These early models have been discarded in favour of more elaborate, systems-based models (see Toates, 1980, for a review). It is interesting that the only motivational model of play to have appeared – the surplus energy model (see Burghardt, above, chapter 1) – is nothing but a resurrected unitary drive theory. The surplus energy theory has been widely criticized, and would seem to be inadequate in the face of the data presented above. For example, it is difficult, under this theory, to account for the hierarchical organization of marmoset play into play bouts and play sessions, or to explain the apparently self-perpetuating effect of play in baboons. Clearly, more sophisticated causal models need to be formulated to account for such phenomena.

THE ONTOGENY OF PLAY

Play ontogeny presents to the investigator two particularly challenging theoretical issues. The first concerns the nature of the ontogenetic processes that control the changes with age in form, frequency and patterning of playful behaviour. The second concerns the age changes in the relationship of play to other aspects of the animal's behaviour. Few studies of play ontogeny have addressed themselves to the first of these issues. A larger number have addressed themselves to the second.

Detailed accounts of play ontogeny are available for wild baboons, *Papio cynocephalus* and *P. anubis* (Owens, 1975; Cheney, 1978; Chalmers, 1980a), for captive rhesus monkeys (Hinde and Spencer-Booth 1967; Harlow, 1969; Mears and Harlow, 1975), and for captive common marmosets, *Callithrix jacchus* (Stevenson, 1978; Chalmers and Locke-Haydon, 1984). In these species, play first appears soon after the age when infants begin to make short excursions away from their mothers (or other caregivers). This may be as soon as one to four weeks after birth. Thereafter, play becomes increasingly frequent. In all three studies of baboons cited above, play has two peaks, one around the middle of the first year of life, the second in the second year of life, or later (figure 5.4). The trough between these peaks in some individuals corresponds with the time at which the mother resumes her sexual cycling, and with a concomitent change in her relationship with her infant. This can be a stressful time for the infant, for its mother may forcibly reject its attempts to contact and feed from her. Although this changed relationship might be expected to depress play the evidence for this is equivocal. Cheney (1978), for example, showed in the baboons that she studied that the troughs in play did not always correspond with peaks in weaning tantrums or with the mother's resumption of cycling.

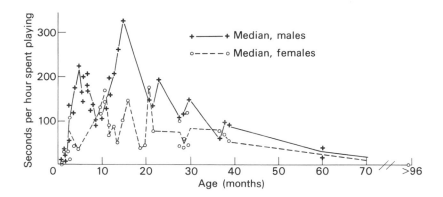

FIGURE 5.4 Age changes in the amount of social play in wild baboons (*Papio anubis*).
(From Chalmers, 1980a)

It has become apparent that if different components of social play are recorded separately, then the time course of their development may not follow the same pattern. In both captive rhesus monkeys (Hinde and Spencer-Booth, 1967) and wild olive baboons, *P. anubis* (Owens, 1975) approach–withdrawal patterns of play increase in frequency relative to rough-and-tumble play with age. An earlier study by Rosenblum (1961) on captive rhesus monkeys also showed that rough-and-tumble appeared earlier in development than approach–withdrawal play, although, once both patterns had appeared they showed very similar developmental changes in frequency. In his study of wild *P. anubis*, Chalmers (1980a) traced the development of rough-and-tumble play (which he termed 'mouth-and-wrestle') from earlier, less elaborate behaviours involving the use of hands and mouth. First to appear, within a day or two of birth in some instances, was the play face; an open-mouthed gesture usually performed at a nearby animal. Later, the infant came to perform this gesture while in contact with other animals, thereby mouthing them. Subsequently, the infant began to grasp its parner while mouthing it, and finally, from 4 weeks onwards, the infant began to add the rotational and tumbling movements typical of wrestling (figure 5.5). The development of running, chasing, jumping and climbing, all of which are vigorous and acrobatic activities that can occur during play, was found to follow a different pattern of development from that of rough-and-tumble and its precursors (figure 5.5). The fact that different components of play show different patterns of

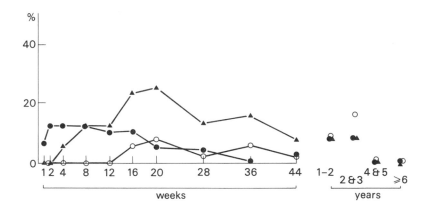

FIGURE 5.5 Age changes in the frequency with which wild baboons (*Papio anubis*) performed the play face (closed circles), rough-and-tumble (open circles) and running (triangles) during social interactions.
(From Chalmers, 1980a)

development is not especially surprising, and has been demonstrated not only in primates, but in other mammals such as cats (Barrett and Bateson, 1978). Both Chalmers and these latter authors suggest on the basis of their observations that play should not be regarded as a unitary behaviour, but can more legitimately be viewed as a multi-component system, within which groups of components are clustered together as sub-systems.

A number of studies have investigated the relationship between play and other kinds of behaviours, notably aggression, sexual behaviour and parental care. With respect to the first of these, several workers have shown that play contains components, such as wrestling and mock biting, which are similar (but not identical) to behaviours performed during intraspecific aggression (see Fagen, 1981, for a review). For example, Levy (1979) points out that in rhesus monkesy (*M. mulatta*), play can contain both wrestling and chasing, but that the extended periods of physical contact that occur during wrestling are much more frequent in play than aggression, and that the accompanying facial expressions, vocalizations, body postures and gaits in the two contexts are different (cf. Sade, 1967; Symons, 1974).

The quality of play changes with age, and some authors have claimed that play becomes rougher in older animals (e.g. Hall and DeVore, 1965). Levy (1979), who used carefully-defined measures of roughness, found no increase in roughness of play over the first three years of life in some wild rhesus monkeys (*M. mulatta*) on Cayo Santiago. She did find, however, that rhesus play came to resemble aggression more closely with increasing age in other respects. True dyadic fights she argued, are asymmetric, in that one animal is consistently the attacker, and the other the victim. In a bout of dyadic play, by contrast, the role of attacker and victim can change backwards and forwards several times between the two animals involved, and much of the wrestling behaviour involves coordination between the play partners. Such play can be referred to as mutualistic. Levy found that when like-age one- and two-year-old males played together, most of their play was mutualistic. On occasions when such males did perform asymmetric play, the role of attacker was equally likely to be taken by the higher-ranking or lower-ranking partner, as was the role of victim. For play between three-year-olds, by contrast, the proportion of asymmetric play increased, and the role of attacker was taken more frequently by the higher-ranking play partner. In these two respects, therefore, dyadic play interactions come to resemble dyadic aggressive interactions more closely with increasing age. The situation proved to be different for females. Most play between like-aged one- to three-year-old females was asymmetric, and the proportion of asymmetric play did not increase with age. However, as in males, there was an increase with age in the tendency for the higher-ranking play partner to adopt the role of attacker.

Owens (1975), although using somewhat different behavioural measures from those of Levy in his study of wild *Papio anubis*, also reported an increase in asymmetry of dyadic play interactions with age.

Just as it is possible to investigate the relationship between play and aggressive behaviour during development, so is it possible to do the same for play and sexual behaviour (e.g. Owens, 1976; Hanby, 1976; Chalmers, 1980b) and for play and parental care (e.g. Lancaster, 1972;

Owens, 1975), since play can incorporate components from both these kinds of behaviour. Rather than outline such relationships here, I believe it is important to broaden the discussion in order to consider some of the theoretical issues involved in such relationships. Implicit in most discussions of developmental relationships between play and other kinds of behaviour are two assumptions. The first is that the behaviour of infants, and also of adults, can be partitioned into a set of categories. The second is that the categories present in infants are developmental precursors of those seen in adults, and hence that there is developmental continuity between the two (figure 5.6 represents these two assumptions at their simplest level).

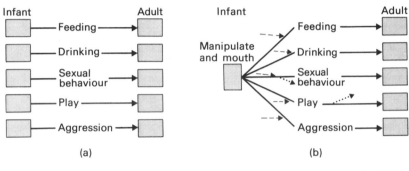

$\longrightarrow$ Indicates that an infant behaviour is a precursor to an adult behaviour

$----\rightarrow$ Category-specific components that appear during development

$\cdots\cdots\rightarrow$ Components that disappear during development

FIGURE 5.6 Theoretical relationships between infant and adult categories of behaviour in (a) one-to-one relationships and (b) more complex relationships.

It is rare in discussion of play for authors to state explicitly the criteria by which they partition infant and adult behaviours into categories, and by which they recognize precursors. Hinde's (1970) well-known discussion of the criteria for classifying behaviour argues that classification can be achieved either on the basis of shared form, causal mechanisms, or functions, and that the classifications produced by these respective criteria need not be congruent. A similar argument can be put forward with respect to developmental precursors (Chalmers, 1980b). An infant behaviour, defined on the basis of its form, can be thought of as a precursor to an adult one, similarly defined by its form, if the two are connected during development by a series of behaviours intermediate in form. Similarly one behaviour might be thought of as the precursor of another if their causal mechanisms or their functions are connected by a series of developmental intermediates. There is, however, no guarantee that developmental relationships defined in these three ways will be congruent (see Oppenheim, 1974; A. Bekoff, 1978).

Most of the studies of play ontogeny in monkeys that have investigated the relationship between play and other kinds of behaviour, have classified the various behaviours involved in terms of their form, and have then gone on to investigate changes in form and function of these behaviours during ontogeny. For example, Chevalier-Skolnikoff (1974) describes how the play face of the infant stumptail macaque (*Macaca arctoides*) develops from sucking and rooting movements of the neonate, and how the play face in turn develops into various adult communicative gestures.

I would argue that, even if we restrict ourselves to classifying behaviour in terms of its form, we do not have an adequate account of the developmental relationships among play and other kinds of behaviour in a single species of monkey, and that with respect to a causally or functionally based behavioural taxonomy, the situation is even less satisfactory. If we study the developmental relationships of behaviour defined by their form, it is clear that the situation outlined in figure 5.6a is far too simple. Figure 5.6b depicts a more complex situation, in which some infant behavioural categories are seen to be precursors to many adult behaviours, each of which in addition incorporates its own specific components. There is some evidence to support certain features of figure 5.6b. Thus Chalmers (1980b) found that in baboons (*Papio anubis*), both feeding and rough-and-tumble play have some ontogenetic precursors in common, namely the grasping and mouthing of objects at 1 week of age, but that by 12 weeks of age the use of these abilities in the two contexts had become quite different (figure 5.7).

If we are to understand the developmental relationships among behaviours in monkeys, or in other animals, we must be prepared to recognize that such relationships may be complicated, and that simple models of the type depicted in figure 5.6a will be inadequate. One particular difficulty that has to be overcome is that it is often most convenient to categorize an adult's behaviour in terms of its consequences, feeding, grooming, mating, and so on. However, much of an infant monkey's behaviour is difficult to categorize in this way. Are we to say that, when a one-week-old baboon grasps and mouths another infant's arm, that it is 'really' playing, 'really' feeding, trying to do both or neither? Clearly, at this very early age, such classificatory terms as play and feeding are not helpful and are better avoided.

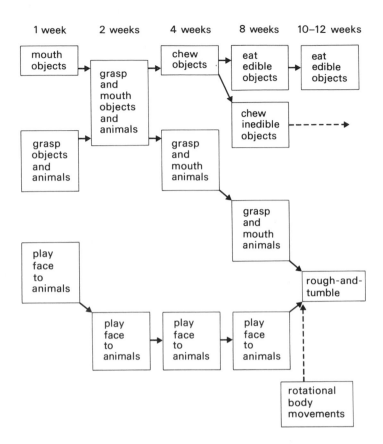

FIGURE 5.7 Developmental relationships between components of feeding and play in wild baboons, *Papio anubis.*
(From Chalmers, 1980b)

FUNCTIONS OF PLAY

When one speaks of the 'function' of a behaviour one normally means the beneficial consequences of the behaviour that have resulted in its selection during the course of evolutionary history (Williams, 1966; Smith, 1982; Symons, 1978). It is not possible to assess the function of a behaviour directly, and indirect methods have to be used instead, of which I shall briefly mention three.

One method is to assume that play confers benefits and also that it incurs costs. Depending upon what further assumptions the investigator makes about the magnitude of these costs and benefits and about the stage during its life history at which they impinge upon the animal, it is possible to devise a model which either predicts as yet unknown properties of play or mimics features that are already evident. If the predictions turn out to be true, or the mimicry accurate, then there is some justification for believing that the assumptions made about the costs and benefits of play are correct. For example Fagen (1977) devises a model in which he assumes that play incurs immediate costs but results in delayed benefits. His model produces several predictions, for example that play should be more frequent in K-selected than in r-selected species, and that behaviour patterns required in adulthood should appear in play as soon as or soon after they appear in the animal's general behaviour repertoire. It also mimics some known features of play; for example, under the model young animals are expected to play more than old ones.

In his review of play Fagen (1981) greatly extends his modelling approach, and generates a multitude of predictions. There is insufficient space here to discuss these models further, but two general comments need to be made. First, the modelling approach is extremely useful in so far as it allows us to discover the implications of assuming that play carries certain costs and benefits, and more particularly, in so far as it helps us to discover the implications of assuming that these costs and benefits vary in specified ways during an animal's life, or from one play strategy to another. Second, the modelling approach does not of itself, nor can it, identify the nature of the costs and benefits involved. It needs therefore to be complemented by other approaches that are better suited to this task.

Another approach is to compare the Darwinian fitness, or a partial measure of fitness such as viability or fecundity, of animals who play, with that of others of the same species who do not, and so to assess the present-day survival value of play. It is then necessary to assume, perhaps without justification, that the present-day survival value of play is similar to that which obtained during the evolution of the behaviour. There have been no studies on any animal species which have compared the viability or fecundity of playful or non-playful individuals within a species. A gross difference of the kind just mentioned is unlikely to be found in nature, especially between animals that resemble one another in other respects such as age and sex. As an alternative, it should at least in principle be possible to conduct a correlational study in which inter-individual variation in viability (or possibly even fecundity) and playfulness are compared. Again, no such study has been published.

Another, less direct, approach is to assess the effects of play, not on

Darwinian fitness, nor on one of its main components, such as viability, but on a specific behavioural attribute which in turn is assumed to affect fitness. There are many theories of play function that operate within this paradigm, and these have been reviewed by Smith (1982). Specific instances of these theories suggest that play promotes physical fitness (Brownlee, 1954; Fagen, 1976; Fagen and George, 1977), competitive social skills (Symons, 1978), cognitive abilities (Einon et al., 1978, Poirier and Smith, 1974), and so on.

It is easier to propose effects of play such as these than to test the proposals, and it is in this area of play research, in particular, that theory greatly outstrips data. Several different research strategies are available to those who wish to test such proposals. The first involves more or less plausible advocacy, based on descriptive information about the form and frequency of play among individuals of different sexes, ages and species across the animal kingdom. The second involves experimental manipulation of play. Individual animals are artifically stimulated to play or inhibited from playing, and the effects of such manipulations on the animals' subsequent behaviour are assessed. The third strategy is correlational: inter-individual variation in playfulness and in measures of behavioural competence is analysed, with a view to discovering whether those animals that of their own accord play a lot do better on the measures of behavioural competence than individuals who play less.

Fagen (1981) has argued that manipulative experiments of the kind just described can tell us nothing about the function of play, in the strict sense of the phrase, because such experiments do not allow us to discover whether the consequences of manipulating play are true functions, for which play was originally selected, or merely secondary effects. In this he is undoubtedly correct (although from an ontogenetic rather than an evolutionary standpoint the discovery of such effects is valuable in itself). I believe he is wrong, when he goes on to argue that an analysis of the design features of play (the descriptive strategy outlined above) can tell us about the functions of play where experimental manipulation cannot. All three of the research strategies mentioned above are directed at theories within the paradigm of specific behavioural consequences of play, rather than within the paradigm of effects of play on Darwinian fitness or on its major components. All three, therefore, suffer from the same difficulty of distinguishing functions from effects.

I shall briefly discuss below the evidence available on the functions of monkey play from these research strategies, and assess their usefulness.

Descriptive evidence

Smith (1982) has reviewed much of the descriptive evidence on the functions of play. As an example of this evidence, consider the hypothesis that play promotes intraspecific fighting skills (Symons, 1978). Smith cites evidence that intraspecific competition is greater among male mammals than among female mammals, and that play-fighting is more frequent among male mammals than among females. Examples to support both of these generalizations can be found in monkeys, such as the rhesus monkey, *M. mulatta* (Symons, 1978). As a result, one can argue that play may be important in developing competitive skills. Similarly, intraspecific competition among males of polygynous mammals is supposed to be more intense than among males of monogamous species. If play is more frequent among males of polygynous than monogamous species, one can again argue that play promotes competitive skills. By contrast, Smith argues that play is unlikely to promote affiliative relationships between specific individuals, or to allow individuals to learn each other's rank in a non-serious context, because animals of many species emigrate from their natal groups during adolescence, and hence sever any relationship that they may have developed with former play partners.

Other authors have argued for particular functions of play on the basis of its form. This approach has the most obvious relevance in the Canidae and Felidae, where young dogs, cats, coyotes etc. perform movements during play that are very similar to those that they use when as adults they catch prey (Vincent and Bekoff, 1978; Caro, 1979). Applying this approach to rhesus monkeys, *M. mulatta*, Symons (1974) was one of the first to compare the movements that monkeys performed in play and in fighting. He found that aggressive gestures and vocalizations were absent from play, and that the gestures and vocalizations given during play were rarely given in other contexts. He argued that play could not, therefore, provide a vehicle for practising these specific aggressive patterns of behaviour. Chalmers (1980a) found exactly the same to be true in wild olive baboons, *Papio anubis*. However, when Symons considered the strategies used by rhesus monkeys engaged in rough-and-tumble play (or 'playfighting', as he called it), he concluded that these strategies provided a useful opportunity for the playing animals to develop skills used in intraspecific aggression and predator avoidance. Symons argued that the main strategy used by a play-fighting animal was to bite without being bitten; for example to grasp the play partner from behind or to get on top of it. This strategy would, he suggests, be very important in real fighting.

Although the descriptive approach outlined above has produced most of our present information on the functions of play it has certain drawbacks.

First, because it depends to a large extent on advocacy, arguments on function based solely on descriptive evidence depend to an unusually high degree upon the skill of the advocate. One sometimes gains the impression from the play literature that a sufficiently skilful advocate could argue for or against any particular function of play that he or she chooses. Second, those arguments that depend upon cross-specific comparisons of play depend crucially upon the quality of the data obtained from studies of the different species. It is, unfortunately, still true that rigorous, systematic, quantitative studies of play are available for only a few monkey species. If we are to make cross-specific comparisons, we therefore have to be careful to select species for which adequate data are available. This has not always been done in the past.

Manipulation of play

The frequency with which animals play can readily be reduced under natural conditions by rain, the presence of predators or other competing activities (see above). It can also be manipulated in the laboratory by maternal deprivation (Hansen, 1966), administration of a tranquillizing drug (Chalmers, unpublished data), by alarming stimuli or competing activities.

Despite the possibility of manipulating play levels, the manipulative approach has not yet been used effectively to analyse the function of primate play. The main reason for this is that it is extraordinarily difficult to manipulate play levels without manipulating the levels of other behaviours as well. Hence, any manipulative experiment on play is likely to introduce confounding variables.

In the field, certain 'natural experiments' occur in relation to monkey play. Thus Baldwin and Baldwin (1973) discovered two troops of squirrel monkeys (*Saimiri sciureus*) in Panama in which food was in short supply, and in which the animals spent most of their waking time foraging for food, and virtually none of their time playing. The Baldwins noted that the animals in the group appeared normal in their social behaviour, and argued that play was not therefore needed for its development. Most theories of play function imply, or explicitly state, that the play performed by young animals promotes skills which persist into adulthood, long after play has become rare or ceased. For the Baldwins' argument to be valid, therefore, it would have to be demonstrated either that the adults in the group that they observed did not themselves play as infants, or that the infants that they observed in the group subsequently matured into normal adults. Since their study of these groups lasted a little over two months, the necessary information is not available.

Another natural experiment comes from Lee's (1981) field study of vervets (*Cercopithecus aethiops*), in Kenya. As previously mentioned, play frequency in the groups she studied correlated positively with rainfall. Infants were usually born at the beginning of the rainy season, and during the first three months of life play was common in the group. During the rest of the year, however, play was very infrequent, but increased when the rains began in the following year. Since the young animals she studied developed normally, despite long periods without play, Lee argues that play is unlikely to have a vital role in promoting the development of skills. Certainly, one can conclude from her study that, if the situation she reports is normal for the species, and if it produces normal adults, then continual play during infancy is not necessary for normal social development.

Correlational studies of monkey play

If play promotes skills, then one would predict positive correlations between scores of playfulness and skilfulness. This approach has been used with cats (Caro, 1979) and coyotes (Vincent and Bekoff, 1978), but not until recently with monkeys. A study by Chalmers and Locke-Haydon (1984), on the common marmoset *Callithrix jacchus*, has revealed significant, positive, age-specific correlations between certain components of play and certain measures of skills. The skills of ten infant marmosets were measured at 4-weekly intervals from 6 to 22 weeks inclusive. Some of the skills measured were derived from the behaviour of the infants in relation to their families in undisturbed family groups. The remaining skills were measured when the infants were required to perform specific tasks involving, respectively, manual dexterity, agility, and competition with their mothers for access to food. The infants' play was measured during the intervening three-week periods. The design of the experiment made it possible to correlate indices of skill at a given age with amounts of play performed over various age ranges.

One of the main findings of this study was that infants who played the most at 11 to 13 weeks of age made the most numerous attempts at 14 weeks of age to take food from their mothers during food competition tests (although they were not necessarily more successful than less playful infants in taking food from the mother). They also used more vocalizations, gestures and avoidance of the mother during the food test than less playful individuals: that is, they appeared to show a greater anticipation of the potential consequences of being in conflict with the mother. Playful animals also did better than others on agility tests at the same age. Significant correlations were not found at other ages, and it is interestng that the age of 10 to 14 weeks, when the significant correlations were found, is one at which infants achieve locomotor independence from their family and switch largely to a solid-food diet (Locke-Haydon and Chalmers, 1983). It is also the age at which play is increasing rapidly (Chalmers and Locke-Haydon, 1984). Chalmers and Locke-Haydon point out that although their results are consistent with the hypothesis that play promotes specific skills, it is also consistent with alternative hypotheses – for example that skilful animals, by virtue of their skill, have more opportunity or ability to play, or that both the measures of skills and of play depend upon some common underlying ability. (They also point out that the frequency of certain non-playful behaviours correlated with skills measures. Hence the associations they revealed were not unique to play.)

This difficulty of interpretation is, of course, commonplace among correlational studies, but this particular study does at least point us to certain specific stages of development for closer investigation and further experimentation.

CONCLUSIONS

Of the three kinds of research strategy mentioned in the last section, the first, which I have called the descriptive approach, has been by far the most frequently used. Its principal advantage is that in many situations, particularly in the field, it is the easiest, and possibly the only practicable, strategy to adopt. None the less it does have its limitations. In particular, it is less well suited than the other strategies mentioned to deal with very specific hypotheses on the functions of play. If, let us say, an adequate cross-species survey of monkeys play were to suggest strongly that play promotes competitive skills in monkeys, we have at best supported no more than a very general hypothesis. We could not say which components or features of play promote which particular components of social competitiveness, nor could we say anything about the mechanisms by which such promotion takes place.

Manipulative and correlational studies are better suited to attack these problems, despite their difficulties, and despite their weaknesses, mentioned in earlier sections. Both play and skills are multi-component facets of behaviour, and we must expect the relationship between them to be complex. Without manipulative and correlational studies it is difficult to see how we can reveal the nature of this relationship.

At the beginning of this chapter I suggested that data on play and theories about play are out of step. I would argue, from the material presented in this chapter that, with respect to the causal mechanisms and ontogeny of monkey play, we have an excess of data over organizing theories, and that, with respect to the functions of play, we have an excess of theories over data. Our understanding of all aspects of monkey play is rudimentary, but I suggest that it will rapidly improve if we seek to achieve a better balance between data and theory.

REFERENCES

Baldwin, J. D. and Baldwin, J. I. (1973). The role of play in social organization: comparative observations on squirrel monkeys (*Saimiri*). *Primates* 14, 369–81.

Baldwin, J. D. and Baldwin, J. I. (1976). Effects of food ecology on social play: a laboratory simulation. *Zeitschrift für Tierpsychologie* 40, 1–14.

Barrett, P. and Bateson, P. P. G. (1978). The development of play in cats. *Behaviour* 66, 106–20.

Bekoff, A. (1978). A neuroethological approach to the study of ontogeny of coordinated behavior. In G. M. Burghardt and M. Bekoff (eds), *The Development of Behavior: Comparative and Evolutionary Aspects*. New York: Garland STPM.

Bekoff, M. (1976). Animal play: problems and perspectives. In P. P. G. Bateson and P. H. Klopfer (eds), *Perspectives in Ethology, Vol. 2*. New York and London: Plenum Press.

Brownlee, A. (1954). Play in domestic cattle: an analysis of its nature. *British Veterinary Journal* 110, 48–68.

Caro, T. M. (1979). Relations between kitten behaviour and adult predation. *Zeitschrift für Tierpsychologie* 51, 158–68.

Chalmers, N. R. (1980a). The ontogeny of play in feral olive baboons (*Papio anubis*). *Animal Behaviour* 28, 570–85.

Chalmers, N. R. (1980b). Developmental relationships among social, manipulatory, postural and locomotor behaviours in olive baboons, *Papio anubis*. *Behaviour* 74, 22–37.

Chalmers, N. R. and Locke-Haydon, J. (1981). Temporal patterns of play bouts in captive common marmosets (*Callithrix jacchus*). *Animal Behaviour* 29, 1229–38.

Chalmers, N. R. and Locke-Haydon, J. (1984). Correlations among measures of playfulness and skilfulness in captive common marmosets (*Callithrix jacchus jacchus*). *Developmental Psychobiology*, in press.

Cheney, D. L. (1978). The play partners of immature baboons. *Animal Behaviour* 26, 1038–50.

Chevalier-Skolnikoff, S. (1974). The ontogeny of communication in the stumptail macaque (*Macaca arctoides*). *Contributions to Primatology* 2, 1–174.

Einon, D. F., Morgan, M. J. and Kibbler, C. C. (1978). Brief periods of socialization and later behaviour in the rat. *Developmental Psychobiology* 11, 213–25.

Fagen, R. (1974). Selective and evolutionary aspects of animal play. *American*

Naturalist 108, 850–8.

Fagen, R. (1976). Exercise, play, and physical training in animals. In P. P. G. Bateson and P. H. Klopfer (eds), *Perspectives in Ethology, Vol. 2*. New York and London: Plenum Press.

Fagen, R. (1977). Selection for optimal age-dependent schedules of play behavior. *American Naturalist* 111, 395–414.

Fagen, R. (1981). *Animal Play Behavior*. New York and Oxford: Oxford University Press.

Fagen, R. and George, T. K. (1977). Play behavior and exercise in young ponies (*Equus caballus* L.). *Behavioral Ecology and Sociobiology* 2, 267–9.

Goy, R. W. and Phoenix, C. (1971). The effects of testosterone administered before birth on the development of behavior in genetic female rhesus monkeys. In C. Sawyer and R. Gorski (eds), *Steroid Hormones and Brain Function*. California: University of California Press.

Hall, K. R. L. and Devore, I. (1965). Baboon social behavior. In I. DeVore (ed.), *Primate Behavior: Field Studies of Monkeys and Apes*. New York: Holt, Rinehart and Winston.

Hanby, J. (1976). Sociosexual development in primates. In P. P. G. Bateson and P. H. Klopfer (eds), *Perspectives in Ethology, Vol. 2*. New York and London: Plenum Press.

Hansen, E. W. (1966). The development of maternal and infant behaviour in the rhesus monkey. *Behaviour* 27, 107–49.

Harlow, H. F. (1969). Age mate or peer affectional system. *Advances in the Study of Behavior* 2, 333–83.

Hinde, R. A. (1970). *Animal Behaviour* (2nd edn). New York: McGraw-Hill.

Hinde, R. A. and Spencer-Booth, Y. (1967). The behaviour of socially living rhesus monkeys in their first two and a half years. *Animal Behaviour* 15, 169–96.

Lancaster, J. B. (1972). Play-mothering: the relations between juvenile females and young infants among free-ranging vervet monkeys. In F. E. Poirier (ed.), *Primate Socialization*. New York: Random House.

Lee, P. (1981). Ecological and social influences on development of vervet monkeys. Unpublished Ph.D. thesis, Cambridge University.

Levy, J. S. (1979). Play behaviour and its decline during development in rhesus monkeys (*Macaca mulatta*). Unpublished Ph.D. thesis, Chicago University.

Locke-Haydon, J. (1983). Infant–caregiver relationships in the common marmoset, (*Callithrix jacchus*). Unpublished Ph.D. thesis, Open University.

Locke-Haydon, J. and Chalmers, N. R. (1983). The development of infant – caregiver relationships in captive common marmosets (*Callithrix jacchus*). *International Journal of Primatology* 4, 63–81.

Mears, C. A. and Harlow, H. F. (1975). Play: early and eternal. *Proceedings of the National Academy of Sciences (U.S.A.)* 72, 1878–82.

Mitchell, G. (1977). *Behavioral Sex Differences in Nonhuman Primates*. New York: Van Nostrand Reinhold.

Oppenheim, R. W. (1974). The ontogeny of behavior in the chick embryo. *Advances in the Study of Behavior* 5, 155–72.

Owens, N. W. (1975). Social play behaviour in free-living baboons, *Papio anubis. Animal Behaviour* 23, 387–408.

Owens, N. W. (1976). The development of sociosexual behaviour in free-living baboons, *Papio anubis. Behaviour* 57, 241–59.

Phoenix, C. H. (1974). Prenatal testosterone in the nonhuman primate and its consequences for behavior. In R. Friedman, M. Richart, and R. L. Van de Wiele (eds), *Sex Differences in Behavior*. New York: Wiley.

Poirier, F. A. and Smith, E. O. (1974). Socializing functions of primate play. *American Zoologist* 14, 275–87.

Rosch, E. (1978). Principles of categorization. In E. Rosch and B. L. Lloyd (eds), *Cognition and Categorization*. London: Halstead Press.

Rosenblum, L. A. (1961). The development of social behavior in the rhesus monkey. Unpublished Ph.D. thesis, University of Wisconsin.

Sade, D. S. (1967). Determinants of dominance in a group of free-ranging rhesus monkeys. In S. A. Altmann (ed), *Social Communication among Primates*. Chicago: University of Chicago Press.

Smith, P. K. (1982). Does play matter? Functional and evolutionary aspects of animal and human play. *Behavioral and Brain Sciences* 5, 139–84.

Stevenson, M. F. (1978). The ontogeny of playful behaviour in family groups of the common marmoset. In D. J. Chivers and H. Herbert (eds), *Recent Advances in Primatology*. London: Academic Press.

Stevenson, M. F. and Poole, T. B. (1982). Playful interactions in family groups of the common marmoset (*Callithrix jacchus jacchus*). *Animal Behaviour* 30, 886–900.

Symons, D. (1974). Aggressive play and communication in rhesus monkeys (*Macaca mulatta*). *American Zoology* 14, 317–22.

Symons, D. (1978). *Play and Aggression: A Study of Rhesus Monkeys*. New York: Columbia University Press.

Toates, F. M. (1980). *Animal Behaviour: A Systems Approach*. Chichester: Wiley.

Vincent, L. E. and Bekoff, M. (1978). Quantitative analyses of the ontogeny of predatory behaviour in coyotes, *Canis latrans. Animal Behaviour* 26, 225–31.

White, L. (1977). The nature of social play and its role in the development of the rhesus monkey. Unpublished Ph.D. thesis, Cambridge University.

Williams, G. C. (1966). *Adaptation and Natural Selection*. Princeton: Princeton University Press.

PART 3
Reflections on Animal and Human Play

The three chapters in this part provide a link between the earlier sections on animal play, and the later sections on human play. Chapter 6, by Dietland Müller-Schwarze, reviews and highlights many of the problematic issues in the study of animal play which the reader will have had some acquaintance with from the previous part. Chapter 7, by Robert Fagen, is more speculative; it attempts to show how social play might foster behavioural flexibility, especially as the individual develops in an interactive way with the environment. Although the argument is ostensibly made for animal play, the extension to human play is suggestive and at times made explicit. Chapter 8, by Dennis Wolf, is on children's play, notably symbolic play; but it deliberately attempts to suggest concepts from the children's play which may be useful in the study of animal play. Also, its concern with the mechanics of how play can foster flexibility can be related back to the previous chapter by Fagen.

A number of provocative points emerge from Müller-Schwarze's chapter. Firstly, it reinforces the suggestion (e.g. from Martin, chapter 3) that some of the benefits of play *may* be immediate (even though they should not be *obvious* immediate benefits, otherwise by functional definition it is not play!). He and Fagen both conclude, in different styles, that juvenile behaviour such as play should not be considered as just a means of achieving the goal of adult behaviour; there may well be a trade-off between immediate, short-term, and long-term benefits.

Secondly, Müller-Schwarze illustrates the difficulties of comparative studies and of assessing the costs and benefits of play. Should we consider 1% of an animal's time budget spent in play as very little, or as quite appreciable when compared to resting metabolism? How can we quantify the benefits of play? Even the measurement of play is made difficult by the problems of whether to split or lump descriptive categories, and whether the behaviour is constrained by an artificial environment. Nevertheless, these difficulties are not insuperable, and comparative studies on closely related species, such as those on deer and caribou, may, as more detailed data are gathered, yield insights not obtainable in other ways. Modest inter-species differences in play may correlate with ecology and social organization; and these correlations may be less beset by problems of interpretation, such as equifinality, than the correlations of play experience with later viability or behaviour across individuals in the same species.

The notions of behavioural flexibility and innovation have often been related to play (see also Smith and Simon, chapter 9). Most commonly, they have been related to play with objects, but Fagen argues the case for social play. Firstly, he develops recent theorizing on the evolutionary stability of cooperative encounters in animals to suggest certain constraints on social play; it should be most complex and cooperative in group-living species where juveniles stay together and repeated encounters are likely. This is a more general case of the point that, for example, play-fighting is best done between friends, so that neither abuses or exploits the play convention (see also Humphreys and Smith, chapter 11).

Secondly, Fagen argues that social play (such as play-fighting) may well be the best way that a young animal has to develop flexible spatial skills *vis-à-vis* a changing environment. For coping with new environments in the future, a youngster might best play with an unpredictable partner than play with the present, familiar, environment. This would predict that play would be advantageous in a group of juveniles before dispersal. In many mammal species the young of one sex disperse from their natal environments as they reach sexual maturity; if Fagen is right, then the sex in question should play more (though other theories, such as that social play functions to develop fighting skills, would make the same prediction). Apart from general plausibility, Fagen's main evidence rests on the play-deprivation studies with rats, carried out by Einon and her co-workers and reviewed by Hole and Einon in chapter 4. Fagen's interpretation of these results with respect to possible functions of play is probably in line with Einon's, though developed further and more explicitly in this chapter.

Finally, Fagen emphasizes that the interaction between individual and environment is a mutually interactive, or dialectic, one. The distinction between social play and physical or object play is thus lessened. The interaction between individual and environment, and the way in which this may enhance flexibility, are also part of the theme of Wolf's chapter, based on the development of symbolic play in human children.

Wolf starts by discussing two ways in which human play may be generally different from animal play. One is that much human play is symbolic. It is consciously symbolic (the child knows that he or she is in pretend play) and thus is different from the presumably unconscious symbolism that may be involved in animal social play (Fagen) or the metacommunicative use of play signals. The other is that human play is culturally transmitted, varying in different societies. However, given what we are learning about traditions in animals (e.g. Mundinger, 1980) and about intra-species variation in play behaviour (Baldwin and Baldwin, 1974; Berger, 1980), there may well turn out to be less of a discontinuity in this latter respect than presently appears.

Wolf then delineates three types of variety in children's play. 'Repertoire' refers to different types or modes of play (such as object, motor, fantasy) which are species-typical. 'Style' refers to individual variation in choice of play modes. Finally, 'format' refers to intra-individual variations in the detailed form of play and how it is structured in relation to goal-directed activity. Wolf suggests that these may be useful concepts to take from human play back to animal play. For example, are some juvenile rats 'play-chasers' and others 'play-fighters'? Ethologists have typically documented age and sex differences in style, but individual differences have received little attention.

Amongst other ideas, Wolf relates the 'theme and variations' format of play to the notion of 'fooling around' with what would otherwise be serious means to an end. This is similar to Fagen's idea of play as being an object of discourse rather than a mechanism controlling behaviour.

The relation of behavioural flexibility to play (and whether it might be a 'weak' or 'strong' function of certain kinds of play in some species) remains controversial. Perhaps some further insight will come from attempting to see whether the concept of play style, and of play formats such as 'loop' and 'theme and variations' can be applied to animal play, in the way that it clearly can be to human play.

REFERENCES

Baldwin, J. D. and Baldwin, J. I. (1974). Exploration and social play in squirrel monkeys (*Saimiri*). *American Zoologist* 14, 303–15.

Berger, J. (1980). The ecology, structure and functions of social play in Bighorn sheep (*Ovis canadensis*). *Journal of Zoology (London)* 192, 531–42.

Mundinger, P. C. (1980). Animal cultures and a general theory of cultural evolution. *Ethology and Sociobiology* 1, 183–223.

6 Analysis of Play Behaviour: What do we Measure and When?

Dietland Müller-Schwarze

In this chapter I would like to urge the search for potential *early* benefits of animal play. To demonstrate such benefits, we have to decide what aspects of play to measure. Unfortunately, generalizations are difficult or impossible at present; different studies of the same or related species have recorded different behaviours at different ages of the animals, and under varying degrees of confinement. As an example of the use of natural history data, a preliminary comparison of three species of deer tries to relate play to the social organization, reproductive strategy and ecology of each species. The role of experiments on play is also briefly considered.

WHY DO ANIMALS PLAY?

The ultimate biological questions about play behaviour are that of its (inclusive) fitness-promoting value, and the selective pressures that have shaped play into its present form.

Subservient to these questions are the more specific ones of the ontogenetic (longitudinal) and short-term functions. What deficiencies are observed in animals that are prevented from playing, or are unable to play? How can such play deficiency be brought about experimentally? If we manipulate play behaviour, what are the most important dependent variables to measure? Is it more important *how* the animal plays, i.e. what play patterns are performed, who its partners are, and what forms the interactions take? Or are later effects (or defects) more dependent on *how much* play occurs, i.e. the amount of play in general, regardless of the form it takes? Specific skill effects would depend on the kind of play patterns. For instance, 'play-fighting' has been postulated to be a biological adaptation for acquiring motor skills that are needed for escalated fights (Symons, 1978). General exercise and practice of the neuromuscular and pulmocardiovascular systems on the other hand, would require frequent and/or continuous performance of unspecified motor patterns.

Taxonomic differences

Among mammals, play behaviour is most elaborate in primates and takes up a higher percentage of their time and energy budgets than in other mammals. Moreover, more papers on primate play have appeared than for any other order of mammals. A computer search of the most recent animal play literature yielded 25 papers on primates, and 24 for all other mammals combined. Ungulates, carnivores, and rodents were listed eight, seven, and six times, respectively. Because of this prevalence of primate studies, the danger of generalization to all mammals is ever present, and a careful look at other groups is needed not only for balance, but especially to appreciate evolutionary trends and specific adaptations. When are the putative effects to be measured? There may be immediate benefits (thermoregulation is a possible, though unlikely, example), caenogenetic benefits (those accruing to the animal while it is immature – *caenogenesis*: 'Appearance of youthful characters not affecting the adult' (Simpson, 1953)) or developmental effects which are fully evident only at reproductive age.

Amount of play and life expectancy

Does the amount of play correlate with the species' life-span so that the returns of the initial investment can be maximized (Smith, 1982)?

First, the amount of play is low and varies within a narrow range for many non-primate species. Captive black-tailed deer (*Odocoileus hemionus columbianus*) spend about 2% of their *time* in play (Müller-Schwarze, 1968), white tailed deer (*O. virginianus*) 1% (Müller-Schwarze et al., 1982), and pronghorn (*Antilocapra americana*) about 0.7% (Müller-Schwarze, unpublished data). Most mammals spend between 1 and 10% of their total time budget in play (Fagen, 1981: 273), though more species are closer to 1% than to 10%. Second, in the longer-lived primates, the value ranges all the way from 0% to 50% (various authors, in Fagen, 1981). Third, the same amount of play can be found in species of different life-spans. For instance, Norway rats (*Rattus norvegicus*) play for 0.4% of their total time (Müller-Schwarze, 1966), whereas in longer-lived caribou (*Rangifer tarandus*), calves play for 0.3% of their total time (Müller-Schwarze and Müller-Schwarze, 1983). Even though the intensity of play can be high for a short time, the portion of the daily energy budget allocated can actually be very low. However, it can be a large part of the energy expenditure *above resting metabolism*.

It seems reasonable to postulate an evolutionary trend, with the primates playing the most, but an exact quantitative scale is not available yet, as some data are from the field, and others from captive animals, or from populations on different nutritional planes. Different ages of the animals, times of day, or observational opportunities confound the difficulties of comparisons. The amount of play should perhaps be better related to the complexity of adult behaviour than to life-span.

Even if such a trend exists, are benefits correlated with the amount of play? Does less play mean fewer benefits, or the same benefits at lower cost (i.e. higher efficiency)? It should be stressed that the notion 'cost/benefit ratio' is misleading, as we are able to quantify only some of the costs, such as energy or time expended, but not risks taken, for example, and none of the benefits.

Early vs delayed benefits

The next point I would like to raise is the question of possible immediate benefits to the immature animal as opposed to delayed benefits for the adult. 'Physical stamina and fitness' (Smith, 1982) are advantageous to the immature animal as well as the adult. There are numerous possible effects on the neuromuscular, skeletal, or cardiovascular systems, and/or on the knowledge of terrain and the ability to negotiate it under varying weather conditions and degrees of alarm or stress. The two following examples are suggestive of such early benefits. I observed caribou calves running in laps, which consisted of an outward stretch up and along the steep slope of an esker with boulders and dwarf birch scrub, and a return run over sheer, level ice at the foot of the esker. Clearly, this behaviour contributes to the ability to handle highly variable terrain, a skill which might already be needed during the following hour, when travelling with the mother for miles with the additional possibility of being harassed by wolves. In caribou, play increases most rapidly during the first week of life (Müller-Schwarze and Müller-Schwarze, 1983). Why so early, if benefits accrue only in adulthood, i.e. two years later?

Black-tailed deer, when experimentally prevented from a high-intensity play bout of short duration at the typical time of day (morning or evening), will instead be active and explore for a longer time during the middle of the day (Müller-Schwarze, 1968). I suggest that this longer activity increases exposure to predators, and that exhaustion via play twice a day may have anti-predator benefits in that the young will remain sedentary for most of the remainder of the time, and still obtain their exercise. These are just two random examples of possible 'immediate', but not necessarily behaviour-specific, benefits. Indeed, practising of adult behaviours in play of the young includes several possible, distinctly different processes: 'honing', in the sense of becoming more precise (more channelled), and hence, more efficient, and the opposite, trying out new variations and combinations of motor patterns, thus becoming more flexible and variable.

What are the most critical components, steps or phases of adult behaviour that need to be rehearsed the most? Which parts of male – male competition, reproductive behaviour or predator-avoidance would benefit most from honing, polishing, or rehearsing earlier in life? Can we identify such 'behavioural bottlenecks' that would be candidates for meticulous practising, behavioural stepping-stones that count? If such critical patterns exist, and if they have precursors in play, the practice argument would be strengthened. If not, play may have general exercise effects, and is less significant as rehearsal of specific motor patterns.

One could make a case that in agonistic behaviour actual combat, and in sexual behaviour copulation, are the decisive steps in the chains of events, respectively. On the other hand, inefficient appetitive behaviours that precede fighting, or mounting, respectively, reduce the chance that an individual will ever have an opportunity to engage in these consummatory activities. Adult animals will far more often engage in threat behaviour, or courtship, than in combat or copulation, respectively. Furthermore, the distance-regulating behaviours of threatening and courting (which by the way, are related) require much more skill, flexibility, inter-individual signalling, and situational assessment (including the actions of third parties). Thus a strong case can be made that these are the behaviours that are most in need of early practising, and not the consummatory acts of fighting or copulation.

In the play repertoire of some sub-primate mammals the motor patterns of threat and courtship are precisely those that are conspicuously absent. In other words, most play is palingenetic, i.e. repeating general patterns common to many species of the taxon, but may be caenogenetic functionally, i.e. provide benefits early in ontogeny. If young animals primarily mount and wrestle in play, why do they 'practise' the wrong behaviours?

MEASURING PLAY

Simply put, we just don't yet know how much play is needed for what. In the absence of clearly recognizable benefits, and although we are unable to measure those postulated benefits, we can at least measure how much play occurs in a young animal under specified conditions. We can measure or calculate how much time and energy are spent in play relative to other activities (Fagen, 1981; Müller-Schwarze et al., 1982; Martin, 1984). From this we can infer its relative importance, on the assumption that the amount of play does indeed reflect its importance.

By necessity much of the data on play are obtained from domestic, laboratory, or captive wild animals. Are the kinds and amounts of play observed in these species and settings representative for wild animals in their natural environment? What light do observed differences of play behaviour in the field and in captivity shed on its functions?

Fortunately, we now have a good body of thorough studies of play across the mammalian orders, the emphasis on primates notwithstanding. Yet it is difficult to compare between studies as the circumstances of the studies vary greatly. In field studies, not all play may be observable, or not in great detail. Moreover, individuals often cannot be distinguished, or their age can only be estimated, as in caribou, for instance (Müller-Schwarze and Müller-Schwarze, 1983). In captivity, on the other hand, these problems can be eliminated, but social groupings are often artificial, and space limited. Recent measurements of play in primates, for instance, come from the field, but also from laboratory cages as small as $1.2 \times 1.2 \times 1.8$ m (e.g. Box, 1975). Similarly, single rats used in play observations were kept in cages $25 \times 20 \times 18$ cm, and groups of nine rats kept in $35 \times 70 \times 80$ cm cages (Leedy et al., 1980). Not surprisingly, running or chasing was not measured in this last study. The point is that play will take different forms, depending on space available, primarily, and cross-study comparisons are difficult to make.

The actual level of analysis varies greatly. Single steps and turns have been counted in ponies (Fagen and George, 1977), while in other species and circumstances the distance covered during running proved to be the most easily recorded variables. In captivity the shape of the pen may prescribe the turns and force the animals into circular patterns, as in a study of white-tailed deer (Müller-Schwarze et al., 1982). In the field where distances can only be estimated, timing of running bouts proved to be most satisfactory for caribou calves (Müller-Schwarze and Müller-Schwarze, 1983). In the latter two species running accounts for over 90% of the play activity, both in terms of time spent, and estimated energy expended. Thus, running can be used here as a measure of play.

In rats, 'pinning', in which one animal holds another to the ground, has been described as a good measure of play (Panksepp and Beatty, 1980); while others (Leedy et al., 1980) measured 'offensive and defensive play fights', mounting frequency and number of 'walkovers'. Müller-Schwarze

(1966, 1971) timed running, jumping, wrestling, plus exploratory sniffing. In other rodents different classifications are called for. For instance, in the yellow-bellied marmot (*Marmota flaviventris*) 'play fighting', chasing, mouth-sparring, grabbing, and wrestling have been distinguished and measured as rates (interactions per marmot hour; Nowicki and Armitage, 1979).

Primates, having the most complex play behaviour, and playing more than other mammals, offer even more diverse opportunities to select, lump together, or split behaviour patterns under study. Voland (1977) distinguished 38 play elements in the common marmoset (*Callithrix jacchus*). For rhesus monkeys (*Macaca mulatta*), one study (Rose et al., 1978) separated as play 'sequences of social interactions that incorporated play faces or invitation (widely open mouth with teeth exposed and rotary movements of the head or torso) or that were in complete sequences repeated in different patterns with frequent interruption and resumption'. This clearly leaves out any solitary play, such as locomotor or object play. A different approach in the same species was taken by Gard and Meier (1977). Forty-three motor patterns were distinguished and grouped into seven categories: rough-and-tumble, approach–withdrawal, object, sex, activity, aggressive and mixed play.

The chimpanzee, finally, has such finely differentiated behaviour that in social play alone the following patterns can be recognized: tickling, wrestling, biting, sparring, hitting and pushing, chasing, butting, kicking, dragging, finger-wrestling, pinching, rubbing, thrusting, play-face, play-walk, and laughing (Merrick, 1977).

Thus, it is clear that play measurements cannot be standardized; what is recorded depends on the question asked, what is recognizable, and what is feasible which in turn depends on field or laboratory conditions.

THREE CASE HISTORIES

It may be illuminating to correlate play behaviour with the social organization and ecology of a number of related, and well-studied, species. Such a comparison will illustrate some of the problems I have discussed, as well as the potential of observational and natural history data.

The caribou

The caribou, *Rangifer tarandus*, lives in an arctic and subarctic climate, and utilizes the tundra with its bogs, hills, eskers, lakes and streams in summer, and largely the taiga in winter. Seasonal migrations typically cover several hundred kilometres.

The life expectancy is 10–15 years, and caribou take three years to attain sexual maturity. The one young born per year is extremely precocial; it will eat solid food on its first day and can follow its mother for kilometres when only a few hours old. On the calving grounds, calves are with their mothers only. Yearlings separate from their mothers prior to calving, and males do not visit these areas. After calving, 'maternity bands' and 'post-calving aggregations', numbering several hundred mothers and calves, may form.

The social system of the caribou is extremely open, with group sizes and composition constantly changing, although mother and offspring, or two particular males, may travel together for years and form the basic social unit in the often large aggregation.

Agonistic behaviour is subtle, especially when groups encounter one another and merge. There is no territoriality. During breeding, a bull accompanies an oestrous cow and her calf for only a few hours. With few bulls and many oestrous cows, harems form for a short period. In captivity, a bull may guard all cows in an enclosure against other bulls, yearlings, or even people.

Predation pressure is variable. Five per cent annual mortality due to wolf predation is considered a high rate. In many areas human influence on caribou as well as wolf populations has changed predation to artificial levels. Predator diversity is low, wolves and man being the main predators. In the west, grizzly bears play a role, as does the lynx in certain areas, such as Newfoundland (Bergerud, 1971).

Play behaviour occurs from the second day of life on, and increases rapidly in duration and complexity until the age of about ten days. The most frequent play patterns are running, leaping, butting, striking, mounting and pawing. Running takes up most of the play time. The calves run at different speeds over various terrain-types such as ice, snow, rock, swamp, meadows, slopes, patches of dwarf birch, sand, or gravel. Since running constitutes over 90% of total play, it alone is used for further considerations.

The total amount of play averaged 0.31% of total observation time over three seasons (Müller-Schwarze and Müller-Schwarze, 1983). Since the calves were active 23.6% of the total observation time (or 5.66 hours per day), play took up 1.33% of their activity time, on the average. From season to season, the total amount of play changed significantly. The cows calved in different geographical areas during the three years, and more play was observed on the better quality range.

Our caribou play study has established benchmark values of play. The population in question, the George River herd, has increased over the past three decades, numbers currently about 300,000, and may well reach a peak soon.

For some mammals it has been shown that agonistic behaviour is significantly more frequent when the population density reaches its peak. This is the case for male voles of the species *Microtus pensylvanicus* and *M. ochrogaster* (Krebs et al., 1973). With increasing importance of agonistic behaviour during a population cycle, play would be expected to be increasingly important, too, if indeed it does prepare the growing animal for adult aggressive behaviour. Such changing frequencies of social play during the population cycle have not been observed yet. However, two countervailing pressures may obscure any effects of population density. The increased importance of agonistic behaviour in adulthood may intensify the 'preparation value' of juvenile play-fighting, running and chasing. On the other hand, an extreme population density may stress mothers and calves, so that play becomes reduced for energetic reasons. These two possible factors are amenable to testing in the field.

The black-tailed deer

The black-tailed deer, *Odocoileus hemionus columbianus*, lives in a temperate climate on the west coast of North America. Its habitat is variable and includes chaparral, forest and savannah. Seasonal migration is altitudinal in the coastal mountain ranges.

Life-expectancy is about 9 to 15 years. Time to sexual maturity is two years, but yearlings, or even fawns, may breed. Typically, two young are born, but fawns and yearlings have singletons. During their first days and weeks the young are *Ablieger*, spending a large proportion of their time resting under cover while the mother forages. Weaning occurs at the age of three months. Mothers separate from conspecifics prior to parturition and join with yearlings and other females to form small maternal bands.

Groups are more stable than in the caribou, and intergroup aggression is frequent, especially when the fawns are still young. There is a rich repertoire of agonistic signals which are shown all the year round. Even fawn–fawn aggression is frequent. Individuals maintain home ranges that may in certain situations be termed incipient territories or 'facultative territories'. At high population densities black-tailed deer are even more aggressive (Dasmann and Taber, 1956). At breeding time, the buck is intolerant of other males and follows one female at a time, as they come into heat. Even in captivity, a buck associates with only one female at a time. Original predator pressure was exerted by coyotes and mountain lions. Today, the main pressure is exerted by man and domestic dogs.

Play behaviour occurs about six days of age on. It increases in intensity until about 2.5 months of age when play bouts become rarer, but remain intense when they occur. The most frequent motor patterns are head jerk, leaping, running, butting, striking, mounting, pushing, neck-craning, neck-twisting, head-shaking, and reclining. Social running can take the form of following, chasing, or intercepting wth striking with one or two forelegs. The duration of running is 3–4 minutes, the other patterns being intermittently distributed over a period of about 20 min.

Two- to four-month-old fawns were active 37% of total observation time, and played for 3.3%. Play thus took up 8.9% of their activity time; it was less in younger fawns.

The white-tailed deer

The white-tailed deer, *Odocoileus virginianus*, inhabits the woodlands of Eastern North America, and various subspecies reach central and northern parts of South America. It uses open fields and forest edges for foraging, and mature forests for cover. Seasonal migrations are elevational and cover from 10 to 12 kilometres. Life-expectancy is 8 to 12 years. Sexual maturity is reached at two years. On the average, 1.2 fawns are born per doe, though older age classes (4.5–7.5 years) average 2.0 fawns. Weaning occurs at the age of four months.

The social unit is a mother with her yearling and fawn(s). Males tend to be solitary, or form small bachelor groups. During mating time, bucks occupy and scent-mark mating areas, which the doe will be attracted to. The social system appears to be more open than that of the black-tailed deer. In Florida the author observed groups frequently splitting up and joining. Group size varies with habitat, with larger bands in more open terrain (own observation; see also Hirth, 1977). Predator pressure over most of the range of the white-tailed deer is exerted primarily by man and domestic dogs.

Play behaviour occurs from about one week of age on, and resembles very closely that of the black-tailed deer, with running, striking, and mounting predominating.

Comparisons

Can comparisons between the play behaviour of these three deer species, with their different behavioural ecology, shed light on the function of play? And, if so in principle, do we have enough data to make valid comparisons?

Thus far, some data come from the field, and some from captivity, and animals have been studied at different ages. Still, despite far-reaching divergences in anatomy, behaviour, and ecology, the patterns and amounts of play that have been measured thus far, are remarkably similar in *Rangifer* and *Odocoileus*. Most of the playing time is spent in motor patterns of escape behaviour, plus some fighting and mounting.

What, on the other hand, are the differences? In *Odocoileus*, we find more agonistic patterns in play, such as striking, butting, intercepting, or mounting than in *Rangifer*. This seems to foreshadow the more open social system of adult caribou. However, we do not know whether the more aggressive play and the more competitive adult behaviour in *Odocoileus* are simply manifestations of the same predisposition or whether the latter is a consequence of the former. We do not know whether play is actually necessary for polishing aggressive behaviour and increasing its efficiency.

None of the three species shows threat or courtship behaviour in play. Threat behaviour in black-tailed deer, for instance, includes ruffling of the entire fur, lowering the head, laying back the ears, spreading the tarsal hair tufts and snorting; another example is rubbing the hocks together and urinating over them ('rub-urinating', Müller-Schwarze, 1971). None of these motor patterns occur in play, although they are precisely the ones whose practising, especially in various pattern combinations, would confer benefits to the individual.

EXPERIMENTATION

Overall, play behaviour has not been particularly amenable to experimental manipulation. This is mainly because play cannot be easily staged; we are not sure whether and which stimuli release or control play. Furthermore, we cannot easily recreate the complex and delicate equilibrium of internal states that favours the occurrence of play behaviour.

In his landmark book, Fagen (1981) is sceptical about the few experimental studies of play available at that time: 'Unfortunately, past experiments on play (e.g., Chepko, 1971; Hansen, 1974; Müller-Schwarze, 1968) were unsatisfactory. These experiments were based on deprivation and isolation paradigms now known to be faulty (Bekoff, 1976; P. P. G. Bateson, 1976), and the interpretation of these experiments is questionable at best (Bekoff, 1976). Experiments as such have done no more to advance play research than numbers as such.'

I shall use this opportunity to reconsider this statement. Bateson (1976) deals with the developmental determinants of behaviour and in particular with the nature of the 'relevant' experience for the acquisition and refinement of behaviours. Bekoff (1976) discusses social isolation experiments and states in this context: 'play experience is not the *only* type of social interaction that is prevented'. Neither author quotes or discusses the play deprivation studies.

The play studies cited by Fagen, on the other hand, have employed selective short-term *play* deprivation, and not long-term *social* deprivation. In fact, the black-tailed deer used by Müller-Schwarze (1968) were raised as a group and never separated, not even during the selective play deprivation. The question asked was whether play can be intensified by prevention of play for hours or days, and not how play develops in the absence of play partners. The play deprivation studies dealt with rebound effects, and not with development, or acquisition of (social) skills.

Recently, however, short-term social isolation has been used as a method to manipulate play behaviour in rats. When put together after either 8 or 24 hours of social isolation, laboratory rats spent more time together and 'pinned' each other more often to the ground (Panksepp and Beatty, 1980).

We now need not only experiments, but also detailed observations under natural conditions. Experiments should not only measure but also manipulate the amount and quality of play of immature animals, and thus the energetic cost relative to other bodily needs. The cost in terms of risk of injury or death should be estimated as precisely as possible. Effects of varying play performance should be monitored at all ages, not only in adulthood.

Where experiments are not feasible, longitudinal observations should correlate play amounts with later behavioural efficiency as they occur naturally in the field. Given the complexity of both play and adult behaviour, the challenge to select the right variables is formidable.

REFERENCES

Bateson, P. P. G. (1976). Specificity and the origins of behavior. In J. Rosenblatt, R. Hinde, E. Shaw and C. Beer (eds), *Advances in the Study of Behavior*, vol. 6, 1–20. New York: Academic Press.

Bekoff, M. (1976). The social deprivation paradigm: who's being deprived of what? *Developmental Psychobiology* 9, 497–8.

Bergerud, A. T. (1971). The population dynamics of the Newfoundland caribou. *Wildlife Monographs* No. 25.

Box, H. O. (1975). A social developmental study of young monkeys (*Callithrix jacchus*) within a captive family group. *Primates* 16, 419–35.

Chepko, B. D. (1971). A preliminary study of the effects of play deprivation of young goats. *Zeitschrift für Tierpsychologie* 28, 517–26.

Dasmann, R. F. and Taber, R. D. (1956). Behavior of Columbian black-tailed deer with reference to population ecology. *Journal of Mammalogy* 37, 143–64.

Fagen, R. M. (1981). *Animal Play Behavior*. New York: Oxford University Press.

Fagen, R. M. and George, T. K. (1977). Play behavior and exercise in young ponies (*Equus caballus* L.). *Behavioral Ecology and Sociobiology* 2, 267–9.

Gard, G. C. and Meier, G. W. (1977). Social and contextual factors of play behavior in subadult rhesus monkeys. *Primates* 18, 367–78.

Hansen, E. W. (1974). Some aspects of behavioral development in evolutionary perspective. In N. F. White (ed.), *Ethology and Psychiatry*. Toronto: University of Toronto Press, 182–6.

Hirth, D. H. (1977). Social behavior of white-tailed deer in relation to habitat. *Wildlife Monographs* No. 53.

Krebs, C. J., Gaines, M. S., Keller, B. L., Meyers, J. H. and Tamario, R. H. (1973). Population cycles in small rodents. *Science* 179, 35–44.

Leedy, M. G., Vela, E. A., Popolow, H. B. and Gerall, A. A. (1980). Effect of prepuberal medial preoptic area lesions on male rat sexual behavior. *Physiology and Behavior* 24, 341–6.

Martin, P. (1984). The time and energy costs of play behaviour in the cat. *Zeitschrift für Tierpsychologie* 64, in press.

Merrick, N. J. (1977). Social grooming and play behavior of a captive group of chimpanzees. *Primates* 18, 215–24.

Müller-Schwarze, D. (1966). Experimente zur Triebspezifität des Säugetierspiels. *Die Naturwissenschaften* 53, 137–8.

Müller-Schwarze, D. (1968). Play deprivation in deer. *Behaviour* 31, 144–62.

Müller-Schwarze, D. (1971). Ludic behavior in young mammals. In M. B. Sterman, D. J. McGinty and A. M. Adinolfi (eds), *Brain Development and Behavior*. New York: Academic Press.

Müller-Schwarze, D. and Müller-Schwarze, C. (1983). Play behavior in free-ranging caribou, *Rangifer tarandus*. *Acta Zoologica Fennica* 175, 121–4.

Müller-Schwarze, D., Stagge, B. and Müller-Schwarze, C. (1982). Play behavior: Persistence, decrease and energetic compensation during food shortage in deer fawns. *Science* 215, 85–7.

Nowicki, S. and Armitage, K. B. (1979). Behavior of juvenile yellow-bellied marmots, *Marmota flaviventris*: play and social integration. *Zeitschrift für Tierpsychologie* 51, 85–105.

Panksepp, J. and Beatty, W. W. (1980). Social deprivation and play in rats. *Behavioral and Neural Biology* 30, 197–206.

Rose, R. M., Bernstein, I. S., Gordon, T. P. and Lindley, J. G. (1978). Changes in testosterone and behavior during adolescence in the male rhesus monkey. *Psychosomatic Medicine* 40, 60–70.

Simpson, G. G. (1953). *The Major Features of Evolution*. New York: Columbia University Press.

Smith, P. K. (1982). Does play matter? Functional and evolutionary aspects of animal and human play. *Behavioral and Brain Sciences* 5, 139–84.

Symons, D,. (1978). The question of function: Dominance and play. In E. O. Smith (ed.), *Social Play in Primates*. New York: Academic Press.

Voland, E. (1977). Social play behavior of the common marmoset *Callithrix jacchus* in captivity. *Primates* 18, 883–902.

7   Play and Behavioural Flexibility

Robert Fagen

INTRODUCTION

Social constraints, spatial skills, and active interplay between organism and environment are three biological ideas that enliven the study of animal play. This chapter is about new research directions that develop from these ideas.

Social constraints

An individual's opportunity to interact repeatedly with the same partner influences the degree of cooperation, interaction, physical contact, and risk of injury in social play with that partner.

Spatial skills

Play experience develops skills important for actively perceiving and creating relationships in space and for using spatially distributed resources.

Organism and environment

Learning animals whose experience and behaviour assemble and alter environments use play to produce experience that enables the player to create, transform, and reconstruct nature according to its laws.

Observed, play is aesthetically eloquent. It fascinates the senses and entertains the mind. On an intellectual stage set by ethology and illuminated by sociobiology, however, play is scientifically mute. It has a bit-part with no spoken lines, and its place is obscure. Sociobiological and quantitative ethological studies of play are still forced and unnatural. It is as if scientists sought to make play conform to a pre-existing stereotype of behaviour, only to find that these contrived scenarios did not capture major features of play and did not yield results of scientific value.

WHAT IS PLAY IN ANIMALS?

The term 'play' is not consistently applied in research on animal behaviour. As I will use it here, play means behavioural performances that emphasize skills for interacting with the physical and social environments and that occur under circumstances under which the function of the exercised skills cannot possibly be achieved. The essential features of play are that it occurs in a paradoxical context (Millar, 1982) and that it embodies cognitive structures in which rules for interacting with, adjusting to, or creating environments are treated actively as objects of discourse rather than as plans controlling behaviour. Play inverts normal relationships between plans and the structure of behaviour, or between experience and behavioural predispositions. In play, the plan is no longer a mechanism controlling behaviour. Rather, it becomes an object of discourse. The behavioural predispositions, and the environment that both creates and is created by them, are the experience. For example, play in domestic cats involves friendly social encounters and object manipulation in which species-typical sequences used in fighting and predation become, in effect, objects whose relationship to the social and physical environment is manipulated, varied and explored. Bateson (1956) sought to express this distinction by saying that play produces the learned ability to set behaviour to 'a logical type or style' in a way that relates to 'the frame and context of behavior'. Altmann (1962) explores these ideas in his analysis of rhesus macaque games.

Two recurrent issues in play research that often surface in definitional arguments are questions of immediate versus delayed effects and of practice versus flexibility (or innovation). In a model of play in the life-history (Fagen, 1977) I assumed that play had immediate costs and delayed benefits. In making this assumption I supposed that play was risky and cost energy and time, so that an individual's probability of survival in a year during which it played, as well as its growth and reproduction during that year, would be decreased as a result of participation in play. Physical training, learning, skill development, and other plausible benefits of play were assumed to be delayed in time relative to the costs of play – perhaps even until adulthood. If play produces a stronger and more skilled juvenile, its benefits will not necessarily be delayed until adulthood, but the point is that they will be delayed, if only slightly, *relative to* the costs mentioned above. For example, on a given day a human might risk injury and spend time in vigorous physical exercise. On that day, survivorship, growth and the individual's chance of reproduction would all possibly be less for that individual than they would have been for that individual in the absence of play. If these 'workouts' continued, over the following weeks the individual would notice some improvement in its physical condition. Relative to a sedentary individual, it would then be better able to meet threats to its physical well-being; it would be able to find more food more efficiently in less time, leading to enhanced growth; and it might find its reproductive chances enhanced as well.

What about play and innovation? Milne-Edward's aphorism 'Nature is prodigal in variety, but niggard in invention' sums up the problem (as Darwin realized, for he approvingly quotes this statement in chapter 6 of the *Origin*). What is really important, in fact, in science and presumably also in individual development, is the ability to recognize the importance of novel behaviours (including ideas) and to capitalize on them (Gould, 1982). Real innovations are generally small and unspectacular. An innovation, although qualitatively new by definition, involves restructuring something that already exists. Reorganization and recombination are the hallmarks of innovation (Barnett, 1953). As biologists, we may be less than comfortable (as was Darwin) with the idea that nature is constantly inventing qualitatively new forms. What is novel about natural variation is its pervasive and persistent richness, and what is interesting about mechanisms for innovation is that they act to recreate and to preserve this variety.

SOCIAL CONSTRAINTS: HARLEQUIN'S DILEMMA AND THE EVOLUTION OF FAIR PLAY

Two central problems in the study of social play are reconciliation of individual self-interest with cooperative play (Fagen, 1981) and the evolutionary significance of repeated interactions between the same play partners (Fagen, 1981). Robert Axelrod and William D. Hamilton (1981), in an important theoretical analysis of the evolution of cooperation, demonstrated that the opportunity for repeated interaction is necessary for cooperation and that close kinship plus repeated interaction can lead to the evolution of stable cooperation between individuals. I think that Axelrod and Hamilton's theory can potentially explain many characteristics of play in a way that leads to respectable scientific research. To me, their theoretical results are especially impressive because they tie together two unsolved problems in play research and offer a simple solution to both.

Axelrod and Hamilton showed that if the same individuals can interact repeatedly in a 'prisoner's dilemma' game of the type often used in models of social behaviour (e.g. Dawkins, 1976), a so-called 'tit for tat' strategy will be evolutionarily stable if the individual's probability of meeting again is sufficiently high. Tit for tat means that if the partner was cooperative in their previous encounter, then the player will reciprocate by cooperating in their current encounter. But a player obeying 'tit for tat' will act selfishly if the partner had behaved selfishly in their immediately-preceding encounter.

Now consider two animals (Fagen, 1981) whose needs and requirements in play do not inevitably agree. Suppose animal A is frequently motivated to play, B only seldom. Or suppose A needs to wrestle, B to chase. Conceivably, the animals could waste the rest of their childhood arguing about how and whether to play. They might even fight over this conflict of interest. The resulting impasse might be called 'Harlequin's Dilemma': to play or not to play with a partner whose favourite game is different from one's own. The situation can be modelled as an evolutionary game using the theory of evolutionarily stable strategies (Fagen, 1981). In real situations, the availability of other partners and the possibility of playing alone lead to additional mathematical complexities. I believe, nevertheless, that reciprocal cooperation in repeated encounters is the most powerful idea we have for understanding sociobiological aspects of play. It leads to the following predictions:

1   The opportunity for repeated encounters is maximized in group-living species when fecundity, juvenile survivorship, and age at dispersal are all high. Often, this combination of demographic parameters occurs in expanding populations in environments where resources are abundant and/or rapidly renewing. We would expect that social play at its most complex and cooperative would occur in such species. This prediction explains many known correlations between adult sociality and complexity of play (Fagen, 1981). For example, social play is most frequent in marmot (*Marmota*: Rodentia, Sciuridae) species with large adult group sizes and relatively great tolerance for young (Barash, 1976). Orang-utans (*Pongo pygmaeus*) on Sumatra are more playful than on Borneo, an apparent consequence of the greater stability of Sumatran orang groups (Rijksen, 1978). Similar gradients occur in cervids (roe deer–red deer, white–tailed deer–black-tailed deer) (Fagen, 1981).

2   Physical contact in play should be facilitated by repeated interaction because close contact is potentially dangerous if animals have a misunderstanding and a fight begins. If we create a scale of physical contact in play, from approach–withdrawal to grappling to wrestling, I would predict, based on Axelrod and Hamilton's theory, that measures of the degree of physical contact in play would be positively correlated with individuals' probability of meeting again.

3   More generally, measures of the degrees of interactiveness and

fairness of play or complexity of the rules of play should be positively correlated with re-encounter probabilities for the same reasons as in (2) and because individuals will only cooperate to learn the rules of a complex game if they trust each other to follow them. Consider, for example, rapid approach–withdrawal play involving tightly interwoven chase–flee sequences and sudden reversals of direction and role. Here, lack of cooperation could lead to injuries through collisions or falls, even though the game itself involves no body contact.

4 If Axelrod and Hamilton's theory (and my interpretation of it) are correct, repeated play encounters will permit the evolution of types of play having certain functions. When repeated play encounters are not possible, (a) other forms of play may evolve to fulfil the same function, or; (b) the benefits of cooperative social play will be impossible and if these benefits are necessary they will have to be produced by other behaviour.

In either case, social constraints will affect the form of play and the function it serves. The action of the behavioural control mechanisms that reflect these social constraints will affect quantitative measures of the diversity of play's control mechanisms. Social factors alone can affect the form, function and control of play.

The theory has yet to be given a full-scale test. There is possibly a minor problem of controlling for group size independent of re-encounter probability. The theory is not a trivial restatement of the tautology that social play cannot occur in solitary species. Rather, it predicts that even in large social groups, individuals will play alone (or not at all) if the same partners are not repeatedly available. Turnover rate is an important parameter to be considered. (Does this explain the apparent lack of social play in giraffe herds, whose membership is quite fluid by artiodactyl standards? What about qualities of play under different arrangements for child day-care?)

Females in many species of cercopithecine primates are born at the same rate as males, survive better than males through their years of immaturity, and disperse much later if at all (Altmann et al., 1977; Dittus, 1980). If Axelrod and Hamilton are correct and all other things are equal, females should play with more body contact and more cooperatively than males, and they should exhibit a greater tendency to social play. However, female cercopithecines appear to be less playful on these measures (e.g. Symons, 1978). Is the reason for this difference in frequency, as Symons suggests, that males have more to gain, in evolutionary sense, from contact play, despite its greater risk?

SPATIAL SKILLS: PLAY AND THE USE OF SPACE

In Norway rats (*Rattus norvegicus*), a fairly clear picture of the effects of social play is now emerging. Flexible spatial skills – the abilities needed to get around in the world – seem to be the key behaviour elements affected by play. Just like a skilled mountaineer, backpacker, hunter, or explorer, an animal has to find its way in an intricate world. How does one travel from point A to point B? Choosing routes, navigating obstacles, and integrating feeding as well as predator and hazard avoidance with the physical features of the habitat are not trivial skills, as Menzel (1978) has convincingly argued and as any skilled mountain-walker can verify. It takes flexibility to perform these tasks with skill, flair, and gusto. The ecological study of habitat (Southwood, 1977), ethologists' and psychologists' approaches to spatial skill (Menzel, 1978; Potegal, 1982), and physiological analyses of underlying brain mechanisms primarily in the hippocampus (O'Keefe and Nadel, 1978) tell a rewarding and increasingly integrated story.

As Einon and Morgan (1977) have argued and experimentally demonstrated, social play in rats appears to have its greatest demonstrable impact on behavioural adjustments of and to what Moermond (1979) has called habitat constraints. Their studies (reviewed in Fagen, 1982) found that social play differentially enhanced rats' abilities to make complex choices involving spatial orientation and locomotor behaviour in a changing physical setting. For example, many kinds of prior experience (including play and exploration) help rats cope with mazes and obstacles in their quest for food, but only social play experience was effective as preparation for situations requiring the rat to reverse a previously learned spatial strategy or to use alternate locomotor behaviours. Einon and Morgan's studies indicate that social play experience was most effective (and uniquely so) in developing spatial flexibility in rats – the ability to adjust properties of their physical environment and to adjust to change in physical properties of the environment.

This hypothesis seems paradoxical – it is roughly equivalent to the statement that the best way to develop as a mountaineer or backpacker is to participate in the sport of wrestling. This claim is certainly not intuitive, but I find it convincing, independently of any evidence that social play does or does not affect fighting skill in rats and independently of the tightening experimental links between play, spatial skill, and the hippocampus. Suppose, as will be argued in the next section of this paper, that the skills of interaction with the physical environment are those of active manipulation, not passive response to fixed a priori stimuli. Then

the best practice for such challenges, in the absence of actual opportunities to range widely and independently, might well be a physical
give-and-take with a complex, responsive but somewhat unpredictable
partner. A monkey who climbs on to a bigger monkey, grabs its hair, and
tumbles off is not conscious that these skills are useful in climbing
unfamiliar rocks and trees. It is probably not pretending to itself that it is
climbing a rock or a tree. It certainly doesn't understand why climbing on
an entertainingly unpredictable friend may actually be better practice for
climbing a new type of tree or a strange rock formation than climbing its
familiar local trees and rocks would be. But we can plausibly understand
how these things could be true in an evolutionary sense and how male
monkeys, who often disperse to new environments, might have especially
great biological needs to play with partners rather than to actively explore
the same physical surroundings that they had already mastered and
played on hundreds of times.

Let us suppose, furthermore, that the physical environment is not a
given, fixed set of quantities but that it is only defined and becomes
meaningful as an individual's experience with it develops or brings out
certain salient qualities in relation to that individual. For example, a rock
with a hollow under it is fundamentally different to an inexperienced
observer, who may merely view it as a blob in the landscape, and to a
play-experienced animal who has used the hollow as a place for hiding
and for ambushing during social play. In particular, social play involving
objects and features of the landscape enables each individual to interact
with a landscape as actively perceived and experienced by that other
individual. The result is not merely familiarity but, much more important, flexibility. By this I mean the ability to experience the spatial
environment using varying frames of reference which are, at least in part,
socially defined; and the ability to manipulate and shape one's own and
others' active formulations of space and of the physical relationships
within actively defined space. I would expect that these skills are
particularly important in future social interactions involving the physical
environment – prey–predator, escalated fighting, as well as courtship and
some kinds of threat displays. Perhaps, then, it is most fruitful to look for
social play as a source of certain kinds of flexible spatial skills – not
necessarily all skills used in interacting with the habitat, but perhaps
especially the ability to make those adjustments that require simultaneous and interacting social and spatial flexibility. Here, as in social play,
the nature of the physical environment in any particular social interaction, depends on what conspecifics or the potential prey (predator) are
doing. Even at the (relatively) mundane level of physical training, the
ability to engage in behaviour in which the particular muscle groups

exercised depend on partners' interactions with a shared, but not identically perceived or experienced, physical environment, could be quite important to short-term survival and long-term reproductive success. Perhaps, then, social play involves learning or reformulating skills in the light of a developing perception (not necessarily conscious) that the physical environment as it affects survival and reproduction is not a fixed, constant unitary thing 'out there' but rather a dynamic process that is defined and even created by the animal's own behaviour and by the behaviour of other organisms. This view will be further expanded in the next section of the chapter.

ORGANISM AND ENVIRONMENT: PLAY AND THE DIALECTICS OF SKILL

Environments, like phenotypes, are not given but made, not interpreted but changed. They are created by an organism's behavioural tendencies and experiences within broad constraints imposed by the laws of nature. There is a sense in which creativity and behavioural flexibility are focal ecological concepts, at least in animals which assemble and alter their environments by learning and remembering. In this view of ecology and evolution, play becomes a central theme: it is the source of those attitudes, experiences and skills which enables the animal to take an active rather than a passive role in its ecological interactions.

This idea of ecological dialectics, expounded most recently by Levins (1979) and Lewontin (1983) (see also Lewontin and Levins, 1978; Levins and Lewontin, 1980) has some antecedents in the pre-Lorenzian, Continental ethology of von Uexküll and Köhler, and parallels in American psychology's responses to behaviourism (e.g. the work of Bruner, Bronfenbrenner, or Krech). Equally, Dawkins's (1981) concept of the extended phenotype owes much to these European ideas. If the true strength of ethology lies in its earliest roots, perhaps students of animal behaviour should first seek out Köhler and von Uexküll for perpetually fresh ethological insight (I do not claim that Köhler or von Uexküll were immune to the prejudices of their time. It is not enough to argue that their philosophies were misrepresented by later ethologists for political purposes. Rather, it is possible to recognize von Uexküll and Köhler despite the fact that they often failed to see and publicize broad biological implications of their ideas and even though ethology as a whole has not always treated their insights kindly).

The idea that ecological interactions follow a dialectical path is a challenge. Developmental psychologists have already learned to view infants as cognitively alert, constantly manipulative agents rather than as passive receptacles for parental care and attitudes. This idea may well appeal to students of play who have sought in vain in current-day mechanistic ethology and sociobiology for concepts even vaguely resembling an active behavioural interchange where organism and environment mutually penetrate. In addition to Bruner and his students, the two commentators who have probably come closest to discovering a dialectical role for play in the life cycle are Eibl-Eibesfeldt (1967: play as an experimental dialogue with the environment) and Sutton-Smith (1971: play as active exercise of voluntary control systems with disequilibrial outcomes).

The new interpretation of behavioural ecology as active reconstruction is abstract and philosophical. Most scientists would probably be grateful for a more tangible manifestation of these concepts. I believe that MacArthur's (1958) classic study of warbler behavioural ecology, which demonstrated behavioural resource partitioning among five closely related warbler species in the same coniferous forest habitat, is meaningful in just this light but has not been correctly interpreted or properly appreciated by most previous commentators. MacArthur, well aware of the ecological dialectic, interpreted his observations to indicate that 'the birds behave in such a way as to be exposed to different kinds of food'. He further identified two of the five warbler species as fugitive species, ecological opportunists that depend on occasional outbreaks of superabundant food for their continued existence and whose numbers accordingly fluctuate dramatically (and often unpredictably) in space and time. These coniferous forest communities would in fact exhibit more lively dynamics than those of equilibrium models based on the Lotka –Volterra competition equations (Holling, 1973; Levins, 1979; Ludwig, Jones and Holling, 1978).

Paradigmatic studies of actual manifestations of the ecological dialectic, whether in behavioural ecology or in play research, remain to be done. Of course, much of the rich field material on complex play interaction is suggestive.

The smoothness, fluidity, grace, or variety of skilled behaviour are possible indicators of the flexibility with which these skills serve to reconstruct both organism and environment: interaction itself as that which is manipulated. Baldwin and Baldwin (1974) noted that squirrel monkeys (*Saimiri* sp.) without recent play experience appeared to have the same physical and social skills as did play-experienced conspecifics in ther populations, but they were exhibited infrequently and performed unceremoniously, in rudimentary form. Copulations, for example, 'consisted of very brief episodes of mounting and thrusting, without any of the consort activities seen in other environments'. Berger (1979) found that playful populations of mountain sheep were more behaviourally diverse, although all populations exhibited the same basic locomotor and social skills. Konner (1982), citing an early study of differential motor exercise in infancy, argues that some effects of early experience may involve qualities such as grace of movement. Perhaps, Konner comments, there are also differences of grace and tone in the cognitive and emotional realms. These subtle characteristics are possible candidates for effects of play and for effects on flexibility of behaviour. Grace and tone are aesthetic qualities. Do they have biological and functional implications as well?

At least in humans, a landscape is, in large part, what we think about it. The trail that led down to the beach from an Alaskan cabin where I once lived is an example. Most of this 'trail' was vertical, a descent via fixed rope down a steep cliff. Formidable though it appeared when viewed as a whole from above or from below, the trail was easy when viewed one step at a time in the mind's eye during actual travel. Each move was technically trivial, although the whole was fairly spectacular. One skill that must be very important for route-finding in learning organisms is the ability to switch perspectives (as in an optical illusion like the Schroeder staircase: Bruner, Postman, and Mosteller 1950). That way it is possible first to plan a route beginning from a general view and exploration of the surroundings, and then to follow that route in person by looking at its details. True, it was also possible to descend the cliff trail stiffly, inch by inch, clinging fearfully and gracelessly to the rope while looking down in terror, but that strategy is a lot less flexible (what if something unexpected happens halfway down?) and not nearly as enjoyable. Incidentally (Tukey, 1977) Bruner, Postman and Mosteller's experiment includes data indicating that human subjects can learn to reverse their perspective and actively switch from one view of an ambiguous optical illusion to another. Does play develop analogous abilities in animals, being used perhaps to make spatial adjustments, or to adjust locomotor behaviour, especially in social situations?

TWO VIGNETTES

In all the rich phenomenology of animal play, the deepest impressions are left by accounts of behaviour involving integrated locomotor and social interactions and incorporating physical objects, features of the living and physical landscape, and characteristics of the terrain. Such complexity may include gamelike interactions characterized by identifiable roles and apparent rules, and it may even involve other species.

Bafflement, delight, and lively intellectual fascination are three human responses to animal play. Although play may be difficult and even unrewarding to study, it is never dull. On the contrary. Play enriches: through the artistry of its movements and contexts, through the intellectual richness of the controversy it engenders, and through still-debated benefits to the player. Take artistry. Young baboons in the East African savannah below Kilimanjaro climb and jump on dead trees, play king of the mountain on stumps, and duck through a maze of tangled thicket or bounce on the springy branches. Joan Luft and Jeanne Altmann (1982) vividly describe the play of two ten-month-old youngsters: 'Giles runs by with a bright feather in his teeth, like a flamenco dancer with a rose, and Putz comes running after him, eager to take the feather away'. In another wilderness, Alaska's Admiralty Island, film-maker Joel Bennett (1982) recorded the play of a young brown bear cub running at and chasing birds, then head-shaking, capering and pirouetting as if elated by this demonstration of its ability to make things happen.

These recent reports document animal play in the wild combining object-oriented locomotor and social elements. Sober facts, to be sure. The style of baboon field study pioneered by the Altmanns and Glenn Hausfater stresses insightful quantitative approaches and stays close to the data, forgoing trendy sociobiological interpretation and extrapolations to human nature. Bennett's brown bear film plainly depicts the cub chasing birds and cavorting. Bennett has no scientific axes to grind. Earlier accounts of young cercopithecine primates in East Africa playing with bright-coloured feathers (Struhsaker, 1967) and brown bear cubs on Admiralty Island exuberantly chasing waterfowl (Holzworth, 1930) might well have been dismissed as imaginative anecdotes or as colourful reminders of the era of rugged individualism in wildlife research. I believe that students of play need to be constantly reminded that such things actually happen, and are important to theory, because noteworthy events may otherwise escape attention or fail to be recorded. A priori behavioural categories, check-lists, and generic statistics such as those of time and energy budgets fail to capture what may be the principal feature of play. Play is performance, in a unique paradoxical context, of active behavioural interactions that enable the player to adjust to and create its own environment, both ecological and social. Anything less may well be interesting (and particularly amenable to quantitative experimental study in the impoverished environments of captivity, in behavioural research laboratories, and under the influence of domestication and provisioning), but whether it is play remains debatable.

WHERE HAVE WE BEEN?

Theoretical sections of the chapter have been consciously eclectic. New developments in sociobiology contribute the idea that social factors, especially the likelihood of cooperation, influence the structure of behaviour and its control mechanism. Sociobiological analysis may serve to explain much existing variation, particularly in cooperativeness, interactiveness, and gregariousness of play.

Recent philosophical analyses in ecology lend biological support to earlier views of Buhler ('functional pleasure'), Groos ('joy in being a cause'), Sutton-Smith, and Bruner that a key to understanding is to emphasize animals' active construction of their environments through play and through play-developed interactive skills. The idea that organisms, unlike machines, actively construct their own environments suggests that play helps intelligent animals develop the skills of active environment-building in a changing, uncertain, incompletely defined world chiefly constrained by their own nature and by physical laws. Intelligence then takes the place of a genetic blueprint or morphological plasticity in shaping patterns of environmental interaction.

The simplistic view of development as optimized progress toward an ideal adult endpoint ought to give way to less Panglossian views more in keeping with the messiness of nature. The idea that behavioural development, unlike automobile assembly or computer programming, is not a mechanical process directed towards an ideal adult endpoint suggests that the study of development in general and play in particular needs to consider what Jerome Bruner (1972) has termed 'the uses of immaturity' from a new biological perspective: the developing organism actively assembles itself and its environment in ways that ensure immediate survival at the cost, if necessary, of some future reproductive success. In general terms, then, the stages of cognitive and skill development should reflect trade-offs between immediate and future adjustment, as well as between the ability to reshape current and future worlds. This point is important for thinking about development. There are many worlds. There are many ways of developing an active mind and each way has its advantages as well as its drawbacks. An open, flexible, stageless strategy of cognitive development that involved continual reshaping and interactive skill would by-pass the dilemma of present versus future adjustments in staged development only to create new problems: false starts, agonizing dissonances, near-disastrous mistakes, and exasperating delays and time-lags. Finally, active minds are not the only kinds of minds that can adjust for survival. A closed cognitive programme gives up the ability to reshape phenotype and environment in return for a guaranteed average return in day-to-day survival. Such a closed strategy is inexpensive in another important way: because strategies of interaction are present, there is no functional reason for consciousness to evolve. A changing or flexible developmental strategy of cognition requires some measure of conscious inner dialogue because there is room in an open mind for conflicts and paradoxes and for their resolution if necessary. A closed cognitive strategy may be completely out of touch with the logic of the interactions that its phenotype has with its environment. This solipsism is of no consequence because the phenotype is going to keep following the same logic regardless of the consequences of its actions and has no biological need to know that it is, in effect, acting out a genetic fantasy.

REFERENCES

Altmann, S. A. (1962). Social behavior of anthropoid primates: analysis of recent concepts. In E. L. Bliss (ed.), *Roots of Behavior*. New York: Harper.

Altmann, J., Altmann, S. A., Hausfater, G., and McCuskey, S. A. (1977). LIfe history of yellow baboons: physical development, reproductive parameters, and infant mortality. *Primates* 18, 315–30.

Axelrod, R., and Hamilton, W. D. (1981). The evolution of cooperation. *Science* 211, 1390–6.

Baldwin, J. D. and Baldwin, J. I. (1974). Exploration and social play in squirrel monkeys (*Saimiri*). *American Zoologist* 14, 303–15.

Barash, D. P. (1976). Social behaviour and individual differences in free-living Alpine marmots. *Animal Behaviour* 24, 27–35.

Barnett, H. G. (1953). *Innovation: the Basis of Cultural Change*. New York: McGraw-Hill.

Bateson, G. (1956). The message 'This is play'. In B. Schaffner (ed.), *Group Processes: Transactions of the Second Conference*. New York: Josiah Macy Foundation.

Bennett, J. (1982). Islands of the Bears (16 mm sound film). Survival Anglia, London.

Berger, J. (1979). Social ontogeny and behavioural diversity: consequences for Bighorn Sheep *Ovis canadensis* inhabiting desert and mountain environments. *Journal of Zoology (London)* 188, 251–66.

Bruner, J. S. (1972). Nature and uses of immaturity. *American Psychologist* 27, 687–708.

Bruner, J. S., Postman, L. and Mosteller, F. (1950). A note on the measurement of reversals of perspective. *Psychometrika* 15, 63–72.

Dawkins, R. (1976). *The Selfish Gene*. New York: Oxford University Press.

Dawkins, R. (1981). *The Extended Phenotype*. San Francisco: W. H. Freeman.

Dittus, W., (1980). The social regulation of primate population: a synthesis. In D. G. Lindburg (ed.), *The Macaques: Studies in Ecology, Behavior, and Evolution*. New York: Van Nostrand Reinhold.

Eibl-Eibesfeldt, I. (1967). Concepts of ethology and their significance in the study of human behavior. In H. W. Stevenson, E. H. Hess and H. L. Rheingold (eds), *Early Behavior: Comparative and Developmental Approaches*. New York: Wiley.

Einon, D. F. and Morgan, M. J. (1977). A critical period for social isolation in the rat. *Developmental Psychobiology* 10, 123–32.

Fagen, R. (1977). Selection for optimal age-dependent schedules of play behaviour. *American Naturalist* 111, 395–414.

Fagen, R. (1981). *Animal Play Behavior*. New York: Oxford University Press.

Fagen, R. (1982). Evolutionary issues in development of behavioral flexibility. In P. P. G. Bateson and P. H. Klopfer (eds), *Perspectives in Ethology, Vol. 5*. New York: Plenum.

Gould, S. J. (1982). On original ideas. *Natural History* 92(1), 26–33.

Holling, C. S. (1973). Resilience and stability of ecological systems. *Annual Review of Ecology and Systematics* 4, 1–23.

Holzworth, J. M. (1930). *The Wild Grizzlies of Alaska*. New York, London: G. P. Putnam's Sons.

Konner, M. J. (1982). *The Tangled Wing*. New York: Holt, Rinehart & Winston.

Levins, R. (1979). Coexistence in a variable environment. *American Naturalist* 114, 765–83.

Levins, R., and Lewontin, R. C. (1980). Dialectics and reductionism in ecology. *Synthese* 43, 47–78.

Lewontin, R. C. (1983). Organism and environment. In F. C. Odling-Smee (ed.), *Multilevel Evolution*.

Lewontin, R. C., and Levins, R. (1978). Evoluzione. *Enciclopedia*. V. Torino: Einaudi.

Ludwig, D., Jones, D. D., and Holling, C. S. (1978). Qualitative analysis of insect outbreak systems: the spruce budworm and forest. *Journal of Animal Ecology* 47, 315–22.

Luft, J. and Altmann, J. (1982). Mother baboon. *Natural history* 91(9), 30–9.

MacArthur, R. H. (1958). Population ecology of some warblers of northeastern coniferous forests. *Ecology* 39, 599–619.

Menzel, E. W. (1978). Cognitive mapping in chimpanzees. In S. H. Hulse, H. Fowler and W. K. Honig (eds), *Cognitive Processes in Animal Behavior*. Hillsdale, NJ: Lawrence Erlbaum Associates.

Millar, S. (1982). Play. In D. J. McFarland (ed.), *The Oxford Companion to Animal Behavior*. New York: Oxford University Press.

Moermond, T. C. (1979). The influence of habitat structure on *Anolis* foraging behaviour. *Behaviour* 70, 118–49.

O'Keefe, J. and Nadel, L. (1978). *The Hippocampus as a Cognitive Map*. Oxford: Clarendon Press.

Potegal, M. (ed.) (1982). *Spatial Abilities: Development and Physiological Bases*. New York: Academic Press.

Rijksen, H. D. (1978). *A Field Study on Sumatran Orangutans* (Pongo pygmaeus Abelii *Lesson 1827*). Wageningen: H. Veenman & Zonen B.V.

Southwood, T. R. E. (1977). Habitat, the template for ecological strategies? *Journal of Animal Ecology* 46, 337–65.

Struhsaker, T. T. (1967). Behavior of Vervet Monkeys (*Cercopithecus aethiops*). *University of California Publications on Zoology* 82.

Sutton-Smith, B. (1971). Conclusion. In R. E. Herron and B. Sutton-Smith (eds), *Child's Play*. New York: Wiley.

Symons, D. (1978). *Play and Aggression: a Study of Rhesus Monkeys*. New York: Columbia University Press.

Tukey, J. W. (1977). *Exploratory Data Analysis*. Reading, Mass.: Addison-Wesley.

8 Repertoire, Style and Format: Notions Worth Borrowing from Children's Play

Dennis Palmer Wolf

Usually, chapters about children's play appear in journals or books about other forms of human behaviour – sociability, symbolization, or language development. In that context, the issue is to describe or quantify changes in the play of young humans which occur with age, exposure, or circumstance. The implied or explicit comparison is between older and younger children, children with more and less training, the young of different classes or cultures, or the same child under different conditions. However, when a chapter about children's play appears in the context of biological or ethological descriptions of play in other species, the familiar developmental questions fade and two questions take shape: first, 'What are the distinguishing characteristics of children's play which set it apart from the "fooling around" that occurs in young cats, monkeys or chimpanzees?' Second, 'What characteristics are common to play, no matter which species carries it out?'

In addressing the issue of what distinguishes human play, one of two hallmarks is typically singled out: either the highly symbolic or the profoundly cultural nature of children's play (Fein, 1981, Schwartzman, 1978). There is much to recommend both of these characteristics as marking the transition from animal to human play. Consider the symbolic nature of children's play: any number of animal species are capable of substituting one object for another in pragmatic, tool-using contexts (Menzel, Davenport and Rogers, 1970; van Lawick-Goodall, 1968). Moreover, some animals can use objects as 'emblems' for situations – bringing a dish to indicate that they want to be fed or a ball to communicate that they want to play. However, it appears that without training, animals fail to use one object simply to *represent* another. Yet precisely this kind of representation becomes available and often central in children's play as early as the second year. In fact, many pre-school children can go so far as to override the conventional uses and associations of particular objects, using a banana as a telephone receiver or a pencil as a rocket ship (Elder and Pederson, 1978; Fein, 1975). Most normal four-year-olds can pretend that there are witches in an empty closet or a cake baking in the open space between four table legs. But even neighbouring species like chimpanzees and gorillas virtually never engage in 'fantasy play', where the player uses 'nothing' as if it were 'something' (Hayes, 1976; Smith, 1982).

The cultural nature of children's play is at least as striking. We have clear evidence that as early as their second year, children draw on the specific play experiences they have shared with others. For example, a boy rounding the corner where he and his father have played hide-and-seek in the past, calls for his father and initiates a new round of the game by ducking down, saying 'All gone' (Wolf, 1982). The play of three-, four-, and five-year-olds is filled with the dramatization of culture-specific scripts. These scripts reflect both the daily routines and the fantasy motives of particular cultures (e.g. playing at driving or being Batman for an American child) (Nelson and Gruendel, 1981). Older children absorb cultural forms, as well as contents. Beginning in the school-years, children learn the concrete rules which govern specific games like marbles and tag. In addition, they pick up 'unspoken' laws about which games are for girls and which belong to boys, which pastimes are for 'babies', what is a clever stretch of the rules and what is cheating (Lever, 1976; Opie and Opie, 1969; Piaget, 1932; Schwartzman, 1978). Observations of animals reveal that the patterns of play they share are more the result of species-specific behaviours than culture: there is little evidence of (or little research on) the preservation and transmission of play forms among different groups within a species.

The symbolic and cultural characteristics of human play are interesting because they establish if not a hard and fast boundary, at least a steep gradient of change, between the play of humans and the kind of fooling around conducted by even closely-related species. But to the extent that human play is set off from or 'above' animal play, we end up with an extremely lop-sided view of the links between animal and human play behaviours. While concepts arrived at in the context of studying animal play are freely imported to studies of human play, the reverse translation, rarely, if ever, occurs. Thus, the distinction between exploration and play that was detailed in animal research has informed research on children's unstructured encounters with novel objects (Hutt, 1979). By contrast, notions which have grown up in studies of children's play – such as concepts of developmental variation or individual styles – are rarely translated into studies of animal play. However, in the spirit of playing with ideas, it seems worthwhile to ask, 'What have we learned in studying children's play that might be worth importing to the study of animal behaviour?'

To make this inquiry productive, we have to shift attention away from the peculiarly human qualities of play and concentrate instead on the commonalities between animal and human players. Since Darwin, we have recognized that the same capacity for variation which eventually differentiates species also provides a fundamental commonality across organisms. Even beyond structural variation, there are variations in behaviour which are common to most species: (1) *developmental variation* or age-related changes in the organism's behavioural repertoire; (2) *individual variation* or differences in the way that single organisms or sub- groups select from a species-specific or developmentally-available repertoire of behaviours; (3) *behavioural variation* or situation-specific shifts in an organism's activities.

In the remainder of this chapter, I outline the evidence for these three types of variety in the play of young humans. First, there is the developmental variety evident in children's gradual construction of a *repertoire* of play modes. This repertoire results from the appearance and preservation of different types of play which children acquire in a fixed developmental sequence starting with the motoric play and eventuating in games structured by rules. Second, there is the variation which shows up in individual *styles* of play evident among young humans. Finally, there is the behavioural variety or the range of distinguishably different play *formats* in which many children engage, ranging from short loops of playful behaviour to carefully marked and elaborate play rituals.

Each of these concepts has helped developmental psychologists to understand the complexity of human play. The notion of a *repertoire* has taught students of human play to see that developmental sophistication might better be understood as having a wide range of playful behaviours rather than just the latest-to-emerge forms. The concept of *styles* has been useful in pointing out the difference between players' characteristic patterns of play and their level of play abilities. The study of different play *formats* has suggested specific types of learning or adaptive significance may be associated with particular types of play.

A PLAY REPERTOIRE

In the course of their first seven years, children's play undergoes several major changes. During infancy, manipulative play with objects dominates, with children beginning to combine objects in what is often termed 'relational play' at about nine months (Fenson et al., 1976; McCall, 1974; Rosenblatt, 1977; Zelazo and Kearsley, 1980). Between 12 and 18 months, simple forms of symbolic play appear. In early pretence play, children are only likely to re-enact familiar schemes out of context, for example, drinking from an empty cup or attempting to comb a teddy bear's 'hair' (Bates, 1979; Fenson et al., 1976; Lowe, 1975; Nicolich, 1977). Gradually, pretence play gains in imaginativeness, such that by the age of three many children can transform simple objects into symbols for other objects or invent completely imaginary items and events (Fein, 1975; Piaget, 1962; Winner et al., 1979). Finally, between five and seven, the free-wheeling spirit of make- believe play gives evidence of a burgeoning concern for rule-governed play, particularly where there is a question of coordinating the actions of multiple players. The first signs of such rules may occur in the form of explicit markers for setting apart pretence from pragmatic or 'real' actions (Garvey, 1974; Wolf, 1981; Wolf and Pusch, in preparation). During the school years, children increasingly organize their social and sometimes even their private play according to either conventional or impromptu rules which govern the objectives, the turn-structures and the boundaries of play activity (Lever, 1976; Piaget, 1932). This sequence of play acquisitions is remarkably stable across diverse populations. For example, the transitions from manipulative to symbolic play to rule-governed play occur across cultures at approximately the same ages (Schwartzman, 1978). Moreover, while occurring at different chronological ages, the transitions to symbolic play and within types of symbolic play occur in the same sequence for premature, abused and neglected, mentally-retarded and Down's syndrome children (Cichetti, 1983; Harmon and Glicken, 1982; Hill and Nicolich, 1981).

However, because the developmental literature stresses the ages of onset of each novel type of play, it is possible to miss the fact that children are adding new play modes to their previously-held approaches. Thus, children do not replace earlier acquired modes of playing, instead they develop a repertoire of play forms which includes later-occurring modes. Consider the following observation of a three- and-a-half-year-old who is playing with a set of wooden building pieces:

> Josh selects a round piece with a hole in the middle and presses a stick into it. Using a slit at the upper end of the stick, he presses a fan-shaped piece in, then plays at making the fan vibrate by flipping it with his thumb. As he does so he chants in rhythmic syllables: 'A peel-a peel- a peepee-el.'

He continues to build several similar pieces. He toys with twirling them in place, 'I gonna turn it . . . I gonna put it . . . I gonna turn the peel on top . . . I keep screwing and screwing and screwing so it will get tight and screw it and screw it, and screw it and screw it and screw it, and screw it, so it can stand up . . . ' He adds several more pieces getting a stack which he calls 'a large boat'. As he builds, the round pieces tend to roll off the table, and he speaks to them calling out 'Where are you going?', as he continues to add new pieces to his structure. Eventually, Josh manages to build an arm leading off his tower to the right. He discovers that he can rotate this arm while the tower remains standing.

'I gonna screw it and screw it and screw it. This is the pump . . . gonna fix it . . . Oh, there is gonna come jelly (as he points to the top of his tower . . . This is a jelly-maker . . . I am making kind of . . . a kind of orange juice jelly . . . ' (The play continues with Josh adding more and more refinements to his jelly-maker.)

When at last, it is complete, Josh assigns the observer the role of the supplier and he takes on the part of the jelly-machine operator. A kind of simple game emerges:

Josh: I'm gonna turn and turn . . . it's all over your hand . . .
Observer: Oh, no, I'll have to take a bath!
Josh: You get it all over your eyeglasses and all over your eyes.
Observer: Oh, no,
Josh: You get it all over your eyes and all over your head.

In this segment of play, Josh combines the same set of elements: turning motions, language sounds and building pieces into several different modes of play. At the outset, these raw materials are used in motoric play where babbling and repetitive motions are the focus. Gradually, relational play, based on combinations of objects, emerges as Josh constructs the tower and arm of his structure. Relational play slowly gives way to symbolic play in which the physical attributes of the structure 'lose out' to the imagined project of making 'a kind of orange jelly'. In the last phase of the play, something approaching rule-governed play appears. Josh and the observer each take on a specified role and develop a routine for 'making jelly' in which the observer's turn consists of putting in 'oranges' and Josh's turn consists of running the 'jelly-maker'.

The sequence in which play skills emerge offers one yardstick for measuring the sophistication of players of different ages and species. Using this approach, a player who only plays at dropping spoons into a pot is judged to be less sophisticated than one who uses those same objects to play out a pretend meal. However, the observations of Josh and the jelly-maker suggest that there is a second way of describing the evolution of play skills. In addition to describing the peak level of a player's activity, an individual's skills as a player can also be described in terms of the breadth of his or her play repertoire. In this light, what is remarkable about human play is not simply that highly symbolic or rule-bound forms eventually emerge, but the fact that such forms exist side-by-side with earlier-emerging forms of motoric and object play.

Clearly, this picture of the development of human play cannot be directly applied to studies of animal play; however, a cross-fertilization could be enriching. The concept of a developmental sequence of play modes might be helpful in describing differences in the quality of 'immaturity' across species. Specifically, animal studies might use the length and complexity of the sequence of play modes to measure how much behavioural development occurs between infancy and adulthood in particular species. Similarly, the notion of a play repertoire might be applied to instances of non-human play. For example, it would be interesting to know which organisms, other than humans, build up a significant repertoire of distinct play modes, any one of which can be activated, once acquired. Conceivably, in less-evolved species, specific forms of play are tied to specific periods in the life-span, appearing and dying out in accord with the appearance and passing of particular age periods. Potentially, among more evolved species, individuals build up a play repertoire which enables them to engage in sequences of play, more limited than, but similar to, Josh's episode with the building pieces.

STYLES OF PLAY: INDIVIDUAL VARIATION IN THE USE OF PLAY REPERTOIRES

As the earlier observations of Josh indicate, even young human players have a repertoire of play modes at their disposal: they can experiment with motion and sound patterns, toy with objects, engage in make-believe, play marbles or 'Go Fish'. Given this option for choice, children often exhibit a second form of variation: individual styles of play.

Any number of studies report group differences in the content and structure of children's play. For example, it is frequently claimed that lower-class children engage in symbolic play more rarely than their middle-class peers and that when they do make-believe, these children are more conservative in their pretence (Smilansky, 1968; Tizard et al., 1976). (The report of differences in play associated with children's class backgrounds is problematic, see Fein and Stork, 1981. Much of the research is based on observations of children of different backgrounds in different settings where contrasting sets of materials existed and where rules for behaviour may have been different. Moreover, the children observed in these studies were rarely matched on intelligence or any other measure of development.) In the same vein, it is reported that boys, as compared to girls, engage in less fantasy play, preferring rough-and-tumble activity and/or constructional games (Goldberg and Lewis, 1969; Matthews, 1977; Pederson and Bell, 1970).

However, in addition to these group preferences for different modes of play there is evidence for considerable variation in the way that individual players engage in the same type of play (Partington and Grant, below, chapter 10; Wolf and Grollman, 1982). The most striking illustration of this within-mode variation comes from the study of the patterns of symbolic play in children. Existing clinical research indicates that some children exhibit 'an imaginative predisposition' which leads them to engage in make-believe play that is both more frequent and more fanciful than that of their peers. Such children tend to play themes like 'witches' or 'space trip' rather than 'house' and they often report having imaginary companions and day-dreams (Hudson, 1966; Singer, 1973). In addition, observational studies of spontaneous free play indicate that individual children use quite different strategies for turning the 'here and now' world of the living room or classroom into a play world. Some children make extensive use of available props and spaces. These individuals have been termed 'material' or 'object-dependent' players. A second group of children tend to ignore the immediate environment, engaging in fantasy or what has been called 'ideational' or 'object-independent' play (Matthews, 1977; Winner et al., 1979; Wolf and Grollman, 1982). Even children of the same age, gender and social background differ along this particular dimension. Moreover, it appears that the individual's predilection for object-dependent or object-independent play is stable across situations and at least from late infancy until the early school years (Wolf and Grollman, 1982). For example, consider the pair of observations, of two girls at ages one and three years, given in figure 8.1.

At each of the ages sampled, both children engage in pretence play. Nevertheless, the way in which each child carries out this project is distinctive. The first child, *Je*, uses words and gestures to create a fantasy that unfolds more or less independently of the immediate physical environment. By comparison, *An's* symbolic play focuses on the concrete objects and spatial arrangements that make up her environment. For example, at three, *Je* is inclined to invent witches and plates while *An* uses the expanse of the rug to signify the water, the

Obs. 1a: At 1:0 the observer presents *Je* with a small toy tea set and several small dolls. *Je*'s attention is attracted right away to a small plastic spoon. She places the spoon in her mouth and wanders about the room with the spoon protruding, mugging for her mother and the observer. *Je* stoops over to pick up a cup. She places the spoon in the cup, stirs it hard, and makes a 'mmmm' sound as if tasting something delicious. *Je* walks over to her mother, takes the spoon from her own mouth, and uses it to feed her mother repeatedly. Her mother enters the game, smacking her lips, saying 'mmmm' and asking for more. *Je* moves away and comes back with a small cup that she holds out to her mother, who obligingly drinks. *Je* then feeds her again. Upon walking away toward the window, *Je* encounters the dolls. She stoops and picks one up, drops it into a nearby chair where she feeds it from both the spoon and the cup. *Je* then takes the cup and, balancing it on her nose, turns to show her mother, who claps.

Obs. 1b: Presented with a small toy tea set and several small dolls, *An*, at 1:2, collects one doll, one cup and one spoon. She sits with them on her lap a moment, but then lifts them into the observer's lap. She is much more interested in the plates of various sizes that are spread out on the floor. She collects the four small ones first, making a neat stack of them. She then collects the four larger ones, also stacking them. *An* then nests the stack of smaller plates inside the set of larger ones. *An* places three remaining spoons on top of her stack; as she does so she makes smacking noises with her lips. She starts to offer the spoon to the observer and to her mother, simply holding it out toward each of them, but instead her attention returns to her previous interests and the process of unstacking and then rearranging the plates resumes.

Obs. 2a: At 3:5 *Je* is asked to play 'going on a boat trip'.
   Je: 'Yeah, let's go in the boat. Oh, I see a wicked witch.'
   O. and *Je* sit on the floor and pretend to look around.
   O.: 'What else do you see?'
   Je: 'I see two plates. They fell down . . . and there's some doors and they are getting ready to saw us.'
   O.: 'Oh no.'
   Je: 'We can go to Snow White's house.'
   O.: 'Okay.'
   O. and *Je* walk across the floor.
   Je: 'Oh, no, don't go in there.' She approaches a small door in the hall and looks in. 'Oh – oh, she's sick. We better fix her up.' *Je* runs for her doctor kit and a different scenario ensues.

Obs. 2b: At 3:8 *An* is also asked to play 'going on a boat trip'. Along with *An*, *O.* settles on a cloth spread out on the living room floor.
   O.: 'What do you see?'
   An: 'I don't know. I want to get something else.' *An* leaves, coming back with dolls and books from her room.
   O.: 'Did you want to read books, or just take them along?'
   An: 'Take them with us. I better get a suitcase.' She does this. She unpacks numerous small toys from the suitcase. ''I'll throw these in the water 'cause all these are fishes.' She packs the dolls and books back into the suitcase. She then surveys the arrangement. She points to the rug area around the cloth where she sits. 'This is the water.' Touching the cloth, she says, 'This is the boat.'

FIGURE 8.1 Longitudinal observations of children with differing play styles (*Je* refers to one subject; *An* refers to a second subject; *O* refers to the adult observer)

position of the cloth on the rug to signify a boat on the water, the small separate shapes of dolls and books to signify fish.

Clearly this variation in symbolic play has no strict counterpart in other species. However, the broad concept of individual player profiles still might be applied to animal play. If the play repertoires of particular species could be described, observations of individual animals' play could yield a picture of the range of play styles open to the members of any particular species. Subsequently, it would be possible to compare the variation in player styles across species. These comparisons might provide a view of the amount of individual behavioural variation characteristic of particular species.

THEME AND VARIATIONS, LOOPS, AND RITUALS: VARIATION IN PLAY FORMATS

One of the recurrent questions about play concerns its contributions to the survival or adaptation of the player. Any number of different theories have been advanced: theorists have claimed that play provides rehearsal for complex sequences of behaviour, social and physical skills needed at later points in the life-span, a way to spend surplus energy. However, part of the problem in defining the rewards of play derives from the fact that we are trying to track down the benefits of an enormous and diverse category of behaviour. Asking about the adaptive significance of play is rather like asking about the adaptive significance of 'goal-oriented' behaviour. Before looking for answers, we must break up the broad category of play into smaller, specific categories which can be investigated independently.

In the past, a number of observers have used differences in content or function to describe different forms of play (e.g. social play, object play, motor play). However, such categories are problematic on two counts. First, they do not help with the fundamental problem of defining types of *play*, as exactly the same behaviours also occur in episodes of pragmatic behaviour. Second, as any observer of play knows, the same contents or functional type of play can be used to quite diverse ends. For example, in the course of a single play episode, a child or chimpanzee may use motor play to practise physical skills or as a way to engage a partner in social play (Smith, 1982).

Partially to escape the problems of traditional content or function categories, theorists have suggested that any behaviour with any material becomes playful as the organism ceases to be dominated by the demands of the environment, forgetting 'ends' in favour of exploring, enjoying, or simply toying with 'means' (Berlyne, 1960; Hutt, 1979; Nunnally and

Lemond, 1978; Piaget, 1962; Reynolds, 1976; Sutton-Smith, 1971). Until recently, this concept has chiefly been used to create broad distinctions between goal-oriented, exploratory and playful behaviours. However, the concept could also be used to create a taxonomy of different types of play. For example, close observation of children's play suggests that human playfulness shades gradually away from (or into) pragmatic activity, such that even within behaviours we recognize as playful, the relation between play and other current pragmatic activity shifts. In order to illustrate this variation in play, consider three moments of playful behaviour in Andrew, age 3: 6.

The first of these observations records a brief, highly-focused type of play. In this type of play, the player backs off momentarily from goal-oriented activity becoming involved with a playful version of that same behaviour. In playing, the child turns up discoveries or insights which modulate the course of subsequent behaviour. Because of this, play behaviours of this kind might be termed *play loops*. In the following observation, a child shifts from 'serious' drawing to playing with lines, and ends up in a 'new' kind of drawing:

> Andrew has been drawing for almost ten minutes, making what for him is a complicated design composed of ovals crossed by and then encircled with lines (cf. figure 8.2a). He begins to 'fool around' with just a large red marker and a stack of coloured paper. In the next drawing, he creates an oval which he crosses with closely spaced lines in horizontal and vertical directions (cf. figure 8.2b). In a suite of four more drawings, he plays with simplifying this pattern. The fourth of these drawings is reduced to nothing more than the quick up and down motion he used earlier to create vertical stripes on his oval. The result is a jagged, wave-like line (cf. figure 8.2c). In a final drawing, Andrew imports this pattern back to the task of drawing. He makes another wavy line, adds a square form and some dots saying, 'A sailboat in the waves and rain' (cf. figure 8.2d).

While drawing, Andrew takes the time to 'back off' from the task of making precise shapes. Because he is only fooling around, Andrew is free to play with the gestural qualities of his marks and, thereby, discover the possibility of representational drawing based on motion and emphasis. This approach to picturing is then reinvested or returned to the project of 'serious' drawing when Andrew makes his boat in the storm. Thus, the 'pay-off' from play *loops* may come in the form of small insights into some recently adopted task. Andrew plays briefly with the elements he has been using for drawing and realizes new uses for those elements. In

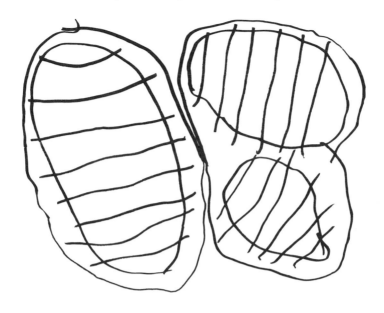

FIGURE 8.2a Andrew's original design of ovals and lines

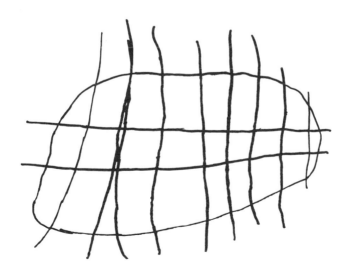

FIGURE 8.2b Andrew's further exploration of line patterns

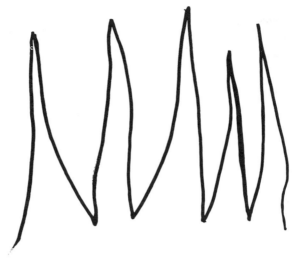

FIGURE 8.2c Andrew's gestural play with up and down lines.

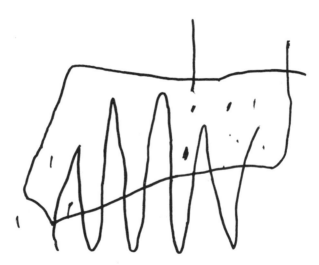

FIGURE 8.2d Andrew's application of knowledge gained in play: 'A sailboat in the waves and rain'

animals, the analogue may be the kind of new vision Köhler's apes won by backing off from too-earnest use of their sticks. As adults, we push back from the typewriter to play with ideas when what's on the paper strikes us as boring, staid or confused.

The second observation records Andrew involved in what could be termed *theme and variation* play. This type of play, which is quite similar to exploration, often occurs as part of the warm-up or epilogue to more goal-oriented behaviour. While engaged in this kind of play the child lets go of specific goals and fools around, for a protracted period, with the 'means' he or she typically uses in pragmatic or serious activity. Here, there is no 'ah-ha' or reversal in the user's perspective on the problem, instead there occurs a kind of systematic toying with the behaviours or materials involved.

Andrew sits down to draw. He makes a design of ovals crossed by and then encircled with lines (cf. figure 8.2a). Once this design is complete, Andrew takes a whole stack of paper and begins to play with the elements he has just used in his design. In short order, he completes a series of five different drawings each of which is an oval patterned over with combinations of verticals and horizontals.

This kind of theme and variation play is not peculiar to Andrew or to the task of drawing. For example, Weir (1962) and Cazden (1976) have recorded similar episodes of language play in children. Having picked out moments when children play at varying the use of materials or the performance of routines, it becomes interesting to ask after the significance of such behaviours. Research suggests that children given the option to play with materials perform equally as well as children trained with materials and better than a control group of children when asked to solve problems involving the materials (Smith and Simon, below chapter 9; Smith and Dutton, 1979; Sylva et al., 1976). Similarly, children allowed to play freely with a set of objects can produce a wider range of alternative uses for those objects than children who have imitated an adult demonstrating possible uses (Dansky and Silverman, 1976). Since there is no evidence that play with specific items produces knowledge or flexibility which generalizes, it appears that theme and variation play makes two rather specific contributions to a player. It provides (1) precise knowledge of the possibilities inherent in a particular object, material, game, etc.; and (2) experience in combining these possibilities in novel, flexible ways.

Compared to theme and variation play, play *rituals* are highly-stylized and self-contained excursions from pragmatic behaviour. Typically, play rituals are instigated by the performer rather than an external event, set off from pragmatic activity by boundary-marking behaviours, and performed with a high degree of dominance over simultaneous environmental events and surrounding objects (Bateson, 1956; Garvey, 1974;

Goffman, 1974). Because of their stylization and distance from previous pragmatic behaviours, the performance of play rituals rarely alters the course of ensuing pragmatic activity. The end of Andrew's drawing session provides an illustration.

Andrew notices Alex looking on. Andrew adds several more wavy lines to his boat picture, making sound effects. 'Pretend it was a real big storm.'

Alex:	adds in some loud sound effects.
Andrew:	makes swift downward lines, 'That's rain.'
Alex:	'Yup, rain.'
Andrew:	again makes more wavy lines accompanied by sound effects.
Alex:	echoes these noises.
Andrew:	makes still more lines and sound effects.
Alex:	echoes these noises.
Andrew:	'The boat's lost!' (mock horror in his voice).
Alex:	'It's lost' (mock horror in his voice, too).

In the near-by block corner a building crashes to the floor.

Andrew:	'It's crashing' (laughs at his own joke).
Alex:	'It crashed' (he also laughs).
Andrew:	'Crash!'
Alex:	'Crash!'

At this point Andrew shoves the markers into the middle of the table. He and Alex go together in search of a third friend. All three of them move on to play in the block corner.

In his play ritual, Andrew makes it clear that he's pretending, thus marking the separation of this activity from 'real' drawing. The ensuing interaction becomes highly patterned. Novelty comes, not from the introduction of new information, but from variations in the performance of stylized responses. Moreover, as he plays with the markers and lines, it also becomes clear that environmental events have very little 'pull' compared to Andrew's interest in performing the play ritual (Wolf and Pusch, in preparation).

At first glance, the stylization and independence of play rituals makes them puzzling behaviours to think about in terms of learning or adaptation. However, the relative predictability of such play sequences may make them excellent frames in which to observe and respond to the subtleties or nuances of behaviour. For example, if Andrew and Alex were to play out this crashing ritual often enough to know the moves 'by heart', small variations in wording, emphasis, or intonation would become significant clues about either player's mood, relation to his partner, level of engagement. Particularly, among organisms who participate in complex social interchanges, the practice and eventual mastery of such subtle clues could have adaptive significance. Among animals, ritualized chase and fighting sequences may provide similar experiences in reading behavioural signals.

These observations indicate that even when a single player uses the same materials, apparently towards the same functional end (e.g. learning more about the skill of drawing), play behaviours vary in the degree to which they are 'uncoupled' from pragmatic activity. On a superficial level, this uncoupling can be measured in terms of the length of the aside. At a deeper level, forms of play can be distinguished by the presence or absence of behaviours also elicited in pragmatic situations, the effects of play on subsequent activity, the degree to which play responds to or absorbs information from the environment (Hutt, 1979; Piaget, 1962). In the *loop*, play occurs almost in the service of the surrounding goal-directed activity. It may be significant as a way for an organism to break set and then return to problem-solving. *Theme and variation* play promotes general knowledge of the specific materials, objects or routines. The stylized behaviours of play *rituals* may alert players less to new content, and more to novelties in the performance of familiar routines.

The observation of a variety of play formats in children raises a number of questions about animal play. Can all species engage in these types of play? If not, which formats (e.g. loops, theme-and-variations or rituals) occur in which species? Can the specific contributions of each of these play forms be more closely determined by examining which species engage in each form? Conceivably, play *rituals* occur in many species because their performance requires little information gathering or variation. By contrast, possibly only higher species, or just primates, exhibit *loops* and *variations*.

CONCLUSION

The statement that children's play is highly varied would seem to imply little more than the fact that, as human beings, they have a huge number of pragmatic activities which can be uncoupled from goal-directed exercise for the purposes of 'fiddling' or pleasurable experimentation. However, there are at least three additional ways in which the notion of variety appears central to the characterization of human play. First, through the course of development, humans construct a *repertoire* of playful behaviours which is preserved throughout the life-span. Thus, at five, a child can draw on any of several modes of playing, each of which appeared and prevailed at earlier times during the development of play skills. Second, given this repertoire of possible modes of play, it appears that children exhibit rather different *styles*, turning to particular modes of play more frequently than others. Thus, among young human players there is considerable variation both across and within the play modes used by individual players. Finally it appears that human play can stand in various relations to other forms of behaviour. One type of playful activity, *loops*, consists of momentary detours from pragmatic activity which may generate information useful to the completion of the activity underway. By comparison, *theme and variation* play promotes diverse knowledge about the particular behaviours or materials at hand. *Rituals*, islands of playfulness which do not lend information to immediately ensuing behaviour, may provide reliable frameworks for noticing the nuances of behaviour.

Biological or ethological analyses of animal play have often informed the study of children's play (Hutt, 1979; Smith, 1982). Somewhat more rarely have studies of children's play raised questions for the investigation of animal play. In part, our interest in describing the qualitative differences between human and animal play has had the peculiar effect of sealing human play off from animal play. For example, while the concepts of development of play skills, individual variation in players' styles and different play processes have become central in studies of children's play, these same concepts appear not to have spread to the study of play in animals.

All three of these concepts might be imported to the study of play in other species. An examination of the sequence of play modes could index the behavioural development occurring in different species between infancy and maturity. Comparisons of the range of individual styles of play evident in juveniles within a species might provide insight into the range of individual behavioural variability characteristic of particular species. Closer studies of the play formats of different species could yield insight into the potential contributions of play behaviours to survival and evolution. Above all, because these concepts can be applied across human and animal play, they could teach us something about what is common and what is distinctive about play in humans and animals.

ACKNOWLEDGEMENTS

The observations in this chapter are taken from earlier research supported by the Carnegie Corporation and the Spencer Foundation. The writing of this chapter was made possible by funding from the Carnegie Corporation and the Mailman Family Foundation.

REFERENCES

Bates, E. (1979). *The Emergence of Symbols: Cognition and Communication in Infancy*. New York: Academic Press.

Bateson, G. (1956). The message 'This is play'. In B. Schaffner (ed.), *Group Processes: Transactions of the Second Conference*. New York: Josiah Macy Foundation.

Berlyne, D. E. (1960). *Conflict, Arousal and Curiosity*. New York: McGraw-Hill.

Cazden, C. (1976). Play and meta-linguistic awareness. In J. Bruner, A. Jolly and K. Sylva (eds), *Play: its Role in Development and Evolution*, pp. 603–8. New York: Basic Books.

Cichetti, D. (1983). Personal communication.

Dansky, J. L. and Silverman, I. W. (1973). Effects of play on associative fluency in preschool-aged children. *Developmental Psychology* 9, 38–43.

Elder, J. L. and Pederson, D. R. (1978). Preschool children's use of objects in symbolic play. *Child Development* 49, 500–4.

Fein, G. G. (1975). A transformational analysis of pretending. *Developmental Psychology* 11, 291–6.

Fein, G. G. (1981). Pretend play in childhood: an integrative review. *Child Development* 52, 1095–118.

Fein, G. G. and Stork, L. (1981). Socio-dramatic play: social-class effects in an integrated classroom. *Journal of Applied Developmental Psychology* 2, 267–79.

Fenson, L., Kagan, J., Kearsley, R. B., and Zelazo, P. (1976). The developmental progression of manipulative play in the first two years. *Child Development* 47, 232–5.

Garvey, C. (1974). Some properties of social play. *Merrill-Palmer Quarterly* 20, 163–80.

Goffman, E. (1974). *Frame Analysis: an Essay on the Organization of Experience*. Cambridge, Mass.: Harvard University Press.

Goldberg, S. and Lewis, M. (1969). Play behavior in the year-old infant: early sex differences. *Child Development* 40, 21–32.

Hayes, C. (1976). The imaginary pull-toy. In J. Bruner, A. Jolly and K. Sylva (eds), *Play: its Role in Development and Evolution*, pp. 534–6. New York: Basic Books.

Harmon, R. and Glicken, A. (1982). Development of free play behavior in infancy. In S. Rogers (ed.), *Developmental and Clinical Aspects of Young Children's Play*, pp. 53–60. Westar Publications: Monmouth, Oregon.

Hill, P. and Nicolich, L. McC. (1981). Pretend play and patterns of cognition in Down's syndrome children. *Child Development* 52, 611–17.

Hudson, L. (1966). *Contrary Imaginations*. New York: Schocken.

Hutt, C. (1979). Exploration and play. In B. Sutton-Smith (ed.), *Play and Learning*, pp. 175–94. New York: Plenum Press.

Lever, J. (1976). Sex differences in the games children play. *Social Problems* 23, 478–87.

Lowe, M. (1975). Trends in the development of representational play in infants from one to three years: an observational study. *Journal of Child Psychology and Psychiatry* 16, 33–47.

Matthews, W. S. (1977). Modes of transformation in the initiation of pretend play. *Developmental Psychology* 13, 212–16.

McCall, R. B. (1974). Exploratory manipulation and play in the human infant. *Monographs of the Society for Research in Child Development* 39 (Serial No. 155).

Menzel, E. W. Jr, Davenport, R. K. and Rogers, C. M. (1970). The development of tool-using in wild-born and restriction-reared chimpanzees. *Folia Primatologica* 12, 273–83.

Nelson, K. and Gruendel, J. (1981). Generalized event representations: Basic building blocks of cognitive development. In M. E. Lamb and A. L. Brown (eds), *Advances in Developmental Psychology, Vol. 1*. New York: Academic Press.

Nicolich, L. McC. (1977). Beyond sensorimotor intelligence: assessment of symbolic maturity through analysis of pretend play. *Merrill–Palmer Quarterly* 23, 89–99.

Nunnally, J. C. and Lemond, L. C. (1978). Exploratory behavior and human development. In H. Reese (ed.), *Advances in Child Development and Behavior, Vol. 8*, New York: Academic Press.

Opie, I. and Opie, P. (1969). *Children's Games in Street and Playground*. London: Clarendon Press.

Pederson, F. A. and Bell, R. Q. (1970). Sex differences in preschool children without histories of complications of pregnancy and delivery. *Developmental Psychology* 3, 10–15.

Piaget, J. (1932). *The Moral Judgement of the Child*. New York: Free Press.

Piaget, J. (1962). *Play, Dreams and Imitation in Childhood*. New York: Norton.

Reynolds, P. (1976). Play, language and human evolution. In J. Bruner, A. Jolly and K. Sylva (eds), *Play: its Role in Development and Evolution*, pp. 621–33. New York: Basic Books.

Rosenblatt, D. (1977). Developmental trends in infant play. In B. Tizard and D. Harvey (eds), *The Biology of Play*. Philadelphia: Lippincott.

Schwartzman, H. (1978). *Transformations: the Anthropology of Children's Play*. New York: Plenum Press.

Singer, J. (1973). *The Child's World of Make-Believe*. Academic Press: New York.

Smilansky, S. (1968). *The Effects of Sociodramatic Play on Disadvantaged Preschool Children*. New York: Wiley.

Smith, P. K. (1982). Does play matter? Functional and evolutionary aspects of animal and human play. *Behavioral and Brain Sciences* 5, 139–84.

Smith, P. K. and Dutton, S. (1979). Play and training in direct and innovative problem-solving. *Child Development*, 50, 830–6.

Sutton-Smith, B. (1971). Boundaries. In R. E. Herron and B. Sutton-Smith (eds), *Child's Play*. New York: Wiley.

Sylva, K., Bruner, J. and Genova, P. (1976). The rule of play in the problem-solving of children 3–5-years-old. In J. Bruner, A. Jolly and K. Sylva (eds), *Play: its Role in Evolution and Development*, pp. 244–57. New York: Basic Books.

Tizard, B., Philps, J., and Plewis, I. (1976). Play in preschool centres–II. Effects on play of the child's social class and of the educational orientation of the centre. *Journal of Child Psychology and Psychiatry* 17, 265–74.

van Lawick-Goodall, J. (1968). The behaviour of free-living chimpanzees in the Gombe Stream reserve. *Animal Behaviour Monographs* 1, 161–311.

Weir, R. (1962). *Language in the Crib*. The Hague: Mouton.

Winner, E., McCarthy, M., Kleinman, S. and Gardner, H. (1979). First metaphors. In H. Gardner and D. Wolf (eds), *Early Symbolization. New Directions for Child Development Vol. 3*, San Francisco: Jossey Bass.

Wolf, D. (1981). Playing along: the social side of early pretence play. Paper presented at the Biennial Meeting of the Society for Research in Child Development, Boston, April.

Wolf, D. (1982). Understanding others: a longitudinal case study of the concept of independent agency. In G. Forman (ed.), *Action and Thought: from Sensorimotor Schemes to Symbolic Intelligence*, pp. 297–327. New York: Academic Press.

Wolf, D. and Grollman, S. (1982). Ways of playing: individual differences in styles of imaginative play. In D. Pepler and K. Rubin (eds), *The Play of Children: Current Theory and Research*. Basel: S. Karger.

Wolf, D. and Pusch, J. (In preparation). Pretend that didn't happen. In L. Galda and A. Pellegrini (eds), *Play and Narrative*. New York: Ablex Publishers.

Zelazo, P. and Kearsley, R. B. (1980). The emergence of functional play in infants: evidence for a major cognitive transition. *Journal of Applied Developmental Psychology* 1, 95–117.

PART IV

The Study of Children's Play

The three chapters in this part discuss three different aspects of children's play; they also exemplify three different predominant methods of study. Chapter 9, by Peter Smith and Tony Simon, discusses research on object play in young children. They review a number of tightly controlled experimental studies which have tried to connect play experience with objects to later problem-solving or creativity. Chapter 10, by John Partington and Catherine Grant, reviews one aspect of children's fantasy play: the imaginary companion phenomenon (other aspects of children's fantasy play are considered by Wolf, chapter 8). Most of the information here is based on interviews with children and parents, and the analyses are usually correlational or employing multivariate statistics. In chapter 11, Anne Humphreys and Peter Smith consider children's rough-and-tumble play. The study of human rough-and-tumble originated from ethological work, and research here has relied mainly on naturalistic and observational techniques.

Previous chapters (Fagen; Wolf) have broached the possible relations of play to behavioural flexibility. This has been a common theme to animal (especially primate) and human studies, but with children a consider-able number of experimental studies on this topic have been carried out. In these studies, a child may be given a play opportunity or experience, for example with sticks and clamps, or with everyday objects such as matchboxes and paper-clips. Later, the child is asked to solve a problem (e.g. to clamp two sticks together into a tool to retrieve a lure) or demonstrate flexible or creative thinking (e.g. to enumerate different possible uses for matchboxes or screwdrivers). Using appropriate non-play experience or control groups, experimental data might yield cause–effect relations better than other sorts of investigation. Indeed, ostensibly, the results of some of these studies support the flexibility hypothesis, and have been quoted as such. Nevertheless, the review by Smith and Simon documents many methodological reservations concerning scoring and yoking procedures, use of control groups, choice of dependent measures, and possible experimenter effects. At present, it would seem that the link between play and creativity cannot be pinned down by experimental studies as easily as at first appeared.

There may be more consensus among the various researches on the imaginary companion or playmate phenomenon, though Partington and Grant too note methodological weaknesses in many studies. Interview data from parents may be inaccurate, and retrospective accounts from older children are subject to memory distortion. From such interview data, it appears that in Western societies, at least, the imaginary companion is a play mode whose presence characterizes some one-quarter to one-third of children, mostly during the preschool and early school years. By and large, children with imaginary companions do not seem to be lonely or poorly adjusted, but to be happy and sociable. These conclusions are born out by the studies reviewed by Partington and Grant, by their own results, and by another study omitted from their review, by Thompson and Johnson (1977).

Historically, the psychological and educational perspectives on fantasy have varied. As Partington and Grant point out, it has been viewed as an escape from reality, or a way of finding security, by some educators and psychoanalysts. Thompson and Johnson (1977) reported that most of their subjects saw their imaginary playmates as 'a close, warm and loving companion who made few demands'. How much practice then, or even challenge, do fantasies such as the imaginary companion provide? In common with many recent theorists, such as Sutton-Smith, the argument of Partington and Grant is that the imaginary companion is a bridge to reality, or a means of experimenting with behaviours; in this case, behaviours of social negotiation and relation. More direct observational data (if they could be obtained) on *how* children interact with their imaginary companions, could be very relevant to this debate.

Rough-and-tumble play in human children is a characteristic play mode but, Humphreys and Smith argue, it has not received the psychological attention given to object and fantasy play. In their chapter, although direct references to animal play are few, much of the methodology runs parallel to animal research: describing the forms of the behaviour and it's distinction from real fighting; the causes of the sex differences; and considering the functional significance of the behaviour in terms of why the predisposition to enjoy this play mode was selected for. The provisional functional hypothesis reached by Humphreys and Smith (that rough-and-tumble originally functioned as practice for fighting and hunting skills), even if correct, does not of course mean that it still functions in this way, or that other effects of this form of play may not now be culturally of greater importance.

Humphreys and Smith supplemented their observational study with sociometric interviews with the children, to gather data on partner choice. Do children play–fight with friends, or those who are perceived as similar in strength? The answer seems to be: both. An extension of the interview method (from ethology to ethogeny; Smith and Sluckin, 1979) involves interviewing children directly about their perceptions of play-fighting. Heaton's results, reviewed in chapter 11, show that some preschool children can make explicit the distinction between real and play-fighting when viewing filmed episodes. Humphreys and Smith did not employ such methods with older children. However Sluckin (1981), in his work with 5- to 13-year-olds in playgrounds, did record the details of encounters, including verbalizations, and also talked to children about their perceptions of, and motivations in, certain episodes. He did not focus specifically on play-fighting, but his general results show that first- and middle-school children are sophisticated in their use and exploitation of play conventions (such as real and pretend); they redefine situations or acts, appeal to friendship rituals and conventions, and tease or show off, in order to achieve their aims (such as getting into a game, or gaining status). It thus seems likely that whatever developmental changes occur, play-fighting might also be used for other ends in older children. (Monkeys can also exploit play conventions; play-wrestling with infants may be employed by rhesus macaque mothers to distract from persistent suckling, or by older siblings to keep the infant from the mother; Breuggeman, 1978).

Finally, the practical relevance of all three sets of research may be noted. For fostering creativity, should certain play curricula be incorporated in nursery or first schools? How does play experience compare with training, in problem-solving? Should having imaginary companions be deliberately encouraged, if they indeed help a child develop socially cooperative skills? What attitudes should parents and teachers have to rough play in children? These are all very real issues which play research can help to shed light on.

REFERENCES

Breuggeman, J. A. (1978). The function of adult play in free-ranging *Macaca mulatta*. In E. O. Smith (ed.), *Social Play in Primates*. New York: Academic Press.

Sluckin, A. (1981). *Growing up in the Playground: the Social Development of Children*. London: Routledge & Kegan Paul.

Smith, P. K. and Sluckin, A. M. (1979). Ethology, ethogeny, etics, emics, biology, culture: on the limitations of dichotomies. *European Journal of Social Psychology* 9, 397–415.

Thompson, E. H. and Johnson, T. F. (1977). The imaginary playmate and other imaginary figures of childhood. In P. Stevens, Jr (ed.), *Studies in the Anthropology of Play: Papers in Memory of Allan Tindall*. West Point, NY: Leisure Press.

9 Object Play, Problem-Solving and Creativity in Children

Peter K. Smith and Tony Simon

Because of the flexible and relatively unconstrained nature of play behaviour, it has often been suggested that one function of play, or at least one prevalent result of play, is an enhancement of problem-solving skills and the kind of innovative behaviour which often helps to solve problems. Such hypotheses have been most often applied to object play, and thus to the higher primates and to human children for whom object play forms a significant part of the behavioural repertoire; although social play can also be considered in a similar way (e.g. Fagen, above chapter 7). In studying vervet monkeys, for example, Fedigan (1972) concluded that play is not '*just* to practice species-specific behavior, or just to learn what the adults of his (her) group have already learned about their social and physical environment, but also to put out as many tests or probes of the environment as possible, to innovate'. Thus, object play in higher primates, besides assisting in the development of tool-using skills already existing in the group or species, could also facilitate learning of quite new behaviours; examples might be the new skills of washing sweet potatoes, and wheat grains, acquired by Japanese macaques on Koshima (Kawai, 1965), or the development of new 'proto-cultural' traditions in chimpanzees (McGrew, Tutin and Baldwin, 1979).

The extent to which play is really important in these ways is under debate. Smith (1982) argued that object play was merely a spin-off of the generally higher intelligence of most primates; but that its potential for practice in tool use was an exaptation (Gould and Vrba, 1982) which became an adaptation in the cebus monkeys and great apes. Similarly, such forms of play had a potential for innovative object use, which was not a specific biological adaptation but which could be (and has been recently) culturally valued in our own species.

In human object play, Bruner (1972) has argued both that play 'is a means . . . of learning . . . in a less risky situation', and also that it 'provides an excellent opportunity to try combinations of behaviours that would, under functional pressure, never be tried'. Such new combinations might then prove to be of functional use in more serious contexts. Bruner was considering play at the level of motor skills and object construction. At a more ideational level, Sutton-Smith (1967, 1977) has emphasized how play can enhance behavioural flexibility. In symbolic play in particular, he suggests, the child tries out new meanings for objects and social relationships; thus play facilitates divergent thinking abilities and role flexibility.

Pepler (1982) suggests that the common themes linking play to problem-solving and divergent thinking are threefold. Firstly, specific exploration would provide initial information about objects (strictly speaking, specific exploration is conceptually different from diversive exploration or play, but characteristically precedes it). Secondly, as both Bruner and Sutton-Smith pointed out, play activities are, by their nature, experimental and flexible. Thirdly, following Vygotsky and Sutton-Smith, symbolic object play could facilitate the transition from concrete to abstract thought, and thus practise symbolic thinking.

There is some amount of correlational evidence that supports the association between playfulness in human children and creativity or divergent thinking ability. For example, Lieberman (1977) has carried out a series of studies linking teachers' ratings of children's playfulness to divergent thinking measures. However, in these and other correlational studies (reviewed by Pepler, 1982) there is always the possibility that some third factor, such as general intelligence or cognitive style, mediates the relationships found.

There are also now a considerable number of experimental studies, which apparently provide a much firmer basis for the hypothesis that play opportunities and play behaviours with objects do foster problem-solving and creative skills. Indeed, such generalizations from these studies have already been made, and at the same time they have come under closer methodological scrutiny which has revealed some weaknesses in design and interpretation (Cheyne, 1982; Rubin, Fein and Vandenberg, 1983). In this chapter, after presenting the details of eleven relevant studies we will consider how strongly various methodological reservations apply, discuss whether any consensus in findings is emerging and conclude with suggestions as to how future progress might be made. The eleven studies chosen all share the same common feature that some children are given a form of play opportunity with objects while others are given some non-play (e.g. observation, training) experience(s). The effects of these experimental manipulations on subsequent problem-solving or divergent thinking are then compared. We have confined ourselves to studies in which only one, or at most a few, experimental sessions are involved (this excludes larger-scale work on symbolic play training, and on different play curricula, see Brainerd, 1982; Johnson and Ershler, 1982).

The studies fall into three groups. The first group comprises those of Sylva (1977), Smith and Dutton (1979), Vandenberg (1981) and Simon and Smith (1983). These employed *lure-retrieval* problems of a convergent nature, i.e. there was only one way to solve the task. Initiated by Sylva, the paradigm follows naturally from Bruner's (1972) theoretical viewpoints while having experimental antecedents in the work of Köhler (1925), subsequently followed by Birch (1945) and Schiller (1952) on previous experience and the solving of lure-retrieval tasks in apes.

A second group of studies comprises those of Dansky and Silverman (1973 and 1975), Li (1978) and Dansky (1980). Following on from Sutton-Smith (1968), who found that children gave more novel uses for toys they liked playing with (but who failed to control for contact time or familiarity), these studies used the *alternate-uses* test of associative fluency as a measure of divergent thinking. Finally, two linked studies by Pepler and Ross (1981) examined both convergent and divergent problem-solving, while Zammarelli and Bolton (1977) looked at symbolic problem-solving as embodied in mathematical concept formation.

The details of these eleven studies are summarized in table 9.1. In addition, the results of a few unpublished thesis studies are mentioned in an appendix to this chapter. We shall leave the reader to peruse the nature of the studies from the table (or from the original sources), and continue by examining the consistency of the reported findings of these studies. We shall then consider three aspects of experimental design in relation to the findings: (1) the nature of the independent variables; (2) the nature of the dependent variables, and (3) the possibilities of experimenter bias.

THE CONSISTENCY OF FINDINGS

(See Columns 3, 7 and 8 of table 9.1.) Amongst the lure-retrieval studies, the general finding is that play and certain non-play experiences are comparable in terms of the number of children who spontaneously solve the problem (i.e. without hints) and the time taken to solution. However, in the earliest three studies, there are some tendencies for the play experience children to do better. In Sylva's study, they apparently needed fewer hints (though full details are lacking in Sylva's published accounts, and see Cheyne, 1982); in Vandenberg's study, for the middle age-group only, the 'play' group had a lower hint-based score on one of the two tasks.

TABLE 9.1 Details of eleven experimental studies which relate play experience to problem-solving skills and creativity. Details of another four unpublished studies are given in the appendix to chapter 9.

Study	Common Pre-test Conditions	Independent Variables and Time of Sessions	Subjects	Procedure	Tests	Dependent Variables	Results	Experimenter Effects
Sylva, 1977	E demonstrated use of clamp on one stick, 1 minute	1 Play; with clamps, and sticks of different lengths — 10 minutes 2 Observe principle; watch E clamp two long sticks together at overlap — 2 minutes 3 Observe components; watch E make constructions, yoked to S's in Condition 1 — 10 minutes 4 Train components; S told by E to make constructions, yoked to S's in Condition 1 — 10 minutes 5 Control; no intervening experience — 0 minutes	180 S's all US mostly white MC. age 3, 4, 5 years. 36 S's (equal b/g for each age group) in each condition	5 E's (3 aware and 2 unaware of hypotheses). One E saw each S individually for Pre-test, Condition and Testing	Lure-retrieval task, to get chalk from box with tool constructed from two long sticks and a clamp	Number of hints given Number of spontaneous solvers Solution time	$1 < 2$, $p < 0.01$, $1 > 3, 4$, $p < 0.05$ $2 = 1 > 4 = 3 = 5$ $(1 > 5, p < 0.01)$ not significant	Testing bias possible Scoring bias possible
Smith and Dutton, 1979	E demonstrated sticks and how stick fits into block. 1 minute. S explored materials, 2 minutes	1 Play; with blocks, and sticks of different lengths — 8 minutes 2 Training; S watches E and imitates in making and seriating double-stick constructions — 8 minutes 3 Control one: S goes immediately to tasks one and two — 0 minutes 4 Control two: S goes immediately to task two — 0 minutes	108 S's all UK age 4 years 36 S's in (1) and (2), 18 S's in (3) and (4) (equal b/g for each condition)	Female E saw each S individually for Pre-Test, Condition and Testing	Lure retrieval tasks, to get marble from box with tool constructed from two long sticks and one block (task one), and then three long sticks and two blocks (task two)	*Task one* No. of hints given No. of spontaneous solvers Solution time *Task Two* No. of hints given No. of spontaneous solvers Solution time	$1 = 2 < 3, p < 0.01$ $1 = 2 = 3$ $1 = 2 < 3, p < 0.05$ $1 < 2 < 3 = 4$, $p < 0.001$ $1 > 2 = 3 = 4$, $p < 0.001$ $1 < 2 < 3 < 4$ $p < 0.001$	Testing bias possible Scoring bias possible
Vandenberg, 1981	S had warm-up period of play with lego bricks for 10 minutes	1 Play; with notched sticks and pipe-cleaners — 10 minutes 2 Question-asking; questions about physical attributes and length of materials — 10 minutes	90 S's all US, ages 4–5, 6–7, and 8–10 years. 45 S's in each condition, matched for age and perceptual-motor abilities	E saw each S individually for Pre-Test, Condition, and Testing, Second E present for Testing	Lure-retrieval tasks to get block from box with tool constructed from two long sticks and a pipe cleaner (task one); and to get sponge from tube with tool constructed from several pipe-cleaners tied together (task two)	*Task one* Hint-based score No. of spontaneous solvers *Task two* No. of spontaneous solvers	$1 > 2, p < 0.05$ (only sig. for 6–7 age groups, $p < 0.001$) $1 = 2$ $1 = 2$	Testing bias possible Scoring bias not possible
Simon and Smith, 1983	E demonstrated sticks and how stick fits into block. 1 minute S explored materials, 2 minutes	1 Play; with blocks, and sticks of different lengths — 8 minutes 2 Training; S watches E and imitates in making and seriating double-stick constructions — 8 minutes	64 S's, all UK age 3:10 to 4:7 32 S's in each condition	First E saw each S individually for Pre-Test and Conditions Second E for testing Second E aware of Condition for half the S's, unaware for other half (balanced with condition); counter balanced with high or low E-S contact	Lure-retrieval tasks as in Smith and Dutton, 1979	*Task one* No. of hints given No. of spontaneous solvers Solution time *Task two* No. of hints given No. of spontaneous solvers Solution time	$1 = 2$ $1 = 2$ $1 = 2$ $1 = 2$ $1 = 2$ $1 = 2$ No main effects of experimental manipulations	Testing bias not found, and not possible in 'unaware' condition Scoring bias not possible
Dansky and Silverman, 1973	E saw each S for one 5-minute colour ing session, 1 week before	1 Free Play; with 7 types of materials — 10 minutes 2 Imitation; watch E do 4 tasks, then imitate, same materials as Condition 1 — 10 minutes 3 Control; colour in four sketches with box of crayons — 10 minutes	90 S's mostly white US, MC/UMC, age 4:0 to 6:1 30 S's (equal b/g) in each condition	Same E (male aged 24) saw each S individually for Condition, and immediately after for Testing. Some independent scoring	Alternate-uses test for each of 4 objects used in Conditions 1 and 2	Standard uses Non-standard uses	$1 = 2 = 2$ $1 > 2 = 3$ $p < 0.01$ for all 4 objects	Testing bias possible Scoring bias unlikely

Study	Conditions	Duration	Subjects	Experimenter procedure	Testing	Measures	Results	Bias
Dansky and Silverman, 1975	Two E's visited S's nursery school for 3 days		36 S's, all white US, MC, age 3:8 to 5:2; 12 S's (equal b/g) in each condition	Two male E's. Both saw S's in pairs for Condition, then each E took one S for Testing to new location in same building	Alternate-uses test for each of 4 objects not seen previously in Conditions			Testing bias possible; Scoring bias possible
	1 Free Play; with 8 types of materials	10 minutes				Standard uses	$1 > 2 = 3$, $p < 0.05$	
	2 Imitation; with E do 4 tasks, then imitate; same materials as Condition 1	10 minutes				Non-standard uses	$1 > 2 = 3$, $p < 0.01$	
	3 Intellectual task; guess object E is thinking of, given clues; same materials as Condition 1	10 minutes						
Li, 1978	E saw each S for one 5-minute colouring session, 1 week before		120 S's, all Canadian, age 4:11 6:1; 30 S's (equal b/g) in each condition	Same E (female graduate student) saw each S individually for Condition, than Testing. Independent scoring	Alternate-uses test for each of 3 objects used in Conditions 1, 2 and 3 and for one new object			Testing bias possible; Scoring bias not possible
	1 Free play; with 3 types of materials	10 minutes				Standard uses	$1 = 2 = 3 = 4$	
	2 Make-believe play; pretend story from E, then make-believe play suggested with same 3 materials as in Condition 1	10 minutes				Non-standard uses	$2 = 1 > 3 = 4$ (sig.)	
	3 Imitation; with E do 3 tasks, then imitate; 6 materials including those in Condition 1	10 minutes						
	4 Control; colour in four sketches with box of crayons	10 minutes						
Dansky, 1980	Four × 2 min observations of each S in pre-school; 'players' spend >25% time, 'nonplayers' spend <5% time, in make-believe play		96 S's, all US wide SES range, mean age 4:7 (54 b, 42 g); 32 S's in each condition (half are 'players', half 'nonplayers')	Two female E's. Both saw S's in pairs for Condition, then immediately after, individually, for Testing	Alternate-uses test for each of 4 objects not seen previously in Conditions	All non-redundant uses	$1 > 2 = 3$, $p < 0.01$ for 'players' only; also $1 > 2 =$ no treatment control, $p < 0.05$ in briefly-mentioned follow-up	Testing bias possible; Scoring bias possible
	1 Free play; with 9 types of materials	10 minutes						
	2 Imitation; watch E do tasks, then imitate; same materials as Condition 1	10 minutes						
	3 Convergent task; guess objects E is thinking of, given clues; same materials as Condition 1	10 minutes						
Pepler and Ross, 1981 Study 1	—		64 S's, all Canadian, mostly MC, age 3:0 to 4:9; 16 S's (equal b/g) in each condition	E saw each S individually for 3 sessions in 5-day period for Condition; then Testing about 4 hours after last Condition session	3 Convergent tasks: form matching, colour-matching, representation matching; 2 Divergent tasks: village task, structure-meaning task	Convergent tasks: No. of correct responses, Time taken to complete; Divergent Tasks: Fluency, Originality	$1 = 2 = 3 = 4$; generally $2 > 1 = 4 > 3$ (sig.)	Testing bias possible; Scoring bias possible
	1. Convergent play; 5 sets of jigsaw pieces with form boards	3 × 10 minutes						
	2 Divergent play; 5 sets of jigsaw pieces without form boards	3 × 10 minutes						
	3 Convergent observation; watch E fit jigsaw pieces into form boards	3 × 10 minutes						
	4 Divergent observation; watch E build structures with jigsaw pieces	3 × 10 minutes						
Pepler and Ross, 1981 Study 2	—		72 S's, all Canadian, mostly MC, age 3:0 to 4:9; 24 S's (equal b/g) in each condition	As above, but Testing done by second E, blind to Condition	4 Convergent tasks: form-matching, representation-matching, two types of colour-matching; 2 Divergent tasks: alternate-uses test, structure-meaning test	Convergent tasks: No. of runs, Correct moves, Incorrect moves, Trial-and-error moves; Divergent tasks: Fluency, Originality	$1 = 2 > 3$ form rep" only, $p < 0.01$; $1 > 2 = 3$ form rep" only, $p < 0.01$; No overall diff $1 < 2 = 3$, n.s.(?); $1 = 2 = 3$; $2 > 1 = 3$, n.s. ($p < 0.06$)	Testing bias not possible; Scoring bias unlikely
	1 Convergent play; 5 sets of jigsaw pieces with form boards	3 × 10 minutes						
	2 Divergent play; 5 sets of jigsaw pieces without form boards	3 × 10 minutes						
	3 Control; read books with E	3 × 10 minutes						
Zammarelli and Bolton, 1977	Pre-tests on modulo-4 concept task. Four days later asked to remember 16 colour combinations		24 S's, all UK, age 10:2 to 12:7; 8 S's in each condition, matched for age, sex and mathematical ability	E saw each S individually for Pre-Test, Condition, and Testing. Independent scoring	Matrix completion task based on modulo-4 concept			Testing bias possible; Scoring bias not possible
	1 Play; explore and play with toy embodying modulo-4 concept	7½ minutes				Memory	$1 > 2 = 3$, $p < 0.002$	
	2 Observation; observe effects on toy, experience yoked to Condition 1	7½ minutes				Conceptual level	$1 > 2 = 3$, $p < 0.001$	
	3 Control; no further experience	7½ minutes						

Key E = experimenter; S = subject; MC = middle class; UMC = upper middle class; b = boy; g = girl; SES = socio-economic status

The most substantial finding is from Smith and Dutton's second task where the 'play' children received many fewer hints than the 'training' children and solved the problem much faster. This second task involved an extension of the training principle and as such was more innovative than the first task which was directly related to the training procedure. However, this specific result was not replicated by the Simon and Smith study.

The general findings of the alternate-uses studies have been that play experience has produced more responses than non-play or control experiences for non-standard uses but not consistently for standard uses. The results of Dansky and, to a lesser extent, Li, suggest that fantasy or make-believe play are particularly efficacious in this respect.

The results of Pepler and Ross's study are mixed, but in general there was little effect of conditions on the solving of convergent problems (though some slight advantage seemed present in the 'convergent play' group in the second study). However, some superiority of the 'divergent play' condition was evident where divergent tasks were concerned.

Overall, these findings suggest that, so far as convergent problems are concerned, play experience is as useful as comparable non-play experiences (such as observation, imitation and questions), but not markedly superior. The principal exception here is the result of Zammarelli and Bolton, who did find play superior to yoked observation or no-treatment controls. In contrast, a general superiority of play over non-play conditions seems evident for divergent tasks. Since it would be for divergent tasks that much of the hypothesized advantages of play would apply (in terms of flexible behaviour and unconstrained combinations), this overall finding is potentially compatible with the prevailing theoretical viewpoint. However, there are some severe methodological shortcomings to most of the studies which prevent immediate acceptance of this conclusion.

THE NATURE OF THE INDEPENDENT VARIABLES

(See column 3 of table 9.1.) All of the studies contrast some kind of play experience with some kind of non-play or control experience(s). In drawing conclusions from the results, it is obviously important to consider what the play experience provided, what the non-play experience provided, and what the control groups controlled for.

The conditions labelled as 'play' or 'free play' have meant that the child is presented with some materials and is allowed to interact with them in an unconstrained matter. The experimenter typically tells the child, for example, 'You may play with all these things; do whatever you would like to do with them' (Dansky and Silverman, 1973). However, this does not guarantee that the ensuing activity is indeed play. Perhaps the biggest problem here is that of intrinsic motivation. Most definitions of play, diverse as they are, agree that one prerequisite of play is that it is an intrinsically-motivated activity. However, the circumstances in which children are given the invitation mentioned above rarely satisfy the requirements necessary for intrinsic motivation to occur, since the child does not actively choose to take part in the experiment (see Deci and Ryan, 1980). Furthermore, only the studies by Sylva, Dansky, Vandenberg, and Pepler and Ross report any observations of the children that show that they were in fact engaged in play.

While it is indeed likely that children do, by some criteria, play with the materials when invited to do so, the problem is not a negligible one. Play is typically preceded by some more specific exploration of unfamiliar materials; only Smith and Dutton, and Simon and Smith, allowed any prior exploration, and then only for an arbitrary period. One of the advantages of play experience might indeed be the opportunity for exploration (Pepler and Ross, 1981) but the relative importance of specific exploration and play are confounded in most of the studies. Observations of what children do in the play condition could allow some insight into the relative importance of exploration, and various forms of play, for problem-solving. The most extensive observations are from Pepler and Ross, who report inter-group differences between their 'convergent play' and 'divergent play' conditions, but unfortunately do not correlate within-group individual differences in play with problem-solving performance. Their 'divergent play' children did engage in more symbolic play, as well as doing better at divergent tasks. This ties in with evidence from Sylva, and Dansky, that non-literal or fantasy play is an important component in any relationship between play and problem-solving.

From a pedagogical viewpoint, at least, the major interest of these studies is whether play experience is in some sense more beneficial for problem-solving than some other kind of experience such as instruction or observation. Obviously the precise nature of the latter may be very important. If one examines the non-play conditions which have exposed the child to the same materials as the play condition, the main types of experience can be classified as training (involving active use of the materials), observation, and questions. The training and observation conditions can be classified as direct (if they deliberately embody the future solution), or indirect. Only two studies (Smith and Dutton, and Simon and Smith; task 1) employed direct training, at least in the sense that the child actively constructed the tool needed (though he or she did not practise the principle of arm extension). A number of studies utilized indirect training where the materials were manipulated but the solution principle was not produced (Dansky and Silverman; Li; Dansky) or only serendipitously in some cases (Sylva). The four alternate-uses studies also incorporated some observation of behaviour not involving the solution before the training began. Indirect observation of this sort was the only form of non-play comparison in two studies (Pepler and Ross; Zammarelli and Bolton), and was present in another (Sylva). One study (Sylva) included a direct observation condition, in which the child observed the future solution. Finally, three studies (Vandenberg; Dansky and Silverman, 1975; Dansky) employed conditions in which children were questioned about the materials. This variety of non-play experiences could militate against consistent findings emerging.

Two studies have employed a yoking procedure to attempt to further link a non-play experience to the play experience. Sylva yoked her 'observe components' and 'train on components' to her 'play' condition, and Zammarelli and Bolton yoked their 'observation' condition to their 'play' condition. This apparently controls more directly for experience with the materials, independently of the play/training or autonomy/ control dimensions which were the principle foci of investigation. Unfortunately, yoked control designs can handicap the yoked children by giving them a variety of experiences which are *not* linked to their ability, whereas they *are* linked to the ability of the play children by definition. The general point is discussed by Church (1964), and it has been discussed in detail in relation to Sylva's study by Cheyne (1982), who shows that on reasonable assumptions as to the effects of yoking, Sylva's yoked children in fact perform no worse than the play children. The Zammarelli and Bolton result is open to similar analysis.

Finally, six out of the eleven studies incorporated some form of control group. In three cases (Sylva; Smith and Dutton; Zammarelli and Bolton) these were no-treatment controls. In three other cases (Dansky and Silverman, 1973; Li; Pepler and Ross, second study) there were alternative materials controls (crayoning or reading tasks for an equivalent period of time to the other conditions).

What is the purpose of control groups in these studies? Given the short duration of the studies (usually less than an hour; though taking place over a five-day period in the Pepler and Ross study) there is no need to control for age effects, or effects of non-specific experience. The obvious factor which is being controlled for is experience of the specific materials to be used later in the tasks. Both no-treatment controls and alternative materials controls are appropriate for this purpose. Surprisingly, in the majority of comparisons, the control groups do not do significantly worse than one or more of the treatment groups. The control group does worse in the Sylva study but *only* on the number of spontaneous solvers measure. The control groups are clearly worse only in the Smith and Dutton study.

These latter two studies both employed no-treatment control groups. Unlike alternative materials control groups, no-treatment controls do not provide any consideration of another factor; that of time with the experimenter and in the experimental situation. Since the children in these studies are mostly quite young, it could well be that suddenly being taken into another room by an unfamiliar experimenter could have anxiety-provoking or concentration-reducing effects. Thus, any inferiority of no-treatment controls is unsurprising and could be due to factors such as these. In contrast, it is worth noting that none of the three studies using alternative materials controls found them significantly inferior to indirect training (Dansky and Silverman, 1975; Li) or, on many comparisons, convergent or divergent play (Pepler and Ross, second study).

THE NATURE OF THE DEPENDENT VARIABLES

(See columns 6 and 7 of table 9.1.) Again, from a pedagogical viewpoint, at least, it would be most valuable to demonstrate any relationship of play to actual problem-solving or creative skills which were potentially of use in real-life situations. In this sense it is a pity that some of the most significant findings favouring play come from the four studies using the alternate-uses test. It is notoriously difficult to measure creativity, and there is no strong evidence to suggest that doing well on the alternative-uses test is going to predict real subsequent creativity or problem-solving ability. The significant results are largely restricted to non-standard uses, which can include far-fetched or bizarre responses (such as using a screwdriver to chop down a tree). The play condition does seem to induce a playful set which produces or disinhibits unusual responses of this kind, but it is not clear that it has any longer-term or practical significance. A set to produce unusual responses in the alternate-uses test can be induced by forms of direct instruction in schoolchildren, as Hudson (1968) found. Some of the other divergent tasks, like those used by Pepler and Ross, seem more convincing in this respect than the alternate-uses test. This is especially true of the task used by Zammarelli and Bolton.

The lure-retrieval tasks, while reasonably close to real-life problems, suffer from a number of drawbacks in procedure and analysis. In all four of these studies, hints were given if children were not seen to be progressing towards the solution. Although the procedure for giving hints is supposedly standardized, in our experience it is extremely difficult not to give hints, or at least verbal encouragement of some kind, in what is inevitably an interactive situation between the child and experimenter. There are also varying procedures or rationales for weighting the various hints. Thus the different hint scores are not as objective as would be desired of such measures. Furthermore, the hints system also affects the other primary measures in these studies. It affects the spontaneous solvers measure since children can be removed from this measure simply by provision of a hint, necessary or otherwise. It can also affect solution time, either by the actual time added on in giving the hint or, if the hint actually helps the child, by reducing overall solution time. Since it seems a fair assumption that the same hints will not help all children to the same extent, then the hint system could be adding more variance to the large individual differences which already exist.

EXPERIMENTER BIAS IN ADMINISTRATION, TESTING AND SCORING

(See column 9 of table 9.1.) The issue of experimenter effects in research is a long-standing and troubling one (see Rosenthal and Rubin, 1978, for a comprehensive review). Its relevance to the experimental studies of play has been broached recently by Cheyne (1982). In fact, all but two of the eleven studies reviewed here are susceptible to possible experimenter effects; in most cases the same experimenter has administered the different treatment conditions, done the testing, and scored the results. The effect of an experimenter who was aware of the study's hypotheses (in a number of cases they even formulated them) could be felt at any one of these stages. This could materialize in the way a play or non-play experience is administered; in the way a test is administered; and in the way the results of the test are scored.

As regards the last of these possibilities, five of the eleven studies *did* control partly or completely for scoring bias (see table 9.1); and in some of the other studies, notably the lure-retrieval designs, the measures used (number of hints, solution time) are sufficiently objective to score that scoring bias is unlikely. Thus, while controls for scoring bias should be applied and this can relatively easily be done (for example, by filming the test situation, as done by Simon and Smith), this is quite likely the least worrisome source of experimenter effects.

If the same experimenter both administers the treatment conditions and the tests, then bias in the administering of both becomes possible. This could appear in the form of unconscious attitudes or cues, either non-specific (e.g. contributing to a relaxed, or stressful, atmosphere), or specific (e.g. contributing solution-relevant information, as in the cues used by the 'genius horse' Clever Hans in 'solving' numerical problems, Pfungst, 1911). Are these realistic worries in the studies here being reviewed? Quite possibly. Non-specific context effects could well be an important problem in the alternate-uses studies, in which a 'playful' or perhaps just a relaxed set or attitude seems to be of major importance for producing non-standard uses. An experimenter not 'expecting' many non-standard uses might well convey a less permissive atmosphere via tone of voice or expression. According to Hudson (1968), in older children at least an individual's fluency score on non- standard uses 'can be modified grossly by quite small adjustments of context'. More specific effects could operate in the lure-retrieval studies. As we have seen, the procedure for giving hints is not very objective. Both the timing of hints, their possible repetition for clarity, and the general kind or level of experimenter interaction with the child could well be susceptible to the experimenter's expectations of performance.

The possibility of testing-bias could be avoided if the experimenter who tested the children did not know their treatment condition. Such a procedure was followed only by Pepler and Ross (second study) and by Simon and Smith. The possibility of treatment bias could only be avoided by using experimenters who had no preconceived ideas about the effects of the treatments (as was done by Simon and Smith).

The issue of testing-bias was specifically investigated by Simon and Smith, who compared results from children with testers aware and unaware of their treatment conditions and with the potential for visual and verbal contact at normal or low levels. The behaviour of the testers to the children did not differ in the aware and unaware conditions, and the performance of the children was not greatly affected by any of the manipulations. Thus this study did not find any *direct* evidence for experimenter testing-bias. However, Simon and Smith did fail to replicate the finding of a superiority for play over training reported by Smith and Dutton in their second (three stick) task. (This failure to replicate is supported by the results of Emberton, 1983, see the appendix to this chapter.) Simon and Smith (1983) hypothesize that there may have been unconscious experimenter bias in Smith and Dutton (1979) in the administering of hints in this second task; specifically, unnecessary low-level hints may have been given to the training children thereby inadvertently lengthening their solution times.

CONCLUSIONS

Having reviewed the studies on play, problem-solving and creativity, and considered various methodological drawbacks which have been prevalent in this area, we will develop the discussion in three ways, Firstly, we will consider improvements which can be made to research in the existing paradigm. Secondly, we will discuss whether any conclusions about the relationship of play to problem-solving and creativity can reliably be drawn from the studies carried out so far. Finally, we will consider alternative research strategies, some of which have already been attempted and some of which might be new directions for future research.

Improvements of the existing paradigm

Although no direct evidence of experimenter effects have yet been proven, there is indirect evidence that they can occur (Simon and Smith, 1983). Clearly, to be convincing, future studies should control for experimenter bias as thoroughly as possible. What is needed is a variant of the traditional 'double blind' technique. In this research there is no problem in the subject (child) being aware of his or her condition, but the experimenter administering the conditions should not be aware of the tests, and the experimenter giving the tests should not be aware of the conditions. Both condition and test administration should be recorded on film, and scored by independent judges.

Filming the administration of conditions also allows for subsequent analysis and re-analysis of what goes on. Do children actually play in the 'free play' condition? Do they actually attend in the 'observation' conditions? A permanent data record also permits subsequent within-group correlations of condition experience with test achievement (although such analyses, being outside the experimental design, are subject to the usual caveats regarding correlational studies).

The actual conditions used should be considered carefully. Ideally, forms of play might be compared with a range of non-play alternatives. The non-play conditions should cover those plausibly helpful for the subsequent task. For example, in the lure-retrieval tasks, helpful training experiences might include reaching out for distant objects with sticks of different lengths, as well as actually constructing tools. The most useful control group will be one which incorporates equal familiarization time with the experimental situation (i.e. alternative materials controls).

What can we conclude so far?

The major provisional conclusions we made earlier were that the effects of play and training were roughly comparable for convergent problem solving; but that play experience, especially that involving symbolic play, may have some advantage for divergent problem-solving. Nevertheless, it would be premature to accept these as firm conclusions, given both the possibilities of experimenter bias already explored, and the curious findings regarding the alternative materials control groups.

As far as the findings on divergent problem-solving are concerned, a sceptic could regard any superiority of play as susceptible to experimenter bias (Smith and Dutton, task 2; Dansky and Silverman, both studies; Li; Pepler and Ross, first study). Where experimenter bias was not possible, the play conditions were not consistently superior (Simon and Smith; Pepler and Ross, second study). Furthermore, the alternative materials control groups did as well as the 'imitation' group in Dansky and Silverman (1973) and in Li; and did not do significantly worse than either of the 'play' groups in Pepler and Ross (second study).

If the alternative materials control group does as well as some of the experimental conditions, then there is one logical conclusion. This is that the specific experience with the materials in the experimental conditions has no impact, or an impact so small that it is swamped by individual variations, or by artifactual effects of the child becoming accustomed to the experimental situation. The duration of these studies should be reconsidered here. Is it the case that a play or training experience lasting only 8 or 10 minutes (in all the studies except Pepler and Ross, where there were three 10-minute sessions) is really not long enough, or the single session not sustained enough, to have much impact? On the most pessimistic assessment, the studies reviewed in this chapter may be showing little more than that children need time to feel secure in a new environment (hence the poor performance of no-treatment controls), and that experimenters can unwittingly affect the performance of their subjects (hence the patchy superiority of the play children in some studies).

Improved studies within the paradigm can tell us whether this assessment is too harsh; but the possibility also prompts us to consider what other directions there may be in the experimental study of play and problem- solving.

Alternative directions for research

One criterion for assessing the value of experimental research, or for considering new directions, is the ecological validity of the study. It may well be the case that the one-session play experiment has poor ecological validity. Some important things may indeed be learnt from a single experience; for example, avoidance of a frightening or harmful event (such as the appearance of a predator, or a nasty food-taste). But what we know of naturally occurring play in animals and humans does not suggest that learning from play is of this kind. Typically, play bouts are repeated, fairly short and often incorporate a fair amount of repetition or overlap of experience with previous bouts. The probable inference is that any learning from play bouts is piecemeal, and cumulative over bouts or episodes.

In fact, other experimental studies of play have used multi-session designs; though these have not specifically or primarily investigated problem-solving or creativity, so they have not been reviewed in detail in this chapter. Some have used a relatively small number of similar sessions, rather as Pepler and Ross (1981) did; for example, the studies on symbolic play and conservation by Golomb and Cornelius (1977), Guthrie and Hudson (1979), Golomb and Bonen (1981), and Golomb, Gowing and Friedman (1982). These still employ a quite short total exposure time (e.g. three periods of 15 minutes in Golomb and Cornelius, 1977), and the lack of replication (Guthrie and Hudson, 1979) suggests that the problem of experimental impact may not have been fully overcome.

Other studies have compared what are effectively play or non-play curricula, in naturalistic studies of play intervention in nursery or infant classes. Typically, such interventions span a term and last at least some dozens of hours (see Smith, Dalgleish and Herzmark, 1981, for a recent example and review). The results can be of quite direct educational relevance, but are more difficult to interpret theoretically. Inevitably, any such experimental curriculum embodies a whole variety of experiences, and it is not possible to say whether any particular component has had a certain effect. Indeed, it is often difficult enough to conclude that any general 'play' aspect to the curriculum has had an effect (Smith, Dalgleish and Herzmark, 1981; Brainerd, 1982). A feasible compromise could be to employ sufficient sessions to make an impact, but not so many that the whole nature of the experiment changes and the interventions become diffuse and less analysable.

Another consideration is that the task(s) and conditions be sensibly matched, and that both, so far as is possible, are educationally or ecologically valid. For example, success with computer games, or computer-operated toys or machines, might be suitable tasks to investigate; they are becoming increasingly important as educational materials. They also permit less experimenter bias, since most interaction is with a machine. At least, it seems to us that tasks where graded success is possible, will be more promising than the lure-retrieval tasks with their confounding problems associated with the giving of hints. Perhaps, too, it is the way the child approaches the problem that will be as informative as the degree of success (some of the Pepler and Ross measures adopted this approach).

Play has been described as an elusive phenomenon. Pinning down the effects of play is proving just as elusive. If indeed the effects of play are slowly cumulative, and perhaps in a sense incidental to the play experience itself, this creates special difficulties, but also special challenges; in this case, challenges to the problem-solving skills and creativity of the investigator.

APPENDIX: UNPUBLISHED THESIS STUDIES SUPPLEMENTING TABLE 9.1

Barnett (1976) used six conditions, with 9 children in each (US, aged 3:6 to 5:9). The task was to assemble a mobile toy and move it up and over a ramp by constructing a tool. The conditions involved visual or physical demonstrations of part of the solution, or free play with relevant or irrelevant materials. The same experimenter administered the conditions and the task. Out of a very large number of analyses, few were significant, quite possibly because of the small sample size.

Zammarelli (1977) carried out a series of studies, one of which was published in Zammarelli and Bolton (1977). Five other studies are reported in the thesis. The first was similar to the published study, but with less rigorous procedural controls. University students performed better after the play experience than after yoked experience or instruction. Another study used a toy embodying base-two operations. Eight children each were assigned to free play, demonstration, or hybrid conditions and then given a written test and interview. The interview rankings, but not the test rankings, showed the free play children to have significantly superior understanding of the base-two operations. Three further studies employed a five-by-five display board with a game similar to 'battleships'. Free play children were compared with yoked experience children. Most results were non-significant, quite possibly because of small sample size (five or eight in each condition). These latter studies used US children aged 9 to 12 years.

Darvill (1982) carried out a lure-retrieval study. There were 90 children (US, aged 4:11 to 7:1) who were given either play or demonstration experiences with materials either appropriate or non-appropriate to the solutions. Tasks were a box problem as in Smith and Dutton (1979) and a tube problem as in Vandenberg (1981). Following the procedure of Smith and Dutton (1979), there was a second version of both problems requiring an extension of the first. However, in this study the demonstration session never included the solution-principle of even the first problem. Furthermore, all children were allowed five minutes of free play between the two problems. Many children used 'unexpected' methods to solve the tube problem. Perhaps for these reasons the results showed no consistent differences between the groups.

Emberton (1983) carried out a close replication of Smith and Dutton, 1979, but incorporated some control for the amount of experimenter/ child interaction. There were 40 children (UK, aged 3:8 to 4:10), assigned equally to play or training conditions and within these two, normal and low experimenter interaction (manipulated by the experimenter's seating position). Scoring was done independently. There were no significant differences between the play and training groups, either on task 1 or task 2. The normal/low manipulation did affect experimenter/child interaction, but did not affect task performance. The results closely parallel those of Simon and Smith (1983).

ACKNOWLEDGEMENT

During the writing of this chapter Tony Simon was supported by a grant from the Social Science Research Council, London.

REFERENCES

Barnett, L. A., (1976). The contrast between play and other forms of learning in preschool children's problem-solving ability. Unpublished Ph.D. thesis, University of Illinois at Urbana-Champaign, USA.

Birch H. G. (1945). The relation of previous experience to insightful problem solving. *Journal of Comparative Psychology* 38, 367–83.

Brainerd, C. J. (1982). Effects of group and individualized dramatic play training on cognitive development. In D. J. Pepler and K. H. Rubin (eds), *The Play of Children: Current Theory and Research*. Basel: S. Karger.

Bruner, J. S. (1972). The nature and uses of immaturity. *American Psychologist* 27, 687–708.

Cheyne, J. A. (1982). Object play and problem solving: methodological problems and conceptual promise. In D. J. Pepler and K. H. Rubin (eds), *The Play of Children: Current Theory and Research*. Basel: S. Karger.

Church, R. M. (1964). Systematic effect of random error in the yoked control design. *Psychological Bulletin* 62, 122–31.

Dansky, J. L. (1980). Make-believe: a mediator of the relationship between play and associative fluency. *Child Development* 51, 576–9.

Dansky, J. C., and Silverman, I. W. (1973). Effects of play on associative fluency in preschool-aged children. *Developmental Psychology* 9, 38–43.

Dansky, J. L., and Silverman, I. W. (1975). Play: a general facilitator of associative fluency. *Developmental Psychology* 11, 104.

Darvill, D. (1982). Object play and problem solving of young children. Unpublished MA thesis, University of Waterloo, Canada.

Deci, E. L. and Ryan, R. M. (1980). The empirical exploration of intrinsic motivational processes. In L. Berkowitz (ed.), *Advances in Experimental Social Psychology, Vol. 13*. New York: Academic Press.

Emberton, R. (1983). Play and problem solving: an investigation of experimenter effects in studies attempting to determine the relationship between the two. Unpublished BA thesis, University of Sheffield, UK.

Fedigan, L. (1972). Social and solitary play in a colony of vervet monkeys *(cercopithecus aethiops)*. *Primates* 13, 347–64.

Golomb, C., and Bonen, S. (1981). Playing games of make-believe: the effectiveness of symbolic play training with children who failed to benefit from early conservation training. *Genetic Psychology Monographs* 104, 137–59.

Golomb, C., and Cornelius, C. B. (1977). Symbolic play and its cognitive significance. *Developmental Psychology* 13, 246–52.

Golomb, C., Gowing, E. D. G. and Friedman, L. (1982). Play and cognition: Studies of pretence play and conservation of quantity. *Journal of Experimental Child Psychology* 33, 257–79.

Gould, S. J., and Vrba, E. S. (1982). Exaptation – a missing term in the science of form. *Paleobiology* 8, 4–15.

Guthrie, K., and Hudson, L. M. (1979). Training conservation through symbolic play: a second look. *Child Development* 50, 1269–71.

Hudson, L. (1968). *Frames of Mind*. London: Methuen.

Johnson, J. E. and Ershler, J. (1982). Curricular effects on the play of preschoolers. In D. J. Pepler and K. H. Rubin (eds), *The Play of Children: Current Theory and Research*. Basel: S. Karger.

Kawai, M. (1965). Newly acquired precultural behavior of the natural troop of Japanese monkeys on Koshima islet. *Primates* 6, 1–30.

Köhler, W. (1925). *The Mentality of Apes*. London: Kegan Paul, Trench, Trubner & Co.

Li, A. K. F. (1978). Effects of play on novel responses in kindergarten children. *Alberta Journal of Educational Research* 24, 31–6.

Lieberman, J. N. (1977). *Playfulness: its Relationship to Imagination and Creativity*. New York: Academic Press.

McGrew, W. C., Tutin, C. E. G., and Baldwin, P. J. (1979). Chimpanzees, tools and termites: cross-cultural comparisons of Senegal, Tanzania and Rio Muni. *Man (NS)* 14, 185–214.

Pepler, D. J. (1982). Play and divergent thinking. In D. J. Pepler and K. H. Rubin (eds), *The Play of Children: Current Theory and Research*. Basel: S. Karger.

Pepler, D. J., and Ross, H. S. (1981). The effects of play on convergent and divergent problem solving. *Child Development* 52, 1202–10.

Pfungst, C. (1911). *Clever Hans: a Contribution to Experimental Animal and*

Human Psychology. New York: Holt.

Rosenthal, R. and Rubin, D. B. (1978). Interpersonal expectancy effects: the first 345 studies. *Behavioral and Brain Sciences* 3, 327–415.

Rubin, K. H., Fein, G. G., and Vandenberg, B. (1983). Play. In P. H. Mussen and E. M. Hetherington (eds), *Handbook of Child Psychology (4th edn), Vol. 4*. New York and Chichester: Wiley.

Schiller, P. H. (1952). Innate constituents of complex responses in primates. *Psychological Review* 59, 177–91.

Simon, T. and Smith, P. K. (1983). The study of play and problem solving in preschool children: have experimenter effects been responsible for previous results? *British Journal of Developmental Psychology* 1, 289–97.

Smith, P. K. (1982). Does play matter? Functional and evolutionary aspects of animal and human play. *Behavioral and Brain Sciences* 5, 139–84.

Smith, P. K., Dalgleish, M., and Herzmark, G. (1981). A comparison of the effects of fantasy play tutoring and skills tutoring in nursery classes. *International Journal of Behavioral Development* 4, 421–41.

Smith, P. K. and Dutton, S. (1979). Play and training in direct and innovative problem solving. *Child Development* 50, 830–6.

Sutton-Smith, B. (1967). The role of play in cognitive development. *Young Children* 22, 361–70.

Sutton-Smith, B. (1968). Novel responses to toys. *Merrill-Palmer Quarterly* 14, 151–8.

Sutton-Smith, B. (1977). Play as adaptive potentiation. In P. Stevens, Jr (ed.), *Studies in the Anthropology of Play: Papers in Memory of Allan Tindall* Cornwall, NY: Leisure Press.

Sylva, K. (1977). Play and learning. In B. Tizard and D. Harvey (eds), *Biology of Play*. London: S.I.M.P./Heinemann.

Vandenberg, B. (1981). The role of play in the development of insightful tool-using strategies. *Merrill-Palmer Quarterly* 27, 97–109.

Zammarelli, J. E. (1977). The use of autonomy in the development of mathematical concepts in primary and middle school children. Unpublished Ph.D. thesis, University of Durham, UK.

Zammarelli, J. and Bolton, N. (1977). The effects of play on mathematical concept formation. *British Journal of Educational Psychology* 47, 155–61.

10 Imaginary Playmates and Other Useful Fantasies

John T. Partington and Catherine Grant

This chapter will discuss the significance of the imaginary playmate fantasy within the context of other fantasies, social behaviours, general development, and coping throughout life. Our concern about this topic is paralleled by changing interests toward fantasy among educators and psychologists.

At the turn of the century, fantasy and sociodramatic play were considered by educators as merely irrelevant escape from reality (Montessori, 1912). Even for a long time after, rote learning the 'three R's' continued to be the major educational approach to prepare children for life; i.e. to take their proper place in the world of work. Equally stultifying was the emphasis, within psychology, of militant behaviourism which muzzled our interests in anything beyond simple S–R phenomena for many years.

Fortunately, thinking has begun to change among those interested in child development. As suggested by Smith (1982), this is perhaps because we recognize that education is becoming increasingly handicapped in preparing children for the future. Education sets contemporary goals for children, which more and more may be generating obsolete learnings due to rapid social change in industrialized societies. Fantasy play, on the other hand, provides innovative learning experiences. These are necessary to equip children with generalized behavioural repertoires appropriate for dealing with the novel roles and relationships to be encountered in whichever probabilistic future may unfold.

Our review will attempt to answer the following questions. What is the imaginary playmate fantasy? Who engages in such a fantasy? When does the fantasy occur? Where does the fantasy fit within the actor's behavioural and imaginal repertoire? Why is the fantasy important, both to the individual, and to those of us interested in human experience, adjustment, and actualization?

Before proceeding, a note of clarification is in order. Although most reports in the literature use the term 'imaginary companion' to designate this fantasy, we prefare the label 'imaginary *playmate*'. We feel that if play can be defined as 'transformation' (Schwartzman, 1978), then the product of the most ultimate transformation, i.e. creating *someone* out of nothing, should at least be semantically linked to the term 'play'.

OVERVIEW

Two streams of research activity concerning this fantasy may be found in the literature, one reflecting the psychoanalytic tradition, and the other incorporating assumptions and methods of developmental psychology.

Psychoanalytic investigators have studied this fantasy primarily through intensive case studies of disturbed children. Until recently they have focused on compensatory and conflict reduction functions of the fantasy. For example, the fantasy has been variously interpreted as a vehicle for the discharge of unacceptable impulses, as a way of prolonging feelings of omnipotence, as a mode of handling trauma or intense stress, and for children with limited synthetic capacities, the fantasy is said to bridge the gap between external controls and internalized superego, and/or to defend against disintegration and thereby assist in psychic integration of emerging aspects of the self. The most complete review of such literature is given in Nagera (1969). Though not included in this review, we should also add to these jaundiced, though perhaps realistic, psychoanalytic views of the role of this kind of fantasy in the lives of threatened children. Specifically, note Freud's (1975, first published 1927) interpretation of the illusion of God as a fantasy father-companion in our lives. Those interested in more recent psychoanalytic perspectives, which emphasize the positive growth potential of this fantasy, are referred to Benson (1980) and Rucker (1981).

Much of the child development research has been reviewed by Masih (1978). Our own impression from the recent literature is that developmental psychologists usually study large samples of normal subjects, and they view this fantasy as a common occurrence which may provide mental rehearsal for social development. We have located only 12 published reports of systematic research focusing directly on this fantasy, as follows: Ames and Learned, 1946; Calderia et al., 1978; Hurlock and Burstein, 1932; Jersild et al., 1933; Manosevitz et al., 1973; Manosevitz et al., 1977; Rosenfeld et al., 1982; Schaefer, 1969; Singer and Singer, 1981; Singer and Steiner, 1966; Svendsen, 1934; and Vostrovsky, 1895.

Although the research methodology of these studies was generally more systematic than that found in psychoanalytic reports, results of most of these studies are clouded by one, or sometimes a combination, of the following weaknesses:

1 *Definitions* There were wide differences in how this fantasy was defined; some investigators included human characters only, others included humans, animals and human-like objects, while some neglected to use and/or report their operational definition of the phenomenon under study.

2 *Data* Studies which relied exclusively on the direct verbal reports of young children could be biased due to a number of 'on-stage-effects', such as need for social approval. This is also true for studies based on retrospective adolescent reports, but these could also be invalidated by selective memory distortions. Finally, studies which utilized parent reports could include all of the above errors, plus the further handicap that knowledge of the child's imaginary playmate depends largely on parents' observations of the child's behaviour: if some of the children in these studies chose to keep their fantasy a secret, then parents' reports would underestimate incidence of the phenomenon; alternatively, if parents were not interested in, or held negative attitudes toward, their child's imaginal processes, then parental observations and reports would be misleading.

3 *Sampling* Samples were often small and select, thus invalidating reports on such features as incidence of the fantasy in the population.

4 *Tests* Some studies used questionable measures of intelligence and other attributes.

5 *Statistical treatment* No evidence from statistical tests was given for some reported results, and sometimes meaningful interpretations were attempted in the face of statistical non-significance.

6 *Design* Correlates of the imaginary playmate fantasy were often difficult to interpret since the scope of the matrix of variables was usually limited.

On a more positive note, however, we can report a gradual trend toward greater research sophistication in this area. Methodological highlights from these studies include Vostrovsky's first attempt to study this fantasy using *both* child and adult reports, Jersild's use of statistics, Svendsen's decision to develop an operational definition for the imaginary playmate fantasy, the work of Singer with blind children, the Manosevitz effort to study the behavioural significance of the fantasy through systematic laboratory observations, the efforts of Calderia and the Singers to identify implications of the fantasy for subsequent social relations in free play, and finally the attempt of Rosenfeld to study how the fantasy fits within a broader array of other fantasy modes.

The chapter plan is as follows: the first section will answer *what* is comprised in the imaginary playmate fantasy and *when* it occurs; the second section identifies *who* invents the fantasy. These descriptive sections are given in the form of a synthesis derived from the twelve empirical sources discussed above. Following this, a third section will show *where* this fantasy fits within the individual's cognitive and behavioural repertoire. Inferences will be drawn from the four most recent programmes of research on this topic, including our own as yet unpublished work. Detailed methodological summaries are included to inform the reader how current research is being conducted in this area. The fourth section explains *why* this fantasy is important. Converging interpretations from developmental and psychoanalytic reports are reported. Finally the fifth section explains *why* we should continue to study this fantasy, and how we should consider doing this in future work.

WHAT IS AN IMAGINARY COMPANION AND WHEN IS IT EXPERIENCED?

What

Most imaginary playmates are human, though a few are animal, or elves and fairies. Generally, they are characters which the children admire, and are usually based on, or borrowed from, stories and pictures in books, films, and more recently television. Most have names of real people, or names appropriate to their source (e.g. 'Tom', after the character Tom Sawyer).

The majority of imaginary playmates are of the same age as the child, although some are older. Most children, especially boys, create only one imaginary playmate of the same sex. This trend also holds for girls, although girls are somewhat more prone than boys to create more than one playmate and to include, in their fantasy, imaginary playmates of both sexes.

Finally, in the vast majority of cases, the imaginary playmate is experienced by the child as very real; for example, children often accommodate for the physical presence of their fantasy friend by yielding one side of their bed, and many children eidetically 'see' and 'hear' their conversations with this playmate. Furthermore, most children report a frequent and enduring, rather than a transitory, relationship with this fantasy friend.

When

This fantasy is triggered either by negative circumstances, such as feeling lonely through lack of companionship, or feeling upset because of being scolded; or it is initiated by the salience of some stimulus cue in a story or picture. Once created, the fantasy playmate is usually not shared with real playmates.

Play episodes with the imaginary friend sometimes include positive feelings such as respect, love, happiness, and peace, but sometimes the feelings are painful, such as shame. One recurring play theme involves parental discipline or reactions to authority in general. The role of the imaginary companion in these episodes includes taking the blame for what the child has done, being allowed to do that which the child was forbidden, or being asked by the child to grant permission to do the forbidden act. For blind children, the imaginary playmate was sighted, and could wander around freely in the world.

Finally, termination of the fantasy is usually associated with a life-change event such as starting school, but in some cases, termination results from intrusion and interference with the fantasy by others. Some children drop the fantasy abruptly while others give it up gradually.

WHO ENGAGES IN THE IMAGINARY PLAYMATE FANTASY?

Modal incidence of this fantasy is 30%. However, estimates range between 13% to 65%, depending on definitions used and samples studied.

Our synthesized profile of the child who creates an imaginary playmate was derived from a review of organismic variables, such as age, sex, general temperament, intelligence, creativity, verbal fluency, and visual acuity; as well as familial and situational variables, such as socio-economic status, parental attitudes toward fantasy, time spent with parents, ordinal position and time spent with siblings, number of pets, television viewing practices in the home, and availability of other playmates. Only replicated, converging findings will be reported, with the exception of the blind–sighted variable for which there was just one study.

Organismic characteristics

The child who creates an imaginary playmate is most likely to be 3–6 years of age; however, some younger children also engage in this fantasy, and it continues for many children into adolescence. Incidence is higher for girls than boys, and for blind compared to sighted children. Finally, children with imaginary playmates seem to have a slight edge over others in verbal-literary skills.

Familial and situational factors

Very few background factors characterize children who invent imaginary playmates: first, they experience less sibling contact, either because they are 'only' children, first-borns, or children in families characterized by large age-gaps between siblings; second, parents of children with imaginary playmates generally feel that the fantasy is good for their child; and third, boys with imaginary playmates watch less television than other boys.

WHERE DOES THE IMAGINARY PLAYMATE FANTASY FIT WITHIN THE CHILD'S BEHAVIOURAL AND IMAGINAL REPERTOIRE?

The purpose of this section is not simply to locate the imaginary playmate fantasy within a behavioural and psychological space, but by doing so, we hope that it will provide an empirical base for us to begin to judge the significance of this fantasy for the overall adjustment of the child.

The following four independent research teams have contributed to this problem: (1) Manosevitz (e.g. Manosevitz et al., 1973; Manosevitz et al., 1977); (2) Singer (e.g. Calderia, et al., 1978; Singer and Singer 1981); (3) Rosenfeld (e.g. Rosenfeld, et al., 1982); and (4) Partington and Grant (e.g. Grant, 1981; Grant, 1982). We will provide detailed summaries of the procedures and findings of each.

Manosevitz

This team has published two studies. The first involved parents of 222 male and female preschool children, aged 3–5 years. Questionnaire data were obtained concerning such matters as whether their child had an imaginary companion, and how the child interacted with adults and played with other children at home. Parents were instructed to think of the imaginary companion as 'a very vivid imaginal character (person, animal, or object) with which their child interacts during his play and daily activities'. Interaction with adults at home was assessed on two dimensions, using seven-point scales, anchored respectively by 'shy and reserved' to 'open and outgoing', and by 'very adept at talking and interacting with adults' to 'talks and interacts much easier with children than adults'. Play behaviour at home was assessed by checking 'yes' or 'no' for each of seven adjectives.

Results showed that 28% of cases were reported by parents as having an imaginary playmate. These children were rated as being more capable of interacting with adults, and their play was judged as more 'self-initiated'.

The second study involved five-year-old children, of whom 42 had imaginary companions and 42 did not, drawn from the sample used in their previous study. Each subject was tested in the privacy of his own room by a 'blind' experimenter. The Peabody Picture Vocabulary Test – Form A was used to assess intelligence, and the Uses and Abstract Patterns Task was given to measure creativity. A behavioural measure of 'waiting ability' was also given which had the child pretend he was driving a car. Boxed-in by a cardboard shield, the child was instructed that, 'to be a good driver, you have to sit real still, watch the road, and not talk or turn around'. The number of seconds after the 'go' signal during which the child kept still was the index of 'waiting'.

There were no significant differences between children with and without imaginary playmates on any of these measures.

Singer

The two studies in this research programme assessed the relationship between the imaginary playmate fantasy and other imaginative play behaviours. In the first study, subjects were 141 three- and four-year-old boys and girls attending day-care and nursery schools. Each child was interviewed concerning imaginative activities in general, and a question was included concerning whether or not the child had a 'make-believe friend'. Data were obtained from parents by means of a questionnaire concerning the play of their children, which included items about the number of imaginary playmates engaged in by their child, and the frequency of such fantasy play.

Pairs of trained observers assessed the child's play in school. They watched each child on two separate days, and independently recorded all activities within a ten-minute period during early morning free play. Protocols included the following variables: imaginativeness, positive affect, concentration, overt aggression, cooperation with peers, mood and social interaction, and verbal behaviour including total number of words used, and mean length of utterance.

Results were based on findings from the 106 children whose parents completed the questionnaire. Compared to girls without imaginary playmates, girls with pretend friends showed more imaginativeness, more positive affect, such as smiling and laughing, more cooperation and sharing with peers, and less anger during free play at school. Boys with imaginary playmates showed more positive affect than those without this fantasy.

The second study in this series involved 111 children, similar to those in the above study. Again, data were obtained from testing and interviews with the child, parental reports of play at home, and objective behaviour ratings of the child's free play at school. However, this study utilized a quantitative index of the imaginary playmate fantasy. It was based on parental responses to the following questions: 'Has your child ever had an imaginary companion? Yes/No/More than one'; 'Did this imaginary friend appear: only once/more than once/or is it a steady companion?'; 'Does your child talk to the imaginary companion? Yes/No'.

Data were analysed according to a series of stepwise multiple regressions. The imaginary companion index was included in a battery of variables comprising child's age, IQ, socio-economic status, ethnicity and level of imagination. This battery was regressed against play variables, language variables, and television viewing.

Results were analysed separately for boys and girls. For boys, the imaginary playmate index was involved significantly in the following outcomes: first, imaginativeness during free play was positively linked with the imaginary companion index and family background, and negatively with watching television cartoons. Secondly, positive affect during free play was strongly related to the imaginary companion index; those with a pretend friend showed fewer signs of fearfulness and anxiety during play. Third, the imaginary companion variable was also the major contributor to behavioural ratings of the child's sharing, helping, and general degree of cooperation with peers, while watching adult television 'action' programmes and news was negatively related to these cooperative acts.

Similar results were obtained for girls concerning the significance of having an imaginary playmate in predicting helping and sharing with peers. In addition, the imaginary playmate index was also positively associated with persistence during play, and to emotions and moods during play; specifically, feelings of anger, fearfulness, and sadness were *less* likely in girls with imaginary companions.

Rosenfeld

The three studies in this series were undertaken to develop a psychometric measure of fantasy behaviour in children. They are reported here to help us identify where the imaginary playmate fantasy fits within the broader framework of the child's overall imaginal processes.

In the first study, an ethnically and socio-economically heterogeneous sample of 713 children in grades one and three were asked, 'Did you ever have a make-believe friend who you talked to and went places with you?' This question was part of a 45-item test-battery designed to assess a wide variety of children's fantasies. Each child was tested in a group of classmates. Questions were read aloud by the experimenter, and the child recorded his answers according to categories provided on the response sheet. The following standard orientation was used for all groups:

> You know how sometimes when you're by yourself, or before you fall asleep at night, or when you're just not doing anything special, you start to think about something just for fun, or because it just pops into your head? Well, this happens to everybody – adults as well as boys and girls. Sometimes these thoughts are big, long, make-believe stories, and sometimes they are just quick little thoughts. We call these make-believe thoughts 'day-dreams'. You know, also, how sometimes you play (by yourself or with friends) and you pretend that you're somebody or something else? Or you pretend that a toy is really something besides the toy? Well, I would like very much to know about your day-dreams, and about the pretend games that you play.

Results of the factor-analysis of the 45 test items were assessed against the original set of constructs used to guide selection of the item pool. On the basis of these empirical and conceptual considerations, 9 of the 11 factors were retained. These were further refined statistically to maximize internal consistencies and face validities.

The imaginary playmate item, 'Did you have a make-believe friend who you talked to and who went places with you?' loaded on the 'Fanciful' fantasy factor, together with the following items: (1) 'Sometimes when you play pretend things, do you feel so happy that you don't ever want the game to end?' (2) 'Do you day-dream about very happy things?' (3) 'Do you play pretend games about how things used to be when you were much younger – before you started to go to school?' (4) 'Does your mother or father, or someone else, read fairy tales to you [third grade, 'Do you read . . . '] – like 'Hansel and Gretel' or 'Snow White?' Subsequently, second-order factor-analysis found that the factor comprising the imaginary playmate fantasy clustered with a 'Vivid' fantasy factor (e.g. 'Do the people and things that you day-dream about sometimes seem so real that you think you can almost see or hear them in front of you?'), and a 'Scary' fantasy factor (e.g. 'Do you play scary pretend games – like 'ghost' or 'monster', or something like that?'). These three factors were said to represent a 'Fanciful–Intense' style of fantasy. Finally, when 540 of these children were retested one year later, all nine fantasy factors showed significant reliability, with the highest stability index ($r = 0.43$) obtained for the Fanciful fantasy factor.

Two validity studies were then undertaken with 73 similar children. Their scores on the nine-factor fantasy profile were related to other measures of day-dreaming, and imaginative play predispositions, as well as with gender and school grade. The day-dreaming index was obtained by asking children to describe or make up a day-dream. This was scored 'blind' by two judges on four dimensions: affect, richness of fantasy, unreality, and fluency. Reliabilities ranged from 0.89 to 0.94. Imaginative play predispositions were assessed by an interview, which included the following items: (1) 'What is your favourite game? What do you like to play most?' (2) 'What game do you like to play best when you are alone? Do you ever think things up?' (3) 'Do you ever have pictures in your head? Do you ever see make-believe things, or pictures in your mind, and think about them? What sorts of things?' (4) 'Do you have a make-believe friend? Do you have an animal or toy or make-believe person you talk to, or take along to places with you?'

Strong positive relationships were obtained between the Fanciful – Intense style of fantasy, which characterizes children with imaginary companions, and the range of imaginative activities as assessed by the Imagination Play Predisposition questionnaire used by the Singer research group. Despite the presence of common method variance, these correlations are impressive since they provide statistical control for measures obtained in the study of fantasy frequency and verbal fluency. Further canonical correlations revealed that those children high on Fanciful fantasy invent day-dreams that are high on affect (e.g. 'The monster came, and I was really scared').

Finally, in a third study, discriminant analyses showed that girls scored higher on the Fanciful fantasy factor, while boys scored higher on an 'Active–Heroic' fantasy factor; and that younger children in the first grade at school, compared to those in the third grade, scored higher on the Fanciful factor.

Taking these three studies together, we can infer with considerable confidence that the imaginary playmate fantasy fits within a stable Fanciful–Intense style of fantasy. This is because the first study revealed that the fantasy factors are stable and internally consistent; the second study evidenced significant concurrent validity for these fantasy factors; and because the results of the third study are consistent with age and sex trends in the literature.

Grant and Partington

The purposes of our investigations were as follows: (1) to examine the reliability and validity of parental reports concerning the imaginary playmate fantasy; (2) to determine the location of the imaginary playmate fantasy within a factor structure derived from a broad array of other fantasy behaviour; (3) to explore the possibility that there may be fantasy types among children, and that the imaginary playmate fantasy may not simply be an isolated phenomenon, but may be part of a more inclusive set of fantasy predispositions; and finally (4) to replicate the important relationship, found by the Singer group, between the imaginary playmate fantasy and the disposition to help and share with peers during free play.

Our initial sample involved 47 children, 20 boys and 27 girls, in the Carleton University experimental preschool. These children ranged in age from 2 years 10 months to 5 years 2 months, with a mean of 3 years 9 months. They were from upper-, and upper-middle-class families of various cultural and ethnic backgrounds. This sample was supplemented by including an additional 33 children from the same preschool assessed in the next year.

Data about the child's imaginary playmate fantasy and other imaginal processes were obtained from a questionnaire survey of parents. Parents were told that we were interested in their child's 'world of make-believe'. They were then given nine descriptions of imaginary play, all represented as 'quite normal activities'. They were asked whether their child engaged in each of these, and how frequently. The nine categories are given below:

1 Imaginary companion. An imaginary companion is an invisible character (person, animal or object) which the child pretends to interact with, and apparently this character interacts with the child. Often this character is named or referred to in conversation by the child.
2 Imaginary inanimate object. An imaginary inanimate object is an invisible object which the child utilizes during play, however, unlike an imaginary companion it does not interact with the child. An example is when the child talks on an imaginary telephone, unlocks a door with a non-existent key, or pretends to ride a horse by galloping around the house.
3 Impersonation or role-playing. The child assumes the role of some character (person, animal or object). The child pretends to be this character and acts as such, e.g. pretending to be a teacher, fireman,

dog, etc. He/she may even insist upon being addressed by the name of the character.

4 Personification. The child attributes human characteristics to objects or animals. The child talks to or plays with the object or animal as though it was a real person, e.g. pretending Teddy is a real friend, or the dolly is a live baby. The child may manipulate the object or animal so as to pretend it moved of its own accord, or speak for the object giving it a voice, e.g. making a doll walk, or 'talk'.

5 Object and place transformation. The child imagines or pretends that an object has characteristics of some different object, or that a place is somewhere else than it actually is. For example, a bathtub is an ocean and the soap is a ship; under the table is a cave; or the bed is a raft, or a horse.

6 Time transformation. The child imagines that he/she is in some other period of time, either past or future. For example, the child may pretend that you can read his/her thoughts while he/she is playing in an imaginary futuristic world where people don't have to speak, they can send 'mind messages', or, the child may pretend to be doing what granny did years ago, such as cooking on a wood stove, or riding to church in a horse and cart.

7 Imaginative speech play. The child invents rhymes, jokes, stories or composes songs or poetry. Any other original word games are also included here.

8 Day-dreaming. The child is usually sitting or lying quietly. He/she is not paying attention to what is going on, and seems to be in a different world. It looks as if he/she is in a trance or deep thought. The child is oblivious to all around him/her and you might have to speak twice before he/she will hear you.

9 Dreaming. Sleep related dreams reported by the child.

Parents of the children in the initial subject pool were asked to assess their child according to these same categories one year later, while parents of children in the second supplementary sample were asked to re-assess their child three weeks later. In addition, all parents were asked to complete an inventory which assessed their own acceptance of day-dreaming (Singer and Antrobus, 1970).

Before describing the fantasy findings, evidence of their reliability and validity will be reviewed. Assessments by parents of their child's imaginary behaviours were very reliable, and seven of the nine expressions of fantasy were found to be very stable. In fact, the imaginary playmate fantasy yielded a test–retest reliability of 0.69, and the stability coefficient of 0.79 was the highest obtained from this fantasy protocol.

Finally, parental reports of the imaginary playmate fantasy were unrelated to their own attitudes concerning the acceptance of day-dreaming (r = 0.12). These findings invite considerable confidence in the results to be reported below.

Factor analysis of the nine-category fantasy questionnaire yielded two factors with eigen-values greater than unity. Table 10.1 shows the varimax rotated solution. Using loadings greater than 0.35 as a guide for interpretation, it may be seen that factor 1 incorporates fantasy based on transformations of given reality (e.g. personification, 0.72; imperson-ation, 0.68; and object/place transformation, 0.60); while factor 2 incorporates the much more dramatic fantasy in which something or someone is invented out of nothing (e.g. imaginary companion, 0.69, and imaginary inanimate object, 0.67).

Findings on this point are consistent with those obtained by the Rosenfeld group; for example, the one-year-apart assessments by parents showed the imaginary playmate to be a stable form of fantasy, and an obtained factor structure showed that the imaginary companion fantasy is associated with other highly fanciful transformations.

TABLE 10.1   Rotated factor solution of the nine-variable fantasy
                 questionnaire

Imaginary behaviours	*Factor 1*	*Factor 2*
Imaginary companion	0.09	0.69*
Imaginary inanimate object	0.17	0.67*
Impersonation or role-playing	0.68*	0.27
Personification	0.72*	0.02
Object and place transformation	0.60*	0.19
Time transformation	−0.02	0.04
Imaginative speech play	0.11	0.04
Day-dreaming	−0.05	0.06
Dreaming	−0.02	0.07

*factor loading exceeds 0.35

A further analysis of these fantasy indices was undertaken to determine whether there are fantasy types among children, and to locate where the imaginary playmate fits within the obtained typology. To this end, a computerized Modal Profile Analysis (Skinner and Lei, 1980) was undertaken. The assumption is that the sample can be differentiated into relatively homogeneous sub-groups. The routine estimates a set of 'ideal types' or modal profiles which best depict the sample in terms of the variables under study.

Results from this analysis should be interpreted with caution, since only 80 cases were involved. In any event, eight modal fantasy profiles were extracted, according to the eigen-value-greater-than-unity criterion. Classification according to these profiles resulted in 96% of the cases being placed. However, the majority of subjects, 71.3%, were classified by three of these modal profiles. The first profile accounted for 26.3% of our sample; they were clustered in terms of modal profile with high peaks for the imaginary companion, imaginary inanimate object, impersonation, and imaginative speech play, and a low index for day-dreaming. The next most frequent type, which classified 25% of the sample, was characterized by high peaks on personification, object/place transformation and imaginative speech play, and a low index on imaginary inanimate object and dreaming. A third profile, which accounted for 20% of our subjects, was characterized by high peaks on imaginary inanimate object and object/place transformation and a low elevation on imaginary companion.

These results from the Modal Profile Analysis (MPA), which derive from a Q-type factor analysis (i.e. an analysis of subjects rather than variables), indicate that one of the subject types includes not only the Imaginary companion fantasy but also other fantasy components, including Imaginary inanimate object, Impersonation, and Imaginative speech play. The combination of Imaginary companion with Impersonation in this subject type may seem inconsistent with the previously reported R-type factor analysis, which showed that these two variables loaded on separate factors. However, Modal Profile Analysis identifies commonalities among *people* in terms of how variables co-vary in individual psychological space, whereas factor analysis identifies co-variations among *variables* in test space. Hence, while the nomothetic factor-analytic model may reveal a certain structure among variables for a particular sample, it may be that this pattern does not faithfully represent the various types of subject profiles within this sample. The idiographic MPA model was developed to detect reliable group profiles.

In sum, results from our application of this novel analysis show that the Imaginary companion fantasy characterizes one modal fantasy type, providing further evidence of the importance of this kind of fantasy in the experience of a significant proportion of children.

Our final purpose, to replicate fantasy and behaviour relationships obtained by the Singer group, was accomplished by supplementing the parental judgement data with behavioural judgements in the preschool obtained according to the following procedure.

After a three-day warm-up and familiarization period, a 'blind' observer rated each child's free play behaviour on a standard observation sheet according to categories given below:

1 Unoccupied. The child is not engaged in any overt behaviour with objects or people. He/she may glance around at things of momentary interest, such as a loud noise, but he/she does not watch for long. It seems that he/she is in his/her own little world.

2 Self-directed. The child is engaged in frequent, almost mechanical repetitious movement, which varies only slightly in form from time to time. This movement is directed towards the child's own body, but does not seem to serve any obvious function, or have a specific goal. Some behaviours include thumb-sucking, hair-twisting, rocking, pacing, etc.

3 Solitary. The child is focused upon his/her own activity, which is pursued independently, without reference to other children. He/she is playing alone and is totally absorbed in what he/she is doing. The child makes no effort to speak to or participate with the other children.

4 Spectator. The child is watching other children. He/she is within speaking distance of others so that he/she can see and hear everything. This child may talk to those he/she is observing, but does not overtly enter into the activities. This type of behaviour differs from 'unoccupied' in that the spectator is definitely observing particular people, rather than just anything that happens to be of momentary interest.

5 Parallel. The child is playing beside rather than with other children. He/she may use the same objects as the others, but plays with them as he/she sees fit. There is no regular exchange of glances or intentional imitation, and the child does not attempt to influence or control the activity of those around him/her.

6 Attention-seeking. The child is trying to attract attention to himself/herself. He/she wants to be noticed, e.g. by following somebody around or yelling 'Look at me!' This type of behaviour invites or demands a response from the other children.

7 Cooperative. The child is interacting with another child or group of children in some common activity, such as singing, dancing, or playing with blocks. Any materials being used are shared and the children are helping or supporting each other in their task. The activity is mutually agreed upon, whether it consists of creating something or destroying it.

8 Non-cooperative. The child is disrupting the activities of other

children. He/she may simply ignore or refuse to comply with others, or block the others' activity. He/she may display more aggressive behaviour such as swearing, arguing, fighting, or destroying something.

9 Competitive. The child is interacting with one or more children in order to achieve some mutual standard or criterion. This is done according to agreed-upon rules among the players. The emphasis is upon achieving or performing beyond the other person, group or team. For example, finishing the task faster, jumping further, scoring more points, etc. This behaviour differs from cooperative in that here some are winners and others losers.

10 Adult-oriented. The child is interacting or trying to interact with an adult. This is done by his/her own accord, e.g. following the adult around, asking a question, initiating a game of catch. This behaviour could include any of the above categories involving others, but here the behaviour centres on adults instead of other children. Note that adult-initiated or adult-prolonged interactions are not included, for they are not free-play activities.

Observations were based on a systematic time sampling. Each child was observed for two 15-minute periods, each divided into 60 15-second intervals. This resulted in a sample of 120 observational units for each child. Observations were made everywhere the child went in the preschool, including both 'active' and 'quiet' areas, 'book', 'science', and 'socio-dramatic' centres, as well as in the washroom, cloakroom, kitchen, and outdoor playground. Care was taken to schedule children for observation according to a random sequence; also, observations were not undertaken on Mondays and Fridays, nor during the first ten minutes of each day, since behaviour in these periods is generally atypical. The result was a complete, systematic, and representative behavioural profile for each child.

Inter-observer reliabilities were obtained by having two independent raters assess four children in an early phase of the six-week observational period, another four children in the middle phase, and yet another four children in the last phase. Reliability (agreement/agreements and disagreements, $\times$ 100), based on a 15-minute observational period for each of four children, was very high, ranging from 78.3% to 91.6%. Average reliabilities across the four children were 83.1%, 83.1% and 84.6% respectively in the early, middle, and late phases of the six weeks of observations. 'Spectator', 'parallel', and 'cooperative' play styles were most frequently occurring, with very little 'competitive', 'unoccupied', and 'self-directed' play being seen.

To examine relationships between the fantasies and free-play behaviours of these children, we conducted a canonical correlation, which yielded no significant relationships. This is not surprising given the large number of variables relative to the small sample size. Accordingly, we undertook univariate analyses of variance, which showed a significant positive relationship between the imaginary playmate fantasy and cooperative behaviour ($F(1,22) = 5.97$, $p < 0.02$). Furthermore, when the ten play categories were grouped into larger classes adapted from Shure (1963), univariate analysis of variance also revealed a significant positive relationship between the imaginary playmate fantasy and scores on the aggregate index of 'social interaction' ($F(1,22) = 8.2$, $p < 0.009$). This index grouped categories 7, 8 and 9 above, and as such, denoted a general predisposition for social contact with peers.

In sum, our own research, based on reliable and valid observations, is consistent with the Rosenfeld findings that the imaginary playmate fantasy is a stable part of a more general imaginative mode. We were also able to identify specific imaginative types, and classify children accordingly. Finally, our research confirms the Singer findings that children who invent an imaginary companion are more likely to engage in cooperative acts during free play; moreover, we find that they are also more predisposed towards social interaction, in general.

WHY IS THE IMAGINARY PLAYMATE FANTASY IMPORTANT TO THE CHILD?

Our interpretation of how this fantasy may function in the service of the child's development can be introduced by reference to some general points concerning fantasy and reality. Breger (1974) says that the private world of fantasy and dreaming allows the child to experiment with new roles and solutions to life conflicts. But he stresses that before true mastery and growth can occur, the advances in self–other relationships, which may have been experienced within fantasy, must eventually be applied and tested with real people and real objects in the public world.

The problem for the child is how to bridge the gap between fantasy and reality. According to Sutton-Smith (1979), play generally helps at this point. Within the play frame the usual power relationships are reversed, and the usually contingencies of reinforcement are suspended. This means that players can experiment with and experience new ways of being, and relating. But Sutton-Smith also notes that young children often have difficulty negotiating play frames with other children. As he puts it, they have trouble 'getting their act on stage'. Hence, developmental advances made prepotent in fantasy cannot be transferred readily into the field of action because they are denied the protected practice which should be available in play.

I believe that this is where the imaginary companion fantasy plays an instrumental role. The playmate fantasy may provide the important first span in the bridge between fantasy and reality. This is because it may help the child enter into play, from which he can then step successfully into real life, with his now practised new behavioural sub-routines. But how can the fantasy help? If the child has difficulty negotiating the roles and rules which frame play episodes with real children, what better transitional step can be imagined than for the child to invent a fantasy playmate with whom this negotiation can take place more easily? Remember that in fantasy the powers of the imaginary playmate are under the child's control.

This truly ingenious stage in solving the problem of developmental application is admittedly just one small step toward more mature adjustment in reality. Its importance lies in providing a safe arena for rehearsing how to negotiate and renegotiate play frames, and how to step in and out of the boundaries of play with 'another'. One would expect that the child who could succeed in becoming more adept at such prepublic-play negotiations, through the invention of a fantasy friend, would also be more likely to appear happier, more mature, and less aggressive in public play episodes, precisely because the roles and rules which frame these episodes would have been more skilfully negotiated in the first place. Observations of the public play of those who have at some time invented such a fantasy confirm this line of reasoning.

Our explanation is similar to recent psychoanalytic formulations in terms of our emphasis on the role of this fantasy as a means for *positive preparation* in normal children, within a *continuum* of private fantasy, public play, and subsequent adjustment in the real world. I will review these psychoanalytic perspectives at this point, not simply to reinforce our own position, but also to help us extend our discussion of fantasy beyond childhood.

There is a new look in the psychoanalytic literature on imaginary playmates. It emphasizes that the fantasy does not necessarily evidence pathology, but serves different functions depending on the adjustment of the child. This position has been cogently developed by Rucker, whose conclusions (1981: 136) are given below:

> In the absence of gross pathology . . . a child who invents an imaginary friend from the fabric of his own internal experience is handling his problems in a marvellously creative manner. He is able to use his strengths to cope with stress in a way that interferes minimally with his accomplishment of age-

appropriate tasks . . . yet for other children, this fantasy may accompany severe problems with synthesis and serves as an adaptation to intense fragmentation. For them, the threshold of disintegration is always close at hand. The creativity that is so delightfully intriguing in a healthier child now represents a desperate attempt to mobilize healthy resources in the interests of survival, and the originality it expresses is lost in the urgency of its importance.

A second emphasis is also apparent in recent psychoanalytic interpretations of fantasy. Within this new perspective, the imaginary playmate is seen as part of a progressive continuum of fantasies, each in the service of establishing a cohesive self. Benson (1980) developed this perspective when he compared, and noted similarities between, idealized vocational fantasies of adolescents, children's imaginary companions, and younger children's transitional objects, such as security blankets.

Benson notes that youth in early and middle adolescence can't gain a sense of perfection and well-being from parents, because at this point they are trying to diminish the importance of parents in their lives. Neither can they totally profit from peer support. This is because they have not matured enough to be able to accept peer love without threat to the integrity of their self. Add to this the fact that most real occupational options, such as becoming a plumber or doctor, involve conflicts associated with success and competition in the job market. In the light of all this, an idealized vocational fantasy, such as being a super-star, actress, or astronaut, would seem like a reasonable fantasy support.

Based on clinical work with several non-psychotic male and female cases, Benson learned that while these adolescents were planning and actively preparing for realistic vocational goals, they simultaneously created, and used for a period of a few months to a few years, a fantasy of an idealized and grandiose vocational role for themselves. Benson argues that these temporary, and usually private, vocational aspirations provide a detour through fantasy, promoting growth. Some of his concluding statements (1980: 262–3) are cited here because they will serve to sweep us ahead toward our final broader reconceptualization of the significance of the imaginary companion fantasy:

> Idealized vocational fantasies are, like the transitional object and imaginary companion, another in the developmental series of narcissistic guardians. They are created by their user, are under his complete control, and are self-objects in the transitional zone of experience.
>
> Narcissistic guardians are created by children and by adolescents in response to developmental needs. They permit the growing young person some immunity from the too soon and too stark realization of his limitations.

Yet, all people, throughout the life cycle, are similarly faced with threats to their very sense of existence. It seems likely that the creation of narcissistic guardians may be found in all stages of the life cycle.

This broad view of the role of fantasy throughout our lives has also been envisioned by Sutton-Smith (1979). He proposes that there are good grounds for arguing that children who 'make-believe', as well as participants in games and sports, and those engaged in rituals and ceremonies of one kind or another, may all be engaged in 'make-*belief*'; that is, in creating flexible social frames. These frames allow them to gain belief in themselves, and in objects and events in the real world, by their voluntary control of their own buffered fantasy versions. The following excerpt (Sutton-Smith, 1979: 319) illustrates the scope of this formulation:

> play, games, sports and ritual are all part of novel frame-making behavior; there can be either a zest to these novelties (called playfulness) or a sobriety (called religious fervour). We conclude that they are more similar in their fundamentally creative response to life than they are dissimilar. And that their differential range and status evokes the charge of make-believe or revelation, but that this has more to do with how they function in the groups in which they are found for the members of the different subclasses, than reveals their fundamentally creative similarity. This makes sense too of the great variety of ways in which play, games, sports and ritual are defined in different societies. The variety is baffling if we take each of these categories as itself the activity which we discuss, rather than as a culturally relative exemplar of the life and times of frame making in that situation.

Finally, though space does not allow a detailed report, it should be noted that a similarly transcendent perspective about our continual striving for meaning and security in life has recently been proposed by Csikzentmihalyi and Rochberg-Halton (1981). Based on data from a large-scale interview survey they conclude that we invent our lives by imputing special meanings to things and possessions. Our rings, photographs, cars, boats, bedrooms, and houses, and the churches, factories, and the entire built environment that we create for ourselves, support whatever illusions about our self and our life which we wish to maintain.

To conclude this section on why the imaginary playmate fantasy is important to the child, it appears that both recent psychoanalytic and developmental interpretations agree that the children and youth who invent imaginary playmates, and then move on to play cooperatively with peers, are engaged in the same kind of activity as are those responsible for advances in the arts and sciences, and are perhaps no less creative. Similarly, those children and youth who choose to 'be with' their imaginary friends, to the exclusion of their siblings and peers, are perhaps no more deluded than those adults who invest inordinate time and effort in prayer, in polishing their new car, or in counting their money. As individuals, and as a culture, we seem to possess the capacity for making beliefs and illusions to frame our lives, which can either nurture our growth, or destroy our future. Each of us, in our own way, is trying to deal with the paradox and promise of the human condition.

WHY SHOULD WE CONTINUE TO STUDY THE IMAGINARY PLAYMATE FANTASY?

More research is necessary on this fantasy because our current understandings rest on a rather limited empirical foundation. Additional work with improved procedures may make it possible to apply our knowledge of this fantasy in early childhood education programmes. We say this because of the convergence in the present review, which indicates that those who create an imaginary playmate fantasy are more likely subsequently to play with real peers in a civilized manner. If we value sharing and cooperation, then it seems unfortunate that less than one third of children engage in this fantasy. To increase the frequency of civilized social interaction perhaps we should try to discover how to encourage more children to invent imaginary playmates. Alternatively, perhaps we should try to learn how to provide children, who don't engage in such a fantasy, with an alternative opportunity for mental rehearsal training to assist their social development. There is evidence that fantasy training does improve the social participation of preschoolers (Smith et al., 1981). Improved study of the imaginary playmate fantasy could identify behavioural scripts and strategies which might then be used to guide fantasy training programmes for children in day-care and preschools.

To satisfy the above objectives our research would have to be considerably improved. We would need to do more than simply correct design and methodological difficulties noted in a previous section of this chapter. We would need far more detailed reports of the texts of interactions between the child and his imaginary playmate. How does the child directly, and indirectly through intentions imputed to his pretend friend, negotiate the framework and understandings necessary for their play to get started? Does the child who gives up his imaginary playmate negotiate play frames with real peers differently than same-aged children who still have, or never had, an imaginary playmate? Do the pre-play negotiations and texts of fantasy play with a pretend friend differ for normal and clinical groups? Such questions demand very detailed and in-depth investigation.

We also need to resort more to multiple data sources, since these fantasy experiences are so ephemeral. Behavioural observations reported by parenting figures should be supplemented by equally detailed reports from siblings and others in the home, as well as baby-sitters, day-care personnel, preschool teachers, neighbours, and all those who know the child well enough for him or her to be natural in their presence. These observations should also be checked against what the child says concerning how and what he or she was doing during imaginary play episodes.

Similar multiple inputs are necessary concerning the reale life contexts of these fantasy play episodes. It may only be through the observation of commonalities in the relationships between text and context of the fantasy play episodes that complete understanding of the coping and rehearsal value of the fantasy will be achieved. This point came to us when recent informal discussions with staff at a nearby children's hospital revealed not a single report of the imaginary playmate fantasy among four- to six-year-old patients, but a high incidence of strong attachment to transitional objects. These observations call forth the possibility that level of fantasy play may interact with degree of contextual stress. Again, we need far more detailed data to examine this possibility.

Assuming that we could obtain such detailed reports, from multiple sources, about the texts and contexts of children's fantasy, future investigators might then seriously consider improving their means of deriving meaning from these data. We recommend the dramaturgical method proposed by Harré and Secord (1972). This involves working iteratively toward an 'authentic' account through continuous negotiated understandings between and among the investigator and all observers. Although time-consuming, and seemingly subjective, such checks and balances seem very desirable because there is such a strong temptation to interpret children's actions in essentially adult terms. There may be something very new and special to learn from young children's private 'social' negotiations with their imaginary friends. It would be a shame to cloud this fresh wisdom by having just one expert pour it into his favourite old bottle.

To recapitulate, the imaginary playmate fantasy occurs frequently among young children. For emotionally disadvantaged children this fantasy provides a buffer against the terror of disintegration. For normal children in non-threatening situations, the fantasy appears to facilitate social development by making possible the practice of play frame negotiation.

This and other modes of fantasy may be viewed as part of a

developmental continuum which includes childhood transitional object and imaginary playmate fantasy, career fantasy in adolescence, and in adulthood it includes games, sports, rituals, ceremonies, and illusions of many sorts. At every point along this continuum, fantasy seems to have two faces; each fantasy mode can either impede or facilitate our growth. The challenge is to develop methods for maximizing the functional face of fantasy.

REFERENCES

Ames, L. B., and Learned, J. (1946). Imaginary companions and related phenomena. *Journal of Genetic Psychology* 69, 147–67.

Benson, R. M. (1980). Narcissistic guardians: developmental aspects of transitional objects, imaginary companions, and career fantasies. *Adolescent Psychiatry* 8, 253–64.

Breger, L. (1974). *From Instinct to Identity*. Englewood Cliffs: Prentice-Hall.

Calderia, J., Singer, J. L., and Singer, D. G. (1978). Imaginary playmates: some relationships to preschoolers' spontaneous play language and television-viewing. Paper presented at the meeting of the Eastern Psychological Association, Washington, DC, March.

Csikszentmihalyi, M., and Rochberg-Halton, E. (1981). *The Meaning of Things: Domestic Symbols and the Self*. Cambridge: Cambridge University Press.

Freud, S. (1975). *The Future of an Illusion*. New York: Norton, 1975 (first published 1927).

Grant, C. (1981). The imaginary companion fantasy: and related background variables, imaginative behaviour, and social behaviour in preschool children. Unpublished BA thesis, Carleton University.

Grant, C. (1982). A topological analysis of imaginative behaviours in preschool children. Unpublished manuscript, Carleton University.

Harré, R., and Secord, P. F. (1972). *The Explanation of Social Behaviour*. Oxford: Blackwell.

Hurlock, E. B., and Burstein, M. (1932). The imaginary playmate: a questionnaire study. *Journal of Genetic Psychology* 41, 380–2.

Jersild, A. T., Markey, F. V., and Jersild, C. L. (1933). Children's fears, dreams, wishes, daydreams, likes, dislikes, pleasant and unpleasant memories. *Child Development Monographs* No. 12. New York: Teachers College, Columbia University.

Manosevitz, M., Fling, S., and Prentice, N. M. (1977). Imaginary companions in young children: relationships with intelligence, creativity and waiting ability. *Journal of Child Psychology and Psychiatry* 18, 73–8.

Manosevitz, M., Prentice, N. M., and Wilson, F. (1973). Individual and family correlates of imaginary companions in preschool children. *Developmental Psychology* 8, 72–9.

Masih, V. K. (1978). Imaginary play companions of children. In R. Weizman, R.

Brown, P. Levinson, and P. Taylor (eds), *Piagetian Theory and the Helping Professions, Vol. 1*. Los Angeles: University of Southern California Press.

Montessori, M. (1912). *The Montessori Method*. London: William Heinemann.

Nagera, H. (1969). The imaginary companion: its significance for ego development and conflict solution. *The Psychoanalytic Study of the Child* 24, 165–6.

Rosenfeld, E., Huesmann, L. R., Eron, L. D., and Torney-Purta, J. V. (1982). Measuring patterns of fantasy in children. *Journal of Personality and Social Psychology* 42, 347–66.

Rucker, N. G. (1981). Capacities for integration, oedipal ambivalence, and imaginary companions. *The American Journal of Psychoanalysis* 41, 129–37.

Schaefer, C. E. (1969). Imaginary companions and creative adolescents. *Developmental Psychology* 1, 747–9.

Schwartzman, H. B., (1978). *Transformations: The Anthropology of Children's Play*. New York: Plenum Press.

Shure, M. B. (1963). Psychological ecology of a nursery school. *Child Development* 34, 979–92.

Singer, J. L., and Antrobus, J. S. (1970). Imaginal processes inventory: 1970 revision. Unpublished manuscript, Center for Research in Cognition and Affect, Graduate Center, City University of New York.

Singer, J. L., and Singer, D. G. (1981). *Television, Imagination, and Aggression: a Study of Preschoolers*. Hillsdale, Lawrence Erlbaum.

Singer, J. L., and Steiner, B. F. (1966). Imaginative content in the dreams and fantasy play of blind and sighted children. *Perceptual and Motor Skills* 22, 475–82.

Skinner, H. A., and Lei, H. (1980). Modal profile analysis: a computer programme for classification research. *Educational and Psychological Measurement* 40, 769–72.

Smith, P. K., Dalgleish, M., and Herzmark, G. (1981). A comparison of the effects of fantasy play tutoring and skills tutoring in nursery classes. *International Journal of Behavioral Development* 4, 421–41.

Smith, P. K. (1982). Does play matter? Functional and evolutionary aspects of human and animal play. *Behavioral and Brain Sciences* 5, 139–84.

Sutton-Smith, B. (ed.) (1979). *Play and Learning*. New York: Gardner Press.

Svendsen, M. (1934). Children's imaginary companions. *Archives of Neurology and Psychiatry* 32, 985–99.

Vostrovsky, C. (1895). A study of imaginary companions. *Education* 15, 393–8.

11 Rough-and-Tumble in Preschool and Playground

Anne P. Humphreys and Peter K. Smith

INTRODUCTION

Rough-and-tumble play refers primarily to play-fighting and chasing. Such play behaviours 'mimic more intentionally aggressive actions' (DiPietro, 1981), but are accompanied by laughter and by a tendency for the participants to stay together rather than separate. Indeed, laughter (or, in high intensity play, screaming) seems to be a play signal which can indicate that the apparently aggressive action is not really aggressive in intent (Aldis, 1975). It has been described in a number of societies: in Britain (e.g. Blurton Jones, 1967), in the USA (e.g. Aldis, 1975), in the Kalahari San (Konner, 1972) and, as 'assaults sociably' or 'horseplay', in Japan, the Philippines, north India, Kenya, Mexico and the USA (Whiting and Whiting, 1975).

Rough-and-tumble play is quite common in children from the preschool period up to adolescence. For example, observations we have made in Sheffield nurseries and schools (Smith and Connolly, 1980; Heaton, 1983; Humphreys 1983) show that some 3 to 13% of children's free-play time may be spent in rough-and-tumble play. In the six-cultures study of Whiting and Whiting (1975), some 6% of behavioural acts coded (range 4 to 8%) was 'assaults sociably', the bulk of this being 'friendly wrestling and back-slapping'.

Agonistic play is common in other social mammals (see Martin, above, chapter 3; Chalmers, above, chapter 5). Indeed, for some species, such as the rat, it is the most distinctive form of play (Hole and Einon, above, chapter 4). It is a very characteristic form of primate play, and agonistic play in the rhesus macaque has been the subject of a very detailed study by Symons (1978). Its prevalence suggests some functional value, but precisely what remains unresolved (Smith, 1982).

Human rough-and-tumble play would appear to correspond fairly closely with mammalian agonistic play, although there are some differences (Aldis, 1975). Its developmental importance and functional significance are also unclear, although whether, and to what extent, such forms of behaviour should be tolerated or encouraged is nevertheless an important issue for parents and teachers (Fraser, 1973; Aldis, 1975).

Play-fighting and chasing were given due consideration by the early play theorists, particularly by Groos, who devoted a large section of *The Play of Man* (1901) to 'Fighting Play'. Indeed, the view of play as being surplus energy is more concordant with a focus on agonistic and physical exercise play than on the quieter kinds of object and fantasy play. Such forms of play could be seen as easily getting out of hand, as when Groos (1901) wrote that 'the child who leaps and hops about or runs with all his might, or scuffles with his companions, is seized with a wild impulse for destruction'; or, in terms of Hall's (1904) recapitulation theory, as relatively crude and primitive instincts, relics of our animal past.

Perhaps for these reasons, and because of the swing against biological or instinctive views of human behaviour in the 1920s and 1930s, rough-and-tumble play received little if any attention from researchers for several decades. Piaget's (1951, first published 1945) categories of functional and dramatic play, and constructive activity, scarcely allow a place for rough-and-tumble. By the 4- to 10-year-old period, when so much rough-and-tumble takes place, children were expected to be involved in sociodramatic play, progressing on to games with rules. Although sociodramatic and rule-governed play often incorporates play-fighting and chasing, the examples chosen have generally involved quieter object play; domestic play, for example, or games such as marbles. It is these most distinctively human forms of play – object play and especially pretend or fantasy play – which have dominated psychological interest in play since the origins of modern child psychology in the 1930s. The primary interest of psychologists and educationists has been in constructive play activities and the choice of appropriate play materials; in pretend play, the development of imagination and the processes of identification and projection; and in the development of social participation in play (e.g. Buhler, 1935; Valentine, 1956; Mussen, Conger and Kagan, 1963).

Most anthropological studies, too, concentrated on children's constructive or dramatic play, usually as an illustration of how play was imitative of adult activities. Play-fighting seems often to have been ignored or else noted briefly in passing as an aimless, unorganized or somewhat undesirable activity. For example, Mead (1930) described how the play of Manus children in New Guinea is 'like that of young puppies or kittens'; in the absence of adult guidance or modelling the children 'have a dull uninteresting child life, romping good-humouredly until they are tired, then lying inert and breathless until rested sufficiently to romp again'. Hattwick (1937), writing of US nursery-school children, noted a tendency for boys rather than girls to 'laugh, squeal and jump around excessively'. Raum (1940) wrote of the Chaga of Tanzania that 'sometimes one sees boys engaged in rough horseplay, tripping one another, kicking out with their heels and treading upon one another. Where such pastimes are orderly and regulated, genuine competitive games are played'. Minturn and Hitchcock (1966) wrote of the Rajput of north India that 'a great deal of the play of younger children consists of almost random activity. They chase each other, tease each other . . . '

It was an ethologist, Blurton Jones, who first explicitly described and discussed 'rough-and-tumble' play in human children while watching behaviour in a nursery school. He took the term from the Harlows' description of play in rhesus monkeys. Further analysis of this kind of behaviour appeared in the volume of ethological studies of child behaviour edited by Blurton Jones (1972). A major contribution was also made by Aldis in his book *Play Fighting* (1975), which covers both animal and human agonistic play. Aldis observed children in school playgrounds, parks, swimming pools and beaches, and filmed play episodes for more detailed study. Most recently, we have completed work in Sheffield on the incidence of rough-and-tumble play, and the choice of play partners, in schoolchildren during recess periods (Humphreys, 1983; Heaton, 1983; Humphreys and Smith, in preparation). Some of our findings, together with those of earlier studies, are reviewed in this chapter.

Five main issues are considered in this chapter: What do the terms 'play-fighting' or 'rough-and-tumble play' include? How do these forms of play change with age? How distinct are play-fighting and serious aggression? Why are there sex differences in play-fighting? and finally, What is the developmental significance of rough-and-tumble play?

WHAT DO THE TERMS 'PLAY-FIGHTING' AND 'ROUGH-AND-TUMBLE' INCLUDE?

It is important to define this kind of play firstly because it surely must not be confused with all the other things which we call 'play' just because they are done by children, and secondly because in investigating its distinctive-ness from other behaviour we may get some idea how it differs from other behaviour in its effects and functions and in its causal organization. (Blurton Jones, 1967)

As with most concepts, there are some examples of play which virtually everyone would agree count as 'rough-and-tumble', other examples which virtually everyone would agree are not, and yet others where there might be substantial disagreement.

The core concept or 'paradigm case' (Matthews and Matthews, 1982) for rough-and-tumble play, as the name indicates, is actual fighting play: grappling, wrestling, hitting or beating in a playful mode. Closely related to this is chasing play which occurs frequently, though not exclusively, in association with fighting play (Aldis, 1975; Humphreys, personal obser-vations). The earlier ethological work also showed that play fighting and chasing tended to occur in close temporal proximity in nursery school children. Blurton Jones (1967) identified a cluster of behaviours – 'laugh', 'run', 'jumps', 'open beat' and 'wrestle' – as co-occurring significantly often within five-minute periods. Blurton Jones (1972) replicated his previous finding and showed that these behaviours tended to occur at different times from 'work' (defined as using objects). A similar cluster of 'laugh', 'smile', 'chase/flee', 'wrestle/tumble' and 'play noise' was identified by Smith (1973), analysing co-occurence within half-minute intervals (see figure 11.1). In this chapter we shall therefore use the term 'rough-and-tumble' to cover play-fighting and play-chasing.

Play-fighting and chasing are clearly playful forms of aggressive behaviour. (The distinction between real and playful aggression may not always be clear, a problem which we discuss further in a later section.) They are very different from sedentary object play, and indeed factor-analytic studies suggest that some children spend a lot of time in rough-and-tumble play whereas others spend a lot of time in object play. Blurton Jones (1972), studying 25 two- to four-year-olds, found a first factor which loaded high on 'wrestle', 'jumps', 'run', and 'laugh/smile' and high in the opposite direction on 'work' (using objects). Principal-component analysis on children of similar age by Smith and Connolly (1972) and Smith (1973) also found that a major dimension of individual difference was between the frequency of rough-and-tumble play and of object play. The distinction is not an absolute one; some play-chasing can employ objects such as pretend guns, and some object play, for example with sand or water, can involve laughing and hitting or throwing. However, the above investigations show that the general distinction is nevertheless a meaningful one.

It is more difficult when we consider physical activity play which does not

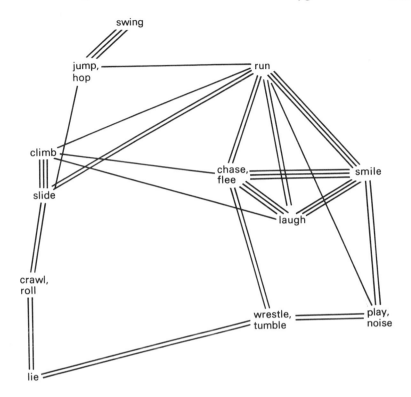

FIGURE 11.1 Temporal associations amongst behaviours of 2- to 4-year-old-children.
(Adapted from Smith, 1973)

directly involve fighting or chasing. Blurton Jones's (1967, 1972) category of 'run' could include episodes of general running, as well as the running involved in chasing and fleeing. Also, his category lists did not include vigorous activity on apparatus, such as climbing, sliding and swinging. Smith (1973, and see figure 11.1) found these co-occurring to some extent with rough-and-tumble items, and his factor-analytic results (on individual differences among 29 two- to four-year-olds) do not give quite such a clear separation as those of Blurton Jones.

Despite some overlap, it seems to us sensible to distinguish 'vigorous activity play' from 'rough-and-tumble play'. Vigorous activity play includes large-scale muscular and bodily exercise play such as running, climbing, swinging, sliding, jumping, pushing and pulling large objects. Aldis (1975) refers to much of this as 'vestibular reinforcement' play, since the activities involve stimulation of the vestibular sense organs of the inner ear which help maintain balance. While it is often social, such play can be solitary. Laughing and screaming often accompany it, but specifically agonistic behaviours, such as chasing, wrestling and hitting, usually do not.

There are thus some graded general distinctions to be made between play-wrestling, play-chasing, vigorous activity play and object play in children. The forms of these types of play obviously depend on the culture and on the specific environment. For example, Aldis (1975) describes play in swimming pools, drawing parallels between 'dunking' (holding under the water), leg-grabbing and pulling, and so on, and play-wrestling on land, whereas many forms of water play could be described as just vigorous physical activity.

Some other forms of play activity may also grade into rough-and-tumble play. Konner (1972) describes a form of social play in Kalahari San children which he calls 'gentle and tumble' play. Common in one- to five-year-olds, it involves clinging and rolling on the ground with tangling of legs. The movements are slow and there is no laughter. He feels that it grades with a mild form of rough-and-tumble involving rolling around on the ground while laughing and hugging.

Groos (1901), in his discussion of fighting play, continued from a consideration of physical play to mental contests such as playful resistance to authority, teasing rhymes, and board games such as chess. Parker (below, chapter 12) takes a similar ontogenetic perspective.

We know little enough as yet about the relationship of these other forms of activity to paradigm 'rough-and-tumble' play to say how important the distinctions and connections are. For the purposes of this chapter we confine ourselves to rough-and-tumble play as involving agonistic behaviours, specifically wrestling, hitting and chasing, in a playful mode as indicated primarily by laughter and by children staying together through and after the episode.

HOW DO THESE FORMS OF PLAY CHANGE WITH AGE?

> Unprovoked tussling merely for the fun of the thing seldom appears earlier than the third year. (Groos, 1901)

Both Konner (1972) and Aldis (1975) suggest that the origins of peer–peer rough-and-tumble lie in earlier parent–infant interactions. Konner (1972) describes how an adult may slowly run from the child, eliciting following, and then turn and chase the child in a play attack. This seems to be a genuine early form of play-chasing, appearing in the second year of life, with both laughter and role-reversal taking place. Aldis (1975) argues that in more general terms, vigorous adult–infant play prepares the child for later rough-and-tumble with age-mates.

Studies of peer–peer interaction in the second year of life show that social play can take place, involving turn-taking, repetition and the signalling of play-intent through laughter and smiles. Some of these social play episodes involve chasing or peek-a-boo, although the majority (in the laboratory situations studied) are object-based activities such as exchanging a ball (Ross, 1982). Goldman and Ross (1978) suggest that given 'the commonality of rough-and-tumble play in slightly older children, the ability to signal play intent and to understand such signals is critical . . . the early development and practise of the various signals of non-literality in play and games that are devoid of any hint of agonism would seem quite adaptive'. Obviously, the even earlier parent–infant play provides a possible context for the initial learning of such signals. The extent to which peer–peer interaction is dependent on earlier parent–infant interaction, or has separate roots, is still a debated issue in developmental research (Vandell, 1980).

While play-chasing seems to be first to appear, play-fighting can be observed in two-year-olds, though it is relatively infrequent compared to its occurrence in older children (Groos, 1901; Konner, 1972; Blurton Jones, 1972; Smith, 1973). Amongst three- and four-year-olds, both play-fighting and play-chasing have been described by Blurton Jones (1967, 1972), McGrew (1972), Smith and Connolly (1972), Smith (1974) and DiPietro (1981).

Some of the rough-and-tumble in this age-range seems to be 'just' wrestling and chasing, but often it has pretend aspects to it. In his observations of Kalahari San children, Konner (1972) reports occasions of one child pretending to be an animal that others play attacked. In contemporary urban societies, roles such as 'monsters', 'cowboys and Indians' or 'witches' are often incorporated into fighting and chasing play (Smith, 1977).

The frequency of rough-and-tumble at this age-range has been clearly shown to be influenced by environmental factors. In a series of experimental studies on preschool playgroups, Smith and Connolly (1980) showed that the frequency was greater when there was a large area available, not very many small toys, a reasonably large (more than ten children) same-age peer group and a permissive 'free play' regime. In some preschool environments, teachers or playgroup leaders often intervene to stop or quieten down rough-and-tumble or monster games (Smith, 1977). Even so, a study of British playgroups (Preschool Playgroup Association, 1982) found that 38% of mothers felt that playgroup was making their child 'boisterous' (*Concise Oxford Diction-ary*: 'violent, rough . . . ; noisily cheerful').

There are considerable individual differences in how much time preschool children spend in rough-and-tumble play. Those who do so a lot tend to be more sociable generally (Blurton Jones, 1972; Rubin, 1982), to engage less in sedentary object play (Smith and Connolly, 1972) and to score lower on aggressive behaviour (Blurton Jones, 1972). The general picture is that, as far as peer relations are concerned, some rough-and-tumble play is a normal and healthy part of the behavioural repertoire. Indeed, there are some indications that young children with behaviour disorders (Campbell and Cluss, 1982) or high hostility levels (Manning, Heron and Marshall, 1978) may have problems engaging in normal rough-and-tumble, possibly through misinterpreting play signals or through responding aggressively to play intentions.

Rough-and-tumble continues into adolescence and beyond but has received comparatively little attention in children of school age, probably at least partly because the greater self-consciousness of this age-group makes ethological observation more difficult. However, studies of rough-and-tumble in the school playground have been carried out by Aldis (1975) and ourselves (Humphreys 1983; Humphreys and Smith, in preparation). Aldis described the various forms of rough-and-tumble occurring among six- to twelve-year-olds. He noted that wrestling might consist either of a struggle for superior position or of brief, detached, low intensity episodes which he called fragmentary wrestling. In the former case, children attempted to attain the superior position by overbalancing the partner, tripping him or throwing him to the ground, and then sitting or lying across his prostrate form to keep him there. (Groos (1901) also noted how 'in this youthful tussling the chief aim is to throw one's opponent to the ground and to hold him in this helpless position'.) Roles might then be reversed, with the previously flattened child toppling his partner and, through further struggling, achieving the superior position. Fragmentary wrestling, as the name implies, covered instances of pushing, pulling, clasping, leg play and kicking occurring mainly amongst standing children, in no particular sequence. Children also engaged in hitting play, which often took the form of an imitation boxing match, 'piling-on', in which they flung themselves on to children already on the ground forming disordered heaps, as well as chasing play, which involved frequent role reversal and commonly occurred in association with other types of rough-and-tumble.

Our own observations endorse Aldis's descriptions. Much of the Sheffield children's rough-and-tumble consisted of trying to 'get some-body down', or in other words to achieve superior position. A number of styles of imitation combat were also fairly common up to about nine or ten years of age, apparently heavily television-influenced: boxing, kung-fu type and spy-thriller type fighting all occurred in which blows rarely connected but lavish sound effects were added. In these cases, the rough-and-tumble incorporated role play since, in adopting a fighting style, individuals might also take on appropriate identities. Some rough-and-tumble behaviours have also been observed in what are usually described as rule-governed games such as tag, Tug-o'-war and Bulldog (Opie and Opie, 1969). In our study, however, the major rule-game was football, which involves relatively little rough-and-tumble behaviour.

The work of Aldis provides a useful document of the behaviours which occur but, being purely descriptive, does not permit formal comparison of ages and sexes. In our own study, we attempted to build on this work by gathering basic quantitative data on rough-and-tumble in the context of other school playground pastimes, and by examining some of the social correlates of the activity. Observed rough-and-tumble partnerships were considered in relation to children's own reported opinions of their playmates. This work was carried out on samples of 7-, 9- and 11-year-olds at a single school. The behaviour of these target children was recorded by an observer in the playground (who, after an initial period of curiosity, came to be accepted as 'that funny lady who always stands outside at playtime').

Information from an initial observation phase produced a breakdown of the proportions of playground time which children allocated to different activities, or 'playground time budget', for the three ages, which is illustrated in figure 11.2. This shows that rough-and-tumble took up about 10% of playground time at all three ages. The major changes appear in the considerable increase in time allocated to rule-games and the virtual disappearance of object and role play by nine years of age. Overall, more active pastimes tended to be chosen as the children got older.

During a more fine-grained phase of observation made later in the year, the occurrence of rough-and-tumble at different ages was examined in more detail. This showed that the proportion of time spent in rough-and-tumble was highest at seven years (13.3%), intermediate at nine years (9.3%) and lowest at eleven years (4.6%). The difference between seven- and eleven-year-olds was significant ($p < 0.01$). By looking at the distribution and length of individual occurrences of rough-and-tumble it is possible to suggest how this overall decline may have been brought about. The mean length of these occurrences did not vary significantly with age, but remained at 7–10 sec throughout. However, the mean number of occurrences per child was significantly less at age nine years than at seven years ($p < 0.05$) and at eleven years than nine years ($p < 0.05$). This

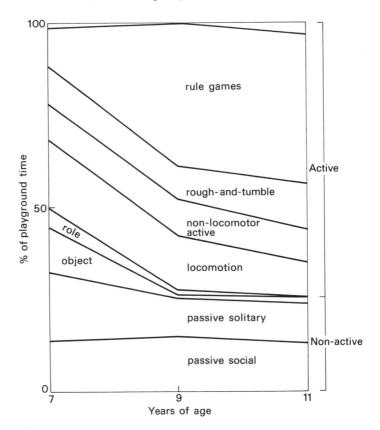

FIGURE 11.2 Time spent in different activities by seven-, nine- and eleven-year-old children during playground breaks. (Unlabelled band at top represents miscellaneous and unclassified behaviour. Further details in text.)

indicates that, once initiated, rough-and-tumble will continue for a similar length of time at all ages, but that it becomes less likely to be initiated as children get older. Thus rough-and-tumble appears to decrease in priority with age, falling lower on the child's list of things to do. The time budget evidence (figure 11.2) suggests that the large increase in rule-governed games, which comes to take up some 40% of the eleven-year-olds playground time, could also be reflecting a shift in priority to more highly structured and socially complex physical activity.

However, it should be remembered that the studies of rough-and-tumble in school-age children mentioned above have been carried out mainly in school playgrounds, which place certain limitations on the child's behaviour. Physical attributes of the playground itself, such as size, shape, texture of surface and variety of objects present, will all influence the activities performed: football is common in flat rectangular open areas, bushes provide cover in which to hide, and, as our own study showed, rough-and-tumble is more common where a soft grass surface is available which does not threaten to remove skin from knees and elbows. Children's activities may also be restricted by the teachers in charge, whose attitudes differ considerably from one school to another. The scope of possible games is widened by the presence of large numbers of children of similar age who are available to take part (25-a-side football was not uncommon). Outside school, such numbers are not forced to share a restricted area in the same way, and the popularity of the different pastimes is probably different in consequence (Opie and Opie, 1969). Konner (1972) has remarked how rough-and-tumble play is relatively infrequent in the small mixed-age peer groups available to Kalahari San children.

HOW DISTINCT ARE PLAY-FIGHTING AND SERIOUS AGGRESSION?

A great difference is observable in the tussling of boys as they approach maturity. While the games of 6-year-olds are uniformly harmless, and proceed amid laughter and fun, as the age of puberty approaches fighting play assumes a much more serious character, and even when only play is intended the whole bearing of the participants is greatly modified. (Groos, 1901)

Rough-and-tumble play and serious aggressive fighting are similar at the level of the motor patterns involved, drawing on a common repertoire of hitting, wrestling and chasing movements upon which specifically playful or aggressive elements may be superimposed. Several studies have found that play and serious fighting can be clearly distinguished in young children. In older children, however, it has been suggested that these two types of behaviour are less easily separated.

In his studies of young children, Blurton Jones (1967, 1972) found that play-fighting and aggression emerged as separate classes of behaviour. In his 1972 study, two of the reliable factors to be shown up were those he calls 'rough-and-tumble' and 'aggression', which were distinct in both context and behaviour. 'Aggression' tended to be concentrated into disputes over possession of objects and consequently included object-specific behaviours such as 'grab' and 'take', while 'rough-and-tumble' did not occur in this context. Although some of these behaviours were similar (and might have been more so had the children been out of doors and therefore at liberty to throw themselves about more), the two factors were loaded differently for facial expression. The playful rough-and-tumble factor was loaded highly for the categories 'laugh' and 'playface', whereas the expressions associated with aggression were 'frown' and 'fixate'.

Aldis (1975) distinguished play-fighting and aggression by considering the outcomes of encounters. He defined the encounter as playful if the participants remained together in friendly social interaction after its cessation. Aggression, on the other hand, was seen as leading to separation of the participants. By this criterion, Aldis found that the vast majority of the fighting behaviour which he saw in school playgrounds and elsewhere was clearly playful, and constituted a part of the children's friendly social interaction.

Facial expression and outcome have thus both been seen as features distinguishing play-fighting and aggression. In a recent study of rough-and-tumble in nursery-school children, Heaton (1983) examined the extent to which these features led to the same conclusion in 4-year-olds. She noted the children's expressions and subsequent behaviour for episodes involving fighting behaviours and classified these for each child as either positive, neutral or negative. The resulting contingency table of expression by outcome is shown in table 11.1. Outcome and expression were found to be significantly related (chi-squared test, $p < 0.001$) and the results show that this relationship was as expected, smiles and playface commonly being associated with positive outcomes while frowns and

TABLE 11.1   Contingency table of facial expression by outcome, for individual preschool-aged children, in episodes involving fighting behaviours

| Facial expression | Outcome | | | |
	Positive	Neutral	Negative	Total
Positive	297	106	6	409
Neutral or unclassified	48	72	24	144
Negative	9	9	26	44
Total	354	187	56	597

insults were associated with negative outcomes. The two diagnostic features therefore showed good agreement and are able, together, to define clearly playful instances (first row, first column in table 11.1) and clearly aggressive instances (third row, third column) more powerfully than either can alone. However, there were a small number of instances when the two criteria clearly disagreed (first row third column, third row first column). Some of these were due to a play invitation being responded to aggressively and others to an apparently serious fighting incident being settled amicably. Other authors (Blurton Jones, 1967; Sluckin 1981) have observed that some children may respond to playful approaches in a non-playful way. Is this because the play signals are misunderstood?

Heaton examined this possibility by showing 4-year-olds video film of 20 interactions involving fighting behaviours and asking them whether each encounter was playful or serious. The film was also shown to the children's two teachers who assessed the encounters in the same way. Most children were found to achieve significant agreement on these judgements with one another and with the adults. A small number failed to agree with anyone else, and these children were also less able to describe the criteria upon which they had based their judgements, suggesting that they were not attending to specific signal features.

Most of the children who agreed reported basing their judgements on properties of the behaviour involved, such as whether A hit B hard or only lightly, while the adults tended to report using other criteria such as facial expression, verbal cues and their knowledge of the children. However, one of the adults, who relied heavily on her knowledge of the children, achieved comparatively low levels of agreement with the children apparently because she was less willing to concede that an encounter was playful.

This variation in adult interpretations of episodes involving fighting behaviours was also apparent among the head-teachers whom we consulted while looking for a suitable school for our study, and underlies their different attitudes towards it. Some saw such activity as harmless fun, and were happy to let it carry on provided nobody was in danger of getting hurt, while at the other extreme, some saw all such behaviour as aggressively motivated and forbade it. All these teachers saw serious fighting and rough behaviour as undesirable, but their views of the boundary between playful and aggressive roughness differed. Sluckin (1981), in his study of playground behaviour at a first and middle school, interviewed a number of teachers and dinner-ladies. Their verbatim accounts clearly illustrate the variation of views on this topic.

Although our own sample of teachers was small, those objecting most strongly to rough-and-tumble tended to be those in charge of older children (9- to 12-year-olds). Is it the case that play-fighting does change in older children as Groos (1901; see quote above) suggested? A study by Neill (1976) supported this possibility. He observed the fighting behaviour of 12- to 13-year-old boys and found that there was considerably greater overlap between play and aggression than was the case for younger children. He subjected the results of his observations to factor analysis, as Blurton Jones (1972) had done, and found that two factors emerged for these activities, one corresponding to 'vigorous fighting, usually playful but often causing distress to the victim' and one to 'playful fighting of low intensity'. This could be seen as evidence that play and aggression merge together as children get older; some behaviour which was previously used in friendly social interaction comes to incorporate real hostility and so to be employed in serious dominance struggles.

In our own study, we examined the outcomes for individuals at each age of episodes involving fighting behaviour. Using a simpler version of Heaton's (1983) method, we looked to see whether the proportion resulting in separation was greater for older children, indicating greater aggressiveness. The proportion of positive outcomes was found to be similar for 7-year-olds (76%), 9-year-olds (64%) and 11-year-olds (80%). It is also comparable to Heaton's finding for 4-year-olds (59%). By this criterion, therefore, the older children in our sample did not come to interpret fighting behaviour as serious more often than younger children did.

Neill's analysis focused predominantly on characteristics of the behaviour itself, with hostility being defined in terms of the recipient's *immediate* reaction. He noted, concerning the high intensity rough-and-tumble factor, that 'the loser might become distressed if the fight continued; conversely the attacker might start vigorously, causing distress, and then become more playful', but did not report the likely state of relations after the episode had ceased. Although there are a number of disparities between Neill's sample and our own (such as sex, age and environment), a cautious comparison of the two sets of results suggests that, while the content of rough-and-tumble is more violent in older boys both in terms of actions carried out and immediate damage inflicted, there is not a corresponding increase in the proportion which is taken as aggressive in a hostile sense. In other words, it seems that older boys put up with rougher behaviour from their playmates, including some pain, without taking serious offence.

In considering the aggressive content of playful rough-and-tumble the nature of serious aggressive behaviour at the appropriate age should also be taken into account. Amongst young children, as Blurton Jones pointed out, fights most commonly occurred in the context of disputes over property. While the older children observed have generally had less property available to argue over, as school playgrounds tend to be devoid of movable objects, it appears that they turn increasingly to verbal means of settling minor disputes. Serious fights were very rare in Neill's study (two instances) and in our own (three instances), and Sluckin (1981) reported seeing only 22 instances in his much longer observation period. In all these studies, serious fights were seen to draw crowds of chanting spectators and appeared to involve an element of ritual. Although physical injuries were not generally greater than those commonly sustained in the playground, an individual's pride could be seriously hurt and major social rifts could result affecting relations between children who were not directly involved.

This very limited comparative evidence suggests that although rough-and-tumble becomes rougher with age, it is still fundamentally distinct from hostile fighting. This view is compatible with that of Groos, as expressed in the quote above, though it does involve some reinterpretation of Neill's (1976) conclusions.

Certain anthropological studies also suggest that the content of play-fighting may change with age. It may become more serious practice, even though it is not hostile in so far as the protagonists stay together in friendly competition. Amongst the Red Xhosa of South Africa, Mayer and Mayer (1970) have described how 'cudgel play' develops from playful beating and hitting with sticks in young children to more regulated cudgel competition from the ages of 8 or 9 on through to about 20 (the age of manhood initiation). Such cudgel play is coached by older people and has certain conventions, rather like boxing in Western society. Although now rather a sport, it used to be a recognized training for proper war. In similar vein, the stick play of the East African Barabaig people is seen as practice for the later use of spears (Klima, 1970).

WHY ARE THERE SEX DIFFERENCES IN PLAY-FIGHTING?

It is well known that boys' play involves more vigorous activities, such as wrestling and tumbling – 'rough and tumble' play – than girls' play, and this difference is observed in cultures very different from our own. (Archer and Lloyd, 1982)

One of the most consistent findings of the studies on rough-and-tumble play is that there is a noticeable sex difference: boys do more of this kind of play than girls. According to Aldis (1975), though without quantitative data, the sex difference is especially marked in 'wrestling for superior position', and less marked for 'fragmentary wrestling' and 'chasing'.

At the preschool age range, a sex difference in the amount of rough-and-tumble play has been reported by Blurton Jones (1967; UK, 5 boys and 5 girls), Smith and Connolly (1972; UK, 20 boys and 20 girls, sex difference greater for play-wrestling than play-chasing), Brindley et al. (1973; UK, 20 boys and 20 girls), Blurton Jones and Konner (1973; UK, 10 boys and 11 girls; Kalahari San, 10 boys and 13 girls), Whiting and Edwards (1973; Mexico, 11 boys and 11 girls; Philippines, 12 boys and 12 girls; Okinawa, 12 boys and 12 girls; North India, 12 boys and 12 girls), Smith and Connolly (1980; UK, two groups, each 10 boys and 12 girls), DiPietro (1981; USA, 30 boys and 22 girls) and Heaton (1983; UK, 16 boys and 10 girls). Most, though not all, of these studies report significant differences. Blurton Jones (1972; UK, 12 boys and 13 girls) reported a higher incidence in younger girls than younger boys, and Whiting and Edwards (1973) reported a higher incidence in girls (Kenya; 8 boys and 8 girls) and in younger girls but older boys (USA, 12 boys and 12 girls). The Whiting and Edwards (1973) six-cultures study covers older children (aged 7 to 11 years) as well as younger children (aged 3 to 6 years). In our own study we found a greater incidence in boys at age 7 and 11 years ($p < 0.05$ and $p < 0.01$ respectively) though not at 9 years (Humphreys, 1983).

The sex difference in rough-and-tumble is thus well substantiated in general terms. What are the causes? Both environmental and hormonal influences have been postulated. Adults may direct rough-and-tumble more towards boys, reinforce it more in boys and provide male models of the behaviour with whom boys can identify. Also, boys may tend to find rough-and-tumble play more rewarding as an effect of sex hormones on the foetal brain.

If differential reinforcement of rough-and-tumble is occurring, it could start at an early age. Studies of parental stereotypes of sex-appropriate behaviour for 2-year-olds show that active physical or rough-and-tumble play is very consistently seen as more appropriate for boys (Fagot, 1973, 1978; Smith and Daglish 1977), although actual sex differences in toddler behaviour are not reported so consistently in these studies. Furthermore it is fathers more than mothers who provide the majority of rough-and-tumble play opportunities for toddlers as a number of USA studies have shown (Lamb, 1977; Lytton, 1980; Parke and Tinsley, 1981), although this may well be culture-dependent. From his longitudinal study, Lamb (1981) found that fathers treated boys and girls similarly at first, but that early in the second year fathers began to direct more social behaviour to sons than daughters. Thus it could be that fathers are encouraging more rough-and-tumble play in boys, both by modelling the behaviour (and by

3 years children are fully aware of their own gender identity, Thompson, 1975), and by directing more of this behaviour towards boys. In addition, the data on parental stereotypes would suggest that both parents might reinforce rough-and-tumble more in boys. The only directly relevant study gives little if any support to this last hypothesis. Fagot (1978), in a study of 12 boys and 12 girls aged 20 to 24 months, in the home, found that parents responded to rough-and-tumble play in boys 91% positively and 3% negatively; in girls 84% positively and 2% negatively (not significantly different). Some other behaviours were reinforced in sex-stereotyped ways, however, and it is quite possible that parental response might become more sex-stereotyped to rough-and-tumble in older children.

A different source of explanation for sex differences in rough-and-tumble play lies in studies of the effects of sex hormones on behaviour. It is argued that exposure to higher levels of male sex hormone in male foetuses during pregnancy has certain effects on the developing brain, one of which is to predispose the child to later enjoy rough-and-tumble activities. The human evidence comes from the effects of anomalous amounts of prenatal sex hormones. Unusual exposure can be due to endogenous causes (such as Turner's syndrome) or exogenous causes (such as mothers given treatment including gonadal hormones during pregnancy). It has been argued especially that girls who were exposed prenatally to a higher than usual level of androgens are more likely to be tomboyish, and to enjoy vigorous physical activity and rough-and-tumble play. Such a result was found by Money and Erhardt (1972) in a comparison of 25 girls who had experienced foetal androgenization with 25 normal matched controls. In a more recent review, Erhardt and Meyer-Bahlburg (1981) suggest that intense physical energy expenditure and rough-and-tumble play 'seems to be an essential aspect of psycho-social development and it appears to be influenced by sex steroid variations before birth'; they regard this as one of the 'best established' influences of prenatal hormones.

Quadagno et al. (1977) suggested some reservations about conclusions from the Money and Erhardt (1972) study. Since the androgenized girls were born with masculinized genitalia, necessitating surgical correction, parental awareness of genital masculinity at birth might have influenced rearing practices. Specifically, it was suggested, the parents might encourage more tomboyish behaviour in these girls. Erhardt and Meyer-Bahlburg (1981) regard the opposite as more likely, that the parents would encourage feminiity in these circumstances. However, the data are based on interviews and not on direct observations. It is therefore the perceptions of the girls and their mothers which have been shown to differ. Such perceptions could be susceptible to rearing expectations, and it would be more convincing to have behavioural data. In another review, Hines (1982) states that 'studies of individuals who were exposed to unusual hormones prenatally, but who were born without abnormalities, have failed in many cases to find evidence of . . . masculinized play comparable to that reported for androgenized girls'. However, these studies have their own weaknesses, and some investigated different hormones (Hines, 1982).

It is clearly difficult for studies of hormonal effects to totally rule out environmental factors such as effects of gender perception on rearing practices. Equally, it is difficult for studies of parental reinforcement to rule out a developmentally-channelled predisposition for boys to enjoy rough-and-tumble more than girls. After all, children respond very positively to fathers' active play (Lamb, 1977), and the evidence so far is that father–son rough-and-tumble play increases in the second year, before differential parental reinforcement as such becomes apparent. Quite likely, the increase in father–son rough-and-tumble play is in part a response to the male child's greater interest in such play. As in many other areas, sexual stereotypes may act to magnify considerably the effects of such predispositions. Even if a hormonal influence on rough-and-tumble play seems likely, cultural factors are surely strong. For example, Blurton Jones and Konner (1973) found that the sex difference in rough-and-tumble was much less in Kalahari San children than in London children. The London girls did much less rough-and-tumble than the San girls, perhaps because of the strong Western cultural stereotype that such play is 'unfeminine' which other investigators have found. An interactionist model (Archer and Lloyd, 1982) is thus the most promising for understanding *how* the sex difference develops, although it does not ultimately explain *why* this difference exists.

WHAT IS THE DEVELOPMENTAL SIGNIFICANCE OF ROUGH-AND-TUMBLE PLAY?

If play does, in fact, tend to increase aggression in adults, perhaps it should be discouraged whatever its other benefits may be. Assuming that playfighting is harmless, parents, playground supervisors, teachers and others are faced, nevertheless, with many vexing problems in dealing with it. Should it be actively encouraged or merely tolerated? . . . The study of play may ultimately be able to give us some answers. (Aldis, 1975)

Recent studies of mammalian rough-and-tumble have been influenced by evolutionary thinking. Given the frequency and distinctiveness of this form of play in many species' repertoire, it is argued that it must have some adaptive significance; it must have some functional benefit for the individual performing the behaviour.

The benefits of rough-and-tumble play in non-human species are still the subject of debate, and a number of viable hypotheses have been put forward (Fagen, 1981; Smith, 1982 and associated Commentary; several chapters in this volume). It is possible to use these as hypotheses for the developmental significance of human rough-and-tumble. In doing so, it is important to bear a number of points in mind.

Firstly, a behaviour could have a number of benefits for the individual performing it. These might vary at different points in the life-span. Even if one benefit is that for which the behaviour was originally selected (i.e. its function in the strong sense of the word), in evolutionary time other, initially incidental, benefits may come to be selected for and these may in turn change the form of the behaviour. Such evolutionary trends are postulated by Byers (above, chapter 2) in his consideration of ungulate play. A behaviour may also have incidental benefits (not strongly selected for) which nevertheless could be of practical relevance. The benefits of play might be essential ones, or they might be benefits which can be obtained in other ways (Baldwin and Baldwin, 1974). They might be highly specific benefits or very general ones (Fagen, 1982). Finally, in human play, there may be cultural values put on play which do not necessarily coincide with any biological function or benefit (Smith, 1982).

Evidence for or against different functional hypotheses can be gathered from the forms of rough-and-tumble play, age changes, sex differences and choice of partners. Deprivation or supplementation experiments could give information on any benefits of play, but are not possible in humans, and any natural experiments in this vein tend to be hopelessly confounded with other variables such as general peer contact.

The original function for mammalian play may well have been physical training (Fagen, 1976), with playful exercise enhancing muscle growth and general physical capacity. This is a plausible function for some human play. Studies of exercise physiology have demonstrated that, while adults can achieve temporary physical improvement through exercise, comparable exercise in children can lead to more lasting developmental changes (Fagen, 1976). Being intensely active, human rough-and-tumble play certainly provides exercise which contributes to physical development. However, if this were its function, it would need to provide a consistently large proportion of total exercise (Fagen and George, 1977). The amount of time spent in rough-and-tumble by the children in our own study (see figure 11.2) suggests that, for them, exercise was not a primary function of the activity. Rough-and-tumble constituted 18.3%, 12.0% and 16.3% of physically active behaviour at the ages of 7, 9 and 11 years respectively. It is probable that, throughout childhood, vigorous activity play, later incorporated into games with rules, is a much more important source of exercise.

Perhaps the most prevalent functional hypothesis is that rough-and-tumble play provides practice in specific skills such as those of fighting or hunting (Symons, 1978). In a playful context, it is argued, individuals can practise and perfect specific motor skills which will later be important for survival, without suffering the serious consequences of their mistakes. Although fighting and hunting skills are of little direct survival value in modern urban societies, the anthropological evidence could give some credence to this hypothesis applied to human rough-and-tumble. We have already mentioned how in some tribal societies, such as the Red Xhosa (Mayer and Mayer, 1970) the forms of play-fighting change with age and seem to grade into more formal, though still non-hostile, practice in fighting skills such as cudgelling or spear-throwing, as well as wrestling. Groos (1901) also provides examples of this from anthropological and historical sources.

Konner (1972) describes an apparent association between rough-and-tumble play behaviours and actions comparable to those of adult hunting in the Kalahari San: 'The interest of both boys and girls in animals continues to expand, and by the age of 5 they take interest and pleasure in bothering and killing them. It is very striking that most of the component behaviours in rough-and-tumble play . . . can be seen in Zhun/twa [San] children annoying large animals . . . or trying to kill small ones.' He concludes that 'In evolutionary terms, the basic primate pattern of rough-and-tumble play has become, in part, specialized in man to serve the acquisition of hunting behaviour.'

It is difficult to separate the functions of practice in fighting and in hunting skills. Both hypotheses explain the distinctive forms of the play behaviour, and both explain the characteristic sex differences, if it is accepted that in the great majority of traditional societies, fighting and hunting are done by males.

It has been postulated for some animal play-fighting (Byers, 1980) that an individual would gain the most effective fighting practice by selecting play partners of similar strength. With this in mind, we examined the choices of rough-and-tumble play partner made by the children in our study (Humphreys, 1983). Previous research has shown that children generally agree in ranking classmates for strength (Omark and Edelman, 1975) though they tend to over-rank themselves, findings which we confirmed. We obtained each child's perceptions of the relative strength of all his or her classmates, from which we calculated a consensus of opinion on relative strength for each class. We then analysed the children's choice of rough-and-tumble partners in terms of both their own and class-consensus relative-strength rankings.

Most interactions (including rough-and-tumble) occurred within rather than between classes, so there is already some degree of assortment by age and presumably by strength. Furthermore, using each child's own perceptions, we found that at all three ages children chose partners whom they perceived as closer to themselves in strength than chance would have predicted ($p < 0.01$). However, using the class consensus on relative strength, it was only the 11-year-olds who chose partners significantly closer to themselves than would have been the case if classmates had been paired randomly ($p < 0.0001$). If this result can be generalized, it provides some support for the hypothesis that rough-and-tumble is suited to practise fighting skills. The hypothesis is best supported for the older children as the class consensus may be thought of as a more objective measure of the children's actual strength.

Another hypothesis is that rough-and-tumble helps individuals 'find their place in the existent social order' (Poirier and Smith, 1974, for primate play), by learning relative-strength or dominance rankings. However, it is unlikely that rough-and-tumble is the only means of assessing other children's strength. At a variety of ages, we and others (Omark and Edelman, 1975) have found that children can rank others for relative strength, and agree on these rankings, even though the group includes children with whom they rarely, if ever, rough-and-tumble (e.g. children of the opposite sex).

An influential set of hypotheses from mammalian research are those suggesting social functions for rough-and-tumble (Fagen, 1981; Byers, above, chapter 2; Hole and Einon, above, chapter 4). Specifically, it may cause animals to stay together longer (social cohesion), or enhance future cooperation by providing an opportunity for individuals to get to know each other. For the young of many mammalian species, play-fighting is one of the major sources of social interaction and a social function for play is plausible. The hypothesis appears less strong for human children, since they have so many other opportunities for friendly social interaction.

The children in our own study chose friends as rough-and-tumble play partners. We obtained children's rankings of their classmates according to personal liking, as we did for strength. We found that at the ages of 7, 9 and 11 years, children chose partners whom they liked significantly better than chance pairing of classmates would have predicted ($p < 001$). This could support a social function for rough-and-tumble. However, the result is also compatible with the theory that play-fighting practises fighting skills if it is assumed that 'safe' fighting practice is best obtained by selecting a friend for a partner.

The final set of hypotheses we shall consider suggest more generalized or complex functions for rough-and-tumble play, such as facilitating general behavioural flexibility (Fagen, 1982, and above, chapter 7) or complex social skills (Hole and Einon, above, chapter 4). These hypotheses are perhaps the least elaborated at present, as far as mammalian play is concerned, and so it is difficult to test them. For humans, flexibility has been primarily postulated as a benefit of other forms of play such as object play (Simon and Smith, above, chapter 9). Complex social skills such as negotiation and bargaining, multi-party alliances, redefining situations, exercising leadership skills and so on may well be practised in the games of older children, some of which incorporate agonistic components (Lancy, 1974; Lever, 1976; Sluckin, 1981; Parker, below, chapter 12). As far as younger children are concerned, rough-and-tumble play (especially when it incorporates fantasy) may involve a large number of participants (Smith, 1977), but apart from this, there is little evidence to support a claim that rough-and-tumble play as such facilitates complex social skills or flexibility.

It seems to us that the most likely original function of human rough-and-tumble play, in an evolutionary sense, is as practice for fighting and hunting skills. This is the only hypothesis which has so far provided a convincing explanation of the forms of the activity and the appreciable sex differences. It appears better substantiated for older children, being supported by evidence from rough-and-tumble partner choice and the general findings on changes with age. Practice in these skills does not receive great positive valuation in our culture, at least in educational circles. Even though there is no evidence that rough-and-tumble play actually fosters aggressive behaviour, such play is discouraged by many teachers and nursery supervisors. However, there is evidence that engaging in rough-and-tumble play is part of the normal development process. It also appears to provide, as incidental benefits, exercise contributing to physical development (also available through other forms of active play) and social bonding (also promoted by other forms of social play and interaction). This leaves unresolved the question of how important rough-and-tumble is for such benefits, whether it has other specific benefits or disadvantages and therefore whether, as Aldis (1975) asked, it should be 'actively encouraged or merely tolerated'. We can hope, with him, that further studies of this form of play can give more advice on these very practical problems.

ACKNOWLEDGEMENT

The research carried out by Anne Humphreys, and the writing of the chapter, were supported by the Foundation for Child Development.

REFERENCES

Aldis, O. (1975). *Play Fighting*. New York: Academic Press.

Archer, J. and Lloyd, B. (1982). *Sex and Gender*. Harmondsworth: Penguin.

Baldwin, J. D. and Baldwin, J. I. (1974). Exploration and play in squirrel monkeys *(Saimiri)*. *American Zoologist* 14, 303–15.

Blurton Jones, N. G. (1967). An ethological study of some aspects of social behaviour of children in nursery school. In D. Morris (ed.), *Primate Ethology*. London: Weidenfeld & Nicolson.

Blurton Jones, N. G. (1972). Categories of child–child interaction. In N. Blurton Jones (ed.), *Ethological Studies of Child Behaviour*. Cambridge: Cambridge University Press.

Blurton Jones, N. G. and Konner M. J. (1973). Sex differences in behaviour of London and Bushman children. In R. P. Michael and J. H. Crook (eds), *Comparative Ecology and Behaviour of Primates*. London: Academic Press.

Brindley, C., Clarke, P., Hutt, C., Robinson, I. and Wethli, E. (1973). Sex differences in the activities and social interactions of nursery school children. In R. P. Michael and J. H. Crook (eds), *Comparative Ecology and Behaviour of Primates*. London: Academic Press.

Buhler, C. (1935). *From Birth to Maturity*. London: Kegan Paul, Trench, Trubner and Co. Ltd.

Byers, J. A. (1980). Play partner preferences in Siberian Ibex, *Capra ibex sibirica*. *Zeitschrift für Tierpsychologie* 53, 23–40.

Campbell, S. B. and Cluss, P. (1982). Peer relationships of young children with behavior problems. In K. H. Rubin and H. S. Ross (eds), *Peer Relationships and Social Skills in Childhood*. New York: Springer Verlag.

DiPietro, J. A. (1981). Rough and tumble play: a function of gender. *Developmental Psychology* 17, 50–8.

Erhardt, A. A. and Meyer-Bahlberg, H. F. L. (1981). Effects of prenatal sex hormones on gender-related behavior. *Science* 211, 1312–18.

Fagen, R. M. (1976). Exercise, play and physical training in animals. In P. P. G. Bateson and P. H. Klopfer (eds), *Perspectives in Ethology, Vol. 2*. New York: Plenum Press.

Fagen, R. M. (1981). *Animal Play Behavior*. New York and Oxford: Oxford University Press.

Fagen, R. M. (1982). Evolutionary issues in development of behavioral flexibility. In P. P. G. Bateson and P. H. Klopfer (eds), *Perspectives in Ethology, Vol. 5, Ontogeny*. New York: Plenum Press.

Fagen, R. M. and George, T. K. (1977). Play behavior and exercise in young ponies *(Equus caballus* L.*) Behavioral Ecology and Sociobiology* 2, 267–9.

Fagot, B. I. (1973). Sex-related stereoptyping of toddlers' behaviors. *Developmental Psychology* 9, 429.

Fagot, B. I. (1974). Sex differences in toddlers' behavior and parental reaction. *Developmental Psychology* 10, 554–8.

Fagot, B. I. (1978). The influence of sex of child on parental reactions to toddler children. *Child Development* 49, 459–65.

Fraser, M. (1973). *Children in Conflict*. London: Secker & Warburg.

Goldman, B. D. and Ross, H. S. (1978). Social skills in action: an analysis of early peer games. In J. Glick and K. A. Clarke-Stewart (eds), *The Development of Social Understanding, Vol. 7*. New York: Gardner Press.

Groos, K. (1901). *The Play of Man*. London: William Heinemann.

Hall, G. S. (1904). *Adolescence, Vol. 1*. New York: Appleton.

Hattwick, B. W. (1937). Sex differences in behavior of nursery school children. *Child Development* 8, 343–55.

Heaton, K. (1983). A study of rough-and-tumble play and serious aggression in nursery school children. Unpublished BA thesis, University of Sheffield.

Hines, M. (1982). Prenatal gonadal hormones and sex differences in human behavior. *Psychological Bulletin* 92, 56–80.

Humphreys, A. P. (1983). The developmental significance of rough-and-tumble play in children. Final report to Foundation for Child Development, New York.

Klima, G. J. (1970). *The Barabaig: East African Cattle Herders*. New York: Holt, Rinehart and Winston.

Konner, M. S. (1972). Aspects of the developmental ethology of a foraging people. In N. Blurton Jones (ed.) *Ethological Studies of Child Behaviour*. Cambridge: Cambridge University Press.

Lamb, M. E. (1977). Father–infant and mother–infant interactions in the first year of life. *Child Development* 48, 167–81.

Lamb, M. E. (1981). The development of father–infant relationships. In M. E. Lamb (ed.), *The Role of the Father in Child Development* (2nd edn). New York: John Wiley & Sons.

Lancy, D. F. (1974). Work, play and learning in a Kpelle town. Unpublished Ph.D. thesis, University of Pittsburgh.

Lever, J. (1976). Sex differences in the games children play. *Social Problems* 23, 478–87.

Lytton, H. (1980). *Parent–Child Interaction: the Socialization Process Observed in Twin and Singleton Families*. New York: Plenum.

McGrew, W. C. (1972). *An Ethological Study of Children's Behaviour*. London: Academic Press.

Manning, M., Heron, J. and Marshall, T. (1978). Styles of hostility and social interactions at nursery, at school, and at home: an extended study of children. In L. A. Hersov, M. Berger and D. Shaffer (eds), *Aggression and Anti-social Behaviour in Childhood and Adolescence*. Oxford: Pergamon Press.

Mayer, P. and Mayer, I. (1970). Socialization by peers: the youth organization of the Red Xhosa. In P. Mayer (ed.), *Socialisation: the Approach from Social Anthropology*. London: Tavistock.

Matthews, W. S. and Matthews, R. J. (1982). Eliminating operational definitions:

a paradigm case approach to the study of fantasy play. In D. J. Pepler and K. H. Rubin (eds), *The Play of Children: Current Theory and Research*. Basel: S. Karger.

Mead, M. (1930). *Growing Up in New Guinea*. New York: Blue Ribbon Books.

Minturn, L. and Hitchcock, J. T. (1966). *The Rajputs of Khalapur, India*. (Six Cultures Series, volume III). New York: John Wiley & Sons.

Money, J. and Ehrhardt, A. A. (1972). *Man and Woman, Boy and Girl*. Baltimore: Johns Hopkins University Press.

Mussen, P. H., Conger, J. J. and Kagan, J. (1963). *Child Development and Personality* (2nd edn). New York: Harper & Row.

Neill, S. R. St J. (1976). Aggressive and non-aggressive fighting in twelve-to-thirteen year old pre-adolescent boys. *Journal of Child Psychology and Psychiatry* 17, 213–20.

Omark, D. R. and Edelman, M. S. (1975). A comparison of status hierarchies in young children: an ethological approach. *Social Science Information* 14, 87–107.

Opie, I. and Opie, P. (1969). *Children's Games in Street and Playground*. London: Oxford University Press.

Parke, R. D. and Tinsley, B. R. (1981). The father's role in infancy: determinants of involvement in caregiving and play. In M. E. Lamb (ed.), *The Role of the Father in Child Development* (2nd edn). New York John Wiley & Sons.

Piaget, J. (1951). *Play, Dreams and Imitation in Childhood*. London: Routledge & Kegan Paul (first published 1945).

Poirier, F. E. and Smith, E. O. (1974). Socialising functions of primate play. *American Zoologist* 14, 275–87.

Pre-school Playgroups Association (1982). *Families in Playgroups*. Reading, UK: Southern Region PPA.

Quadagno, D. M., Briscoe, R. and Quadagno, J. S. (1977). Effect of perinatal gonadal hormones on selected nonsexual behavior patterns: a critical assessment of the nonhuman and human literature. *Psychological Bulletin* 84, 62–80.

Raum, O. F. (1940). *Chaga Childhood*. London: Oxford University Press.

Ross, H. S. (1982). Establishment of social games among toddlers. *Developmental Psychology* 18, 509–18.

Rubin, K. H. (1982). Social and social-cognitive developmental characteristics of young isolate, normal and sociable children. In K. H. Rubin and H. S. Ross (eds), *Peer Relationships and Social Skills in Childhood*. New York: Springer-Verlag.

Sluckin, A. (1981). *Growing Up in the Playground: the Social Development of Children*. London: Routledge and Kegan Paul.

Smith, P. K. (1973). Temporal clusters and individual differences in the behaviour of preschool children. In R. P. Michael and J. H. Crook (eds), *Comparative Ecology and Behaviour of Primates*. London: Academic Press.

Smith, P. K. (1974). Ethological methods. In B. Foss (ed.), *New Perspectives in Child Development*. Harmondsworth: Penguin.

Smith, P. K. (1977). Social and fantasy play in young children. In B. Tizard and D.

Harvey (eds), *Biology of Play*. London: S.I.M.P./Heinemann.

Smith, P. K. (1982). Does play matter? Functional and evolutionary aspects of animal and human play. *Behavioral and Brain Sciences* 5, 139–84.

Smith, P. K. and Connolly, K. (1972). Patterns of play and social interaction in pre-school children. In N. Blurton Jones (ed.), *Ethological Studies of Child Behaviour*. Cambridge: Cambridge University Press.

Smith, P. K. and Connolly, K. J. (1980). *The Ecology of Preschool Behaviour*. Cambridge: Cambridge University Press.

Smith, P. K. and Daglish, L. (1977). Sex differences in parent and infant behavior in the home. *Child Development* 48, 1250–4.

Symons, D. (1978). *Play and Aggression: a Study of Rhesus Monkeys*. New York: Columbia University Press.

Thompson, S. K. (1975). Gender labels and early sex role development. *Child Development* 46, 339–7.

Valentine, C. W. (1956). *The Normal Child and some of his Abnormalities*. Harmondsworth: Penguin.

Vandell, D. L. (1980). Sociability with peer and mother during the first year. *Developmental Psychology* 16, 355–61.

Whiting, B. and Edwards, C. P. (1973). A cross-cultural analysis of sex differences in the behavior of children aged three through eleven. *Journal of Social Psychology* 91, 171–88.

Whiting, B. B. and Whiting, J. W. M. (1975). *Children of Six Cultures: a Psychocultural Analysis*. Cambridge, Mass.: Harvard University Press.

PART V

Varied Perspectives on Play and Games in Humans

The chapters in this final part consider human play and games in different societies and through the life-span; though from varied and sometimes contrasting points of view. Sue Parker (chapter 12) applies concepts from evolutionary biology and Piagetian theory to examine the structure and content of human games, and to explain sex differences which are characteristically found. David Lancy (chapter 13) uses his detailed anthropological research in New Guinea to test empirically some theories of game variation in different societies. Finally, Brian Sutton-Smith and Diana Kelly-Byrne (chapter 14) use a more historical and sociological perspective to question many of the prevailing assumptions we have about play and games, and in particular the validity of and the motives for what they term the prevalent 'idealization of play'.

Parker provides an ambitious framework for categorizing both the structure and content of human games, from infancy to adulthood. The structural analysis is based on Piagetian theory, assuming that the development of logical thinking ability will be paralleled by the development of game structure and complexity. The content analysis covers social and object contingency games, make-believe games, agonistic exercise games, and games with rules (the last category being further subdivided by the type of competition involved). Parker goes on to argue that most or all play and games incorporate play attack or fear, and rule-mediated competition; and that they practise skills, including competitive skills, for later use. This leads her to hypothesize that sex differences in the frequency and complexity of (in particular) agonistic exercise games, and games with rules, are products of sexual selection, as preparation for male–male competition. This is a much broader version of the specific hypothesis put forward by Humphreys and Smith (chapter 11) for rough-and-tumble play in middle childhood.

There certainly are sex differences in children's games in Western societies. For example, Lever (1978), in a US study, showed that boys played games which were more complex in a number of ways: the number of roles, interdependence of players, size of play group, explicitness of goals, number of rules, and team formation. She too saw these differences as helping to promote sex differences in adulthood, in such areas as interpersonal competition, leadership, and styles of human relationships. Lever, unlike Parker, argued that there were primarily historical and cultural grounds for these differences, based on sexual stereotypes and their influence on the encouragement of, and provision for, resources for boys' and girls' games. This is an alternative, though not necessarily opposing, hypothesis to Parker's. Rapid changes in sex differences in games (e.g. Parker, note 9) would support a cultural explanation, though Parker could argue that environmental scaling (the grading of a behavioural predisposition to environmental demands) could have been selected for, biologically.

Parker ends with predictions about the types of games likely to occur in different societies. Lancy too is concerned with this question, and he also utilizes a cognitive approach. Using anthropological data gathered on ten traditional societies in Papua New Guinea, he correlates game complexity with cognitive test scores and an index of societal complexity. The correlations are small. What Lancy concludes is that play groups in small tribal societies may not facilitate the maximum expression of game complexity. As Konner (1975) has also observed, in hunter–gatherer and small tribal groups there will generally be a limited number of children who can play together, and they will be of mixed sex and age composition. This would tend to lessen the expression of sex differences, and to bring in a 'lowest common denominator' of play complexity. As far as we know, human evolution was characterized by such small groups or bands. This would suggest that, while some limited predisposition for certain games (and for sexual differences in game expression) may be rooted in natural selection operating through biological evolution, the expression of game complexity and marked sexual differences found in modern societies must be very strongly influenced by cultural factors. It may well be that some gene-culture co-evolutionary approach (e.g. Durham, 1982) would have useful application here.

Sutton-Smith and Kelly-Byrne develop the importance of cultural ideas in a different sense; how they have affected the attitudes to play and games of both academics and the public generally. They argue that over the last century, factors such as the work ethic, the social status value of team games, the toy industry, and also academic play theories, have tended to idealize play as being voluntary, of positive affect, egalitarian, flexible and functional. They then proceed to argue that these characteristics are *not* necessary for play. For example, in maintaining that play can be non-egalitarian and characterized by negative affect, they describe how a good deal of playground activity involves struggles for power, attack and defence, chase and escape. Highlighting the competitive nature of play is compatible with Parker's analysis; though, as Lancy points out, some games are primarily cooperative. In contrast to Parker and many other theorists, though, Sutton-Smith and Kelly-Byrne are sceptical about the functional view of play as practice for adult activities. They argue rather for an autonomous world of childhood, in which play can threaten conventions and express subjective worlds not permitted by adults. The prevailing emphasis on the importance of play for adult life is, from this viewpoint, a means adults use to control the challenge in children's play.

Adults do indeed use games for socializing functions (e.g. Orlick, 1981), and adult-organized games differ in social context from peer-organized games (Polgar, 1976). However, is this view of children's play as a challenge also historically and culturally limited, for example to urban societies with large groups of children cut off from participating in adult life? Is it an opposing theory to that of play as practice, or a supplementary theory? In any event, Sutton-Smith and Kelly-Byrne provide a refreshing challenge to all of us who think about play: to re-examine our preconceptions about what play is, and what it might be for.

REFERENCES

Durham W. H. (1982). Interactions of genetic and cultural evolution: models and examples. *Human Ecology* 3, 289–323.
Konner, M. (1975). Relations among infants and juveniles in comparative perspective. In M. Lewis and L. Rosenblum (eds), *Friendship and Peer Relations: The Origins of Behavior, Vol. 3*. New York: Wiley.
Lever, J. (1978). Sex differences in the complexity of children's play and games. *American Sociological Review* 43, 471–83.
Orlick, T. D. (1981). Positive socialization via cooperative games. *Developmental Psychology* 17, 426–9.
Polgar, S. K. (1976). The social context of games: or when is play not play? *Sociology of Education* 49, 265–71.

12 Playing for Keeps: An Evolutionary Perspective on Human Games

Sue Taylor Parker

Now we see that youth probably exists for the sake of play.
Animals cannot be said to play because they are young and frolicsome,
but rather they have a period of youth in order to play; for only by so
doing can they supplement the insufficient hereditary endowment with
individual experience in view of the coming tasks of life.

Karl Groos, 1898

Play is primarily a behaviour of young mammals. It is characterized by vigorous and pleasurable activity with no immediate purpose. Although the particular motor patterns of play vary from species to species they are always fragments of longer functional sequences involved in such adult activities as fight, flight, subsistence, or predation. These 'prefunctional' play motor patterns are distinguished from the adult patterns by their frivolous   context   and   incomplete   performance,   and   also   by species-specific play signals. The dog's wagging tail, extended forepaws and cocked head; the monkey's bouncing gait and relaxed open mouthed face; the child's bouncing and laughter, are all examples of such signals.

These and other signals, such as bouncing, tagging, and running off with a backward glance, often serve as invitations to another animal. When two animals play together they alternate between simple reciprocal roles such as chaser and chased, attacker and attacked. These reciprocal roles involve the emotional states of play attack and play fear, both of which are pleasurable at moderate levels (Aldis, 1975). When they are safe and well fed, young animals devote considerable time and energy to play. If a playmate of the same age and sex is unavailable they will handicap themselves in order to keep a younger or weaker animal in the game. They will even play with young animals of another species (Groos, 1898; Huizinga, 1955; Loizos, 1967; Millar, 1968; Smith, 1982; van Hooff, 1972; Dolhinow and Bishop, 1972).

Because it consumes so much energy to no immediate practical purpose, play has puzzled those who have tried to understand its adaptive significance. (Indeed, one school of thought interpreted play as an outlet

TABLE 12.1 Piaget's model of cognitive development

| | | Domains of Cognition | | |
	Types of Logic	*Physical*	*Interpersonal*	*Intrapersonal*
Sensorimotor period (birth to 2 yrs)	sensorimotor trial-and-error; experimention; discovery of new means; circular reactions	object permanence; externalized time, space, and causality	deferred imitation of novel schemes; sensorimotor contingency games	first evoked images
Preoperations period Symbolic sub period (2 to 4 years) Intuitive sub period (4 to 7 yrs)	nonreversible interiorized action schemes, i.e. preconcepts with transductive reasoning	object identity; topological space; graphic collections incipient projective and Euclidean non-graphic collections	make-believe games; unilateral respect for authority	static evoked images
Concrete operations period (7 to 12 yrs)	reversible in teriorized action schemes, i.e. true concepts with deductive reasoning about concrete phenomena	object quantity; true classification with inclusion	games with rules;concept of winning and losing	dynamic evoked images
Formal operations period (12 yrs on)	abstract reasoning, systematic hypothesis formation and testing, inference concerning hidden variables	true measurement	universal rules based on abstract concepts of justice	anticipatory imagery of events never witnessed
	INRC group 16 binary operations	proportionality, conservation of weight and volume, understanding density, equal action and reaction, etc.		

for 'surplus energy', a bizarre idea in light of the selective premium on efficient allocation of a limited supply of energy.) The most widely accepted answer to this puzzle is that play is practice for adult activities that cannot be practised directly.[1] Taking this idea as a starting point, I will try to explain the adaptive significance of the various types of games played by human children. I will begin my effort with a definition of games and an elaboration and extension of Piaget's typology of play in relation to cognitive development (Piaget, 1962).[2] (see table 12.1).

Games are a uniquely human form of play involving the ritualization of roles and the enactment of predictable predetermined scenes. In games, the loosely defined unpredictable sequences characteristic of play are transformed into a ritualized repetitive cycle of action with a beginning, a middle, and an end. In conjunction with this process, the informal alternation of roles characteristic of play is transformed into regularized turn-taking between competing individuals and/or groups. Games differ from other forms of play in requiring that at least one of the players have a conception of the scenario and the rules of its enactment, and that the other players have the cognitive ability to follow the rules.

It is no coincidence then that we are both the most playful and the most intelligent of animals. The relationship between intelligence and play is both systematic and structural: the games of infants are a manifestation of sensorimotor intelligence; the make-believe games of young children are a manifestation of preoperational intelligence (Piaget, 1962); the rule-bound games of older children are a manifestation of operational intelligence (Piaget 1962, 1963, 1965; see table 12.2).

CONTINGENCY GAMES

Human infancy is characterized by contingency games, i.e. by games relying on the infant's understanding that his actions create contingent effects (Piaget, 1963; Watson, 1972). These games take two forms. In social contingency games, such as peek-a-boo, adults respond to vocal, facial, and hand signals from the infant with playful attacks such as tickling and spinning, or hiding and popping up (Watson, 1972; Stern, 1978; Bruner and Sherwood, 1976).[3] In physical contingency games, such as rattle-shaking and object-dropping, physical objects respond to actions of the infant by producing interesting noises and/or spectacles. Both forms depend upon the achievement of the secondary and tertiary circular reactions characteristic of the third and fifth stages of sensorimotor intelligence (Piaget, 1963).

During social contingency games adult and infant alternate roles: the

TABLE 12.2 Games of each type, according to Piaget's development periods

Game Typology	Sensorimotor	Symbolic	Intuitive/Concrete	Formal
Social contingency games	'peek-a-boo', 'the conversation game'	'Why?' Verbal teasing games, hide-and-seek	Verbal teasing games, jokes	flirting, courting
Object contingency games	2nd circular reactions, e.g. shaking rattles; 3rd circular reactions	noise-making	explosives/fireworks	building and launching of rockets and weapons
Make believe games	imitating simple actions like 'pat-a-cake'	making little scenes of simple daily activities, e.g., playing 'house', 'horsey', school'	making bigger scenes of more complex routines, e.g. war games	inventing codes, languages, cities, nations, planets
Agonistic exercise games	looming, tickling, spinning, rocking	running, jumping, sliding, climbing	contests: wrestling, chasing, throwing	
Games with rules	simple simultaneous alternating games, e.g. 'peek-a-boo', 'pat-a-cake'	group action and follow the leader games 'hokey-pokey', 'London Bridge', 'Mother May I', 'Ring Around the Rosy'	simple field games, simple iconic games	iconic and field strategy games with inference

infant smiles or coos or raises his brow, the adult responds by poking or tickling or talking, and the baby repeats his preceding action, etc. (Watson, 1972). These games are the earliest manifestations of the turn-taking scheme which is characteristic of later conversations and of make-believe and rule-bound games. It is likely that they are adaptations for practising this vital turn-taking scheme (Stern, 1978).

The turn-taking scheme is ubiquitous in human interaction beginning in the earliest weeks of life. It plays a central role in language, games, and social organization generally. It is apparently motivated and reinforced by pleasure in 'contingency control' and 'reverse contingency control', i.e. pleasure in the ability to produce contingent responses in others, and to respond contingently to others (Parker, 1977).

Although turn-taking is natural to human beings, it is not natural to other primates: great-ape mothers and infants engage in a simple form of social contingency play in which the mother tickles and dangles the infant, but they do not display the elaborate face-to-face contingency games characteristic of human mothers and infants (Parker, 1977). The turn-taking schemes of monkeys seem to be limited to the alternation of roles in play-fighting and chasing.

Just as social contingency games focus the infant's attention on people's faces and voices, so physical contingency games focus the infant's attention on the actions of objects and their spatial and causal relations with other objects. Through physical contingency games, or, strictly speaking, physical contingency play, such as shaking, banging, and later dropping, rolling, and poking objects, the infant begins to learn about spatial relations, forces, and instrumental functions of objects. Physical contin-gency play is also displayed by great-ape infants, who share with us the ability to use tools (Parker, 1977; Parker and Gibson, 1979). This fact strongly suggests that these games are adaptations for practising tool use.

Although they begin in infancy, both social and physical contingency games continue into later age periods. Teasing games and noise-making games, for example, are later manifestations of this type of play. Playing with fire and fireworks seems to be a popular, if covert, form of contingency play among young boys between the ages of 6 and 12 years. The contingent response of adult startlement and outrage is apparently highly satisfying to boys of a certain age. Such games obviously entail both play attack and play fear motivation as well as contingency and reverse contingency controls.

The enduring role of fire and explosives in human subsistence and agonistic activities suggests that fascination with fire and explosives may have been shaped by sexual selection for hunting and combat. If so, it must have come relatively late in human evolution, because fire appears with *Homo erectus* in the middle Pleistocene. The invention of fire-making seems to require systematic trial-and-error experimentation with combustible materials, an understanding of friction, and of transformations of matter which come with later Piagetian stages of concrete or early formal operational reasoning (Parker, in press).

MAKE-BELIEVE GAMES

Even before they have mastered two- and three-word utterances, young children mimic simple daily activities such as sleeping, eating, travelling, etc. As they grow older and more linguistically competent, children enact ever longer and more complex scenes from everyday life (Piaget, 1962). These scenes typically revolve around domestic and vocational themes, such as food preparation, shelter construction, child-care, transportation, medical treatment, apprehension of wrongdoers, defence against enemies, etc., and are sex-role specific. Make-believe games typically involve the use of real or imaginary objects such as dolls, guns, etc.

Like contingency games, these make-believe games are manifestations of intellectual development; specifically they are manifestations of the interiorization of action characteristic of preoperational intelligence (Piaget, 1962). Later manifestations of make-believe play, such as the invention of private languages and codes, and even inventions of imaginary cities and planets, depend upon operational intelligence. Many kinds of make-believe play (e.g. cowboys and indians, 'doctor', and cops and robbers) involve play fear, play attack, and contingency motivations.

The ability to engage in make-believe games seems to be an adaptation for practising domestic and extra-domestic subsistence tasks and associated sex-role differentiations (Parker and Gibson, 1979). Rosenstiel reports, for example, that many games of the Motu children of Papua New Guinea 'are in direct imitation of the activities of adult life: birth, feeding, widowhood, pot and basket making, fishing and sailing. At eight to twelve years of age boys are already adept at handling the fish spear, using a toy spear about two-thirds the size of the adult spear' (Rosenstiel, 1976: 56). Fortes (1976) reports similar patterns of play in Talensi children, as do DeVore and Konner (1974) in Bushman children.

AGONISTIC EXERICSE GAMES

I prefer the term 'agonistic exercise games' to Piaget's term 'practice games' because I think all games practise some adaptive skill or activity.

The term 'agonistic' comes from the Greek word for contest, *agōn* (Caillois, 1961). Ethologists use the term to include play-fighting, play chase, and play escape (Aldis, 1975). This form of play is characterized by the exercise of the whole body, and by the two reciprocal motivations of play attack and play fear as well as contingency motivation. Play attack motivates and is reinforced by surprising, chasing, or attacking the playmate; play fear is stimulated by falling and jumping, running away and hiding, and submitting to attack. Both motivations are pleasurable at moderate intensities, but can be unpleasant if they grade into real attack and real fear. Vestibular stimulation through falling and rotary motions of spinning also elicit play fear (Aldis, 1975; Caillois, 1961).

Agonistic exercise games begin in infancy with parental attacks of poking, bouncing, spinning, and tickling. As children become mobile they actively invite these play attacks and begin to initiate their own. They also seek thrills on swings and other playground equipment.

Sex differences in play are already apparent by thirteen months of age: boys of this age are more active and vigorous and spend more time away from their mothers; they also play a greater distance from her; they are more likely to try to get around barriers; they prefer to play with toys susceptible to gross motor movements (while girls prefer to play with toys requiring fine motor coordinations); and they tend to attack toys with other toys, for example, by banging on them or running them over (Goldberg and Lewis, 1973).

By the age of five or six, sex differences in play are even more apparent: boys of this age cover more space, run in larger groups, are more aggressive, and begin to wrestle with other boys more or less exclusively (Freedman, 1976). Wrestling follows a fairly predictable course, beginning with tripping and ending with pinning the opponent's wrists to the ground (Aldis, 1975; Humphreys and Smith, above, chapter 11). Human play-fighting apparently practises human-specific male fighting skills of disarming and immobilizing, just as macaque play-fighting practises species-specific fighting skills of biting (Symons, 1978).

Contests of strength and skill, such as racing, aimed throwing, high jumping, etc., are also forms of agonistic exericse play. Aimed throwing is particularly characteristic of male agonistic play and is unique to our species. It correlates with our use of objects as weapons.

Aimed throwing follows a complex developmental course: beginning at age 2 with very inefficient unaimed throwing in the anterior posterior plane from above the shoulders, and ending at 7 years with a mature throwing pattern involving maximum arm rotation and leverage and maximum trunk rotation. Girls and women rarely develop the mature form of throwing (Espenschade and Eckert, 1967). These sex differences in throwing ability correlate with sex differences in the shoulder–hip ratio, which begins to show up by age 7 and becomes very marked at puberty. At this time, male sex hormones stimulate specially primed cartilage cells in the shoulder. From early childhood boys have broader chests and longer forearms (Tanner, 1978; Espenschade and Eckert, 1967).

Aimed throwing first appears in early childhood as an isolated motor pattern. During the years of early and middle childhood this pattern is integrated into simple tossing-and-catching games and then into simple aimed throwing and missile-launching contests. In late childhood these more elaborate patterns are integrated into complex goal-directed sequences in field games such as football, baseball, and soccer or the prehistoric mexican game *peloya*. The basic play-attack motivation expressed in aimed throwing is apparent in all these contexts. Indeed, aimed throwing seems to be one of the three or four basic motor patterns of attack in our species.

In addition to the skeletal and muscular specialization, efficient aimed throwing probably requires cognitive skills of straight-line construction through line-of-sight aiming along two points, which emerges at the end of the preoperations period (Parker and Gibson, 1979). The fact that great apes do not display effective aim is consistent with the argument that aimed throwing arose in early hominids as an adaptation for hunting and for combat with weapons (Parker and Gibson, 1979).[4]

The importance of aimed throwing in our species is suggested by the universal importance of hand-launched or hand-operated machine-launched missiles in human combat, and by the apparently universal occurrence of aimed-throwing games in young human males (Fortes, 1976; Dennis, 1940; DeVore and Konner, 1974).

GAMES WITH RULES

Although games with rules are primarily the province of children above the age of six, they have antecedents in the simpler games of infancy and early childhood. Even infant games, such as peek-a-boo and pat-a-cake have structures that could be called 'prerules' (Bruner and Sherwood, 1976). Despite their simple structures, early childhood games, such as follow-the-leader and hide-and-seek, and circle games, such as London Bridge and hokey-pokey, can be recognized as games with rules. It is notable, however, that most of these games require initiation and supervision by an adult or older child who 'knows the rules'. This is consistent with Piaget's observation that preoperational children think of rules as coming from authority figures and do not remember or understand their content. It is also notable that children of this stage do not understand the relationship between rules and winning and losing (Piaget, 1965).

By the time they enter concrete operations at about 6 years of age, children do understand the concept of rules and their contractual basis, although they tend to forget the specific rules and to change them as they go along; they also understand the concepts of winning and losing by the rules. It is not until they achieve formal operational reasoning, at eleven or twelve years of age, that children apply rules universally and consistently (Piaget, 1965).

There are thousands, perhaps millions, of games with rules, but most of them fall into four categories: field games, floor and table games, iconic games, and word games[5] (see table 12.3).

Field games such as basketball, football, soccer, and polo are played by moving around a large open rectangular arena marked by lines denoting boundaries and goals. Two teams play against each other with the aim of carrying or propelling a missile into the opposing team's goal area by successfully circumventing or overcoming its defensive manoeuvres in accordance with the rules. Defence of the two territorial goals typically alternates with bouts of play in order to equalize any special advantage or disadvantage of a given part of the field. Teams in some field games, like baseball and softball, alternate in their occupation of a single arena and the off-field team plays the offensive role of trying to launch a ball into the defensive team's territory in such a manner that one or more players can run through the field and back 'home' without being intercepted. The defensive team, of course, tries to prevent this.

The rules of the games specify every detail of behaviour involved in propelling and passing or blocking and intercepting the ball. They specify the initial positions and specialized roles of various players; the parts of their bodies they can and cannot use under specific conditions of play; the conditions under which the ball is in or out of 'play'; the basis for awarding the ball to one team or another; the number of points awarded for particular methods of scoring; the penalties for fouls; the length of the game and each of its segments. They also specify the types of clothing and equipment and the marking of the field (White, 1961).

Complex team games like these depend upon the cooperation of several individuals playing interdependent roles. These games practise functional divisions of labour and cooperative strategies of offence, defence, and diversion. They condition players to accept specialized statuses and to subordinate their tactics to the overall strategy of the team (Harragan, 1977). Success in these games depends upon a combination of physical, intellectual, and social skills.[6]

TABLE 12.3 Typology of games with rules

Type of competition	Field games	Floor and table games	Iconic games		Word games
			Board games	Card games	
Territorial invasion with or without capture	football lacrosse rugby, soccer basketball polo, hockey	shuffleboard skittles	Monopoly Siege of Paris chess Go checkers		
Territorial raiding	baseball cricket				
Obstacle racing	golf croquet		Snakes and Ladders Gold Rush backgammon		
Simple contest skills	archery boxing bowling fencing tennis handball	darts billiards pool horseshoes ping pong marbles, jacks	Scrabble Pac Man Asteroids dominoes Mastermind	bridge poker pinochle	crossword puzzles twenty questions geography the dozens
Contests of chance			roulette bingo		

Although these games are highly codified in modern industrial nations, they have more rough-and-ready precursors in violent contests between villages in many areas of the ancient world including Iran, Rome, the British Isles, and Mexico (Atyeo, 1981).

Other field games such as archery, tennis, squash, fencing and bowling are ritualized versions of contests of strength and skill between individuals. Still others, such as golf and croquet, are ritualized versions of obstacle races involving use of aimed missiles.

Floor and table games such as billiards, pool, and marbles are like field games in that they are played with balls or other missiles on fields, but are unlike them in that they are played exclusively with the hands and arms on very small arenas. These games typically have a goal of displacing the opponent's ball or of getting a missile closer to a target than the opponent can.

Both floor and field games are striking in their emphasis on contest and combat via aimed missiles. They differ from aimed throwing games primarily in their elaborate rules and their team work.

Iconic games are games that represent resources iconically in the form of 'pieces' or cards depicting objects and people or more abstract quantities such as money. These games include board games and card games.

Board games such as checkers, chess, and Go, for example, are played with pieces representing members of opposing groups arrayed on boards representing their two territories. Each player begins with an equal number of resources and strives in his turn to capture and/or surround all his opponent's pieces. The rules of these games specify the original positions of the pieces and the conditions under which they can be moved (Bell, 1979). They also specify the conditions for alternating offensive and defensive roles and the bases for scoring and winning. In these regards they duplicate the rules of some field games. Some board games, such as snakes and ladders, represent obstacle courses; others like bingo, lotteries; and still others, like Scrabble, and video games such as Pac man, contests of skill. The iconization of contests and territorial invasion is an interesting expression of the interiorization of reversible actions characteristic of concrete operations.

Card games are even more abstract than board games in that their representations of people and resources are reduced to pictures and numbers. Like board games they begin with the allocation of an equal number of cards to each player. The values of these cards, however, are unequal and randomly determined by shuffling a deck of cards with different face values. The rules of the game specify the number of players, their roles, the number of cards given to each one, and the techniques each player can use to maximize the value of his hand, etc. Scoring in these games typically requires the concrete operational ability to classify objects simultaneously according to two criteria (Inhelder and Piaget, 1964), and the formal operational ability to calculate probabilities (Piaget and Inhelder, 1975). They are contests of memory, classification, seriation, and quantification.[7] Board games also exercise most of these skills.

It seems likely that both board and card games practise skills of classification, quantification, and prediction that are vital to successful competition through trade and commerce. If this is so we should expect the rise of these games to be highly correlated with the rise of civilization.

Word games are another important category of games with rules. Because they require no equipment, games such as 'twenty questions', 'the dozens', and 'geography' are more likely to be passed on solely by oral tradition. Most of these games are straightforward contests of memory, wit, and fluency. They practise skills of verbal combat that are highly important in the political arena.

Another category of games with rules that is generally inaccessible to adult observers is 'club games'. These games, which are highly fashionable among pubescent boys and girls, are the occasion for making elaborate rules of eligibility, initiation, secret codes, insignia, and conduct of membership. These games apparently practise political skills in a very direct manner. Indeed organizations of this sort continue to be formed by adult men and women.

The role of chance in games with rules

Playful competition is easier than serious competition because the rules of the game are designed to equalize the positions of the opponents: handicapping superior individuals is one device for achieving equality; randomly determining the first individual or team to play is another such device; randomly determining the winner of the game is the most extreme device for equalizing the position of players.

Chance plays a variety of roles in games with rules: in some games, like roulette, chance determines the winner; in other games, like chess, chance determines who will play first; in still other games, like Monopoly, chance determines how many spaces a player can move his icon, and hence what obstacles he will encounter.

In many games, such as poker, chance interacts with skill: formal operational children and adults are able to use their knowledge of the laws of probability to play games based on random distributions of known numbers of elements. On the basis of a full knowledge of their own hands, and a partial knowledge of their opponents hands, they can infer the probable identity of the unknown cards and base their strategy on that knowledge.

Motivational bases of games with rules

All games with rules seem to involve play attack and play fear and contingency motivations. Contingency-control motivation is revealed in the ritualized turn-taking between individuals and teams. Play attack motivation is evidenced, for example, in propelling aimed missiles in field and floor games; in fighting among players and spectators at field games (Atyeo, 1981); in the hazing at initiation ceremonies and the aggressive exclusion of non-members from clubs; and in the throwing down of a hand in the challenge of poker. Play fear motivation is evidenced in keeping secrets from outsiders, in keeping a 'poker face' while bluffing, in thrilling to the sight of a little marker stopping on the roulette wheel. Both the motivational structures and the competitive goals of games with rules are like those of agonistic exercise play; in some cases even the motor patterns are the same (see table 12.4).

Table 12.4 Expression of motivation in games with rules

	Expressions of		
	Play attack	Play fear	Contingency control
Field games	running, bumping, aimed throwing (long distances)	running away, darting	alternation of possession of missile
Floor and table games	aimed throwing (short distances	vicarious move- ment with target	alternation of possession of missile
Board games	advance and capture	retreat and relinquishment	alternation of right to move or capture icons
Card games	taking and throwing down icons	showing a bad hand	alternation of right to take or throw down icons
Word games	teasing, name calling, laughing		alternation of utterances

A sexual-selection model of games with rules

Just as rough-and-tumble play is primarily a male activity in monkeys, apes, and humans, so games with rules are primarily male activities.

Piaget commented on this in his famous study of the rules of marble games: 'We did not succeed in finding a single collective game played by girls in which there were as many rules, and, above all, as fine and consistent organization and codification of these rules as in the games of marbles examined above' (Piaget, 1965: 77).

Traditional girls' games, such as hopscotch, skip-rope, and jacks, are much simpler in their rule structure than boys games. They are not characterized by teams with specialized roles and umpires, etc. 'The only rule I remember in girls' games is "no touching." When two or more girls play such games together, they are not playing with each other or against each other; they are mutually engaged in isolating solitary activity' (Harragan, 1977: 72). Among 10- and 11-year-old children, boys' games have a higher 'skill ceiling', and are more competitive and longer-lasting than those of girls. Boys of this age also play in larger groups with a greater spread of ages (Lever, 1976). Even in preschool girls engage more in parallel play, while boys interact more with their peers (Harper and Sanders-Huie, 1978).

Sex differences in moral development parallel those in games with rules (Piaget, 1965): Kohlberg's (1971) research into moral development revealed a greater emphasis on universal abstract rules among males. Gilligan (1977), in her study of moral development in females, emphasizes the greater weight females give to specific contextual factors and to interpersonal relationships and the balancing of conflicting responsibilities.

Sex differences in games with rules correlate with sex differences in spatial abilities (Witkin, 1977). These differences may be products of prenatal organizing effects of male sex hormones on the brain (Goy and McEwen, 1980). Such organizational effects of androgens are known to produce sex differences in play-fighting in male and female monkeys (Goy, 1968; Symons, 1978). Studies of the behaviour of prenatally androgenized human females suggest that the same mechanism operates in our own species (Money and Ehrhardt, 1972; see also Humphreys and Smith, above, chapter 11). Like many other sex differences, these differences in play-fighting are ultimately caused by sexual selection for male ability to compete by fighting or intimidating rivals (Symons, 1978).

Although play itself is disarming both figuratively and literally, and employs many devices such as role-reversal and handicapping to equalize disparate abilities, it provides the basis for ranking male dominance hierarchies. This apparent paradox can be explained as follows: the experience of playing inevitably informs young males of their abilities and disabilities (physical, mental, and temperamental) relative to those of their playmates (Dolhinow and Bishop, 1972; Freedman, 1976); each male can gain this knowledge at the lowest risk to himself through play (Symons, 1978); handicapping, and age-, sex-, and ability-specific grouping in play are based, implicitly or explicitly, on a recognition of differential abilities.

In other words, although play itself is relatively non-hierarchical, emerging hierarchies are expressed in the segregation of play groups by age, sex, and ability, as, for example, with first string, second string, or major and minor league teams, and also by position within teams. Paradoxically, the ranking of play groups helps maintain relative equality of ability within groups and hence the non-hierarchical quality of play. Homogeneous grouping within play groups facilitates continued testing of relative abilities among closely matched opponents.

In some insect, avian and mammalian species, adult males compete with each other for copulations, for control of females, for control of scarce resources required by females to nourish their offspring, and to make labour investments necessary for female reproductive success (Borgia, 1979). They compete through a variety of means ranging from direct combat and physical intimidation to indirect social manipulation through courtship displays and friendly overtures to potential allies.[8] Animal communication in general can be viewed as a mechanism for selfish manipulation of conspecifics (Dawkins and Krebs, 1978), and human language can be viewed as a particularly sophisticated elaboration of this mechanism. Rules are a unique form of social manipulation made possible by language and higher intelligence (Parker, in press): males in every society seek to invent and impose rules favourable to their own interests and those of their close kin. When they are able to do so they interpret the rules in the most advantageous manner. When this is impossible, they cheat or even resort to revolution or other forms of violence. They use rules of incest, exogamy, dowry, and bride price, for example, to control access to marriage; they use rules of dowry, bride price, taxation, property, and inheritance to control scarce resources; they use laws of bride service, apprenticeship, etc., to compete with their labour.

The threat of retribution is the ultimate sanction behind all rules. In the case of secular laws, these sanctions are exercised by representatives of the corporate body (Hoebell, 1954). The threat of violence lies behind all negotiations between groups. Clausewitz (1962) considered it an instrument of policy. As he pointed out, war strategies and tactics are themselves rules, and it is not insignificant that they are known as 'war games'.

Viewed from a sexual selection perspective, field and board games practise rule-mediated competition for scarce resources such as territory, slaves, and women. Soccer, basketball, and football, for example, practise strategies of territorial invasion; baseball practises territorial raiding; Go, checkers and chess practise invasion and capture of enemies (this is very explicit in the case of a game called 'Siege of Paris'); games such as Snakes and Ladders practise overcoming a series of obstacles; others, such as Gold Rush, practise racing to gain a scarce resource; card games such as poker practise bluffing and calculation of odds (see table 12.3). All games with rules practise skills of rule manipulation, memory, quantification, and strategic coalition. Many games with rules, such as field games and contests, sumultaneously practise physical skills such as aimed throwinig and running (see table 12.3).

If this sexual-selection model of games with rules is correct, we would expect that in any given society the types of games with rules would correlate with the primary types of resource competition, and that the importance of such games would vary with the intensity of sexual selection.[9]

Societal differences in games with rules

Cross-cultural studies of games with rules are in their infancy; they are one part of the newly emerging field of ethnography and ethnology of play (Norbeck, 1976). Even so, it is clear that 'the different sorts of cultures and the different sorts of games are not randomly assorted, but rather, some sorts of games tend to be associated with some sorts of cultures' (Heider, 1977: 73).

On a more specific level, Sutton-Smith (1977) argues that the complexity of games is an index of cultural complexity. In particular, he thinks that games of chance are associated with conditions of economic uncertainty (especially common among nomads); that games of skill are associated with hunting; and that games of strategy are associated with social stratification.

Sutton-Smith contrasts societies with very little play with societies such as the Taira of Okinawa, and the Rajputs of India, who have highly elaborated games. He suggests that play is infrequent in groups such as the Nyansongo, where children are an important source of labour: 'This does not mean that all relatively simple cultures do not play, because the records of play amongst the Australian aboriginal groups are very extensive. What seems to be critical is whether or not the adults have a direct economic need to train the children in highly normalized means of survival' (Sutton-Smith, 1977: 228).

He also suggests that different varieties of play are important in different cultures: 'It is impossible to look at, for example, the aborigines and not see that most of their play involves exploration and testing; whereas, in a symbolic and achievement culture like ours, most play involves make-believe and contesting' (Sutton-Smith, 1977: 229).

According to his 'conflict-enculturation hypothesis', conflicts in the child's experience make him responsive to games which enact these same conflicts. A related idea is developed by Teague-Urbach (1982), in her study of Little League baseball in Santa Cruz, California. She believes that this game mirrors value conflicts basic to American society: 'Every participant in Little League, from the smallest to the eldest, performs various balancing acts between seemingly opposing forces. The children are supposed to learn to win and lose; to care a lot about victory, yet be "good sports." They are supposed to "take the edge" but play fair. They are to be independent, think for themselves and take chances, yet respect and obey authority without question. They are to achieve, be good at playing ball, without "grandstanding," they must work with the team, yet stand out' (Teague-Urbach, 1982: 38).[10] She points out that these opposing values characterize many of our institutions, particularly the legal system. (Huizinga, 1955, also comments on the similarities between the rules of play and legal systems.)

In addition to practising rule making, rule bending, and rule breaking, games with rules may also practise skills of combat or warfare. In his comparison of ten warlike and ten peaceful societies, Sipes (1973) found that combative sports were typical of the warlike societies and atypical of the peaceful societies.

His criterion for classifying a sport as combative was the involvement of 'actual or potential body contact between the opponents, either direct or through real or simulated combat weapons' (Sipes, 1973: 69–70). Using this criterion, he classified boxing, hockey, football, wrestling, fencing, and hunting as combat sports, while baseball, golf, and bowling were classified as non-combative sports.

This research sheds an ominous light on the alleged shift in the United States from baseball toward football: in his study of changing preferences for different sports in the United States from 1920 to 1970, Sipes found that football and hunting and betting on horses became more popular during World War II and the Korean Conflict, whereas baseball became less so.

CONCLUSIONS

I began this paper with a definition of games as a uniquely human form of play that depends upon a concept of rules. I discussed four types of play – contingency games, make-believe games, agonistic exercise games, and games with rules – emphasizing their common motivational features. I also presented a detailed typology of games with rules, dividing them into field games, floor and table games, iconic games, and word games. I argued that like agonistic exercise games, games with rules have been favoured by sexual selection because they practise skills important to male–male competititon.

Specifically, I argued that field, floor and table games represent territorial conquest and contests of combat skill based on aimed throwing; that iconic games represent territorial conquest and obstacle races; and that word games represent verbal battles. All games with rules practise skills – such as strategy, rule making and manipulation, memory, classification, quantification, and calculation of odds – that are important for success in political and economic competition. They all share a common motivational base of play fear, play attack, and contingency-control motivation. The sexual-selection interpretation is based on reports of sex differences in all forms of play, but most particularly in agonistic exercise play and games with rules.

EPILOGUE

A Piagetian model for the development of human play implies coevolution of new levels of complexity of play and cognition through the process of terminal addition (Parker and Gibson, 1979; Gould, 1977). The terminal addition model for the evolution of human play suggests that the long period of playfulness typical of our species cannot be ascribed to a simple prolongation of behaviours that were typical of the immature stage of an ancestor. If the human play pattern were simply neotenous, we would expect to see a continuation of the ancestor's infantile or juvenile play pattern in the descendant's juvenile and/or sub-adult periods. Instead we see new patterns of play developing in conjunction with higher cognitive abilities. The fact that these patterns are lacking in all the great apes suggests that they were also absent in the common ancestor of apes and man, and that they subsequently evolved in the hominid lineage.

ACKNOWLEDGEMENTS

I want to express my gratitude to Peter Fisher, David Gordon, Edward Mooney, and Steven Pulos for their careful reading, and helpful criticisms and comments on earlier drafts of this paper.

NOTES

1   Practice entails exercise; exercise develops and maintains neurosensory and
    neuromotor systems by stimulating neurotransmitter and hormone production

during ontogeny. It could be argued, therefore, that play has been selected just because it mediates growth and development, and not because it practises adult skills. This argument, however, overlooks an important point; any individual in a population of animals who play for exercise alone, will have an advantage over his fellows if his play simultaneously practises skills important to his reproductive success. Another way of saying this, is that playing for exercise alone is an evolutionarily unstable strategy whenever practice is advantageous.

2 Piaget distinguishes three major categories of play: practice play, symbolic play, and games with rules, which he associates primarily with sensorimotor, preoperational, and operational intelligence respectively. My typology differs from his in several ways: first, I have added an additional category which I call 'contingency games'; second, I have substituted the term 'agonistic exercise games' for his term 'practice play' because I believe it is more descriptive and because I think all play is practice; and third, I have emphasized the fact that each type of play cuts across developmental periods. Mouledoux (1976, 1977) compares Piaget's categories of play with those of Roger Caillois and finds them wanting. She criticizes Piaget on the grounds that his typology is incomplete and that it subordinates play to cognition and therefore neglects affective and social components. She also objects to Piaget's developmental approach because it emphasizes the primacy of particular types of play during particular developmental periods. Although I agree with this latter criticism I prefer to expand Piaget's categories across his developmental periods rather than abandon his approach altogether.

3 According to Aldis (1975), the vestibular stimulation produced by falling and rotary forms of acceleration is the stimulus mediating play fear. It is the pleasure in play fear which motivates a whole class of social and solitary agonistic exercise games. These games apparently fall into the category Caillois called vertigo games. The sensation of 'falling in love' seems to be akin to 'play fear'. The 'victim' of love is the subject of 'play attack' by Cupid's arrows. He or she feels all the sensations of vertigo associated with falling or swinging or spinning.

4 This interpretation is supported by the fact that great apes do not display effective aim in their missile throwing. Their use of missiles seems to fall into the category of agonistic displays which increase apparent size and ferocity. Their failure to aim efficiently is consistent with the fact that they do not surpass the level of symbolic thinking characteristic of the first subperiod of preoperations (Parker and Gibson, 1979).

5 Games with rules may also involve agonistic exercise, but they are classified as games with rules because rules require greater cognitive abilities than agonistic exercise games do.

6 In his paper 'Cognitive structure in sports tactics', Stevens (1977) analysed the cognitive complexity of basketball plays of children from the seventh to the twelfth grades. Using Sutton-Smith's scheme of primary, secondary, and tertiary levels of play interaction, he showed that children of these ages display complex tactics during basketball games: sets of actions coordinating several players, coordinations contingent on previous coordinations, and coordinations of these coordinated coordinations. It is worth noting that these coordinations involve cooperation between team-mates. Although such cooperation is an important part of competitive games, I emphasize the competition element because I think it is primary. Cooperation, on the other hand, is paramount in simpler games with rules such as follow-the-leader and circle games, and in make-believe games such as playing house.

7 Score keeping in card games, like other games with rules, depends on counting and arithmetic. The fact that boys are more prone than girls to play these games may relate to the male tendency to quantify experience (a tendency charmingly depicted in the recent Scottish film, *Gregory's Girl*). Men show off by spouting numbers; batting averages; stock market averages; auto performance figures; economic indicators; weapons inventories; historic dates, etc.

8   Because their parental investment is lower than that of females, and because they are assured of a female's parental investment after she is fertilized, mammalian males benefit from competition to inseminate females. Because their investment in each offspring is greater than the male's, and because they are not assured of a male's parental investment after fertilization, female mammals do not benefit from competition for copulations, in fact they benefit from reluctance and coyness (Trivers, 1972). Females may, however, benefit from competing for male investment in their offspring. This is true of human females. Females of our species compete for marriage to high ranking males and for other less desirable forms of male parental investment through epigamic displays such as full breasts and hips, clear skin, youthfulness, and through maternal-fitness displays of skill and vigour in maternal and domestic tasks (Low, 1979; Symons, 1979). Human females also apparently compete for strategic alliances that give them and their female kin access to various desirable social groups (such as elite churches, clubs, schools, and jobs) and social events (such as débutante balls) where they can display themselves to high ranking males. While make-believe games such as 'dress up' and 'house' may practise physical displays and domestic fitness, the only games with rules that seem to practise the relevant skills of status recognition, social climbing, and social exclusion are the 'club games' of pre-teen and teenage girls.

9   An increasing number of girls are playing team sports, such as baseball and basketball, and an increasing number of women are holding high-status positions in politics, business, and education in the United States today. These phenomena do not contradict this model: selection will favour direct competition by females for scarce resources (such as money and power) when this strategy increases their reproductive success more than other available strategies would. Since the supply of high status males with control of resources is limited, many females may do better to get the resources for their offspring directly. This is only possible, of course, when their labour is sufficient to garner those resources. To the extent that this is true, females will compete in the market-place with males rather than, or in addition to, competing with each other for high-status mates. Under circumstances favouring a directly competitive strategy, we would expect to see a greater pay-off for participation in agonistic exercise games and games with rules. To metastasize Stephen J. Gould's quotation of a little girl's remark that dogs would be shaped like elephants if they were the size of elephants: to the extent that women are competing with men, they will behave like men.

10 Teague-Urbach speculates that football may be eclipsing baseball as the preferred embodiment of American cultural values. She suggests that baseball represented the values of small-town America, with its farmers, craftsmen, and small businessmen, while football enacts the territorial expansion characteristic of monopolistic capitalism. Harragan (1977) notes that football is the game of choice of corporate executives in the 1970s.

REFERENCES

Aldis, O. (1975). *Play Fighting*. New York: Academic Press.
Atyeo, D. (1981). *Violence in Sports*. New York: Van Nostrand Reinhold Co.
Bell, R. C. (1979). *The Boardgame Book*. Los Angeles: Knapp Press.
Borgia, G. (1979). Sexual selection and the evolution of mating systems. In M. S. Blum and N. A. Blum (eds), *Reproductive Competition in Insects*. New York: Academic Press.
Bruner, J. S. and Sherwood, V. (1976). Peekaboo and the learning of rule

structures. In J. S. Bruner, A. Holly and K. Sylva (eds), *Play: Its Role in Development and Evolution*. New York: Basic Books.

Caillois, R. (1961). *Man, Play and Games*. New York: Free Press. 1961.

Clausewitz, K. von (1962). *War, Politics and Power* (selections from *On War, and I Believe and Profess*) tr. and ed. E. M. Collins. Chicago: Henry Regnery Co.

Dawkins, R., and Krebs, J. R. (1978). Animal signals: information or manipulation? In J. R. Krebs and N. B. Davies (eds), *Behavioural Ecology: an Evolutionary Approach*. Oxford: Blackwell Scientific Publications.

Dennis, W. (1940). *The Hopi Child*. New York: John Wiley & Sons.

DeVore, I. and Konner, M. (1974). Infancy in hunter–gatherer life: an ethological perspective. In N. White (ed.), *Ethology and Psychiatry*. Toronto: University of Toronto Press.

Dolhinow, P. C. and Bishop, N. (1972). The development of motor skills and social relationships among primates through play. In P. C. Dolhinow (ed.), *Primate Patterns*. New York: Holt, Rinehart and Winston Inc.

Espenschade, A. S. and Eckert, H. M. (1967). *Motor Development*. Columbus, Ohio: Charles E. Morrill Pub. Co.

Fortes, M. (1976). Social and psychological aspects of education in Taleland. In J. Bruner, A. Jolly and K. Sylva (eds), *Play: Its Role in Development and Evolution*. New York: Basic Books.

Freedman, D. G. (1976). Infancy, biology and culture. In L. P. Lipsett (ed.), *Developmental Psychobiology*. New York: John Wiley & Sons.

Gilligan, C. (1977). In a different voice: women's conceptions of self and of morality. *Harvard Educational Review* 47, 481–517.

Goldberg, S. and Lewis, M. (1973). Play behavior in the year-old infant: early sex differences. In L. J. Stone, H. T. Smith and L. B. Murphy (eds), *The Competent Infant*. New York: Basic Books.

Gould, S. J. (1977). *Ontogeny and Phylogeny*. Cambridge, Mass.: Harvard University Press.

Groos, K. (1898). *The Play of Animals*. New York: Appleton.

Goy, R. W. (1968). Organizing effects of androgens on the behaviour of rhesus monkeys. In R. P. Michael (ed.), *Endocrinology and Human Behaviour*. London: Oxford University Press.

Goy, R. W. and McEwen, B. S. (1980). *Sexual Differentiation of the Brain*. Cambridge, Mass.: The MIT Press.

Harper, L. V. and Sanders-Huie, K. (1978). The development of sex differences in human behavior: cultural impositions, or a convergence of evolved response-tendencies and cultural adaptations? In G. M. Burghardt and M. Bekoff (eds), *The Development of Behavior: Comparative and Evolutionary Aspects*. New York: Garland STPM.

Harragan, B. L. (1977). *Games Mother Never Taught You: Corporate Gamesmanship for Women*. New York: Warner Communications Co.

Heider, K. G. (1977). From Javanese to Dani: the translation of a game. In P. Stevens Jr (ed.), *Studies in the Anthropology of Play: Papers in Memory of Allan Tindall*. West Point, NY: Leisure Press.

Hoebell, A. (1954). *The Law of Primitive Man*. Cambridge, Mass.: Harvard University Press.

Huizinga, J. (1955). *Homo Ludens*. Boston: Beacon Press.

Inhelder, B. and Piaget, J. (1964). *The Early Growth of Logic in Children*. New York: Norton.

Kohlberg, L. (1971). From is to ought: How to commit the naturalistic fallacy and get away with it in the study of moral development. In T. Mischel (ed.), *Cognitive Development and Epistemology*. New York: Academic Press.

Lever, J. (1976). Sex differences in the games children play. *Social Problems* 23, 478–87.

Loizos, C. (1967). Play behaviour in higher primates: a review. In D. Morris (ed.), *Primate Ethology*. Chicago: Aldine.

Low, B. S. (1979). Sexual selection and human ornamentation. In N. A. Chagnon and W. Irons (eds), *Evolutionary Biology and Human Behavior*. Massachusetts: Duxbury Press.

Millar, S. (1968). *The Psychology of Play*. Baltimore: Penguin Books.

Money, J. and Erhardt, A. (1972). *Man and Woman, Boy and Girl*. Baltimore: Johns Hopkins University Press.

Mouledoux, E. C. (1976). Theoretical considerations and a method for the study of play. In D. F. Lancy and B. A. Tindall (eds), *The Anthropological Study of Play: Problems and Prospects*. West Point, NY: Leisure Press.

Mouledoux, E. D. (1977). The development of play in childhood: an application of the classification of Piaget and Caillois in developmental research. In P. Stevens Jr (ed.), *Studies in the Anthropology of Play: Papers in Memory of Allan Tindall*. West Point, NY: Leisure Press.

Norbeck, E. (1976). The study of play – Johan Huizinga and modern anthropology. In D. F. Lancy and B. A. Tindall (eds), *The Anthropological Study of Play: Problems and Prospects*. West Point, NY: Leisure Press.

Parker, S. T. (1977). Piaget's sensorimotor period series in an infant macaque: a model for comparing unstereotyped behavior and intelligence in human and nonhuman primates. In S. Chevalier-Skolnikoff and F. Poirier (eds), *Primate Biosocial Development*. New York: Garland STPM.

Parker, S. T. (in press). Language and play as adaptations for social manipulation through rules and requests. In S. K. Ghosh (ed.), *Human Language: Biological Perspectives*. Ghent: E. Story Scientia.

Parker, S. T. and Gibson, K. R. (1979). A developmental model for the evolution of language and intelligence in early hominids. *Behavioral and Brain Sciences* 2, 367–407.

Piaget, J. (1962). *Play, Dreams, and Imitation in Childhood*. New York: W. W. Norton.

Piaget, J. (1963). *The Origins of Intelligence in Children*. New York: W. W. Norton.

Piaget, J. (1965). *The Moral Judgment of the Child*. New York: Free Press.

Piaget, J. and Inhelder, B. (1975). *The Origin of the Idea of Chance in Children*. New York: W. W. Norton.

Rosenstiel, A. (1976). The role of traditional games in the process of socialization among the Motu of Papua New Guinea. In D. F. Lancy and B. A. Tindall (eds), *The Anthropological Study of Play: Problems and Prospects*. West Point, NY: Leisure Press.

Sipes, R. G. (1973). War, sports and aggression: an empirical test of two rival theories. *American Anthropologist* 75, 65–86.

Smith, P. K. (1982). Does play matter? Functional and evolutionary aspects of animal and human play. *Behavioral and Brain Sciences* 5, 139–84.

Stern, D. (1978). *The First Relationship*. Cambridge, Mass.: Harvard University Press.

Stevens, T. R. (1977). Cognitive structure in sports tactics: a preliminary investigation. In P. Stevens Jr (ed.) *Studies in the Anthropology of Play: Papers in Memory of Allan Tindall*. West Point, NY: Leisure Press.

Sutton-Smith, B. (1977). Towards an anthropology of play. In P. Stevens (ed.), *Studies in the Anthropology of Play: Papers in Memory of Allan Tindall*. West Point, NY: Leisure Press.

Symons, D. (1978). *Play and Aggression: a Study of Rhesus Monkeys*. New York: Columbia University Press.

Symons, D. (1979). *The Evolution of Human Sexuality*. Oxford: Oxford University Press.

Tanner, J. M. (1978). *Foetus in Man: Physical Growth from Conception to Maturity*. Cambridge, Mass.: Harvard University Press.

Teague-Urbach, J. W. (1982). 'The rite of spring': a look at Little League baseball. Paper presented at the Kroeber Anthropological Society Annual Meetings, University of California, Berkeley. Unpublished BA thesis, University of California, San Diego.

Trivers, R. (1972). Parental investment and sexual selection. In B. Campbell (ed.), *Sexual Selection and the Descent of Man*. New York: Aldine.

Van Hooff, J. A. R. A. M. (1972). A comparative approach to the phylogeny of laughter and smiling. In R. Hinde (ed.), *Non-verbal Communication*. Cambridge: Cambridge University Press.

Watson, J. S. (1972), Smiling, cooing, and 'the game'. *Merrill-Palmer Quarterly* 18, 323–39.

White, J. R. (ed.) (1961). *Sports Rules Encyclopedia*. Palo Alto, Calif.: The National Press.

Witkin, H. A. (1977). *Cognitive Styles in Personal and Cultural Adaptation*. Heinz Werner Lecture Series, No. 11. Worcester, MA: Clark University Press.

13   Play in Anthropological Perspective

David F. Lancy

INTRODUCTION

A number of investigators (e.g. Brewster, 1955) have gathered collections of games in particular societies with little or no attempt at further analysis. More commonly, play has been described and examined for its contribution to other spheres of human life, thus there are, in fact, several anthropological perspectives on play. These include evolutionary biology (Parker, above chapter 12; Lancy, 1980a); child development (Dennis, 1940; Lancy, 1975); cultural integration (Hogbin, 1946; Lancy 1980b); and cultural evolution and change (Roberts et al., 1959; Lancy, 1979) among others. Space does not permit a review of all the strands in the anthropology of play. In any case, Schwartzman (1978) in a thorough and up-to-date volume has identified each of the primary perspectives and related them to the kinds of questions asked, the methods employed and the findings which have emerged. This chapter presents a case study typical of studies found in the anthropology of play literature and, in the process, touches on and further elucidates two of the perspectives. More specifically, I will apply an analytical framework to a collection of games from Papua New Guinea. This framework has been developed to shed light on the role of play in child development and in cultural evolution.

THE ANALYTICAL FRAMEWORK

Brian Sutton-Smith has created a number of schemes for analysing game collections. I have chosen to test his 'structural grammar' (1976, see also Sutton-Smith and Roberts, 1981). The grammar is based on Piaget's theory of cognitive development (in particular Piaget, 1970). It has seven levels, each higher level corresponding to a shift in the logical operations underlying the game and an increase in organiz ational complexity. The major qualitative change that occurs as one moves from lower to higher levels involves adding decisions a player must make concerning the role he or she will play and the actions he or she will take within a particular role. A summary of the structural grammar is shown below:

Game type A   Pastimes
               Level O
Game type B   Central Person Games: primary interactions (actions)
               Level 1: role-reversals (Hide-and-Seek)
               Level 2: role and action reversals (Release)
Game type C   Competitive games: secondary interactions (signals)
               Level 3: internal coordinations (Dodge-ball and Mark)
               Level 4: external coordinations (Prisoners' base and Marbles)
Game type D   Sports: tertiary interactions (sub-group differentiation)
               Level 5: external to players (coaches, audiences, etc.)
               Level 6: internal to one team, the defence (Baseball, etc.)
               Level 7: between both teams, attack and defence (Football)

Sutton-Smith (1976) first used the grammar to test Piaget's invariant sequence hypothesis. As applied to games the hypothesis would predict that the oldest children (11+ years of age) will play (have played) games at all levels, slightly younger children will play games at all but the highest level and so on. Applying the grammar to several North American game collections, Sutton-Smith concludes 'within the limits of the empirical data, the first four levels at least seem to arrange the games in the chronological order in which they actually occur' (1976: 125). Strictly speaking Sutton-Smith does not test the invariant sequence hypothesis but only reports an association between the level of the games played by children and their presumed level of cognitive development based on their age at the time.

The invariant sequence hypothesis has also been invoked by anthropologists with respect to cultural evolution and development. Morgan (1877) for example, argued that societies moved from the stage of 'savagery' through 'barbarism' to 'civilization' with numerous sub-stages in between. Sutton-Smith (1976) following Roberts, Arth and Bush (1959) attempts a test of the weak version of this hypothesis, namely that societies can be scaled in terms of overall complexity and that the structural organization of the games played in a society will be consistent with and predictive of its rank on the scale. Sutton-Smith utilizes collections of games from Congolese forest-dwelling pygmies; aboriginal societies in Australia; Eskimo; sedentary horticulturist societies from North America; and societies from Polynesia, scaled from simple to complex in that order. The grammar seems up to the task. That is, Sutton- Smith reliably finds that as the society becomes more complex the game inventory expands and games at higher levels predominate. His remarks (1976: 133) about games found in North American Indian groups are representative:

> What impresses one about the games in this group is the much clearer level of organization throughout. There are clear specifications for the selection of the players, for their preparation and the game time and space is organized as is the scoring and the equipment. In addition, instead of team games being a small minority of all the games played, they are the major tradition.

An interesting question is raised by these studies, namely the locus or origin of game complexity. Sutton-Smith, following Piaget, seems to imply that as children's logical skills develop, they will invent or use ever more demanding games to exercise and perfect these skills. This certainly seems to be the case in modern European and American societies. However, just as cross-cultural research on cognitive development points to limitations to the generality of Piaget's theory (e.g. Lancy et al., 1981), Sutton Smith's (1976) findings imply that the nature of children's play may be as much or more under the influence of cultural forces as the force of child development. For example, Eskimo games, regardless of the age of the player, almost all reflect 'level four individual self-testing' (Sutton-Smith, 1976: 131); the Mbuti have only five recorded games while in Polynesia one finds 'an incredible abundance of games' (ibid: 134). His analysis was quite preliminary, however, as he admits and this question is not addressed. A somewhat more robust data base, recently established in Papua New Guinea, holds out the possibility for a more rigorous evaluation of the utility of Sutton-Smith's 'grammar' and a more thorough examination of questions concerning play, child development and cultural complexity.

THE DATA BASE

From 1976 to 1980, data were collected in ten traditional societies in Papua New Guinea under the auspices of the Indigenous Mathematics Project (Lancy, 1978). A multidisciplinary team administered a battery of cognitive tests adapted from the work of Jean Piaget and Jerome Bruner among others to children of varying ages and levels of education; interviewed native informants and conducted fieldwork to establish both general ethnography and specifically 'cognitive' features of each society such as counting and classification systems; undertook various analyses of school-based mathematics instruction and achievement; and observed and collected children's play activities including games.

The societies selected for intensive study vary along a number of dimensions but all are at approximately the same level of acculturation. That is, there is no wage-employment in any of the villages and cash-cropping is minimal. All of the villages are physically isolated and far from urban centres. Virtually none of the adult population is literate and subsistence practices are largely unaltered from the pre-contact period. Five of the sites are located on or near the coast; of these, three depend heavily for their livelihood on fishing and trade. Three of the inland sites use hunting and gathering to supplement a diet which is otherwise made up of various starches and occasionally greens and pork. At one extreme are villages with reasonably complex and stable patterns of administration, interaction and kinship, at the other extreme, small bands living in scattered hamlets which interact only under the uneven impetus of 'big-man' contests; warfare; and marriage exchanges. Although the societies can be ordered in terms of overall complexity, we were able to create only a single quantitative measure of complexity. Based on our analysis of hierarchies in the respective languages we calculated a *classification index* for the ten societies. The index ranged from 4 to 12. An admittedly casual analysis of tool inventories in the respective societies utilizing Oswalt's (1976) model suggested that the variety and complexity of 'subsistants' in each society is closely associated with complexity as measured by the classification index (Lancy, 1983).

Turning now to the cognitive test data, performance varied as a function of the child's age, level of education and society. This last variable yielded the most stable and predictable effects. That is in some societies children were very close to Western norms, in others they fell far below these norms. An important underlying factor was the extent to which children readily applied a taxonomic strategy to the solution of test problems. A strong positive association was found between the classification index rating of the society and the tendency for children raised in that society to use the taxonomic and other 'higher order' strategies to solve problems (Lancy, 1983).

In six of the ten societies we undertook a survey of playforms (Roleasa-malik, 1979). Playform was used as an organizer rather than 'games' in order to include certain recurrent activities that might otherwise be considered 'make-believe' or 'pastimes'. Each society yielded about 25 playforms, most were named in the vernacular and all were played out so that a full description and photographs could be obtained. Information on the age and gender of players was also obtained.

ANALYSIS AND RESULTS

The first pass through the data revealed that Sutton-Smith's (1976) framework, while appropriate in a general way, provided insufficient range to analyse this particular sample of games. On the face of it, all of the games appeared to fall within levels O–2 (see Sutton-Smith's (1976) list of game levels, above). The framework was difficult to apply, however, because it does not specify, in detail, the game attributes associated with each level. I developed an alternative framework composed of very specific elements which were either mentioned by Sutton-Smith or were found to be present in my initial analysis of the Papua New Guinea games. Each game was coded for the presence or absence of eight attributes as follows:

1   outcome not prescribed
2   specially selected/constructed props; specially designated/prepared playing area
3   turn-taking within team or group
4   teams
5   role-reversal
6   scoring, points
7   referee, score-keeper, judge
8   coordinated activity within team

A couple of examples will illustrate how the games were analysed. In the first example, seven of the eight attributes were found; in the second example, only one attribute was found. Numbers in parentheses refer to the attributes in the above list.

Toaripi children (aged 8–15, both sexes) play a game called *oveapo*. It is played in a large cleared area about 50 m × 10 m with a post driven into the ground at each end (2+). Two teams (4+) are formed and the children gather in the centre of the playing area. At a signal from the referee (7+) a player from one team tries to get past members of the opposing team, who try to tag him, and get to the opposing team's post. If he succeeds his team gets a point (6+), if he is tagged, no point is awarded. His turn taken (3+) he returns to his team and goes on the defensive (5+) as a player from the opposing team now has to make the attempt. The team with the most points accrued after everyone has had a turn wins the game (1+). Imonda boys (age 7 to 13) play a game called *tiam*. The group selects some object that is lodged in a tree such as a branch, a snake, a grasshopper, a bird's nest. After they have agreed on the target they group themselves around the base of the tree and with a shout all begin to climb, the boy who reaches the object first wins the contest (1+).

Each of the 151 games was scored in this manner, scores ranged from 0 to 7, with a mean of 2.7. The frequency of occurrence for the various attributes was as follows: $1 = 84\%$; $2 = 57\%$; $3 = 40\%$; $4 = 36\%$; $5 = 26\%$; $6 = 20\%$; $7 = 15\%$; $8 = 5\%$. Game attributes *did not* form a particularly good scale; knowing that a particular attribute was present did not allow one to predict with certainty the presence or absence of other attributes.

The average number of attributes found in the games of a particular society was taken as the complexity of the game inventory. This game complexity index is shown in table 13.1, which also shows that the complexity of the game inventory did not vary much across the six societies $(F(5,145) = 0.827$, n.s.$)$. Furthermore, it does not show a very strong relationship to either the cognitive development or cultural complexity measures mentioned earlier.

TABLE 13.1 Game complexity, cognitive development and cultural complexity

Society	Average game complexity	Number of games	Average on cognitive battery	Classification index
Mandok	3.28	25	12.94	10
Ponam	2.93	27	15.00	12
Toaripi	2.85	26	9.98	11
Melpa	2.81	26	8.46	6
Imonda	2.58	24	9.67	4
Tauade	2.48	23	9.04	7

Another, quite different approach to the comparative analysis of game inventories is labelled 'projective' by Schwartzman (1978). Derived from the psychoanalytic school of psychology, investigators (e.g. Roberts and Sutton-Smith, 1962, 1966) look for relationships between patterns of play and the important psychological themes in a society. Dominant values in a society like aggression, independence and envy are 'projected' on to the play of children. We have very few data on the dominant ethos of our ten Papua New Guinea sites; however, two of our sites represent extremes on a cooperation/altruism (Ponam) to competition/aggression (Tauade) continuum as reflected in the ethnographic record and in children's responses on a variety of tests of social behaviour (Lancy and Madsen, 1981). Analysis of playforms showed that Ponam games are slightly less likely to involve winners and losers than Tauade games (70% vs 87%) and considerably more likely to include turn-taking (67% vs 13%).

The relationships between features of play and cognitive development, cultural complexity and social values can be found but they appear very weak. In fact, the commonalities across the six game inventories are far more striking than the differences. Aside from the fact that the total number and the average complexity of games does not vary much across societies, the actual content of the games is remarkably similar. As I have previously noted: 'All have bow-and-arrow or spear and target games; mock battles with mud, sand, or water; sliding games in grass, mud and water with leaves or boards as the sliding devices; string figures and tops; mock hunting exercises; singing-dancing lines; hide and seek; and hand-hidden shells or pebbles' (Lancy, 1983: 119).

It may very well be, as Sutton-Smith and Roberts suggest 'that a psychologically universal competence to *game* exists, which, like the competence to *speak*, is a part of the human condition' (1981: 447). It is probably not true, however, that games, or even play, serve the same functions in every society or even in every species (Lancy, 1980a). Cognitive development is probably an 'incidental benefit' (cf. Smith, 1982) of play, meaning that whatever benefits conferred by play to the individual's cognitive development, these can probably be acquired in other ways in the absence of play. There is one very compelling factor which helps to explain the absence of a strong relationship between game complexity and cognitive development in these data. That is, that virtually all the games are played by groups of children who vary widely in age (and usually involve males and females, as well). This being the case, the cognitive demands of the game cannot exceed the capacity of the youngest member of the play group (aged 8 years approximately). In Piagetian terms the games do not require concrete operations. This 'lowest common denominator' effect is also apparent when a foreign game is introduced into the society, a process I observed with the Kpelle (Lancy, 1979). Soccer or football is a level 5 game in Sutton-Smith's framework; however, it was not played at level 5 by Kpelle children. The number of players was not fixed, there were no assigned 'positions', score-keeping was erratic and so on. This is because children from the age of 8 to 16 all played together and strong sanctions operated to ensure that every player got a chance to handle the ball.

Mixed-aged play groups are typical of societies whose overall population is low as in the Kpelle and Papua New Guinea villages. Since population size is also correlated with other measures of cultural complexity, it is possible that this accounts for the positive correlations between game complexity and cultural complexity found in earlier studies (e.g. Roberts et al., 1959). Another variable, which has not received a great deal of attention, may also affect this relationship, namely role differentiation. Although the Kpelle live in small villages, the society displays far greater adult role differentiation or occupational specialization (Lancy, 1974) than the Papua New Guinean societies with a correspondingly larger and more complex game inventory. As I have shown in a comparison of play behaviour in two American sub-cultures, the range of adult role models in the society is directly related to the range of roles which children 'try on' in play (Lancy, 1982). These suggestions about population size and role differentiation merely point to the obvious. Cultural complexity, a favoured topic of anthropologists interested in play, is probably less tractable as a variable than we would like.

Comparative studies of play face an uncertain future. Children, as the least conservative members of society, often abandon traditional play-forms for more interesting or existing foreign alternatives (Lancy, 1979). The cultural context for play is also changing rapidly. In non-Western societies play is woven into the fabric of community life and is supported by ritual, ceremony, and custom, which gives it its distinctive character. As this foundation erodes, many games will be abandoned or altered. Most of the more interesting playforms will be preserved to be sure (Parker Brothers produces a version of the African *Mankala* game, for example) but their meaning and purpose will be changed beyond recognition. It is unlikely that anthropologists will abandon the study of play, quite the contrary, the field is enjoying a veritable renaissance at the moment, but the topics chosen for investigation and the questions asked will be very different in the future.

REFERENCES

Brewster, P. G. (1955). *American Nonsinging Games*. Norman: University of Oklahoma.
Dennis, W. (1940). *The Hopi Child*. New York: Appleton-Century.
Hogbin, H. I. (1946). A New Guinea childhood: from weaning till the eighth year in Wogeo. *Oceania* 16, 275–96.
Lancy, D. F. (1974). Work, play and learning in Kpelle society. Unpublished Ph.D. dissertation, University of Pittsburgh.
Lancy, D. F. (1975). Developmental implications of a West African playform. *The Association for the Anthropological Study of Play Newsletter* 2, 18–21.
Lancy, D. F. (ed.) 1978. The indigenous mathematics project, special issue. *The Papua New Guinea Journal of Education* 14.

Lancy, D. F. (1979). The play behavior of Kpelle children during rapid cultural change. In D. F. Lancy and B. A. Tindall (eds), *The Anthropological Study of Play: Problems and Prospects* (rev. edn). West Point, NY: Leisure Press.

Lancy, D. F. (1980a). Play in species adaptation. *Annual Review of Anthropology* 9, 471–95.

Lancy, D. F. (1980b). Becoming a blacksmith in Gbarngasuakwelle. *Anthropology and Education Quarterly* 11, 266–74.

Lancy, D. F. (1982). Sociodramatic play and the acquisition of occupational roles. *Review Journal of Philosophy and Social Science* 7, 285–95.

Lancy, D. F. (1983). *Cross-Cultural Studies in Cognition and Mathematics*. NY: Academic Press.

Lancy, D. F. and Madsen, M. C. (1981). Cultural patterns and the social behavior of children: two studies from Papua New Guinea. *Ethos* 9, 201–16.

Lancy, D. F., Souviney, R. and Kada, V. (1981). Intra-cultural variation in cognitive development: conservation of length among the Imbonggu. *International Journal of Behavioral Development* 4, 455–68.

Morgan, L. H. (1877). *Ancient Society*. Chicago: Kerr.

Oswalt, W. M. (1976). *An Anthropological Analysis of Food-Getting Technology*. NY: Wiley.

Piaget, J. (1970). *Structuralism*. NY: Basic Books.

Roberts, J. M., Arth, M. J. and Bush, R. R. (1959). Games in culture. *American Anthropologist* 61, 597–605.

Roberts, J. M. and Sutton-Smith, B. (1962). Child-training and game involvement. *Ethnology* 1, 166–85.

Roberts, J. M. and Sutton-Smith, B. (1966). Cross-cultural correlates of games of chance. *Behavior Science Notes* 1, 131–44.

Roleasamalik, P. M. (1979). *Traditional Games of Papua New Guinea*. Port Moresby: Govt Printer.

Schwartzman, H. (1978). *Transformations: the Anthropology of Children's Play*. New York: Plenum.

Smith, P. K. (1982). Does play matter? Functional and evolutionary aspects of animal and human play. *Behavioral and Brain Sciences* 5, 139–84.

Sutton-Smith, B. (1976). A structural grammar of games and sports. *International Review of Sport Sociology* 2, 117–37.

Sutton-Smith, B. and Roberts, J. M. (1981). Play, games and sports. In M. C. Triandis and A. Heron (eds), *Handbook of Cross-Cultural Psychology: Developmental Psychology, vol. 4*. Boston: Allyn and Bacon.

14   The Idealization of Play

Brian Sutton-Smith and Diana Kelly-Byrne

The aim of the present chapter is to demonstrate, albeit historically and anecdotally, that what currently passes for the science of play is culturally relative. It is an ideology of play rather than a scientific theory of play. For example, beginning with Huizinga (1955), a cultural historian and the most influential of all modern play theorists, play has often been defined as: free, outside of ordinary life, not serious, of no material interest, not for profit and absorbing. More recently, psychologists Krasnor and Pepler (1980), who have done considerable experimental work with children's play, contend that they can define it as: flexible, having positive affect, being intrinsically motivated and not literal. Anthropologist Peter Loizos (1980) suggests that the same kind of reading of play is characteristic of our common-sense use of language and extremely difficult to avoid. It is taken for granted by most, he says, that play must be voluntary, refreshing, spontaneous, egalitarian, not serious, informal and done for oneself. To this kind of defining, in particular to the influential work of Huizinga, Gregory Bateson (1979) retorted 'I assert that Huizinga's definition of play is a red herring, swimming tail first and muddying the water.' Bateson went on to imply that most of the terms used by Huizinga were culturally relative applying to the class aspirations of selected groups of Europeans, and could in no way cover either the 'play' activities of animals or the vast array of phenomena to be found in anthropological data.

Yet the tendency to see play as necessarily voluntary (intrinsically motivated), of positive affective value, egalitarian, flexible and functional is both widespread and difficult to budge. In a recent effort to avoid the problem of such 'operational definitions', for example, Matthews and Matthews have adopted what they call the paradigm case procedure in which a random sample of activities is presented on video tape to a non-trained group of judges who are asked to note when they can say 'That is a case of fantasy play if anything is' (1982: 26). And yet these authors begin by talking about their study as on 'children's spontaneously occurring fantasy play' thus presupposing in their use of the term 'spontaneous' what they are undertaking to discover. The paradigm case as they use it can sample only the values of the culture-bound judges.

We proceed in the rest of this chapter to study first, why these positively toned views of play have come to be predominant in both social science and everyday discourse, and secondly to show that examples can be produced from history, anthropology and present day play data to demonstrate that there is indeed nothing universal about these particular connotations.

HISTORICAL SOURCES OF IDEALIZATION

1 The primary source of the idealization of play has to be the *work ethic* itself, and its concomitant development of the notion of leisure, as anything which sloughs off the obligations of work. The mass of human leisure is given over to a negation of the obligatory clock-controlled work system. Its focus is largely idleness. As Ken Roberts (1978) has shown, the major forms of British leisure are watching television, smoking, gambling, drinking and having sex. Anything which is not work, such as recreation, play, sports, etc., tends within this modern industrial climate to take on the positive hue of an escape from such obligatoriness. We would credit this cultural situation as the major force behind the increasing idealization of children's play. The compulsions of work-obliged time have, in a secularized age, made any kind of activity freed from these obligations appear increasingly romantic and less alienated. And play, as a form of leisure, has become exalted for its freedom. But what is confused here is the issue of being free from work with being free to choose to do whatever you wish. Play has been exalted as an arena where you can do whatever you wish, whereas as we shall see that is often not the case at all.

2 The second major factor in the idealization of play is the *social status value* acquired by team games and athletics because of their original association with the education of the wealthy. There is a representation of this value system in the contemporary film *Chariots of Fire*, where the aristocrat is the one who balances the glasses of champagne on his hurdles as he goes about his most leisurely pursuit of glory in his own sumptuous estates. He is the one who can afford to drop out of one of the Olympic contests to allow his compatriot to compete in his place. His behaviour and value-system contrast strongly with those of the other two main characters in the film, the one overwrought by religion and the other by

ambition, although as we now know the future was to be theirs. This aristocratic use of leisure as a demonstration of conspicuous consumption and superiority contrasted markedly with the work-oriented developments of the industrial age.

Quite incidentally, the industrial age gave to some team games a repute they certainly had not acquired in their more barbarous pursuit by medieval folk. For example, with children roaming the urban streets in the nineteenth century as their fathers went into the factories and with the children disenfranchised from their former apprenticeships in village and family economies, reformers turned first to schools to bring these children under social control. Those involved in playground movements of the first twenty years of this century turned to the use of team sports to bring these urchins, vagabonds, these depraved immigrants, under control. As Goodman (1979) puts it, through team games they could be colonized into the dominant way of life. It was a play ideology of the rich for the poor, and it turned out to be the most successful play ideology that the modern world has had (Sutton-Smith, 1982a).

Buttressed by some evolutionary chatter provided by Stanley Hall, particularly about working through primitive atavisms on swings and roundabouts, such an ideology led to the spending of millions of dollars on playgrounds and on industrial recreation programmes. It was believed that delinquency would decrease amongst minors as they acquired the upper-status virtues of character and teamsmanship and that factory norms would improve in the work place. Both of these outcomes were claimed subsequently to have taken place. The arrest rate certainly dropped when children were not playing their heathen folk-games on the streets, but were playing sports on playgrounds. And although for many years sceptics in sociology have been trying to demonstrate that if you make it on the team you do not necessarily gain a better character or success in life, the majority of parents are still with Stanley Hall, John Dewey, Thorndike and Baldwin, all of whom believed that team games were the answer to child development, although they did not much agree on anything else (Cavallo, 1981).

Most of us are so familiar with the play ideology which we have just mentioned that we do not think of it as a serious theory of play. It has become a folk practice rather than a theory. It could be argued, however, that it has been the very ideological success of team sports as a genre of play, that has made it possible for academic play theories of an idealizing kind also to succeed. And there are not any academic play theories that do not idealize child play.

3 In general, *academic play theories* have been created by professionals who work with children in nursery schools, in therapy clinics or in

laboratories. One might tentatively call them play theories for the rich. Not surprisingly all these theories preach that the child who plays in his or her solitary way is better prepared for life. Whether this play is regarded as a kind of evolutionary preparation, a better adjustment to conflict and anxiety, the development of cognitive operations, the increase of one's exploratory activity or as a facilitation of communication and social innovation, all modern social scientific theorists of play have seen it as contributing to child development in one way or another. In fact, there are now programmes for training children through imaginative play so that they will be better able to inhibit aggression, delay response and learn to read (Sutton-Smith and Sutton-Smith, 1974; Singer and Singer, 1978). What sports has done for the depraved, we are told, imaginative play will do for the deprived.

4 There are many *other forces* at work in the idealization of children's play, such as the older nurturant Froebel kindergarten tradition; the women's movement with its emphasis on teaching children collaboration, and its offspring The New Games Movement (Fluegelman, 1976) with its emphasis on the family and upon collaborative play; and even the works of some women scholars who treat play as something basically overlooked by men scholars and who criticize men's tendency to view play only through the spectacles of games and sports (Schwartzman, 1978). The toy industry also has a vested interest in having us believe that children need to be given the appropriate toys to play with if they are to achieve their most in this life (Caplan and Caplan, 1973).

5 Finally, we would like to focus briefly on the very innovative work of *Mihaly Csikszentmihalyi* (1979) which has had such impact on all our thinking. Mihaly suggests that the usual distinctions between work and play are decreasingly valid; that there is a quality of life which he chooses to call *flow* which can be found in any context whether of work or play. This state of being is characterized by a merging of action and awareness, by a centring of attention, by a loss of self-consciousness, and by being under one's own control; it is self-chosen and gives one immediate and unambiguous feedback on the success of one's own actions. It is the kind of phenomenon which occurs when one is completely involved in a game, and Mihaly's major illustrations are from chess, rock climbing, and dancing. But he also seeks to show that the same involved and blissful state of affairs can happen in work and uses surgery as his example. He has the anecdote of the surgeon whose wife took him to Acapulco for a vacation and after a couple of days he was so bored he reported into the local hospital, volunteering for surgery, which was for him the truly exciting life-form.

In addition to flow there is also *micro flow* which is a small-scale example of the same kind of thing. His study shows that the dominantly reported kind of micro flow is of a *social kind* and is the involved satisfaction that people get from browsing, shopping, galleries, talking or joking with others, social events such as eating, parties and sexual activity. Next in order is the *kinaesthetic* kind which includes walking, running, small muscle movements, touching, rubbing and fiddling with objects, playing games or sports. Thirdly, we have *imagining*; daydreaming, music in the head, talking to one's self, caring for plants and pets, humming, whistling and singing. Fourthly, there is *attending* to things, like watching people or things, or watching television or listening to radio or records, or reading books or magazines or the paper. Fifthly, there are the *oral pleasures* of snacking, smoking, chewing or drinking. Finally, there is *creative work*, musical instruments, sewing, crafts, writing letters or just doodling.

What is happening here is that in Mihaly's work we are being wrenched from the older dichotomies of work and play in which work is said to be valuable and play not. We are being asked implicitly to concentrate on our own *consumer pleasure values* regardless of their historical source or their physical context. And although the data show that in general one can more easily achieve 'flow' at the executive level than at the labouring level, there is also incidental information about some workers who, while doing extremely routine tasks, nevertheless indulge in flights of fancy which they find amongst the most pleasurable parts of their day's activities, particularly if they are wearing earphones sounding out their favourite music.

If one puts together, then, the now traditional view of sports, the functional views of play in social science play theory and this new emphasis on the value of certain *play-like* states of pleasure, which are incidentally quite consonant with the advertising ideology of consumer civilization, a case can be made for the increasing ideological idealization of play in our day and age. We are being led to think of play as 'flow' as being possible at any time, and, moreover, even a workaholic can achieve it at work.

In saying all this, we have not bothered to make our case by referring to those play idealizations occurring in sport sociology upon which Gruneau (1980) has commented so sceptically. Nor have we focused on the idealization of play as man's true exemplar of freedom, which one finds in the phenomenological writings of Derrida, Gadamer and most of all in the recent book by Hans, *The Play of the World* (1981).

What we are contending is that in this century we have, bit by bit, moved away from the traditional view that play is trivial or irrelevant to the major economic and religious culture, towards the view that it is a positive and pleasant aspect of human character, intelligence, pleasure and freedom.

PLAY AS NOT VOLUNTARY

The major turning point in recent realization that play is not necessarily voluntary, spontaneous or intrinsically motivated came from the anthropological work of Victor Turner (1974) who contended that in pre-modern times the important distinction to make was between activities that were sacred and activities that were profane, and not as in modern society between those that are obligatory (work) and those that are optional (play). By and large, what a modern would see as optional because not work, a pre-modern person might see as sacred and obligatory because part of the work of the Gods. When sacred games were play all members of the appropriate age and sex cohort would be expected to participate in order to placate the gods, the dead, the weather, the sick or the infertile or whatever the case might be. Historical anthropology is rife with bloody and brutal but playful customs. There were the Eskimos who competed at twisting each other's ears off; or who attached a piece of leather to each other's testicles to see who could outpull the other in a tug-of-war, all the time smiling and if possible laughing to indicate their playful intent (Agar, 1976). There were the Mayans who played ball games in which the captain of the losing team had his head chopped off; there were Indian tribes in which masses playing at lacrosse injured, brained and brutalized each other as the game proceeded; and then there were those medieval English football players at similar games. Michael Salter (1980) has had the acumen to call some of these 'terminal games'. Even Huizinga who has written so idyllically about the play spirit in civilization cites many examples of contestive plays (the primary form in which civilizing occurs, he believes) which involve enduring pain, fighting, mutual bragging and execration, derision and scurrility, slanging, squandering goods, bloody and fatal conflict and duels fought through to the death. Our modern notions of optional behaviour hardly seem appropriate to these kinds of play.

Perhaps the modern notions derive to some extent from the situation in nursery school in which the adults provide a setting with toys, etc. where under their supervision, children are supposedly 'free' to make choices within the limited array available. When we see children on the playground, however, that freedom is primarily freedom from the classroom. There is limited freedom of choice in the actual play of the playground itself because of the obligations to friends and to powerful other children, etc. (Sluckin, 1981). What is more remarkable about playground play is the necessary conformity of the players to seasonal pastimes or to the activities of the dominant children. Even more intimate play at home with one's best friends is often strongly influenced by commercially instigated activities involving the imitation of television dramas or the use of advertised toys (Kelly-Byrne, 1983). The typical scene in many modern homes is of the child playing in front of the television set with a television-advertised toy. The history of the twentieth century can be written as an illustration of the gradual socialization of children's leisure to bring it from the more unruly folkways of the nineteenth century into the more domesticated forms of the organized and adult-influenced recreation, sport and play with which we are now familiar.

In sum, notions of freedom or voluntariness, etc. are not sufficient to account for play. One can still play even if one has been required to play in the first place. There are a host of ways in which degrees of personal autonomy are or are not expressed in the phenomena called play, and it is an empirical matter to decide what these have to do with it. What has been assumed as the most fundamental characterization of play by modern specialists must therefore be brought into question.

PLAY AS NEGATIVE AFFECT

In *A History of Children's Play* (Sutton–Smith, 1982b) we have detailed a host of ways in which what went on in the playground and what was commonly called children's play was often brutal and unpleasant for some of the members of the 'play group', as the following examples show.

Fights were arranged for the amusement of older children. They were arranged by school bullies in a paddock where one even had to fight one's friends. Everybody had to fight. Anyone who lost was *crowned*, i.e. the victor patted him three times on the back and spat over his head, usually aiming too low! Though the fights were amongst boys, girls usually scratched the eyes of their brothers' opponents if they lost. Girls usually fought in their own way by hair-pulling. In other fights, the prisoners of a gang were held by force. They had their shirts torn and fingers bent back. An observer of the time writes: 'The individual and gang fights of the day were often very harsh and the younger, less virile members of the playground were often terrorized by those stronger ones.' The harshness did not stop there! In many places there were initiation ceremonies as well. Ducking under the tap was the most widespread form but there were others. In 'King of the Golden Sword', the initiate was made to face the fence with his hands behind his back. There was a long ceremony about his crowning and entry into the school and finally the golden sword which had been dipped into the latrine was pulled through his fingers. In the rite of 'Pee Wee Some More Yet', the initiate was blindfolded and ordered to pee into another boy's cap. The cap turned out to be his own; or the initiates would have their pants taken down and the initiators would spit on their private parts. Another ceremony included taking the initiate to the stables, waiting until a horse was urinating and spinning the boy under the stream. In 'Tug O'War', a cap was held in the teeth of the new boy and a bigger boy. The former had his hands tied behind his back. While the war was in progress, the big boy peed on his young opponent who could not see what was going on but gradually felt the wet warmth on his clothing.

If these examples are indicted as rare, antiquated and unfair, we can turn for examples to the modern and comprehensive folklorist work by the Opies (1959) and the Knapps (1976), the story of English playgrounds by Sluckin (1981) and to recent examples of play in nursery schools and other play spaces for children in the US (Sarrett, 1981). Two-thirds of the contents of play in these examples is occupied by struggles for power, by the play of attack and defence or chase and escape. Once again there are in these relatively rare sources multiple instances of brutality, callousness and all-round unpleasant behaviour.

But there is also much obscene and erotic behaviour, which although it might not cause much immediate negative affect in the child players, usually does when they are caught at it by their parents, or by the teachers. Sarrett's study suggests that while middle-class teachers seek out and try to remedy verbally such obscene behaviours, lower-class teachers tend to ignore it unless it becomes behaviourally intrusive and then the child is punished physically. The Knapp's work shows the widespread occurrence of the following games amongst children aged 6–13 years.

In the game of 'Giving a Boy Titties', girls twist a boy's T-shirt so that it looks as if he possesses tiny breasts or giant nipples. The Knapps write that this is a common game. In 'Playing Radio', boys, on the other hand, ask girls if they wish to play radio. If they say 'yes' the boy puts on an imaginary set of earphones, bends over her chest and chants 'come in Tokyo' meanwhile pretending to twist her breasts as if they were dials and then ducking. 'Snapping bras' is also an ambush game and boys creep up on girls and do this to the accompaniment of 'pop goes the weasel' or 'Pearl Harbor sneak attack'. 'Playing Bases' is another sexual game where one is dared to go through more daring phases of sexual activity (kissing, flashing and making it). If you are too scared you are taunted for being a 'greenie'. Even at nursery school Sarrett (1981) found eroticism;

thus she reports that lower-class girls stuff their T-shirts, wiggle their hips suggestively and report instances of sexual activity boasting that 'they did it'. They engage in erotic fantasies of men raping them and pretend to peek through imaginary windows and see a couple making love as they whisper 'they gettin' down'. Games called 'Fathers' involve girls surreptitiously setting up house and getting down on one another 'at night time'.

Similarly, Kelly-Byrne (1983) in her year-long longitudinal participation in the play of a middle-class 7-year-old found that the girl and her play companions were often preoccupied with sex in their play, both in veiled and more explicit forms.

PLAY AS NOT EGALITARIAN AND NOT FLEXIBLE

Although the notion that play, especially collaborative play, is egalitarian, is not widespread amongst social scientists it is found in some quarters (Fluegelman, 1976; Schwartzman, 1978). The view that it is the domain *par excellence* for flexibility training is also found amongst some theorists (Lieberman, 1979; Fagen, 1981 and above, chapter 7). Yet these views must contend against two other positions. On the one hand there is the older view that children's play is highly routine and rule-bound; and on the other there is the newer socialization perspective which says that a major function of children's play is the establishment of dominance – subordination hierarchies. Indeed if one looks at Sluckin, the Opies or the Knapps there is abundant anecdotal evidence of playground bosses, of harassment specialists, of the fact that some games are 'owned' by some children while other children are simply excluded. There are leaders and followers with the former acting very often like dictators of what is allowed to transpire. *Playground bosses* and *harassment specialists* are well-known figures amongst children. Children who wish to enter other's games often barge in, threaten to bash another's face in and often will knee kids in the stomach. Children also use play to terrorize each other. That is to say, they often move between pretending and actually being aggressive. This turns out to be an extraordinarily powerful way of controlling others, for the recipients of such conflicting information have difficulty in predicting what will happen next and become uneasy. Children who engage in this rush up to others and shout 'You asked for it now you stinking fucker' and let their faces melt into a smile. Alternatively, they grab kids, usually smaller than themselves, round their neck and ask, 'Wanna fight?' When the other says 'No' they retort 'I'll let you off this time', smirking. These examples are typical of the way 6-year-olds terrorize each other in play on the playground, according to

Sluckin (1981). All this suggests that there are *dominant and dominated children in play*. Andy Sluckin's work is rife with ferocious descriptions of fights on the English playground (e.g. 1981: 86–90). One is reminded more of the *Lord of the Flies* than of collaboration and flexibility.

PLAY AS DYSFUNCTIONAL

In rehabilitating play from its former neglect, the scholarship of this century has followed the direction of both anthropological and psychological functionalism in seeking usages to which play might contribute. Basically, the bulk of the evidence has consisted in drawing formal parallels between a play or game activity and some analogous form of adult functioning. The search for isomorphisms between play structures (for example, games of strategy) and cultural structures (for example societal complexity) has been held to support the contention that play and games are indeed a functional contribution to socialization in one way or another.

The problem with this simple assumption, however, is that the issue of play's dysfunctionality is never fully reckoned with. Fagen (1981), who is a promoter of play's contribution to evolution and development, is one of the few who also point out that in the course of prolonged separations from the caretaker while playing, animals become entrapped in rocks and mud, have dangerous falls, break their limbs, as well as sustain serious injuries in their play-fighting. According to Fagen the amount of risk that a species can tolerate varies with their conditions of survival probability. When these are low play is too risky. When predation is high, food short, and conditions crowded, there is less play. More play is associated with more territory and more food.

On the human level Alford (1983) has been demonstrating cross-culturally how many festival and playful events are associated with dangerous consequences. She describes the beer-drinking festivals of the South American Tarahumara in which it is not uncommon for the besotted participants to injure each other in fights, fall off steep cliffs, tread on sleeping babies, die from pneumonia due to exposure on mountain sides and be involved in sexual licence with severe implications for their normal relationships. Similarly, Clifford Geertz (1973) is famous for his reintroduction to modern discourse of J. S. Mill's notion of *deep play* which is the kind in which the stakes are so high that it is irrational to participate. When we have questioned our own University students about their examples of deep play it is clear that the phenomenon is alive and well and that thinking about play needs to take into account the centrality of considerable risk-taking. For example, from a 19-year-old female:

For me my most exciting play was going to Las Vegas with a middle-aged stranger whom I had met two hours previously in a bar in Philadelphia. He could have killed me, raped me, or left me stranded there with no money. I didn't know anything about his character. However, none of this happened and it was tremendously exciting. Who knows when I'd get another chance to go to Las Vegas. It was dangerous and degrading and I'd never do it again. But I don't regret having done it once. Being a 'gold digger' is one option for a life style and it was interesting to try it on for myself for a day. We went without luggage and only stayed about ten hours. By going with someone I didn't care about I was able to gamble with his money and truly not care when I lost at the tables.

From a 23-year-old male:

As an active brother in my fraternity there is one weekend each year in which I am required to forgo my activities at school and go away with all of my brothers to an isolated campsite miles from Philadelphia. Traditionally we have made it a point to make this travel and the rest of the evening an unforgettable experience of drinking and pleasure (until we pass out). In order not to continually stop for beer we took with us a keg in the backseat. After all, we were seniors and decided to do it in the right way. By the time we arrived we had a soaking wet car full of six drunken, stoned, thoroughly wasted guys ready to hit some bars. Never mind that it is illegal to have a single open beer can in a moving vehicle, let alone a tapped keg and a multitude of empty cups and mugs. Never mind that it is illegal to smoke pot alone in a private home, let alone in a moving car filled with incredibly intoxicated fraternity brothers shrieking obscenities out the window in a 'Can you top this' fashion. Never mind speeding and passing on the wrong side, over solid lines on single lane roadways, all illegal. And never mind that road signs depicting curves and intersections are meant to remain on their metal posts and not in the trunks of passing cars. These are all a part of our play.

From a 21-year-old male:

My favorite play is climbing buildings, water towers and rock faces after a night at the bar. The risk involved is obvious and not lessened by the effect of alcohol. This is an occupation in which a few of us compete to be first to get to the highest point such as a church steeple. For example, the one at 42nd Street and Spruce is particularly difficult and takes complete concentration particularly after a night at the tavern. Drinking as a precursor to this kind of play is extremely important, not only to decrease inhibitions about being shot down by the police but also to increase concentration. While this would seem to be a paradox, knowing that you have been drinking creates a counter response that makes one even more careful than usual. Before any step which seems precarious there is a mechanism which hesitates and causes you to evaluate whether the step is really practical or seems practical only because you are drunk. A re-evaluation takes place and only when you are satisfied that it really is a prudent maneuver do you take the step.

By our count from several hundred students the largest category of deep play volunteered by males involved physical danger, often in speeding cars or in sports play, and often with drinking added to deepen the risks. Given that 50,000 are killed in motor accidents each year in the USA and a quarter of a million are injured, and that half of these accidents are said to be due to driving under the influence of alcohol, we must also conclude that some of those killed or injured were only playing. In our survey, sports dangers and risks were also important for females. We especially noted the young woman who went mountain climbing in the last stages of her pregnancy and the girl evangelist who liked the excitement of seeking to save souls amongst motor-cycle gangs. The largest category for females, however, involved various forms of blind dating, flirting with strangers, provoking jealous boyfriends and rough sexual activity. Quite surprising in these days of the pill, the diaphragm and the vasectomy, the most widely reported instance of deep play (puns apart) was sex without contraception.

CONCLUSION

The intent of this paper has been largely negative. We have sought to counter the idealization of play which on the everyday level is expressed by saying that the child's play is its work, or that sports build character, and on the academic level by finding the essence of play in voluntariness, positive affect, flexibility and socialization. These characteristics may be present in some play in some circumstances. Unfortunately the opposite characteristics of obligatoriness, negative affect, rigidity and dysfunctionality are also characteristic of some play in some circumstances.

Part of the reason that play could be idealized has been the global manner in which it has been denoted. For whatever reasons researchers have been more inclined to give the concept support than to define it carefully. There are important exceptions to this criticism. The work of Berlyne (1960), Ellis (1973), Hutt (1979) and others has led to useful distinctions between exploration and play. Piaget's (1951) distinction between accommodation and assimilation is of parallel import. Piaget further distinguishes between play and creative imagination. The work of various linguists (Weir, 1962) makes it necessary to recall the older concept of practice or exercise, the repeating of acts to some point of functional habituation. In sum, when we are talking about the learning of children (or epistemic activity), we can sometimes distinguish the analytic functions of intelligence from the synthesizing functions of intelligence (exploration from construction) and we sometimes can distinguish these functions from mere practice. When it comes to mental activity, we can sometimes distinguish spontaneous analytic thought from spontaneous creative thought or the imagination. In adulthood also distinctions can be made between dreams, reverie (day-dreams), and the imagination. Although it would take a major conceptual and research effort to fully sort out these various distinctions, I believe there are already sufficient ground for *not* calling them play. This is true even realizing that it is not always easy to distinguish amongst them, or between them and play; realizing also that in the synaesthesic world of childhood, such distinctions are not always present. Further, realizing that even when such distinctions are made, it is still possible for such additional phenomena to occur as exploratory play, constructive play, playful practice, etc.

Our having said all that, however, the reader must still feel that it would be useful to be given something more positive about the nature of play to buttress the present arguments. Realizing the very tentative nature of what can be said, we would venture the following. First, play is *always a 'framed' event* and everyone concerned knows that that is the case (Bateson, 1972). There are special communications (signals, messages, negotiations, requests) by which the play is established and this is as true of animals as it is of humans. One of the reasons that one can get more observer agreement about play's presence and absence than one can get about its definitional connotations has to do with the elusive character of human signalling systems in which proxemics, kinesics and paralinguistics all play their part. While this is very obvious to most communication theorists it still seems to have eluded many other play investigators. In addition to its framed character (which is true of all other communicated realms), *in play the metacommunicative function always retains primacy*. It is apparently essential to keep in the minds of the players that they are indeed playing, otherwise the activity will break down into anxiety or violence as indeed it often does. To this end, play requires a display of sufficient cues to keep the distinction between this realm and others in the forefront of awareness. There are many kinds of such cues, some have to do with action (which may be exaggerated and endlessly repeated in a cyclic fashion), with objects (which may be miniaturized), with the physical scene (which may be a nursery, a playground, a fort, a sports stadium), with vocalizations (there are peculiar play 'registers' as when iconic sounds are made to represent cars or aeroplanes or babies), with characters (there are stock figures –

mother, father, baby, cowboys, Superman, etc.), and with attitudes (e.g. this is pretence). When one considers this array of cues by which the player is able to continue maintaining this separate realm of activity, the often repeated suggestion that play involves only a change in attitude and that anything can be play, has to be regarded as an oversimplification. There are many clusters of features which combine together, as above, in various intensities to guarantee that those gathered together know that they are playing. Perhaps apart from the historical and ideological reasons for insisting on play being voluntary (work ethic or upper-status privilege), the intrinsic reason may be that there is in everyone the 'knowledge' that play involves transition from one realm of being to another realm of being. Even if that other 'play' realm does not have quite the separation from other spheres that Huizinga contends and even if it isn't always without material interest, without profit, and is seldom not serious, it is truly an 'otherness'. It would be our preference to say that the true locale for all these connotations has to be in the fact of framing and in the maintenance of that primacy.

It follows that if this realm of human affairs must be so carefully framed its events must be of considerable importance. What, we may ask, is the significance of so much repetition, exaggeration, miniaturization, changed register, stock character, special location and guaranteed illusion? Unlike the work on play as a special kind of communication, however, the investigation of what play is as a kind of experience is less theoretically coherent even though almost every kind of scientist and humanist has had something to say about the matter. We might argue that for Csikszentmihalyi the reason for the framing would be that the crucial 'flow' experience which may be contained in the play is itself so gratifying. There is something special about the 'flow' experience, as he describes it, which perhaps makes it as fundamental as sex or eating. His description of that experience, however, is in terms of the 'players'' reports and is his attempt to make a 'structure' (a phenomenological structure) out of these reports. Others have suggested similarly that the heart of the matter has to do with the special kinds of excitements or arousal that are to be found in play, but have couched their descriptions largely in neurological terms, as in Shultz's (1979) description of play as a kind of arousal modulation; for others the central delight has to do with the players' enjoyment of their own skill or mastery; for yet others it is the uncertainty and risk or chanciness of the matters over which the players seek to establish control which is said to be the inherent gratification. Others focus their attention to the 'deep' structure and discuss the unusual relationships of means and ends behaviours, or the dialectical oppositions of approach and avoidance behaviours endlessly repeating themselves in cyclical displays

(Sutton-Smith, 1978). Whether the 'to and fro-ness' of the young child's play (Gadamer, 1982) is indeed akin to the sportsman's attack and defence is a matter for conjecture. While there are clearly many claimants to play's description and none has hegemony, once again it would seem futile to say that play is simply a change in attitude, and is not characterized by special structural features which mark it off from other kinds of human experience.

Finally, no account of play would be sufficient which did not take into account the assertions of the major child psychologists, Freud, Vygotsky and Piaget, who have all in their own way asserted that play is a playing-out of frustrations, or subjective worlds, not permitted expression within the more conventional norms of the societies of which they are a part. Further, if one follows Bateson again, the very point of play's paradoxes are that they permit us to communicate such subjectivity to others in a disguised fashion. They permit us to say the opposite of what we mean in order to mean the opposite of what we say, as he contends. Being weak we (child or adult) play at being powerful in order both to disguise that we feel weak and yet to reveal to any other that weakness is our problem. The other player in like predicament joins with us in a similar mutual expression, release, modulation, chanciness, and mastery of these feelings and behaviours otherwise not symbolized in the daytime domain, but here sufficiently 'marked' by exaggerations, etc. so as not to raise the threat that their appearance in other realms would do. In these terms play is a very special kind of 'language of expression' within which we share our secrets with others (Kelly-Byrne, 1983). It proceeds by paradox and dialectic in order that our subjective worlds, our wish-fulfilments, can see the light of day and enter into the human community without directly overthrowing or directly tampering with the everyday order of normative expectations. Through sharing these secrets of infirmity and desire we are bonded to those with whom we play and feel the validity of our membership in their community.

When the matter is couched in these terms one can see that the idealization of play in this century is not without psychological point. There is intrinsic psychological reason why this kind of human expression might well be felt to be threatening to the normative order and why it might be helpful from an upright and respectable point of view to confuse the functions of play with those of normative learning (educational games, game simulation, exploration and construction). Which is to say that whatever history, in terms of work-ethic ideology and status ideology, might have contributed to our idealization of play, the phenomenon itself as a kind of expression leaves much to be desired from a morally or conventionally orthodox point of view. The Puritans tried to get rid of this inconvenient form of expression. The Kurds still throw stones at their children if they see them playing (Feitelson, 1954). The Aymara consider their children are not adults until they have given up playing (Miracle, 1977). We who have idealized play have clearly developed a yet more cunning defence.

REFERENCES

Agar, L. P. (1976). The reflection of cultural values in Eskimo children's games. In D. F. Lancy and B. A. Tindall (eds), *The Anthropological Study of Play: Problems and Prospects*. West Point, NY: Leisure Press.

Alford, F. (1983). The social structuring of expressive activities in two cultures. In D. Kelly-Byrne and B. Sutton-Smith (eds), *The Masks of Play*. West Point, NY: Leisure Press.

Bateson, G. (1972). *Steps to an Ecology of Mind*. New York: Ballantine.

Bateson, G. (1979). Communication. In B. Sutton-Smith (ed.), *The Newsletter of the Association for the Anthropological Study of Play* 5, 3.

Berlyne, D. E. (1960). *Conflict, Arousal and Curiosity*. New York: McGraw-Hill.

Caplan, F., and Caplan, T. (1973). *The Power of Play*. New York: Doubleday.

Cavallo, D. (1981). *Muscles and Morals: Organized Playgrounds and Urban Reform, 1880–1920*. Philadelphia: University of Pennsylvania Press.

Csikszentmihalyi, M. (1979). The concept of flow. In B. Sutton-Smith (ed.), *Play and Learning*. New York: Gardner Press.

Ellis, M. J. (1973). *Why People Play*. Englewood Cliffs: Prentice-Hall.

Fagen, R. (1981). *Animal Play Behavior*. New York: Oxford University Press.

Feitelson, D. (1954). Childrearing practices in the Kurdish community. *Megamot* 5, 95–109.

Fluegelman, A. (1976). *The New Games Book*. New York: Doubleday.

Gadamer, H. G. (1982). *Truth and Method*. New York: Crossroad.

Geertz, C. (1973). *The Interpretation of Cultures*. New York: Basic Books.

Goffman, E. (1974). *Frame Analysis*. Cambridge, Mass.: Harvard University Press.

Goodman, G. (1979). *Choosing Sides: Playground and Street Life on the Lower East Side*. New York: Schocken.

Gruneau, R. S. (1980). Freedom and constraint. The paradoxes of play, games and sports. *Journal of Sport History* 7, 68–85.

Hans, J. S. *The Play of the World*. Amherst, Mass.: University of Massachusetts Press.

Huizinga, J. (1955). *Homo Ludens*. Boston: Beacon Press.

Hutt, C. Exploration and Play. In B. Sutton-Smith (ed.), *Play and Learning*. New York: Gardner Press.

Kelly-Byrne, D. (1983). A narrative of play and intimacy. In F. E. Manning (ed.), *The World of Play*. West Point, NY: Leisure Press, 1983.

Knapp, M., and Knapp, H. (1976). *One Potato, Two Potato*. New York: Norton.

Krasnor, L. R. and Pepler, D. J. (1980). The study of children's play: some suggested future directions. In K. Rubin (ed.), *Children's Play. New Directions for Child Development, Vol. 9*. San Francisco: Jossey Bass, Inc.

Lieberman, J. N. (1979). *Playfulness: its Relationship to Imagination and Creativity*. New York: Academic Press.

Loizos, P. (1980). Images of man. In J. Cherfas and R. Lewin (eds), *Not Work Alone: a Cross-Cultural View of Activities Superfluous to Survival*. Beverly Hills, California: Sage Publications.

Matthews, W. S., and Matthews R. J. (1982). Eliminating operational definitions: a paradigm case approach to the study of fantasy play. In D. J. Pepler and K. H. Rubin (eds), *The Play of Children: Current Theory and Research*. Basel: S. Karger.

Miracle, A. W. (1977). Some functions of Aymaran games and play. In P. Stevens Jr (ed.), *Studies in the Anthropology of Play: Papers in Memory of Allan Tindall*. West Point, NY: Leisure Press.

Opie, I., and Opie, P. (1959). *The Lore and Language of Schoolchildren*. New York: Oxford University Press.

Piaget, J. (1951). *Play, Dreams and Imitation in Childhood*. New York: Norton.

Roberts, K. (1978). *Contemporary Society and the Growth of Leisure*. London: Longman.

Salter, M. (1980). Play in ritual: an ethnohistorical overview of nature in North America. In H. B. Schwartzman (ed.), *Play and Culture*. New York: Leisure Press.

Sarrett, C. (1981). A translation of class socialization patterns into children's media related play behavior. Unpublished Ph.D. dissertation, University of Pennsylvania.

Schwartzman, H. (1978). *Transformations: the Anthropology of Children's Play*. New York: Plenum.

Shultz, T. R. (1979). Play as arousal modulation. In B. Sutton-Smith (ed.), *Play and Learning*. New York: Gardner Press.

Singer, J., and Singer, D. (1978). *Partners in Play*. New York: Random House.

Sluckin, A. (1981). *Growing Up in the Playground: the Social Development of Children*. London: Routledge & Kegan Paul.

Sutton-Smith, B. (1978). *Die Dialektik des Spiels*. Schorndorf: Verlag Karl Hoffman.

Sutton-Smith, B. (1982a). Play theory of the rich and for the poor. In P. Gilmore and A. Glathorn (eds), *Children in and out of School*. Philadelphia: University of Pennsylvania Press.

Sutton-Smith, B. (1982b). *A History of Children's Play: the New Zealand Playground, 1840–1950*. Philadelphia: University of Pennsylvania Press.

Sutton-Smith, B. and Sutton-Smith, S. (1974). *How to Play with your Children*. New York: Hawthorne Books (now E. F. Dutton, New York).

Turner, V. (1974). Liminal to liminoid in play. Flow and ritual: an essay of comparative symbology. *Rice University Studies* 60, 53–92.

Weir, R. H. (1962). *Language in the Crib*. The Hague: Mouton.

Notes on Contributors

Gordon M. Burghardt is at the Department of Psychology, University of Tennessee, Knoxville, Tenn., USA. He is co-editor with M. Bekoff of *The Development of Behavior: Comparative and Evolutionary Aspects*, 1978, and with A. S. Rand of *Iguanas of the World: their Behavior, Ecology and Conservation* (1982). He is one of the editors of the journal *Zeitschrift für Tierpsychologie*.

John A. Byers is at the Department of Biological Science, University of Idaho, Moscow, Idaho, USA. His main research interests are in play and development, especially in ungulates, and he has published articles on ibex, peccaries, and pronghorn.

Neil Chalmers is at the Department of Biology, The Open University, Milton Keynes, UK. He has researched on play and social development in primates, notably olive baboons, and marmosets. He is the author of *Social Behaviour in Primates* (1979).

Dorothy Einon is at the Department of Psychology, University College, London, UK. Her main research interest is play and social development in animals and, more recently, in children. She has published a number of articles on the effects of social isolation on play and social behaviour in rodents.

Robert Fagen is at the School of Fisheries and Science, University of Alaska, Juneau, Alaska, USA. He has researched extensively on play, and the mathematical modelling of play behaviour. He is the author of *Animal Play Behavior* (1981).

Catherine Grant is at the Department of Psychology, Carleton University, Ottawa, Canada where she is a graduate student. Her research interests are in imaginal processes, and the imaginary companion phenomenon.

Graham Hole is at the Department of Psychology, University College, London, UK. He is a research assistant, working on early social behaviour in rodents, with especial regard to play and sexual behaviour.

Anne P. Humphreys is at the Department of Psychology, University of Sheffield, Sheffield, UK. She has researched on play in rodents, and rough-and-tumble play in schoolchildren. Her current work is with autistic children.

Diana Kelly-Byrne is at the Graduate School of Education, University of Pennsylvania, Philadelphia, USA, where she is the Director of the Program in children's literature. She is author of several articles and co-author with Brian Sutton-Smith of *The Masks of Play* (1983).

David F. Lancy is at the College of Education, Utah State University, Logan, Utah, USA. He worked among the Kpelle in Liberia, and is author of *Cross-cultural Studies in Cognition and Mathematics* (1983). He has published on the anthropology of play, and is currently researching the impact of video games in a computer adventures laboratory.

Paul Martin is at the Sub-Department of Animal Behaviour, Madingley, Cambridge, UK, where he is University Demonstrator. His main research interests and publications are on various aspects of behavioural development, including play, and the energetics of behaviour.

Dietland Müller-Schwarze is at the Department of Environmental and Forest Biology, State University of New York, Syracuse, NY, USA. He and his wife have researched on play in deer and caribou. He is the editor of *Evolution of Play Behavior* (1978).

Sue Taylor Parker is at the Department of Anthropology, Sonoma State University, Rohnert Park, Calif., USA. Her main research interests are in the evolution of language and intelligence, and in the application of Piagetian cognitive theory to primate development.

John T. Partington is at the Department of Psychology, Carleton University, Ottawa, Canada. He has researched on personality types, person perception, and imaginal processes.

Tony Simon is at the Department of Psychology, University of Sheffield, Sheffield, UK, where he is a graduate student. He has researched on play and problem-solving in children, and in the use of computers in education.

Peter K. Smith is at the Department of Psychology, University of Sheffield, Sheffield, UK. His research interests are in early social development and play in children, and in human sociobiology. He is co-author with Kevin Connolly of *The Ecology of Preschool Behaviour* (1980).

Brian Sutton-Smith is at the Graduate School of Education, University of Pennsylvania, Philadelphia, USA. He has researched extensively on play and games in children. His publications include *How to Play with your Children* (1974) and *A History of Children's Play: the New Zealand Playground, 1840–1950* (1982). He is editor of *Play and Learning* (1979).

Dennis P. Wolf is at the Graduate School of Education, Harvard University, Cambridge, Mass., USA, where she is part of the Project Zero research team. She is co-editor with H. Gardner of *Early Symbolization: New Directions for Child Development, Vol. 3* (1979), and has researched on styles in the development of children's fantasy play.

Index

Figures in italic indicate bibliographical references